Leadership in the Secondary School

Frederick M. Raubinger
Professor, The University of Illinois

Merle R. Sumption
Professor, The University of Illinois

Richard M. Kamm
*Administrative Assistant,
Willowbrook (Illinois) High School*

CHARLES E. MERRILL PUBLISHING COMPANY

A Bell & Howell Company

Columbus, Ohio

MERRILL'S SERIES FOR EDUCATIONAL ADMINISTRATION

Under the Editorship of

DR. LUVERN L. CUNNINGHAM, Dean
College of Education
The Ohio State University

and

DR. H. THOMAS JAMES, President
The Spencer Foundation
Chicago, Illinois

Published by
Charles E. Merrill Publishing Co.
A Bell & Howell Company
Columbus, Ohio 43216

Copyright © 1974, by Bell & Howell Company. All rights reserved. No part of this book may be reproduced in any form, electronic or mechanical, including photocopy, recording, or any information storage and retrieval system, without permission in writing from the publisher.

International Standard Book Number: 0-675-08796-1

Library of Congress Catalog Card Number: 74-75444

1 2 3 4 5 6 7 8 9 10 — 78 77 76 75 74

PRINTED IN THE UNITED STATES OF AMERICA

Contents

Preface vii

Introduction xi

PART ONE   THE AMERICAN SECONDARY SCHOOL

1. Background of the American Secondary School — 3
2. Current Trends in Secondary Education — 24
3. The School as a Democratic Institution — 40
4. The Principal as a Leader — 57

Selected Readings
 The School as a Factory, *Warner Bloomberg, Jr.* — 67
 The Coming Death of Bureaucracy, *Warren G. Bennis* — 77
 The School Principal: Key Man in Educational Change, *Kenneth A. Tye* — 87
 Freedom Must Be Taught, *Walter Cronkite* — 94

PART TWO   THE SECONDARY SCHOOL STUDENT

5. The Youth Revolution — 101
6. Student Rights — 115

Selected Readings
 Wanted: A Humane Education, *The Montgomery County Student Alliance* — 137

In Partnership With Youth, *Unesco Courier*   154
Three Court Cases   157

PART THREE   THE STUDENT AND THE SCHOOL

7. The Curriculum   171
8. Student Activities   204
9. Student Personnel Services   220

    Selected Readings

       An Educational Imperative: The Human Dimension,
          Arthur W. Combs   241
       The Gill Plan 1., *John H. Wright and John C. Littleford*   256
       Academic Freedom and the Student Press, *H. C. Hudgins*   261
       Guidelines for the Collection, Maintenance, and
          Dissemination of Pupil Records, *Arthur Ruebhausen*
          and others   263

PART FOUR   THE SCHOOL STAFF

10. Staff Selection and Organization   267
11. The Principal Works with the Staff   285

    Selected Readings

       Hierarchical Impediments to Innovation in
          Educational Organizations, *Max G. Abbot*   325

PART FIVE   SCHOOL-COMMUNITY RELATIONS

12. The School Community   339
13. The Principal Works with the Community   371

    Selected Readings

       Community Relations, *J. Lloyd Trump*   393
       America's Social Imperative, *Ernest O. Melby*   394
       Toward a Dynamic Administration, *Ernest O. Melby*   400
       Community Education and its Organization,
          Clyde M. Campbell   403
       What Could We Build if We Worked Together, *U Thant*   406

PART SIX MANAGEMENT IN THE SECONDARY SCHOOL

  14. The Principal and Management Functions   411

      Selected Readings
        The Dominion of Economic Accountability,
        Ernest R. House   425

      Looking Ahead   438

      Index   445

Preface

This book is directed primarily to those who are preparing themselves for careers as principals of secondary schools and to those who are beginning their careers. It is centered on the leadership role of the principal because in times of change leadership is more important than management alone. Since all effective leadership is *shared* leadership, the book will, it is hoped, be valuable to all who work in the school.

What is written here is not without bias. While acknowledging the solid accomplishments of the secondary school in America, we believe that at present and in the future the school must *change* in a number of respects and adapt itself to the needs of a society in flux and to a student population that is restless, frustrated, often confused, and sometimes alienated. We express dissatisfaction with a school modelled after the factory and favor instead a school modelled after the democratic community.

In the early days of the nation the public secondary school found support among thoughtful leaders who believed schools could be social agencies which preserved and advanced the principles upon which the nation was founded. In the ebb and flow of change, these enduring values can serve as a guide through periods of transition. We hold no simplistic views about what is required if the school is to be a model of democracy. Much more is demanded than the observation of patriotic holidays, the concession to minor student demands, and the memorization of historical facts and heroic exploits; much more is required than the uncritical assimilation of the practices of politics and the forms and procedures of government; and more is needed than the transmission of the culture from one generation to the next. The way the school is organized, and the relations of principal to staff, staff to staff, staff to students, and students to staff must conform to convictions about the importance of the individual and to tolerance for diversity and divergent thinking. School organization must be based on good will, rationality, civility, and respect for students and teachers as persons.

The good school, we believe, should be humane. This implies that those who administer and teach should honestly care about all the students in their schools. They should not attach negative labels, pass hasty judgments, adopt prejudicial attitudes, disparage or discourage. They should strive to develop good self concepts and feelings of worth and belonging. This has implications for grading practices, tracking and grouping, the use of norms in judging individual students, and for the involvement of students in their own education and in the overall governance of their schools.

The book is also based around certain beliefs about the place of the secondary school in the school system. One such belief is that change can take place more quickly, intelligently, and effectively at the level of the secondary school. It is at the school that the principal and staff and students associate day to day, get to know one another, and are in a position to judge what is good and what needs to be improved. We do not believe any justifiable end is served by having curricula, study guides, and books determined or selected by those not closely identified with the school. We believe school rules and regulations should be developed by those who live together in the school community. Progress is served when individual schools have considerable latitude to be themselves and to be different.

If one accepts these beliefs, the role of the principal as leader is enhanced and, at the same time, tested. To maintain comfortable status quo, to keep things quiet, and to keep out of any kind of trouble usually means that nothing too important is happening. On the other hand, honest self-examination by a principal and staff often discloses that some things need to be done differently. The status quo must be altered. Some risks must be assumed. Some mistakes may be made. Good leadership not only calls for objective, critical examination and appraisal, but also demands the courage and willingness to accept and act upon the evidence.

We believe the school cannot be isolated from the community it serves. Dialog between school and community needs to be continuous and must be carried out on the level where purposes are examined, evaluated, and modified. Such association of school and community rises far above the concept of selling the school to the citizens in order to receive money or buildings. It is far more than using a public relations approach to keep the community placated and unquestioning with regard to controversial issues or what the school is doing. People in the community and community agencies can make valuable contributions to the school. The school can extend itself into the community. In the final analysis, the effective school is closely identified with all those it serves. Thus is the role of school leadership extended.

We believe in the future of our democratic form of government and in the vital role which education must play if that future is to be realized in the

Preface

richest and fullest sense. We share the opinion of the late Robert F. Kennedy, that

> The future does not belong to those who are content with today, apathetic toward common problems and their fellow man alike, timid and fearful in the face of new ideas and bold projects. Rather it will belong to those who can blend vision, reason, and courage in a personal committment to the ideals and great enterprises of American society.

Introduction

As stated in various ways throughout its pages, this book is aimed toward the future. Although no one can say with certainty what the future will hold for society and its institutions, it can reasonably be predicted that one constant which will characterize the future is *change*. A variety of influences are already combining to change the public secondary school in the United States. These will affect the way schools are administered and taught and will alter the roles and functions of those in leadership positions—especially those in the position of the secondary school principal. The only questions concern the direction and extent of the changes which will occur.

When social institutions are not capable of adapting themselves to change, and when confidence in them erodes, they become dysfunctional. The greater the degree of change buffeting against the institution, the more difficult it becomes to maintain the status quo. Attempts to do so result in internal tensions and conflicts as well as outside disaffection.

In this period of our history, all our institutions suffer to some extent from a crisis of confidence. The secondary school is not alone in this respect. How to adapt the institutions to new demands while maintaining some stability in the process is the central question with which those in leadership positions will have to come to grips in the decade ahead.

A French proverb tells us that as things change the more they remain the same. A good case could be made to show that this has applied to the American secondary schools over the past eighty years. It is, of course, possible that this tendency of schools to move back and forth within a narrow range will be evident in the decades ahead, but we think it is doubtful.

Clark Kerr, Chairman of the Carnegie Commission on Higher Education, alluded to this question in the David D. Henry Lecture at the University of Illinois in October, 1972. He described historically the movements in college and university education. He showed how practices and philosophies in higher education have swung back and forth, " ... vibrating within the same boundaries, but with a reduced swing each time; each time approaching what might be considered to be the long-term normal in-between 'Golden Mean' position." In fact, Kerr said,

> faculty members are already seeking to draw back on the concessions made to students in recent years. Proponents of the view that change vibrates back and forth within a narrow range note that, despite the great pressures of the student movement in recent years, relatively little has changed on campus by way of governance or academic conduct; that the student movement has turned out to be an unguided missile that soon spent its force; that faculty members are at all times and in all places on the side of the internal status quo; and that administrators do not actively seek the trouble that almost any change entails. As a consequence, having moved slightly in one direction, we shall not move even more slightly back again. The vibrations that started in 1870 (away from a highly controlled student environment to the fully independent student, for example) will continue but with constantly diminishing amplitude.

This, Kerr said, may turn out to be the realistic view of how things will be, but he questioned if this would be so. He stated his belief that higher education is not now just still vibrating from the great "climacteric" of 1870 but that it is entering a new climacteric which will lead to new developments. Kerr pointed out that

> Other changes are also taking place. The "cultural revolution" may turn out to be a decisive event in world history, as was the Renaissance or the Reformation, and also the democratic revolutions in the United States and France. But it is too soon to say whether this is true or not and the "cultural revolution" is, as yet, too diffuse to speculate much about its impacts if it is true: Does it mean a new emphasis on the sensate as against the work ethic? Or that "politics takes charge" in the sense of the supremacy of absolute ideologies? Or that the old culture must be abolished? Or that a new leveling of society into workers and soldiers and peasants will take place? I do believe, however, that new mentalities—new approaches to society—may be in the process of being born.
> While standing with the second view that (higher) education will move in new directions, I do not believe that these directions will be as clear cut as those of 1870. We face a more confused and uncertain period of change.

The secondary schools face the same possibilities. In secondary schools as well as in colleges and universities, many staff members and administrators seem to want most of all to retain the status quo or to return to a status quo ante which seems in retrospect to have been more peaceful and orderly. They are comfortable and reassured with the thought that no matter what the stress of change, actual or proposed, things will sooner or later return to "normal".

On the other hand, some inside the schools and more, perhaps, outside, seem to be convinced that the future will demand something more than short swings of the pendulum.

These questions will be explored in the pages which follow.

Part One

The American Secondary School

1

Background of the American Secondary School

Although we shall not dwell unnecessarily long on the past, we believe some understanding of the history of secondary education in the United States is valuable as a screen against which to measure the present and project the future.* As Santayana reminded us, "those who cannot remember the past are condemned to repeat it."

The American secondary school has a history of its own. Only in the recent past has it evolved into an institution which is (theoretically at least) open to all, free to all, and which embraces almost all of the American boys and girls of secondary school age. What follows is not an attempt to write a history of secondary education in the United States. Rather, it is intended to trace a few of the salient trends and check points that have led to the secondary school of today.

The public, tax-supported secondary school, open to all youth, came late in the history of education in America. The early colonial secondary schools were neither open to all nor were they intended to be. The colonists brought with them the European concept of a class system of education, with one kind of education provided for the masses and another kind reserved for the upper classes. These early schools were described in a publication of the American Council on Education.

> The secondary schools established by the early American colonies followed the pattern of the secondary schools of Europe, which had been the dominant educational institutions of all Western European countries since the medieval period. The colonial secondary schools were variously known as "Latin Schools," "grammar schools," or "Latin Grammar Schools." The chief item in their curriculum, as

---

*Adapted from *The Development of Secondary Education,* by Frederick M. Raubinger, Harold G. Rowe, Donald L. Piper, and Charles K. West (New York: Macmillan Publishing Co., 1969). Copyright © 1969, by Macmillan Publishing Co.

indicated by their name, was the Latin language. They were distinct from the schools which served the sons and daughters of the common people. The schools for ordinary boys and girls limited their instruction to teaching how to read the vernacular—the Latin schools prepared for college. The pupils of these Latin schools were a small select group of boys who were looking forward to careers in the professions; at first, in the ministry, later, in the law, and still later in medicine.[1]

The first of these schools, the Boston Latin School, was established in 1635, and was supported by free subscriptions from forty-five inhabitants. It has a long history, and may be used to illustrate the selectivity of this type of school. In the period 1815–1861 the school sent on to college an average of fewer than thirteen graduates per year. This may be put into perspective when it is seen that in 1861 the population of Boston was 178,000 and the enrollment in the common (elementary) schools was 28,000.

The first public high school was established in Boston in 1821, almost two centuries after the founding of the first Latin school. A three-year school, it was first known as the English Classical High School. Entrance, at age twelve, was by way of examination. The first public high school in Philadelphia was founded in 1838; in Cincinnati, in 1847; and in Chicago, in 1856, the latter being the first which admitted girls. A report of the Chicago superintendent of schools in 1857 showed that the school was built to accommodate 320 students and had a first year enrollment of 151. At that time, Chicago had a total population of 108,000 and a common school enrollment of 8,577.

Perhaps as many as 300 public high schools were in operation in 1860, but they were small, selective, and served very few of the boys and girls of secondary school age.

Although taxes had been levied since Colonial times for support of common schools, it was not until 1872 that the legal right of a board of education to tax citizens for the support of a public high school was established by court decision. This occurred in the famous *Kalamazoo* case whereby the Supreme Court of Michigan affirmed the right of communities to tax themselves for the support of secondary schools. Nevertheless, the seeds for what was to much later become the free, tax-supported secondary school were sown early in the history of the country—first in the Latin schools, and later in the academies.

FRANKLIN AND THE ACADEMY

Benjamin Franklin, self-tutored genius, was the first person of prominence to suggest a different kind of school which would have different purposes from

---

[1] American Council on Education, *What the High Schools Ought to Teach* (Washington, D.C., 1940) pp. 1–2.

Background of the American Secondary School

the Latin schools. Although he is frequently overlooked in discussions of those who influenced the direction of secondary education, Franklin outlined and gave credence to an alternative kind of secondary education. Had Franklin been writing today, the chances are that he would be labeled a "progressive" educator. In 1749, he wrote and distributed a tract, "Proposals Relating to the Education of Youth in Pennsylvania." He urged public-spirited citizens to apply for a charter to "erect an academy for the education of youth." English was to be the chief medium of instruction. He proposed that students be taught to write legibly, clearly, and concisely, to speak well, and to learn arithmetic and accounts and some of the first principles of geometry and astronomy. His proposed curriculum embraced what might be called the social studies: the history of men and nations, of commerce, arts, manufacturing, trade, and religions, as well as political science and geography. He advocated natural sciences so that merchants and mechanics would know more about the commodities and materials of their trades. He proposed practical experience in agriculture through planting and tending gardens, and visits to farms.

Franklin had ideas about how students in his proposed academy should be treated. The trustees, he said, would

> look on the students as in some sort their children, treat them with familiarity and affection, and when they have behaved well and gone through their studies, and are to enter the world, zealously unite, and make all interest that can be made to establish them, whether in business, offices, marriage, or any other thing for their advantage. . . . [2]

He said the schools should be pleasant, with a garden and orchard, and should have books, maps, globes, scientific instruments, and machines. He proposed what would now be called a physical education program, and advocated wrestling, running, leaping, and swimming. Butts and Cremin summarized the proposal:

> Franklin's real hope was to enlarge and make respectable an education for civil and occupational life that would not need to rest upon religious instruction or the classics. He hoped his academy would have an English school that would be on a level of equality and even more valuable than its classical school. [3]

Franklin's proposals were widely read and his proposed academy was eventually established. However, after it was in operation, the "Latinists" in the school attempted to dominate it, according to Franklin, and he was so

---

[2] Benjamin Franklin, "Proposals Relating to the Education of Youth in Pennsylvania" (Philadelphia: University of Pennsylvania Press, 1931) pp. 7–8.

[3] Freeman R. Butts and Lawrence Cremin, *A History of Education in American Culture* (New York: Henry Holt and Co., 1953) p. 79.

disappointed that in exasperation he demanded that the corporation be dissolved.

His ideas, however, survived. Phillips Andover, the first chartered academy in New England, was founded in 1778 and incorporated in 1780. Exeter Academy was incorporated in 1781 and opened in 1783.

The account of Franklin's proposals is included for two reasons. First, his ideas represent a line of thought about secondary education which was a departure from the earlier concept of the elite, selective college preparatory school represented by the Latin schools; they also represent a thread of thought which may be traced through the developing fabric of secondary education from Franklin's time to the present. Second, the growth of the academy was the most important feature of secondary education during the first three quarters of the nineteenth century. It has been estimated that by 1850, 6,000 academies were in operation. In numbers and in enrollment, the academy was the dominant institution for secondary education. It was not until 1880 that the enrollment in the public secondary schools equalled that of the academies.

Much as the academies contributed to the education of boys and girls of high school age, they were not tuition-free, tax supported, or open to all who wished to attend. Many were proprietary schools; some were endowed; some received grants of land on which to erect buildings; many were chartered. But at best they were only quasi-public.

By 1890, though it was still small in number and had a total enrollment of only slightly more than 200,000, the public high school had emerged as the dominant type of secondary school. In 1890, enrollment in the common schools was twelve and a half million. The age of the academy was over. The era of the public high school had begun. Its astonishing growth in the next eighty years was paralleled only by the revolutionary changes in American society and ways of life.

THE FIRST NATIONAL STUDY

The National Teachers Association was founded in 1857. In 1870 the name was changed to the National Educational Association. Although departments of higher education, primary education, and elementary education were established early in the history of the organization, a department of secondary education was not added until 1885. An offspring of the Association was the National Council of Education, organized in 1880. With a membership of sixty, the Council studied various aspects and problems of education and reported regularly at annual meetings of the National Educational Association.

In 1891 a committee of the National Council of Education made a report on the general subject of school programs and college admission requirements. The Committee was then requested to arrange a conference on the subject, and such a conference was held in Saratoga, New York, on July 7–9, 1892.

The conference recommended the establishment of the Committee on Secondary School Studies, since known also as the Committee of Ten. We will comment on this committee's report briefly because it exerted a powerful influence on the schools for twenty-five years afterwards, and its influence is still felt today in arguments about what secondary schools should do, how they should be organized for instruction, and about what uses of subject matter should be continued.

No evidence exists to indicate that parents, other citizens, or boards of education had anything to do with the findings and recommendations of the Committee of Ten. The chairman of the committee was Charles W. Eliot, then president of Harvard. Nicholas Murray Butler, then a professor of philosophy at Columbia (later to become president of that institution) although not a member of the committee, was influential in choosing the subcommittees for the various subject fields. The ten members of the central committee included five college or university presidents, one college professor, two headmasters of private schools, one public high school principal, and the United States Commissioner of Education.

What were some of the concerns of the committee? First, that too many subjects were being taught (forty, according to their survey); second, that many were taught for too short a period of time; and third, that the time allotted to the subjects varied widely.

Conferences were therefore organized on the following subjects: (1) Latin; (2) Greek; (3) English; (4) other modern languages; (5) mathematics; (6) physics, astronomy, and chemistry; (7) natural history; (8) history, civil government, and political economy; and (9) geography. The upshot of the reports of these conferences was a series of recommendations which fixed a quantitative value and time allotment to each subject for years to come. A four or five period per week allotment per subject, each period forty-five minutes in length, was fixed firmly on the secondary school curriculum. Then, just as in the later Sputnik era, all of the subject matter conferences wished their subjects to be moved down into the earlier grades. The recommendation that the secondary period be extended from four to six years was the forerunner of the junior high school movement.

Faculty psychology guided the thinking of the committee—the mind was to be trained like a muscle, on "hard" subjects. Emphasis was mainly on the processes of education, that is, on the subjects to be taught. No thought was given to purpose. It was assumed that study of recommended subjects, taught for the time allotted, would result in desirable ends.

THE CARNEGIE UNIT

It is sometimes almost by accident that practices are cemented into institutions. Such is the case with the Carnegie Unit, which, more than a half century after its inception, is probably the single greatest obstacle to flexibility in the secondary school. The Carnegie Unit had its roots in concerns of colleges over admission requirements, and, to some extent, in the subject matter prescriptions and time allotments suggested by the Committee of Ten. It was, however, money that brought the "standard unit," popularly known as the Carnegie Unit, into national use.

Andrew Carnegie gave $10,000,000 to the Carnegie Foundation for the Advancement of Teaching, the income from which was to be used to provide retirement allowances for college professors. In the early 1900s, it was not always clear whether an institution was a secondary school or a "college." In order to decide which institutions could benefit from the Carnegie money, it became necessary to define a college and a high school. The high school was defined as a four-year *preparatory* institution, not connected with, or part of, a college or university. For college entrance, a minimum of fourteen "units" of high school academic preparation was required. A "unit" was a college entrance subject which was studied five periods per week for a school year. The adoption of the unit measurement by the Carnegie Foundation in 1909 almost immediately set the pattern for all secondary schools in the nation. It remains the typical pattern today.

EVIDENCE OF UNREST

In the twenty-five years immediately following the Report of the Committee of Ten, things changed. More boys and girls began to attend public high schools. High school principals began to assert themselves on the question of what a high school should be and what it should do. Various committees of the Department of Secondary Education of the National Education Association began to examine their own purposes and consequently found the recommendations of 1893 outdated.

One such committee, reporting in 1913, had this to say about the relationship of the high schools to the colleges:

> It has been our aim to make our plea general for the granting to preparatory schools greater freedom in planning their courses of study to fit local needs, and to develop interests, tastes and abilities of their students whom they serve.[4]

The principals spoke of citizenship education, vocational education, an enriched curriculum, and more attention to those students (then a majority) who did not plan to go on to college.

The Commission on the Reorganization of Secondary Education began its work in 1913. It culminated in the 1918 publication of "The Cardinal Principles of Secondary Education," a landmark in the history of the secondary schools. The Commission showed that the schools did not have holding power. One-third of the pupils who entered the first year of elementary

---

[4]National Education Association, *Addresses and Proceedings* 11 July, 1911, p. 729.

school reached the four-year high school; a third of these left before the second year began; half left before the beginning of the third year. Fewer than a third who entered remained to graduate. This was the state of affairs the Commission discovered, and for this reason, along with others, reorganization of the secondary school was imperative. The dropout problem was an early phenomenon.

In supporting the need for reorganization, the Commission reported that, "Secondary education ... like any other established agency of society, is conservative and tends to resist modification." The Commission found this to be true in spite of the fact that "society is always in process of development; the character of the secondary school population undergoes modification; and the sciences on which educational theory and practice depend constantly furnish new information."[5]

The report called attention to (1) individual differences and aptitudes among pupils; (2) the need to reexamine and reinterpret subject values and teaching methods with reference to the theory of "general discipline"; (3) the importance of applying knowledge; and (4) the need for continuity in the development of children. The central question of the purpose of education in a democracy was also examined in the report.

Finally the Cardinal Principles (objectives) were stated. Answers to questions concerning goals and purposes took precedence. Once the goals were established, it was decided how subject matter should be used to achieve the goals, and how a school should be organized to further the goal aspirations. Purpose came before process. The goals, simply stated, included (1) health; (2) command of the fundamental processes: reading, writing, arithmetical computations, oral and written expression; (3) worthy home membership; (4) vocation; (5) civic education; (6) worthy use of leisure; (7) ethical character.

The first general reference to the comprehensive high school was made in the report, as was the first specific reference to dividing the secondary period into junior and senior high schools, each three years in length. Finally, the report asserted, this emerging public high school should be for all youth of secondary school age, and not for a few only.

CHANGES IN AMERICAN SOCIETY

Later we shall return to other reports, primarily those of the 1930s. Here we pause to comment on the change in America which had great impact on the secondary schools, as well as upon other social institutions.

"Within the past few decades," the authors of the Cardinal Principles wrote, "changes have taken place in American life profoundly affecting the

---

[5]Bulletin No. 35, *Cardinal Principles of Secondary Education: A Report of the Commission on the Reorganization of Secondary Education* (Washington, D.C.: Bureau of Education, 1918) p. 7.

activities of the individual. As a citizen he must to a greater extent and in a more direct way cope with problems of community life, State and National governments, and international relationships. As a worker, he must adapt to a more complex economic order."[6]

What were some of the forces that were so profoundly to affect life in America and America's schools in the twentieth century? The second industrial revolution created profound and drastic changes in America—in ways of life, in ways of making a living, and in customs and traditions. The America of the Latin schools, the academies, and the early high schools was uprooted by the forces of industrialization. The day of the small farmer, the small town and village, the small business, and the individual craftsman came to a close. The small factory gave way to large manufacturing industries. Rural America was transformed into metropolitan America, as those who lived and worked on the farms and in the small towns were forced by economic necessity to migrate to the cities or their environs. In 1870, three-quarters of all the people in the country lived in rural areas. A hundred years later the proportion was reversed. In the thirty years from 1940 to 1970, 30 million persons migrated from small towns to cities or areas adjacent to cities. A new word, *megalopolis,* was coined to describe the concentration of population in vast metropolitan centers. Among the later migrants were the blacks, leaving the rural south for the northern cities in search of employment and what they hoped would be a better way of life. As blacks moved into the cities, large numbers of whites moved to the suburbs. A new phrase "the black ghetto" was used to describe the concentration of blacks in the inner cores of the cities. Ghetto areas were typified by poverty, overcrowding, and high incidence of crime and delinquency. Severe problems confronted secondary schools in the ghettos. Millions of Americans became mobile wanderers, and being mobile, often became rootless also.

Bigness characterized the American business corporation. As the United States emerged as a world power, and as domestic problems grew in scope and complexity, bigness also came to characterize American government. Forced by necessity to retain some power and identity, workers joined together in big unions. The face-to-face relationships of an earlier time became more difficult to retain, and associations of the individual with his employer and with his government became more remote and more impersonal. These changes seriously affected the young. Child labor laws kept the young off the labor market, and compulsory education laws progressively raised the age at which a boy or girl could legally leave school. Except for jobs on the assembly lines, unskilled workers found a rapidly shrinking market for their labor.

All of these changes resulted in an astonishing increase in the number of secondary-school-aged youth who remained in school. They also placed great stress on the secondary schools. At the time of the report of the Committee

---
[6]*Ibid.*

Table 1-1
Youth, 14-17 Years of Age in Public and Private Secondary Schools

Year	Number Enrolled	Percentage
1890	359,959	6.7
1900	699,403	11.4
1910	1,115,398	15.4
1920	2,500,176	32.3
1930	4,804,255	51.4
1940	7,123,009	73.3
1950	6,453,009	76.8
1960	9,599,810	86.1
1969	14,200,000	94.4
1971[a]	15,146,899	94.5

Source: U. S. Office of Education, "Progress of Public Education in the United States" (Washington: U. S. government printing office, 1970).
[a]Taken from Statistical Abstract of the U. S. 1972.

of Ten, only one in fifteen of the age group fourteen to seventeen was in school. The others had left to enter the world outside the school. Many who became leaders in commerce, industry, government, and the arts were among those who did not enter or who left the secondary school. The biographer of Mark Twain records that he finished his formal education in 1847 at age twelve, but also points out that this was not unusual, since as late as 1890 the average adult had completed only the fifth grade. The boy and girl of this era entered the adult world early, and formed an association with adults which was in its own way an education. They were inducted early into the decision-making process. But economic and social change forced more and more of the young to remain in school for a longer period of time, thus prolonging dependence.

From 1890 until 1970 the number of those in the fourteen to seventeen-year-old age group who were enrolled in secondary schools increased dramatically, as shown in Table 1-1.

REPORTS OF THE THIRTIES

We now return to some of the reports and studies which mirrored the rapid social changes and reflected the responses educational leaders made to new conditions facing the secondary school.

The decade of the 1930s was a period of deep probing and analysis of secondary education. The Great Depression had shaken the nation. Unemployment was a spectre that haunted most families, and jobs for high school-aged boys and girls were almost nonexistent. With the advent of the New Deal, federal agencies attempted to provide some opportunities. The Civilian Conservation Corps was established in 1933, and some older youth were used in reforestation projects and similar works. The National Youth Administration, established in 1935, provided assistance in made work projects, often in the schools themselves, but also in resident centers. Until appropriations were withdrawn in 1942, the government spent more than 3 billion dollars on those agencies which served perhaps 10 percent of the nation's youth. Young persons also returned to school or chose to remain in unprecedented numbers because no alternative was open to them.

Abroad, disquieting events turned the thoughts of educational and political leaders back to fundamental questions of democracy. The rise of Fascism in Italy, Nazism in Germany, and Communism in Eastern Europe saw totalitarian governments suppressing the freedoms Americans had long cherished. The optimistic belief that the form of government established in the United States would inevitably be adopted as the model elsewhere was diminished. Toward the end of the decade, the threat of another World War hung ominously over the nation. It was during this period of national crisis that some of the most penetrating examinations of the purposes, goals, and practices of secondary education were made.

The Committee on Reorientation

In 1932, the Department of Secondary School Principals of the National Education Association authorized appointment of a Commission "to study and restate the principles and objectives of secondary education." The group formed to carry on the study became known as the Committee on the Reorientation of Secondary Education. The Committee issued a report in 1936, and presented ten issues and ten functions. As in the Cardinal Principals, the emphasis was on goals and purposes. As an introduction to the issues and functions, the Committee said:

> It is especially notable in our history that provision was so early made for secondary education. But the pride with which we have celebrated this phenomenon should not blind us to the fact that it was for a long time provided in only a few localities and for a very small number of highly selected boys, that it was frankly and fully imitative of an institution already a relic of largely outgrown needs in a civilization far different from that in America, and that it could have had small significance to the pioneer people. It did prevent learning of a sort from being buried in the grave of our fathers, but at the same time it stifled the imagination of educators and made them content to follow outworn practices without planning soundly and comprehensively for what the New World needed.
>
> Proposals for improvement and adaptions to the demands of new conditions were few, spaced at long intervals, and, except for those by Benjamin Franklin in the middle of the eighteenth century, singularly small and lacking in inventiveness to meet new needs. Although the academies made wide curricular experimentation, there was a continuing lack of any attempt to prepare a sound, comprehensive, and long

Background of the American Secondary School

sighted program for secondary education. This lack has continued to the present time. Although the several committees of the National Education Association have made valuable contributions, the need for agreement on fundamental principles and definitions of secondary education in our country today is almost as great as it ever was. This need is especially imperative in light of the many and significant changes that have come in our civilization.[7]

The more things change, the more they remain the same; changes in education vibrate within a narrow range. These aphorisms the Committee had discovered were true. The issues perceived by the Committee were:

1. Shall secondary education be provided at public expense for all normal individuals or for only a limited number?
2. Shall secondary education seek to retain all pupils in school as long as they wish to remain, or shall it transfer them to other agencies under educational supervision when, in the judgment of the school authorities, these agencies promise to serve better the pupils' immediate and probably future needs?
3. Shall secondary education be concerned only with the welfare and progress of the individual, or with these only as they promise to contribute to the welfare and progress of society?
4. Shall secondary education provide a common curriculum for all, or differentiated offerings?
5. Shall secondary education include vocational training, or shall it be restricted to general education?
6. Shall secondary education be primarily directed toward preparation for advanced studies, or shall it be primarily concerned with the value of its own courses, regardless of a student's future academic career?
7. Shall secondary education accept conventional school subjects as fundamental categories under which school experiences shall be classified and presented to students, or shall it arrange and present experiences in fundamental categories directly related to the performance of such functions of secondary schools in a democracy as increasing the ability and the desire better to meet sociocivic, economic, health, leisure time, vocational and preprofessional problems and situations?
8. Shall secondary education present merely organized knowledge, or shall it also assume responsibility for attitudes and ideas?
9. Shall secondary education seek merely the adjustment of students to prevailing social ideals, or shall it seek the reconstruction of society?
10. Granting that education is a "gradual, continuous, unitary pro-

---

[7]The National Education Association, Department of Secondary School Principals. Bulletin No. 59, *Issues of Secondary Education: Report of the Committee on the Reorientation of Secondary Education* (January 1936) p. 20.

cess," shall secondary education be presented merely as a phase of such a process, or shall it be organized as a distinct but closely articulating part of the entire educational program, with peculiarly emphasized functions of its own?[8]

In the discussion of the issues and functions, the Committee agreed upon a number of general principles, some of which are paraphrased here:

1. The secondary school should be universal, not selective.
2. Too many boys and girls were dropping out of school. In respect to dropouts, the Committee said:

> The Curricula usually involves sitting on hard chairs four or five hours a day, reading and writing, discussing and reciting, learning the facts of history, grammar, science, mathematics and the like. Tension is created by severe competition in which many children are destined never to succeed, and by high standards of achievement which they can never meet. Normal social communications and cooperation are forbidden. It is no wonder that many children rebel against this regime with almost hysterical violence and drop out of school.[9]

3. Admission to secondary schools should be open to all: to those who graduated from elementary school; those who did not but who seemed likely to benefit from secondary school, assuming the secondary school provided more flexible programs; to those who had left but who wished to return.
4. Teachers should have to define competence in other ways than mastery of "facts."
5. The use of external motivation, such as marks, and passing and failing grades should be reexamined.
6. The school should provide in its program both integration (education common to all) and differentiation.
7. Vocational education should be a respected part of the curriculum.
8. Adults should have the privilege of using school facilities.
9. The secondary school should be primarily concerned with its own courses.
10. The idea that a single pattern of courses required by colleges is necessary for success in college should be rejected.
11. Considering knowledge gained from psychology, a curriculum using conventional subjects as the only categories of school experiences is

---
[8]*Ibid.*, p. 5–6.
[9]*Ibid.*, p. 25.

not defensible. More fundamental categories of organization and learning experience should be used.
12. The schools should get rid of the notion of one school "preparing" for another.
13. The fault of the educator has been in misjudging what the real needs of youth are.
14. The secondary school has too often disappointed rather than satisfied the eager minds of youth.
15. Interests should be recognized as the dynamics of education.

The Eight-Year Study

Two years before the Committee on Reorganization began its work, the question before the annual convention of the Progressive Education Association was: "How can the high school improve its services to American youth?" The concerns of both groups were similar in most respects, the most important ones being the slowness with which the schools were responding to the needs of young people in a changing world, and the tendency of schools to perpetuate outworn beliefs and practices in the face of urgent reasons to alter them.

The membership of the Progressive Education Association included many private as well as public secondary schools. The member schools had come to the conclusion that proposals for improvement in the high school program were met with the objection that changes would jeopardize the chances of students being admitted to college. In response to this objection, a Commission on the Relation of School and College was established, "to explore possibilities of better coordination of school and college work and to seek an agreement which would provide the necessary freedom for secondary schools to attempt fundamental reconstruction." Their study was begun in 1933 and was terminated in 1941.

As a preliminary to the study of school and college relationships, the Commission reported on what was wrong with secondary schools as they then existed. They acknowledged the tremendous growth in the number of boys and girls enrolled, and the billions of tax dollars invested in buildings and operating expense; they urged the expansion of a limited curriculum consisting mainly of foreign languages, history, mathematics, science, and English to include the social studies, commercial subjects, the arts, home economics, industrial arts, and many other courses. Finally, they emphasized the need for the development of extracurricular activities.

The Commission was not pleased with the fact that only half of those who entered high school remained to graduate. The dropout problem was still at hand, just as it had been in 1918. Turning then to shortcomings of the schools, they expressed the judgments which are summarized here:

1. Secondary education did not have clear, definite, central purpose.
2. Schools failed to give students appreciation of their heritage as American citizens.
3. Schools did not prepare students adequately for the responsibilities of community life.
4. Schools seldom challenged students of first-rate ability to work up to the level of their intellectual powers.
5. Schools did not know their students well or guide them wisely.
6. Schools failed to create conditions necessary for effective learning (teachers persisted in assigning meaningless tasks and listening to recitations.)
7. Creative energies of students were seldom released and developed.
8. The conventional curriculum was far removed from the real concerns of youth.
9. The traditional subjects of the curriculum had lost much of their vitality and significance.
10. Many high school graduates were not competent in their use of the English language.
11. There was little evidence of unity or continuity in the work of the typical high school.
12. Complacency characterized the high school.
13. Teachers were not well-equipped for their responsibilities.
14. Seldom were principals to be found who thought about their work in terms of democratic leadership of the community, teachers, and students.
15. Principals and teachers worked hard, but they had no comprehensive evaluation of the results of their work.
16. The high school diploma signified only the accumulation of required units.
17. The relationship of high school and college was unsatisfactory.[10]

It is impossible to condense in a few paragraphs the story of the Eight-Year Study, which was fully reported in five volumes. Essentially, the study was intended to determine if high schools freed from traditional course and unit requirements could send on to college students who would succeed as well in college as those prepared in the traditional way.

Thirty public and private secondary schools made up an experimental group. Three hundred colleges and universities agreed to accept recommended

---

[10]Wilford M. Aiken, *The Story of the Eight-Year Study* (New York: Harper and Brothers, 1942) pp. 4–10.

graduates from those schools and to waive the traditional course requirements for admission. Freed from college requirements, the thirty schools could proceed to experiment with changes in learning patterns.

The thirty schools, as they planned their experimental program, realized that many changes in ways of teaching, as well as in organization and curriculum, were necessary if attendance at school was to become the stimulating, meaningful experience it could be for each student. It was believed that the high school in the United States could rediscover its chief reason for existence—to lead young people to understand, to appreciate, and to live the kind of life for which the people of the United States have been striving throughout our history. The best way to give youth an understanding of and appreciation for the way of life called democracy is to live that kind of life every day in school.

The researchers also believed that the curriculum of the secondary schools should deal with the present concerns of young people as well as with the knowledge, skills, understandings, and appreciations which constitute our cultural heritage. They wanted to achieve greater unity and continuity in the curriculum. Finally, they believed that the schools must know each student well in order to guide him wisely. Thus, they recognized the importance of measuring, recording, and evaluating students' work. (The story of how the schools planned and carried out new kinds of programs and reorganization during the eight years is contained in one volume of the report.)

What were the results of the Eight-Year Study? The research design matched 1,475 pairs of students, one group including students from the experimental schools, the other group including students from schools in which traditional college preparatory programs were followed. These students were carefully followed into college, for varying periods of time: those entering in 1936 were watched for four years; in 1937, for three years; in 1938, for two years; and in 1939, for one year.

The final report showed that the graduates of the thirty experimental schools earned a slightly higher total grade average; specialized in the same academic fields as the comparison students; did not differ from the comparison group in the number of times they were placed on probation; received slightly more academic honors each year; were more often judged to possess a high degree of intellectual curiosity and drive; were more often judged to be precise, systematic, and objective in their thinking; were more frequently judged to have developed clear or well formulated ideas concerning the meaning of education, especially in the first two years of college; more often demonstrated a high degree of resourcefulness in meeting new situations; did not differ from the comparison group in ability to plan time effectively; had about the same problems of adjustment as the comparison group, but approached their solution with greater effectiveness; particpated in the arts more frequently, and enjoyed more appreciative experiences; and earned, in each college year, a higher percentage of nonacademic honors. The experimental group did not differ from the comparison group in the quality of their adjustment to their contemporaries. They had a somewhat better orientation toward the choice of an occupation, and demonstrated a more active concern for what was going on in the world. Over and above the general comparisons, it was revealed that the graduates of the most experimental of the thirty schools, to use the words of the report "were more strikingly successful than their matchees."

Youth Tell Their Story

The American Youth Commission, which was appointed by the American Council on Education, began its work in 1935. One of the principal projects of the Commission was a report issued in 1938 called "Youth Tell Their Story: A Study of the Conditions and Attitudes of Young People in Maryland between the Ages of 16 and 24." Although the young people questioned in this study responded to inquiries about their attitudes toward home, school, work, leisure, and religion, much information obtained related to school, directly or indirectly.

The study was based on a sampling of Maryland youth, but for good statistical reasons it was asserted that the sampling could be generalized for young people of the entire nation. The generations studied were those who in a few years would enter the armed services in World War II or would work in the industries that supported the war effort at home. They are also the parents and grandparents of students now in our schools.

What did the report say about that generation?

> They (the pages of the report) will reveal the activities and the thinking of a generation that is still making an effort to adjust itself to the educational, social, and vocational realities of an era that is past. With what looks very much like apathetic docility, youth are trying somehow to find adequate satisfaction in such things as a secondary educational system that too often persists in preparing them for colleges they will never enter, a system of vocational training that too frequently trains them for jobs they will never find....
>
> If there is anything in the present situation for sober adults to view with alarm, it is not that youth will rise in revolt against the programs and policies of antiquated institutions that are intended to serve them, but that they will, with a supreme meekness, continue to accept those programs and policies exactly as they inherit them.[11]

On equality of opportunity through education:

> The facts in this study indicate that our present secondary school is still a highly selective institution adapted to the needs of a small minority of our population. The public schools of this country have been supported by the theory that they serve as an instrument for the

---

[11]*Youth Tell Their Story* (Washington, D.C.: American Council on Education, 1938) p. 6.

maintenance of equality of opportunity. In view of the very great inequalities in educational opportunity that exist at the present time, one may well question whether this end is, in fact, being accomplished. There is grave danger that the public school system, if present tendencies exist, may become a positive force in creating those very inequalities in the condition of men it was designed to reduce.[12]

As to the need for guidance and vocational training:

> Guidance is one of youth's most pressing necessities. Under present conditions only a small minority of youth are receiving anything like vocational guidance.[13]

This study revealed the lack of appropriate and adequate vocational training. The study further revealed that the program of general secondary education was in need of thorough reorganization. More care needed to be given to health education; civic education (as was reflected by a reported indifference to the ballot and other kinds of civic responsibility) was in need of fundamental improvement; an urgent demand to focus all the agencies of society on the individual youth and his needs was apparent.

As for those who dropped out of school:

> Our data reveal that with several groups of youth, unsatisfactory school adjustment—by which is meant a combination of lack of interest, disciplinary problems, and too difficult subjects—is a more general reason for leaving school than a lack of family funds.[14]

The Regents' Inquiry

Under a grant from the General Education Board, the Board of Regents of the State of New York authorized, in 1935, a broad study known as the Regents' Inquiry into the Character and Cost of Public Education in the State of New York. The study was completed and published in 1938.

One important phase of the study examined the secondary school. Many of the conclusions are remarkably similar to those of other reports of the period and, indeed, to those of the period 1913–1918. Thus, what we include may seem repetitious. Yet the persons who prepared the studies were different, and the locale was not the same. One can only conclude that the realization that secondary schools lagged behind cultural change was general, regardless of what group studied the school, or where a particular inquiry was made.

The Regents' Inquiry took note of the rapid expansion of secondary school enrollment. In New York State in 1938, it was observed that eight pupils entered the secondary school for one who entered in 1900. The secondary school had progressively become a less selective institution. The

---

[12]*Ibid.*, Foreword.
[13]*Ibid.*
[14]*Ibid.*, p. 67.

question was raised as to whether the secondary school could adapt itself to the varied needs of the study body, or whether it would be overshadowed by an educational unit more responsive to social pressures.

> What has become increasingly clear is that school experiences must be planned in terms of the life goals of adolescent boys and girls, rather than traditional academic patterns, and that these goals must be suited to the astonishing diversity that exists in respect to abilities, needs and interests. Some years ago the success of the secondary school might have been estimated from the subsequent college careers of its students; today the criterion must be sought in the relevancy of high school offerings to the needs of the entire population.[15]

The investigators came to a number of conclusions:

1. It is often difficult to establish any clear relationship between classroom experiences and present-day problems.
2. Evaluations have usually only analyzed the "flower" of the system, which is judged by those who succeeded, ignoring the many who dropped by the way.
3. Most ... educators are ready to agree that the functions of secondary education have changed, but few have made comparable changes in the program of their schools.
4. Students have very little contact with adults outside of school, nor do adults know students.
5. Students, on the whole, know almost no one to whom they can go for advice. As a matter of fact, many students feel that to acknowledge the need for advice is a sign of weakness.
6. Educational and recreational activities begun in school are seldom continued after boys and girls leave school.
7. After students leave school, they have little further contact with it.
8. Those who work in the schools know little about the home lives of their students.
9. Former pupils have a low regard for the school as a place to get dependable advice outside of scholastic matters.
10. Guidance is inadequate, particularly vocational guidance.
11. The school does not affect choice of leisure activities to any important degree.[16]

EDUCATION FOR ALL AMERICAN YOUTH

The Educational Policies Commission was established in 1935 as a joint effort of the National Education Association and the American Association of

---

[15]Ruth E. Eckert and Thomas D. Marshall, *When Youth Leave School* (New York: The McGraw-Hill Book Co., 1938) pp. 3–4.

[16]*Ibid.*, pp. 310–15.

Background of the American Secondary School

School Administrators. In the following years, the Commission published a number of significant reports on various aspects of public education. One of these, *Education for All American Youth,* appeared in 1944. It was aimed at the secondary schools. It was also the last of the major reports in the idealistic tradition which reached back to the early part of the twentieth century.

The emphasis in the report, as expressed also in the title, was on the word "all".

> When we write confidently and inclusively about education for all American Youth, we mean just that, we mean that all youth, with their human similarities and their equally human differences, shall have educational services and opportunities suited to their personal needs and sufficient for the successful operation of a free and democratic society. . . .
>
> Each of them is a human being, more precious than material goods or systems of philosophy. Not one of them is to be carelessly wasted. All of them are to be given equal opportunities to live and to learn.[17]

The Commission was sanguine about the possibilities of changes necessary to adapt the secondary schools to the boys and girls who attended them. The Commission stated that while tradition and certain established interests hindered change in education, such hindrances did not stem from any active opposition to educational advancement, and would be done away with by the vigorous movement to shape education to the needs of all youth, when once that movement gained momentum.

The report envisioned two possibilities for the postwar period. One, titled "The History that Should Not Happen," imagined a situation in which the federal government would step in to control education and to provide the broadened opportunities which the former state and local system of school control had not been able or willing to provide. Among the reasons for federal control of education, in addition to inadequate local and state funding, and failure of local districts to foresee and plan for the shift from a wartime to a peacetime society, was an incapacity of secondary education to adjust because of the tremendous pressure of the traditional program.

> Although its enrollment doubled, redoubled, and redoubled again, during the first four decades of this century, and although its declared purpose had been broadened far beyond college preparation, equally fundamental changes in the secondary school curriculum and in the preparation of teachers were not made. The heroic efforts and revolutionary changes in procedure which the secondary schools made in

---

[17]Educational Policies Commission of the National Education and the American Association of School Administrators, *Education for All American Youth* (Washington, D.C.: 1944) pp. 17–18.

the national crisis of war could not be sustained. The slow prewar processes of minor piecemeal adjustment were quite inadequate for a situation requiring extensive changes and prompt, unified action.[18]

The Commission believed, however, that the history of federal control of education need not be written if the schools of the nation anticipated the needs of youth after the war, had a plan to meet these needs, and if local schools became agencies which served all American youth, whatever their educational needs, right through the period of adjustment to adult life.

Models of schools for rural and urban areas were constructed. In both instances, the models encompassed a span from grade seven through the thirteenth and fourteenth years, the last two grades constituting the Community Institute, with functions quite similar to what has now developed into the two-year community college. The keystone of the entire model system was individual assistance to each boy and girl in making his or her plans and decisions about career, education, employment, and all sorts of personal problems.

The models reflected earlier recommendations: preparing for occupations, civic competence, personal development in areas of health, family life, leisure, democracy, economic processes, sciences, and literature and the arts. They suggested flexible scheduling following joint planning by the staff, with the schedule reviewed monthly, and with changes made as needed. The school plant was to be used as a community center.

A summary of the report was prepared and published by the National Association of Secondary School Principals, and included a list of "Imperative Needs of Youth":

1. All youth need to develop saleable skills and those understandings and attitudes that make the worker an intelligent and productive participant in economic life. To this end, most youth need supervised work experience as well as education in the skills and knowledge of their occupations.

2. All youth need to develop and maintain good health and physical fitness and mental health.

3. All youth need to understand the rights and duties of the citizen of a democratic society, and to be diligent and competent in the performance of their obligations as members of the community and citizens of the state and nation, and to have an understanding of the nations and peoples of the world.

4. All youth need to understand the significance of the family for the individual and society and the conditions conducive to successful family life.

---
[18]*Ibid.*, p. 6.

5. All youth need to know how to purchase and use goods and services intelligently, understanding both the values received by the consumer and the economic consequences of their acts.
6. All youth need to understand the methods of science, the influence of science on human life, and the main scientific facts concerning the nature of the world and of man.
7. All youth need opportunities to develop their capacities to appreciate beauty, in literature, art, music, and nature.
8. All youth need to be able to use their leisure time well and to budget it wisely, balancing activities that yield satisfactions to the individual with those that are socially useful.
9. All youth need to develop respect for other persons, to grow in their insight into ethical values and principles, to be able to live and work cooperatively with others, and to grow in the moral and spiritual values of life.
10. All youth need to grow in their ability to think rationally, to express their thoughts clearly, and to read and listen with understanding.[19]

Although, as we shall see, the report of the Commission was obscured by unforeseen events in the years following its issuance, many of its ideas reappeared in the era of "reform" and "innovation" of the 1960s.

Bibliography

Conant, James B. *The American High School Today.* New York: McGraw-Hill Book Co., 1959.

Gulick, Luther H. *Education for American Life.* New York: McGraw-Hill Book Co., 1938.

National Association of Secondary School Principals. *Background for Choice Making.* Washington, D.C., 1961.

Sizer, Theodore. *The Age of the Academies.* Bureau of Publications, Teachers College, Columbia University, 1964.

U.S. Department of Health, Education and Welfare. *The Carnegie Unit: Its Origin, Status, and Trends.* Bulletin No. 7. Washington, D.C., 1954.

---

[19]"The Imperative Needs of Youth of Secondary School Age," *Bulletin of the National Association of Secondary School Principals* 31, No. 145 (March 1947): 6–144.

2

Current Trends in Secondary Education

The period immediately following World War II witnessed an attack on many of the principles and goals for secondary schools which had been promulgated since 1913. The studies and recommendations made during this time had centered around concerns for the student as a person. They deplored a system that spawned so many dropouts, and they called for an education more relevant to the needs of the individual student and to the times. They rebelled against the domination of the secondary school curriculum by the subject requirements and entrance demands of colleges and universities—requirements which they believed to be unrealistic and which bound the schools to patterns of courses, subject content, and time requirements that prevented the creation of more imaginative responses from schools. They were deeply concerned about the future of American democracy, and they emphasized the importance of better types of instruction, more vital school experiences, and school organizations and administrations which would lend themselves to the development of thoughtful, participating, involved, responsible citizens. They reflected alarm at the long delay between school and meaningful employment, and at the lack of intelligent personal and vocational guidance. They examined and outlined purposes and goals, placing purpose ahead of process, and calling to account the traditional subjects as ends in themselves.

The direction in which schools were being urged to move, the philosophy underlying the proposals, and the changes in schools which had occurred came under increasingly sharp criticism.

Some critics blanketed all of the previous proposals for reform under the label "progressive education," and excoriated the schools which had allegedly fallen under the influence of the "progressivists" for being "soft," for neglecting the fundamentals, and for graduating students who were incompetent. Titles of books such as Bestor's *Educational Wastelands: A Retreat from Learning,* Lynd's *Quackery in the Public Schools,* and Hutchins' *The Conflict in Education* were clues to the kind of sharp rebuke characteristic of the late 1940s and the early 1950s.

Unprepared for the intensity of the onslaught, secondary school principals and other leaders were in considerable disarray, a condition made more confusing because of two facts. First, despite the many arguments for needed change made by the leaders of the earlier period, little fundamental change had actually occurred in the majority of secondary schools, as the reports themselves indicated. Progressive education, the target of the attack, had had little effect on most of them. So school personnel in many instances found themselves defending something which had never really happened. Second, many principals and teachers in the secondary schools were as annoyed as the critics at what had been urged on them by leaders and educational spokesmen. They had resisted change in traditional practice, and many were now ready to testify that proposals to abandon the old tried and true curriculum had indeed brought chaos to the schools.

It would be interesting to speculate how the debates of the period following World War II and continuing into the late 1950s would have been settled had it not been for an event that occurred in October, 1957, which cast the balance. That event was the launching of Russia's Sputnik I. It should be remembered that the high hopes for a stable world order which had risen during the period immediately following World War II were dashed shortly after the war was ended. Nations which had been free prior to the war were dragged behind what Winston Churchill described as the Iron Curtain. Germany lay divided between East and West. The Soviet Union and the United States eyed each other coldly and warily. Trouble flared in Korea, and five years after the close of the Great War, the United States found itself involved in a major conflict in the Far East. The United States, in possession of hydrogen bombs potentially many more times as devastating as the bomb that destroyed Hiroshima, flexed its diplomatic muscles, confident in its superiority in weaponry.

Thus, the United States entered the era of the Cold War. Given the circumstances, it is not surprising that the nation reacted with a sense of shock when the Soviet Union announced that it had succeeded in launching a satellite which was circling the earth. Public reaction was intense. The President was criticized because he had not forcefully supported efforts to launch a missile program. Congress was blamed for failure to provide funds. Space officials and the military were criticized. A sense of shame developed. The Soviet Union had been first in a technological contest in which it had always been believed the United States excelled.

Suddenly, the accusing finger pointed to the schools, as if it was here that the failure lay. National magazines, television, radio, and the daily press focused on alleged shortcomings in the schools. Official delegations were dispatched to the Soviet Union to visit schools. Unflattering comparisons were made between secondary schools in the United States and those in the

Soviet Union. Hyman Rickover, then Admiral of the United States Navy, who had helped develop the atom-powered submarine, became a principal spokesman for those who looked with favor on the selective secondary schools of Europe. Academic excellence became the phrase of the moment, and the gifted, usually defined as the academically talented, became the center of attention. Education became associated in the minds of the public with national security. Congress passed the National Defense Education Act, providing federal funds to strengthen the teaching of science, mathematics, and foreign languages.

Secondary school principals and their staffs responded. They acknowledged guilt. Homework assignments were doubled. For the able, five "solid" subjects became the mode instead of four. Pressures on students increased, and for many became almost intolerable. Tracking and homogeneous grouping became standard practice.

The Conant Study

The Carnegie Corporation, seeking to make its contribution to the reshaping of the secondary schools, persuaded James Conant to undertake to examine some of the critical problems facing the high schools. Mr. Conant, a former president of Harvard, had gone to Germany in 1953, first as high commissioner, later as ambassador to the Federal Republic of Germany. He returned to the United States in 1958 to carry out the assignment, and in 1959 he published *The American High School Today*. The widespread criticism of secondary schools had been so devastating that principals welcomed the Conant book, which seemed moderate in contrast to much that had been written. Above all, they welcomed his support of the comprehensive secondary school, a position that pretty well silenced those who had been advocating separate, selective schools for the academically elite.

In their emphasis on subjects to be studied, Mr. Conant's values and proposals were more in accord with those of the Committee of Ten than they were with intervening reports and studies. He developed an academic inventory of subjects which in his judgment all secondary schools should include. He proposed subject curricula for the academically talented. He espoused advanced placement classes, and ability groupings.

In order not to oversimplify the parallel, however, it should be recognized that Conant was influenced by a whole set of conditions which had not existed in earlier events. The climate created by the Cold War was one of these conditions. Another was a series of projections of manpower needs, some of which were government reports, while others were predictions made by private research organizations and industries. Such projections, which forecast a future need for large numbers of engineers and scientists, had a natural relationship to secondary schools which was reflected in their subject emphasis and in the guidance given to the more academically-able students.

Conant's recommendations received national attention, and for a while his judgments were the dominant influence on secondary education. Subsequent experience a decade later indicated the need to place less absolute reliance on manpower need projections than was placed during the earlier period.

Hindsight seems always to be better than foresight. Looking back to the late 1960s and early 1970s the earlier projections for employment possibilities in the engineering and scientific fields proved, at least in the short run, to be overly optimistic.

The post-Sputnik era spanned roughly the period from 1958 to the middle 1960s. One may wonder why the changes wrought as a result of the clamor over the Sputnik episode were not sufficient to quiet the uneasiness about secondary schools. The schools had done what they believed they had been asked to do. They had singled out the academically talented. They had introduced "rigor" in the form of heavy homework, they had concentrated on hard subjects, and they had succeeded in creating schools with strong emphasis on achieving, as measured by competition for marks, grades, and rank in class. The "fads and frills" had been reduced, and students found little time for art, music, or drama, or for many extracurricular activities.

YOUTH PROBLEMS REEMERGE

By the middle of the decade of the sixties, old, unresolved problems surfaced to destroy the illusion that all was well. Youth unemployment, rising delinquency rates, youthful crime, the increasing number of dropouts, the use of drugs, and the explosive anger of blacks in city ghettos and particularly in ghetto secondary schools all signaled a dysfunction that could not be ignored or explained away. Problems arose in suburban schools, where, above all other places, they were least expected.

The next major federal act of legislation, after the National Defense Education Act was the Vocational Act of 1963. With an appropriation of close to a quarter of a billion dollars, the federal government authorized the creation of area vocational schools, work-study programs, the development of appropriate programs for those with academic, socioeconomic or other handicaps, and programs for out-of-school youth and persons in need of retraining.

The next year, the National Defense Education Act was amended to provide assistance in English, reading, history, geography, and civics. The Office of Economic Opportunity created the Job Corps and the Neighborhood Youth Corps, reminiscent of the Civilian Conservation Corps and The National Youth Administration of the 1930s. The Elementary and Secondary Education Act of 1965 reflected a belief of the federal government that it had an obligation to enlarge the educational opportunity for the children of poverty.

What is intended in this brief account is not to present a detailed history or to describe in detail various laws directed to improving the schools; rather, it is an attempt to illustrate the theory that was mentioned earlier, namely, that changes in education tend to vibrate within a narrow range. The Sputnik period brought schools closer to the same general concepts and set of beliefs which motivated those who wrote the reports of the Committee of Ten. The period after the Sputnik period had many concerns similar to those expressed in the various reports from 1913–1944: the plight of the child from the impoverished home, the dropout, the need for realistic vocational education, better personal and vocational guidance, and broadened course offerings.

The question to be asked now is whether this movement within a narrow range will characterize changes in secondary education in the future, or whether, as some predict, we are facing a new era, with a distinctive kind and dimension of change that is sweeping but is not yet clearly defined.

A NEWER CRITICISM

We now turn to a newer type of criticism, which addressed itself not only to schools *per se,* but also to the larger society, of which the schools are but a part. Before describing some of this criticism we make note that in 1967, 1968, and 1969, unprecedented protests and disruptions occurred in junior and senior high schools throughout the country. These will be discussed in some detail in Chapter 6. For the first time ever, large numbers of students became highly vocal about their school experiences.

Some of the criticism directed at schools in the 1940s and 1950s carried strong overtones of disparagement toward those who taught in and administered the schools. As might be expected in a system of schools so diverse, some of the personal kind of criticism was probably justified. Much, however, was not, since failures ascribed to the schools were as much a mirror of flaws in the larger society as they were of imperfections in the schools themselves.

A later kind of examination, accompanied by proposals for change, was directed more toward the system itself. To those who work in the system, the illustrations which follow may provide a distinction without much of a difference; however, we believe that they are different in motivation and aim, and are worthy of objective appraisal by principals and others who are engaged in the educational enterprise. This is not to say that we are here expressing value judgments. We do believe that some of this criticism is shared fairly widely.

Deschooling

Ivan Illich, director of the Center for Intercultural Studies which is based in Cuernevaca, Mexico, and author of *Deschooling Society,* represents the most radical thought concerning modern schooling in the 1970s. He believes that schools should be disestablished just as the medieval church was disestablished. Schooling is presently used as a screening device for entrance to favored occupations and leadership positions in society, and controls important aspects of a person's life from entrance age to graduate work in the university. Its system, based on hours and years spent in school, credits given, and success in pre-packaged curricula, confuses schooling with education—which it is not, in Illich's opinion. In such a system, knowledge becomes a commodity kept in scarce supply, to be dispensed only by those society has licensed to dispense it. The myth is created that the only learning of any value is that which takes place in a school, in a class, in a "subject" presided over by a teacher. The pupil, he says, is " 'schooled' to confuse teaching with learning, grade advancement with education, a diploma with competence, and fluency with the ability to say something new."[1]

Illich would repeal compulsory education laws and provide a "law forbidding discrimination in hiring . . . or admission to centers of learning based on previous attendance at some curriculum."[2] In a deschooled society, ways would be created or developed by which a person would learn by exchange of skills between persons and peers, and by having access to all kinds of facilities for specialized learning and skills: museums, libraries, computers, tool shops, laboratories, closed circuit television, records, films and the like. A part of the money now spent on schooling would be used to make such laboratories for learning readily available to everyone.

Illich's objections to the schooled society are so fundamental that he looks with skepticism on the efforts of others to reform the system of education from within, by free schools, open universities, alternative choices within the system, or application of technology in a school setting to enhance learning possibilities. His analysis is bold and some of his points are well-taken. However, for the purposes of this book we are assuming that, in one form or another, society will stand by a system of formal schooling, however modified it may be, at least in the lifetime of those who will read this book and work in leadership positions. Therefore, what follows is predicated on that belief, and other references to change will be those made within the framework of the school as a social institution.

Task Force Report on Compulsory Education-NEA

The Report of The Task Force on Compulsory Education of the National Education Association was published in 1972. It addressed itself to one aspect of the deschooling argument: compulsory education. Using *compulsory* in the sense that life in a modern society requires a certain level of learning if a person is to function within and as a part of that society, the Report concluded that compulsory education is not a matter of present

---
[1] Ivan Illich, *Deschooling Society* (New York: Harper and Row, 1970) p. 1.
[2] *Ibid.*, p. 11.

decision. The Report, however, drew a distinction between compulsory education as described, and compulsory attendance, as presently conceived. It urged greatly-increased flexibility in school attendance requirements through new or amended legislation. While everyone needs education, this does not necessarily mean six hours a day, thirty hours a week, thirty-six weeks a year in a building called a school. It should be possible for schools to provide options for students in terms of hours, days, and weeks required in attendance in school buildings. Further recommendations in this area include:

1. Provision for ease of exit and reentry into the educational system
2. Increase in number and variety of work study experiences
3. Consideration of the promising possibilities of alternative schools and free schools within and outside the educational establishment
4. Major revision of present school curriculum
5. Greatly altered teaching methods for many educational purposes
6. Sharing with students decisions about programs, curriculum and teaching methods
7. More and different types of school personnel to provide more individualization and personalization of educational offerings
8. Major reorganization of the institution called school
9. Inclusion in the concept of school business, industries, social agencies, the community at large
10. Reorganization of the base of financial support
11. Massive increases in funds for education[3]

To further elaborate on the definition of compulsory education (as used in the Report) a broad concept of education was established:

> Different people need education of different forms as well as different content. They learn best in different ways, within different structures of the educational system.
>
> Everyone, however, needs the guarantee that the school will offer him the kind of education he needs to carry out his plans. Everyone knows that when he leaves the school system he is competent to survive, to look forward to a life free of the fear of hunger and cold. He must be enabled to earn or win the economic freedom to make some choices about his life if he was born without that freedom.
>
> Everyone also needs respect for himself, his ideas, his opinions, his feelings. One way for the school staff to show that respect is to accord students more and more responsibility in making decisions about the school and about their own education as they grow older. Although the form and content of education must vary, the attitude of the staff towards the student must be unswerving human respect.[4]

---

[3]*Report of the Task Force on Compulsory Education,* National Education Association. Washington, D.C., 1972, p. 2.

[4]*Ibid.,* pp. 2–3.

The National Commission on the Reform of Secondary Education

The National Commission on the Reform of Secondary Education, established by the Charles F. Kettering Foundation in 1972, published its report in 1973. The report asserts that the Commission was established only after most of the organizations involved in the education of secondary school youth had been consulted. Members of the Commission included officials of public and private educational associations, The National Congress of Parents and Teachers, school board associations, an official of a regional accreditation agency, a private college president, students, teachers, a state legislator, a state school superintendent, and a professional writer.

During the course of its deliberations, panels of teachers, parents, students, and school administrators were established. Membership was drawn from all sections of the country. Public hearings were also held, and visits were made to schools.

"The American high school has become a beleaguered institution," the report states. "Everyone agrees that the high schools are in difficulty, but there agreement ceases; even before they arrive at proposals, experts find themselves arguing about what is wrong and about the source and the size of the trouble. While educators ponder the problem, the high school environment deteriorates further."[5]

The Commission advocates the development of new goals with the active participation of students, parents, other citizens, and educators. Other recommendations include revising the traditional curriculum content, eliminating racial and ethnic bias in textbooks and in counseling, offering some courses in late afternoon or evening, providing better career guidance with active involvement through advisory councils and those working in various careers, eliminating discriminating attitudes and practices, and instituting more effective job placement. The report recommends the lowering of the compulsory education age to fourteen.

The Commission proposes that credit for out-of-school accomplishments in work settings or community service be granted, and urges that alternative kinds of education be organized to provide a variety of paths to completion of graduation requirements. The Report further recommends that time schedules should be made much more flexible; that student rights and responsibilities should be clearly understood; that corporal punishment should be abolished everywhere by statute; and that scholarship should not be set as a prerequisite for taking part in extracurricular activities. It urges that biases against women as students, teachers, and administrators must be eliminated, and the rights of students to the privacy of their records must be preserved.

This report is likely to be widely discussed and debated. Many of the issues raised by the Commission are examined in various sections of this book.

---

[5]The National Commission on Reform of Secondary Education, "A Report to the Public and the Profession" (New York: McGraw-Hill, 1973), p. 8.

The Voucher System

Milton Friedman, an economist, proposed a voucher system by which parents would be given vouchers equal to the per pupil cost of education in the district in which they resided. This voucher could be used to purchase education at any public or private school which, in the judgment of the parents, provided a desirable alternative to the education their children were getting in the public school they were required to attend. The reasoning behind this proposal is that under the present system of governing public education, parents and pupils have no real choices. Schools are everywhere alike, homogeneous in style and operation. Parents have no way to change the system without going through a difficult political process. The voucher system would provide leverage not otherwise available. It is, Friedman argues, "the way to stimulate variety and diversity ... to broaden the range of alternatives open to children."[6]

The voucher system was espoused by the Office of Economic Opportunity and funds were made available to develop pilot projects. The first recorded experiment with educational vouchers was begun in the Alum Rock Elementary School District, San Jose, California. In the absence of enabling state legislation, vouchers could not be used in private or parochial schools, and the experiment was administered by the local board of education instead of by an autonomous voucher agency. Parents of 4,000 children were given choices among alternative educational programs offered at six different schools. It is too soon to know whether the voucher plan will be adopted on any substantial scale, but the prospects of this occurring are doubtful. It is mentioned here because underlying its mechanics is a form of criticism of the system—of its alleged slowness to change, to offer alternatives, or to accommodate itself to the needs of a diverse pupil population.

HUMANIZING THE SCHOOLS

Another kind of criticism, pervading much of what is said about secondary education, is that the schools have become dehumanized and impersonal. Therefore, the argument goes, changes should be made in the direction of humanizing them. This has implications for the curriculum, for the kinds of rules and regulations that are developed to manage the conduct of the schools, and the processes by which such rules and regulations are established or modified. The emphasis on humaneness goes to the heart of the teaching-learning process, to the relationships between teacher and student, teacher and teacher, student and student, and directly to the role of administrative

---
[6]Milton Friedman, "Decentralizing Schools," *Newsweek*, 18 November 1968, p. 100.

Current Trends in Secondary Education

leadership, in creating a school climate in which human considerations are paramount.

Many writers have addressed themselves to this topic, approaching it from various viewpoints. Silberman wrote:

> ... when schools become warm and humane, teachers grow as human beings as well as teachers. The lesson is clear; Dewey stated it two-thirds of a century ago. What is needed, he wrote, "is improvement of education, not merely by turning out teachers who can do better the things that are necessary to do, but rather changing the conception of what constitutes education."[7]

In his book, Silberman refers to the "grim, joyless classrooms" he observed and regretted that students seldom seemed to have the opportunity to confront their teachers.

> By and large, they are expected to learn what the faculty wants them to learn in the way the faculty wants them to learn it, and no nonsense, please. Freedom to explore, to test one's ideas as a means of finding out who one is and what one believes—these are luxuries a well-run school cannot afford.[8]

Edgar Friedenberg and John Holt addressed themselves to the need for a more humane education. "The whole experience of secondary education," Friedenberg wrote, "is set up in such a way that individual adolescents will become alienated from their own inner life; they are given no opportunity to examine it, and are punished if they permit it to direct their actions." He goes on to say

> What has been violated is not so much freedom as dignity. I do not mean that someone has been unnecessarily rude—quite the opposite. Assaults on dignity are usually very friendly and well meaning—that is part of the strategy. But the action taken has been basically contemptuous of students, negligent of their real characteristics as human beings and indifferent to their needs and feelings as individuals. In the blandest possible way they have been pushed around. They have been pitted against one another in strategically organized committees, seduced with little awards of leadership and contributions to school life; taught gamey old political tricks for ensuring the triumph of good government; playfully spanked for displaying undue and unreasonable disorder. If this is not enough, playfulness abruptly ceases and is replaced by pious sorrow that heedless young people are ruining their chances with their record in school. The record is being very carefully kept.[9]

---
[7]Charles Silberman, *Crisis in the Classroom* (New York: Random House, 1970) p. 552.
[8]*Ibid.*, p. 336.
[9]Peter Schrag, "Education's Romantic Critics," *Saturday Review*, 18 February 1967.

John Holt urges that schools be deemphasized in importance, that compulsory attendance be abolished, and that recognition be given to the opportunities for learning outside the classroom, joining learning with life.

He deplores the pressures put on boys and girls, not for their good, but to enhance the prestige of the school. The pressures create "an exaggerated concern with getting right answers and avoiding mistakes; they drive them into defensive strategies of behavior that choke off their intellectual powers and make real learning all but impossible." An adolescent, he says, "needs time to talk and think about who he is and what he would like to be and how he can get there. He needs time to taste experience and to digest it. We don't give him enough."[10]

Much of the movement to humanize the secondary school comes from inside the system of education. The authors quoted in this chapter are teachers. In addition, professional organizations such as the National Education Association, the Association for Supervision and Curriculum Development, and the National Association of Secondary School Principals, have in one way or another addressed themselves to this objective. A publication of the American Association of School Administrators, "Labels and Fingerprints," was addressed to the question:

> It is not in the might of the military, the productivity of industry or the efficiency of transportation and communication that the true greatness of America lies. Rather, it is the high esteem accorded the individual personality. Here, indeed, is our greatest contribution to men everywhere, and here is America's secret weapon. Our philosophy of government from its very beginning, our deepest convictions, and our highest ideals have sought to clothe the individual with a sense of dignity, to recognize his potentialities, to unloose his creative powers, and to stimulate his initiative. It was on this platform that Jefferson, Adams, Lincoln and Wilson rose to greatness.
>
> And yet, despite these fundamental concepts and ideas, we seem to be drifting into impersonality in every sphere of our culture. . . .
>
> Caught in this cultural drift, the schools, too, are veering toward impersonal solutions to vital educational problems. Mass grouping, standard curriculums, standard examinations, standard test scores, and standardized institutions are squeezing individuals into a common mold. Standard school products are demanded by shortsighted and frightened adults and frequently accepted by school boards and teachers . . . schools are departing from their historic character by manipulating pupils and teachers into organizational patterns and by leaning on administrative and mechanical devices that tend to destroy the very quality that has made them great.[11]

---

[10] John Holt, "The Fourth R: The Rat Race," *New York Times*, 1 May 1966.

[11] Joint statement of the American Association of School Administrators, the Association for Supervision and Curriculum Development, the National Association of Secondary School Principals and the National Association of Elementary School Principals, Washington, D.C., 1961.

The Bulletin of the National Association of Secondary School Principals for February, 1972, was devoted to the topic "Humanizing the Schools," with special emphasis on the role of the principal. The 1970 Yearbook of the Association for Supervision and Curriculum Development carried the title *To Nurture Humaneness.* This was followed in 1971 with a publication titled *Removing Barriers to Humaneness in the High School,* which included such topics as "A Vision of a Humane School," "External Management as a Barrier to Humanizing Schools," "Can Education Be Relevant?" "Teaching and Learning in the Affective Domain," and "Design of the Curriculum." (One of these topics, "Can Education Be Relevant?" by Arthur W. Combs, appears in the Reading Section.)

The School As a Factory

The way schools are organized and administered is a determining factor in whether education can in fact be humanized. The organization and administration of schools are also implicit or explicit expressions of their functions and purposes. Patterned after the bureaucratic model which began to characterize organizations during the later phase of the Industrial Revolution, schools came to resemble industrial, military, and other governmental organizations. The bureaucratic model of organization is in the form of a pyramid, with the chain of command running from the top to the bottom of the pyramid: it has a system of procedures and rules dealing with all contingencies relating to work activities; a division of labor based on specialization; promotion and selection based on technical competence; and it is characterized by impersonality in human relations.

A number of writers have drawn an analogy between the modern school and a factory. We shall attempt to describe the analogy. It goes something like this: The school is a work place. The raw material is the boys and girls. As they proceed through the years in school, they are sorted and graded and processed. Teachers and others processing the material use the language of the factory or assembly line. A boy or girl is referred to as "poor material" or "good material" or as "college material" or "not college material." The good pieces of material are gradually shaped and finished into "products." We speak of the "products" of our schools. This or that school "turns out a good product," we say. The poor material is cast aside as something of little value. Schools have adopted words from industry, such as "inputs" and "outputs."

Teachers are workers on the assembly line. They work on and shape the material, judging, with the help of others (those who test the material, for instance), the best, the average, the poorest. Labels are put on the material: slow learner, underachiever, high achiever, gifted, "ready" or "not ready" for the next stage of production—the grade, the course, graduation. The principal is the foreman, managing the factory, keeping the assembly line moving, reporting on the process, keeping records of the product, keeping the workers at their tasks of sorting, grading, and shaping the product. He is evaluated by the efficiency with which the factory is operated.

So far as the school is concerned, the analog breaks down in part because in the school the "material" being processed is both object and worker. It is the student who is being processed. At the same time, the tasks he is set to do (as worker), and how well he performs the tasks, determine in great measure the value or worth placed upon him, conditions how well and how fast he moves toward the end of the production line, and into what kind of product he is eventually packaged. As worker, he is paid in grades, gets advancement by moving from grade to grade, and, if he does his assigned tasks very well indeed, is honored by awards, scholarships and the like. Some such description as this is common to all "school as factory" analogies. (One such analogy appears in the readings section which appears at the end of Part One.

The Study of Inequality

The book *Inequality: A Reassessment of the Effect of Family and Schooling in America,* by Christopher Jencks and his colleagues in the Center for Educational Policy Research at Harvard, also refers to the factory model. The authors challenge many of the cherished beliefs about schools and schooling, and their conclusions are sure to be the subject of controversy for a long time to come. One of their central themes is that the long-term effect of schools in making adults more equal in income and position is negligible. So, it is argued, it is more reasonable to judge schools by their immediate effects on pupils while they are still in school.

> These arguments suggest that the "factory" model which pervades both lay and professional thinking about schools probably ought to be abandoned. It is true that schools have "inputs" and "outputs," and that one of their nominal purposes is to take human "raw material" (i.e., children) and convert it into something more "valuable" (i.e., employable adults). Our research suggests, however, that the character of a school's output depends largely on a single input, namely the characteristics of the entering children. Everything else— the school budget, its policies, the characteristics of the teachers—is either secondary or completely irrelevant.
>
> Instead of evaluating schools in terms of long-term effects on their alumni, which appear to be relatively uniform, we think it wiser to evaluate schools in terms of their immediate effects on teachers and students, which appear much more variable. Some schools are dull, depressing, even terrifying places, while others are lively, comfortable, and reassuring. If we think of school life as an end in itself rather than a means to some other end, such differences are enormously important. Eliminating these differences would not do much to make adults more equal, but it would do a great deal to make the quality of children's (and teachers') lives more equal. Since children are in school for a fifth of their lives, this would be a significant accomplishment.

Looking at schooling as an end in itself rather than a means to some other end suggests that we ought to describe schools in a language appropriate to a family rather than to a factory. This implies that we will have to accept diverse standards for judging schools, just as we do for judging families. Indeed, we can even say that diversity should be an explicit objective of schools and school systems. No single home-away-from-home can be ideal for all children. A school system that provides only one variety of schooling, no matter how good, must almost invariably seem unsatisfactory to many parents and children. The ideal system is one that provides as many varieties of schooling as its children and parents want and finds ways of matching children to schools that suit them. Since the character of an individual's schooling appears to have relatively little long-term effect on his development, society as a whole rarely has a compelling interest in limiting the range of educational choices open to parents and students. Likewise, since professional educators do not seem to understand the long-term effects of schooling any better than parents do, there is no compelling reason why the profession should be empowered to rule out alternatives that appear to parents, even if they seem educationally "unsound."

The argument that school life is largely an end in itself rather than a means to some other end does not mean we believe schools should be run like mediocre summer camps, where children are merely kept out of trouble. We doubt that a school can be enjoyable for either adults or children unless the children feel they are doing something purposeful. One good way to give children a sense of purpose is to give them activities that contribute to their becoming more like grownups. Our findings suggest that a school's choice of objectives has rather little long-term effect on what kinds of grownups the children become. That is determined by outside influences. But since we value ideas and the life of the mind, we favor schools that value these things too. Others, who favor discipline and competitive excellence, may prefer schools that value high reading and math scores. Still others, more concerned with teaching children to behave properly, will prefer schools that try to do this. The list of competing objectives is nearly endless, which is why we favor diversity and choice.[12]

So accustomed are those who work in schools and those who send their children to them to the sorting, classifying, tracking procedures, to the predigested curriculum, to the grading system, and to the production line process, that seldom do teachers or parents consider the possibility there may be alternatives to the school as a factory.

To balance the presentation, it should be noted that school "reform" carries with it a variety of intents and meanings. Probably relatively few in the total population would respond favorably to proposals to deschool society, although some might accept certain aspects of deschooling. The Report of The NEA Task Force referred to earlier is a move in this direction.

---

[12]Christopher Jencks et al., *Inequality: A Reassessment of the Effect of Family and Schooling in America* (New York: Basic Books, 1972) pp. 256–57. Used with permission.

So are efforts to change from "credentialing" to basing readiness for employment on demonstrations of particular competencies.

Not everyone would endorse the aim of humanizing the schools. In many school districts, a sizable and vocal part of the community demands more "discipline" in response to the rising restlessness of young people. Requests by students for an open campus, for easing of rules and regulations governing conduct and dress, and similar changes are not always met with approval, either by professional teachers and educators or by lay people of the community. Indeed, it is usually quite the contrary.

The image of the school developed by many adults, out of their own experience in schools, is not susceptible to change without considerable stress. This image includes a vision of the good school as a quiet school where students go about their assigned tasks in ways that disturb no one, either physically or intellectually. The view that learning can be a stimulating, enjoyable experience, or that a school can be a pleasant place, is alien to many adults as well as to many teachers and administrators. Many, but not all of those who see the future of schooling carried on largely with the use of advanced technology-teaching machines, talking typewriters, programmed instruction, television, and computers think of learning primarily as the acquisition of facts and the ability to recall what facts have been learned. Thus, the didactic, emotional pedagog would be replaced by the didactic, unemotional machine.

Beginning in the late 1960s, and continuing with increased tempo in the 1970s, is the emphasis on accountability. The aim to hold schools accountable, or liable, or responsible for what they do is no doubt good. The question to which no complete answer has been provided is, "accountable for what?" The answer to this question determines whether the goals of the schools are narrowed or broadened as a result of accountability. Early attempts to measure accountability are not encouraging to those who seek to broaden school goals. These efforts are discussed in more detail in Chapter 7.

When schools are in the process of changing, cross currents develop, as old concepts encounter newer ones. The leader-administrator must master the skills of navigation.

Bibliography

Association for Supervision and Curriculum Development, National Education Association. *Freedom, Bureaucracy and Schooling.* Washington, D.C., 1971.

Friedenberg, Edgar L. *Coming of Age in America.* New York: Random House, 1965.

_____. *The Vanishing Adolescent.* Boston: The Beacon Press, 1959.

Goodman, Paul. *Compulsory Miseducation.* New York: Horizon Press, 1964.

Holt, John. *How Children Fail.* New York: Pitman, 1964.

———. *How Children Learn.* New York: Pitman, 1967.

"Humanizing the Schools." *The Bulletin of the National Association of Secondary School Principals,* February, 1972.

National Education Association, Association for Supervision and Curriculum Development. Council on Secondary Education. *Removing Barriers to Humaneness in the High School.* Ed. J. Galen Saylor and Joshua L. Smith. Washington, D.C., 1971.

National Education Association, Association for Supervision and Curriculum Development. *To Nurture Humaneness: Commitment for the 70's.* Washington, D.C., 1970.

Silberman, Charles. *Crisis in the Classroom: The Remaking of American Education.* New York: Random House, 1970.

3

The School as a Democratic Institution

A CONCEPT OF DEMOCRACY

An understanding of the secondary school as a democratic institution must be predicated on an understanding of the basic principles of democracy as a social as well as a political concept. The late Boyd Bode referred to democracy as a way of life. The concept is all-pervasive, and affects all the interrelationships of individuals as well as those of nations and societies.

American democracy is based upon a system of values, beliefs, ideals, and aspirations. This system has derived from the diverse groups who came to America as minorities seeking adventure, wealth, a haven from religious persecution, and a variety of other goals. This diverse population of minorities was welded together as a free society under the leadership of such men as Washington, Jefferson, Hamilton, and others of like mold. Evidence of this system of beliefs appears in the Constitution of the United States, the laws by which we govern ourselves, the court decisions which we abide by, the institutions which we support, and the values to which we subscribe.

One basic tenet of the democratic concept is respect for the individual as a person with rights and privileges, with strengths and weaknesses of character, and with the hopes and fears, and prejudices and biases which characterize all human beings. This tenet is, perhaps, best expressed in the Golden Rule, "Do unto others as you would have others do unto you." That is, grant your fellow men the same privileges, rights, and tolerance that you expect from others.

In a democracy no one is above criticism—least of all public officials who are charged with a public trust. In fact, it is the responsibility of citizens to be critical of that which they believe to be wrong or not in the best interests of the nation or the society. However, to be intelligently critical requires knowledge upon which to base criticism, and it is the duty of critics to acquire sold facts as a basis for criticism.

Intelligent, constructive criticism, freely expressed and properly received, is an effective means of improving a democratic society. It provides a check upon leadership, and is a constant reminder that the leader is responsible to his followers. This points up quite well the essential difference between a democracy and a totalitarian state. While in the former the leader is responsible to the people, in the latter the people are responsible to their leader. Included in this tenet is the belief that human life and well-being are more important than material values. This means that issues are to be decided, and policies determined, on the basis of the promotion of human welfare and individual equality of opportunity. The opportunities of life are to be made available to all through equal education, economic and political opportunity, and undeviating equality before the law.

A second major tenet—a closely related one—is the belief that people have the capacity and the innate desire to govern themselves and determine their own destinies. They can be architects of their own fate and should carve out their own destinies without artificial barriers and restrictions of caste, royalty, class, wealth, or divine right. This tenet rejects all forms of totalitarianism. The people are sovereign and government has only those powers given it by the people. They are the masters and the state is the servant.

Closely allied to this philosophy is the belief in the right of man to be free. The concept of freedom is broad, including freedom of thought, expression, assembly, appearance, and movement, as well as the freedom to embrace any religion or none at all. All individual freedom is, of course, subject to the restriction that it does not deny the same freedom to others or impinge upon the general welfare. As Justice Oliver W. Holmes once said, "Freedom of speech does not give a person the right to shout fire in a crowded theatre." This concept of the free man not only permits, but encourages the search for truth in the social and political realms as well as in the scientific.

The foregoing gives rise to a fourth tenet of the democratic ideal, namely, a faith in human intelligence. Our belief is that given the freedom to think, inquire, discuss, and criticize, men will improve their own lot. The unrestricted play of man's intelligence upon man's problems generates the best solutions. It is essential that human intelligence must be completely free and must never be subverted or distorted for the purpose of arriving at preconceived goals or substantiating the merits of the status quo. This tenet places a high value on the accuracy and integrity of knowledge and those who search after it. Erroneous and fictitious information, however generated, tends to prevent new insights, curtail discovery of new horizons, and, at worst, enslave the human intellect, which in turn leads to human slavery.

A fifth major tenet of the democratic ethic is the belief in the rule of law as developed by those who are to be ruled. We subscribe to a written constitution and to legislative enactments which uphold the rights of people and enforce their obligations. The rule of law is universal in a democratic society where it equally affects the lowliest citizen and the highest official. Law and order are not to be imposed on us by higher authority, but by our common acceptance of their necessity in the achievement of common justice.

Another important principle of democracy is that of majority rule with adequate protection of the rights of minorities, as set forth in the Constitution and legislative statutes. We subscribe in general to the theory of providing the greatest good to the greatest number. However it is not only the well-guarded privilege, but also the responsibility of minorities to work to become majorities, and by persuasion and other peaceful and ethical means promote the merits of their position. In the meantime it is their duty to abide by the rule of the majority, even as they work to change it.

A corollary principle is that all citizens who are affected by a rule or decision should participate in the making of that rule or decision. Such participation is a right, and should be exercised in the best interests of all concerned. This serves to help insure that all points of view are represented, and that the rule or decision is then made with due regard to the general welfare. The adherence to this principle insures the involvement of people in decisions affecting their destiny, and tends to promote a feeling of unity among them.

Another well-established belief is that of the desirability of peaceful and orderly social and political change. A democracy, by its very nature, is a creature of change. Only through change can there be improvement. Change is a built-in characteristic of a social system which encourages the development and employment of human intelligence in the enhancement of human life. Change is continuous and inevitable, but how change is effected differs from society to society and from nation to nation. In a democracy, change is effected around the conference table, in the legislative halls, in the courts, and, finally, at the voting booth. The democratic system of government is the only one now extant which provides for the ultimate change, that of discarding itself if a majority of the people determine that they wish to try another form of government.

While not all-inclusive, the foregoing describes the basic beliefs on which our democracy rests. These beliefs are reflected in our political and social systems, and they form an interwoven fabric of the democratic way of life. Needless to say, in many cases these hallmarks of a democracy more accurately represent our aspirations than they do our achievements. And yet they are generally accepted as our commitment, and they serve as criteria by which to judge our success. They are the ideals to which most American citizens subscribe.

The fact that we have always had anti-democratic elements in our society is testimony to the vitality of the democratic system. Violence, bigotry, crime, prejudice, and jingoism have all been in evidence in our history. And yet they have never attained any permanent ascendency in our national scale of values.

THE ROLE OF THE SCHOOL IN A DEMOCRACY

The country in which we live and work may be defined as a representative democracy. Its history, which reaches back over two centuries, is one of democratic government—a rule of the people through their elected representatives. The Constitution, and specifically the Bill of Rights, has as its purpose the safeguarding of the rights of the people. The concept of power, originating with the people and conferred by them, on a temporary basis only, to those of their number who are chosen to exercise authority, is well-established in American history. This delegation of power is for the purpose of effective regulation of society, and is not for the enrichment or enhancement of the fortunes of the power-figure at the expense of those he serves. The public official is a servant, not a master. In such a society, the role of the school is a magnificent one. It must provide the opportunity for the people to become effective members of society. This requires the fullest development of individuals with values consistent with the democratic ideal.

Societal Values

In a democracy, the education of the citizenry serves a dual purpose in that it seeks to develop and enhance the abilities of the individual, which in turn develops and enhances a form of government which benefits and protects the individual. The public school system is tangible evidence of the belief that education is fundamentally a state responsibility; it also demonstrates the fact that through the development of effective citizens democracy receives its greatest benefits.

Democratic citizenship is, or should be, a primary objective of public school education. Private schools likewise have a responsibility to develop good citizens. In a democracy, education must recognize its responsibility to both the individual and to his society.

The task of the school as an institution to promote democracy is broad and comprehensive. Its accomplishment is vital to the welfare of society. A free government of free people cannot long survive in ignorance. As Thomas Jefferson said, "If a nation expects to be ignorant and free, in a state of civilization, it expects what never was and never will be." A democratic society has the right to expect its educational system not only to teach democratic values, but also to be constructively critical of those values, in the hope that constant reappraisal will enhance those values which are good, strengthen those which show weaknesses, and revise those which have not adequately met the test of time and trial. Beyond this, it is the responsibility of the school to measure the action and conduct of society against the values which have been tested by time and forged in the crucible of discussion and debate. In such a context, the public school serves all the people, not just those who enter its doors. It is an institution of all the people, educating all the people, and responsible to all the people.

The democratic concept of the role of the school makes it an institution of inquiry. It must be free to raise questions about established practices, to explore alternatives to such practices, and to search always for what is true, instead of accepting that which is as sacrosanct. Society can be improved only through change, and the school can and should explore possibilities for change.

The public school is a public enterprise. As an enterprise, its responsibility reaches far beyond simply transmitting the culture. It must also stimulate and motivate critical analysis of the values of the culture and of society's adherence to those values in its political, social, and economic life. If the school is to accomplish this, it must be a center of controversy. As a center of controversy, it will encounter many hazards and will face criticism from those who regard the school as an agency of the "corporate state." Similar criticism will also come from those who regard the school as simply an agency to transmit the most popular values, customs, and mores, so that the youth entering society will adjust quietly and obediently to the generally accepted patterns of social action or inaction.

In accepting the role of an agency which encourages controversy, the school should not become a protagonist or a promoter of a particular point of view or social, political, or economic program. Its task is to explore issues, to accumulate pertinent information, to assess democratic values, and to promote discussion so that decisions may be made on a cognitive level. Since decisions are constantly being made, by the individual student as well as by the community, the state, and the nation, the school must not confine itself within its own walls. It must be a community educational agency. The role of the school may be described as that of an intellectual catalyst for the community. It is the place where people may go for information on issues which confront the local community and the larger community as well.

Of course, the major share of the work of the school is with its students. It must, in the classroom, encourage free inquiry, promote critical analyses and evaluation, and promote discussion and debate on relevant issues. The student must feel free to challenge accepted standards and at the same time keep an open mind to what may be said in their favor. During the process he will learn to make his own judgments, based on the relevant facts that are available and measured against the democratic values of our society. Hopefully, through this process he will accumulate relevant knowledge, learn to analyze and evaluate it, become acquainted with the prevailing cultural patterns, acquire the ability to search for truth, and, finally, he will be able to make independent judgments—judgments on which decisions about himself and the social order will be based.

If the school accepts its full responsibility as a public enterprise, it will not confine its efforts to youth, but will also serve those who have gone beyond high school age—the adults of the community. Education of adults occurs on both formal and informal bases. The responsibility of the school does not have to stop with adult afternoon and evening classes; the informal educational function is of at least equal importance. It is a function which should, of course, be shared with other social agencies. However, it is the school which is most strategically located to encourage and provide for community discussion and evaluation of social, political, and economic issues. For example, a community may be faced with a decision which involves a conflict between environmental health and economic wealth. In such a situation, the effective school can provide a forum for the discussion of the issue. Experts on both sides of the issue, as well as local people, may be invited to openly debate the issue before the people. Such a debate may be held in the school auditorium. There the people of the community may hear both sides of the issue, raise questions, and become better informed on the issue so that they can base their opinions and consequent decisions on more than rumor, personal prejudice, and propaganda.

Individual Values

The democratic concept of respect for the individual has important implications for the public school. If we recognize that every person has strengths and weaknesses which are unique to him as an individual, we must also recognize that he has unique educational needs. It follows that the school must shape its program to meet educational needs, rather than expect and require uniformity regardless of needs, or assume that educational needs are pretty much the same for everybody.

While recognizing that as human beings we have common educational needs as well as common physical needs, the democratic ethic demands that we give equal recognition to unique individual needs, and, by so doing, stimulate and encourage the varied potentials of students. In this way, the school contributes to the development of creativity, imagination, and initiative in the individual, and helps to make possible the development of his unique potential, thus benefitting himself and the democratic society in which he lives.

The democratic concept of education is diametrically opposed to the totalitarian practice of forcing all people into a common mold, the nature of which is dictated by the state. Such a mold is designed to secure an obedient conformity which allows the state to control individuals like robots. At the same time, it stifles initiative and discourages the pursuit of individual goals. Learning in such a situation is oriented toward state goals and neglects and even suppresses individual goals. However successful totalitarian educational practices may be in the short run, they carry with them the seeds of their own destruction. They do not allow for criticism, they destroy initiative, and only reluctantly yield to change; and change, when it does occur, comes about largely through the pressure of outside forces rather than from generation within. This is often fatal when leadership is headstrong and imbued with missionary zeal.

The democratic state, by its very nature, is best served by the initiative and enterprise of individuals whose unique abilities provide both impetus and direction to change. It is adaptable to change and thrives on internally generated growth. It welcomes new ideas, new adaptations, and new ways of doing things which improve society.

The implications for the school as a democratic institution are clear. It must foster individuality, encourage initiative, and give every possible assistance to the development of individual ability. When this philosophy is adopted it will be reflected in the attitude not only of the administration, but also in the attitudes of the teachers as they go about the business of education. It will be revealed in the relationships between the students and the professional staff of the school. The whole atmosphere of such a school reflects a concern for the worth and dignity of the individual, and a commitment to see that he has the best possible opportunity to develop to his full potential.

THE SECONDARY SCHOOL AS A DEMOCRATIC INSTITUTION

As an important integral part of the public school system, the secondary school has an essential role to play in the development of democratic citizenship. High school students are at an age where they are conscious of values and societal issues. The adolescent is characteristically idealistic, and during the high school period many personal and social values are established which may persist through life.

In its broadest sense, the development of democratic citizenship includes not only a knowledge and appreciation of democratic values, but also the ability and initiative to appraise these values and to measure personal and social conduct against them. In order to do this, the individual must have the ability and desire to search for truth for himself and for his society. Such inquiry requires the acquisition of many skills which are necessary to analyze, evaluate, and accumulate relevant facts and figures on which to base that analysis and evaluation. Thus, the inclusion in the secondary program of such subjects as mathematics, history, English, and social science contributes to the development of the democratic citizen because they help supply the tools he needs. Courses in health, physical education, recreation, mental hygiene, and similar subjects are also important because they teach the individual how to maintain health and well-being so that he may effectively pursue the goals of democratic citizenship.

The number of youth graduating from high school has increased steadily both in numbers and in percentage of total school-aged youth over recent years. Thus, the secondary school is in a strategic position in our educational system. It represents the final stage of formal education for many. For these youth, the high school is the principal source of their knowledge of the history, values, and responsibilities of democratic citizenship.

As has been indicated earlier in this chapter, the democratic society welcomes and thrives on change. Only through change can improvement come about; therefore, the secondary school must adopt and maintain an orientation which accepts change as a necessary and desirable characteristic of its structure. In short, while the program of the secondary school is rooted in the past, it should orient itself to the future. The future is, of course, built upon the past, and we must know of the past if we are to effectively design the future. There is a vast reservoir of cultural knowledge from which the secondary school can draw in order to enrich the lives of its students and provide them with the tools to function in the existing social order. However, it should never become so preoccupied with the past that it forgets that youth will live in the future. The secondary program must be oriented so that the knowledge of the cultural heritage provides insights that help predict and shape the future.

The program of the secondary school must be broad and comprehensive if it is to meet the educational needs of a variety of individuals. As a democratic institution, it must recognize that educational needs differ widely, and that each individual has a right to a secondary education suitable to his needs and aspirations. The implications of this principle are far-reaching. In order to effectively provide broad and comprehensive school experiences, secondary schools must be reasonably large. The very small high school simply cannot provide this. The traditional program with its emphasis on college preparation cannot do it either. The secondary school as a democratic institution which efficiently and economically provides a wide variety of educational experience both within and without its walls *can* do it. It must do it if it is to meet all those whom it serves, and if it properly discharges its responsibility as a democratic institution.

One of the basic principles referred to earlier in this chapter deals with wide participation in decision-making. If we accept the democratic principle that all who are affected by a decision should have some voice in making it, then there will have to be some significant changes in the traditional high school. There will have to be an expansion of the human base upon which decisions are made. This means greater participation of teachers, students, and community in planning, policy-making, and programming. It is apparent today that people in general and youth in particular are concerned with decision-making and wish to participate in it—this fact becomes most obvious when decisions are handed down to people which are distasteful to them.

In one community, the local board of education, by formal action, summarily changed the name of the high school. The action was met with vigorous protests from the student body. The new name was not found objectionable in itself, but the fact that seven men and women changed the name of their school without even seeking student opinion was resented. The teachers joined in the protest in a more subdued fashion. The point which they all made was that they disliked having the name of the school in which they lived and worked changed without their even knowing about it, much less expressing an opinion about it. In other words, they wanted to take part in, and be informed about, the making of changes and decisions which directly affected them.

The board defended itself by explaining that its members were the chosen representatives of all the people and therefore empowered to act on the behalf of those people. The students made the point that as minors they had no voting rights and thus had no voice in choosing those who presumably acted on their behalf. Their spokesman went even further and suggested that any public body ought to seek out the opinions of those they serve before acting in their behalf. The effect was not lost on the board, which sent its president to meet with teachers and student body to discuss the change. Fortunately for all concerned, the matter was amicably settled through compromise, and all profited by the experience.

The democratic secondary school should itself be a model of democracy. It should be a laboratory in which students learn to practice democracy as well as learn about it; however, to do this the school must have an openness and a flexibility which are not characteristic of the traditional high school. Innovation must be encouraged, the evaluation of existing practice must be provided for, and change which is consciously directed toward improvement must be welcomed. The school should offer a challenge to students and teachers alike to find a better way to live, and to achieve finer goals.

MAJOR IMPLICATIONS FOR SECONDARY SCHOOL ADMINISTRATION

The concept of the secondary school as a democratic institution which serves as an agency of a democratic society with certain values and aspirations has many and varied implications. This section will deal with the broad general implications, while succeeding chapters will deal with the more specific implications as they are revealed in administrative practice.

If we accept the democratic concept of the role of the secondary school in our society, then the school administration should embody the ideals and practices of the democratic way of life. The school can be a community of learners, with the primary leadership role vested in the principal. However, leadership should not be confined to one person, or the professional staff, but should be shared throughout the membership of the school community, to include the nonprofessional and students.

The secondary school, whether we like it or not, is in many respects a reflection of the society in which we live. Sometimes that reflection is distorted or appears to be out of focus. This may be due to the influence of pressure groups, divergent theories of professional educators, or the persistence of outmoded practices. In any case, the goals of the school, its administrative structure, the decision-making process, and the way teachers and students work and learn and live together tells us much about our society. It is the structure of the school which perhaps has the greatest influence upon students, and which provides a substantial share of the education they receive. Therefore, it is difficult to overestimate the importance of the structural model of administration which the secondary school adapts.

For example, the way students participate in decision-making regarding the time and length of lunch periods, the scheduling of public performances of the band, or the presentation of the class play will probably have a greater effect upon their conception of decision-making in our society than will a civics lesson on the same subject. The actual practice is relevant and meaningful, while the book learning may not be.

CURRENT SCHOOL MODELS

Modern secondary schools may be said to operate along the lines of three models or combinations of these models. They are popularly known in the order of their development, as the "family" model, the "factory" model and the "corporation" model. These models originated in various sectors of our society and have been adopted in varying degrees and in diverse combinations in our secondary schools. No single model is likely to be found in its pure form in any school because of the many counter-influences which prevail in the community, and also because of the fact that teachers, fortunately, are individuals, and adopt different procedures and techniques to the extent that the administrative structure permits. However, in most schools a model pattern may be easily discerned by the competent observer.

Family Model

The "family" model had its origin in the era of progressive education. It was most popular in the elementary school during its early history. Although the early colonial school exhibited some of the essential features of the family model, it was not until the time of John Dewey that the "family" model became a distinct pattern for the operation of the school. He proposed that the school take on the pattern of the ideal family home, where the wise parents see that the children develop habits of honesty, thrift, punctuality, truthfulness, and due regard for the rights of others. Parents and children converse, and childish inquiries are answered and misconceptions corrected. Family excursions to parks and fields are taken to provide opportunity for children to learn about nature first-hand and to visualize a world of vast opportunities as well as dangers outside the sheltering walls of the home. Then, if we generalize this and organize these experiences into an educational pattern we have an ideal school. In view of the fact that parents are not always wise or imaginative, and familial experiences are often haphazard, the school that adapts the family model should seek to enrich and broaden the learning experiences, and should arrange them systematically so as to produce the most effective learning situation. The watch-words of the family-model school would be, "Learning by living."

While the "family" model was originally conceived as a model for the elementary school, and was displayed as such in Dewey's Chicago Laboratory School, it has had adaption mainly by rural and small urban secondary schools, although it is not unknown in large urban centers, particularly in private and parochial schools.

Factory Model

On the other hand, the "factory" model (as described in the preceding chapter) has been a very significant influence in secondary education. The "factory" model, as the name implies, likens the school to a factory into which raw materials in the form of children are taken, and, after processing, are turned out as finished products in the form of graduates. In such a school, students work at a uniform pace and curricular content is standardized. The educational process is largely one of assigning work and having students recite. Rote learning is characteristic of the process. The teacher is a taskmaster who sees students study and listens to them recite. The dialogue is *between* teacher and student, rather than *among* students and teacher. Students are evaluated by identical set standards and are graded on the basis of the amount of material they master.

Students in the "factory" model are induced to regard learning as a standardized process to acquire knowledge which may or may not be relevant or meaningful. They are told that if it is not now relevant or meaningful, it will be later, or that it will exert an unseen influence for good upon them even though they may not realize it. The "factory" school encourages competition among students in a standardized form and on somewhat limited grounds. Individual initiative, imagination, and creativity are not fostered, nor is inquiry encouraged.

The "modus operandi" of this type school, unlike the democratic model, does not encourage collaboration of students in planning projects, nor does it recruit their cooperation in working on them. It is only in extracurricular activities such as athletics and dramatics that cooperation and group discussion of problems are generated. Students are expected to put in a designated number of hours in the school and to be at certain stations at designated times. Monotony and tedium characterize the school program, with youthful exuberance breaking out in the halls only occasionally, and most often reserved for the time that school "lets out" and students rush to freedom.

The all-pervading atmosphere of the "factory" model is punitiveness. The teacher is obliged to punish the student for aberrant conduct, as the principal will punish her if she fails to mete out the prescribed penalty. Students often take pride in outwitting the teacher and administrator, and avoiding the penalty for substandard or forbidden conduct. The popular students are often those who can "get away with" flaunting the school rules and regulations which are handed down by administrators. In brief, the school operates in a series of standardized procedures to which pupils must adjust or suffer prescribed penalties.

The Corporate Model

The third model, the "corporate" school is a quite different species from either of the other two models. It is first of all largely a "teacher-centered" school, where teachers are systematically organized, and instruction and procedures are highly rationalized. Innovation and the variation of instructional procedures are encouraged. Team teaching is characteristic of this type of school. Teachers engage in workshops and seminars in which they cooperatively plan, formulate, and evaluate instruction.

The importance of instructional materials is emphasized. The "corporate" model abounds with teaching machines, computers, projectors, tape-recorders, films, and other audio-visual learning aids. In addition, teachers are encouraged to develop specialized instructional materials of their own for use in their classes. Differentiated ways of evaluating student progress and achievement result from the activated ingenuity of the teaching staff.

While students and teachers are often grouped together for learning experiences, the major emphasis is on the teacher and her methods, instructional materials, and evaluation techniques. There is a recognized hierarchy in which the principal occupies the top spot and the teachers come next, followed by teacher aides and noncertified personnel. Responsibility for decision-making is distributed among the hierarchy with the most important decisions left to the principal. Teams of teachers often are given broad controls over curricular content and programming.

Students themselves have little or no control over administrative practice, school structure, curriculum content, instructional methods, or evaluative procedures. The administration and teachers spend so much time in detailed planning that there is little left for students to plan or propose. The "corporate" school gives the impression to students that the work of education is highly specialized, and that innovation and improvement of educational experience are largely a function of institutionalized processes and therefore involve students to a very limited degree. The "corporate" school is a reflection of the "establishment" and is seldom responsive to the frustrations and protests of the students.

In the "corporate" school, teachers teach and students learn. Little recognition is given to the need for and the desirability of teachers learning from students who in turn would become teachers in an informal manner. This type of school emphasizes the importance of achievement as represented by the acquisition of specialized knowledge and skills. Little attention is given to personal and social development, and social issues are not explored to any great extent. There is an impersonality about the "corporate" school which generates an atmosphere of machine-type efficiency which has little place for the human aspects of life. In this atmosphere, the self concepts of students are not likely to be enhanced.

The insistence on accountability in the school is symbolic of this atmosphere. The school must be held responsible, since it is consuming tax monies. Accountable for what? The answer is often that it must be held accountable for what we can readily measure. This means achievement tests which measure how much knowledge has been achieved, and how high the stockpile of facts in the student's brain has become. His personal adjustment, moral character, interpersonal relationships, social ideals and values, and his outlook on life are of no concern in this form of measurement.

The Democratic Model

The authors of this book reject much of the philosophy embodied in the factory and corporate models briefly—and somewhat unfavorably—described in the preceding sections. Instead they propose the "democratic" model, which is a reflection of the basic values and highest aspirations of our democratic society briefly set forth in the first section of this chapter.

It is characteristic of the human being that he seeks satisfaction, self-realization, social significance, and real meaning through effective participation in the social institutions of the society in which he lives. Of all societies, the democratic one gives him the greatest opportunity to do this. Such participation involves the right and the duty to rebel against social practices and institutions which are considered unfair, outmoded, or dehumanizing. The rebel is justified in utilizing every legitimate means to combat these practices and institutions; but he is also obligated to sponsor better ones unless such practices and institutions have no useful function.

The democratic model, therefore, is characterized by the broadest participation, the utmost freedom to question the status quo, and the responsibility to contribute to constructive change. Participation includes not only teachers and administrators but also students and citizens of the school community. This does not mean that everyone participates in all decisions about the school, but rather that all who are directly concerned and affected by a policy or decision have an opportunity to be heard. In some cases this will mean an expression of opinion; in others, it could mean sought advice or a decisional vote. In all cases, however, it will represent an attempt to secure a consensus through acquisition and dissemination of information and rational discussion. Some decisions will be made by the principal and his staff, others by administrative and teaching staff, others by administrators, teachers, and pupils, and still others will involve citizens, as well as school personnel. It will be the responsibility of the administrators of the secondary school to establish and maintain a system of policy formation and decision-making which is consistent with the democratic principle of participation. This is a responsibility of leadership in the democratic-type secondary school.

Students will be involved in the establishment of the goals of the school. Appropriate citizens and teachers will also share in this function. By involving students in goal-setting, planning, and evaluating, students will learn about these processes in a real and meaningful manner. When students share in these processes, they are more likely to understand their significance and value, and, hence, to accept and help implement them. If, on the other hand, all planning and evaluation is done by others, the students tend to become dependent on others, which prepares them more for living under a dictatorship than in a democracy where they must be decision-makers.

In the democratic model, major emphasis will be given to helping students develop both school goals and personal goals. Students will be assisted in planning ways to achieve these goals and in appraising their progress toward worthy goals. They will be encouraged to examine the goals of the local community and of the nation itself. In a democratic community as well as a democratic school, people will be expected to be self-critical, not only personally, but with respect to the community and nation. It is through such criticism that constructive change is brought about.

As may be expected from the preceding, the democratic model will seek to encourage student initiative, imagination and creativity. Students will be encouraged to think for themselves and to learn to communicate their thoughts clearly and accurately. Communication skills will be learned, not by rote, but by the necessity to express thoughts effectively so as to influence the attitudes, opinions, and actions of others.

The democratic model will be characterized by recognition of each student as a person with unique qualities and unique needs. Teachers will display an attitude of respect for the student as a person, and in turn will be respected by him. There will be an atmosphere of humaneness about the school. The depersonalization which characterizes the "factory" model will nowhere be seen. Counseling and guidance will be prominent in the program. Every attempt will be made to insure that each student succeeds, not only in his educational pursuits, but also in his personal and social life.

The democratic model will be characterized by a great deal of student activity. Student councils, student clubs, student project teams and student liaison groups will be in evidence. Individual students will represent the student population on advisory councils and committees. Student organizations will plan and carry out projects, with teachers acting as advisors and resource persons. Student groups will sponsor and participate in worthy efforts of both school and community. Every student can and will be expected to contribute in a manner consistent with his preferences, interests, and abilities.

The school community can be a resource region for the school. It can reach out and bring these resources to bear on the program of the school. Professional and business people can come to the school to teach and to learn. They can act as resource people in their fields, and can give individual counselling and guidance in vocational choices. They can participate in the program of the school in the areas of their unique qualifications, thus providing a service to the community.

The school-community presents a rich laboratory for learning which the democratic model fully utilizes. Field trips of many types characterize the school program. Students learn by observing court trials, welfare programs, police and public safety operations, park and recreation administration and the many other governmental activities. They can visit private businesses and industrial plants, thus learning how the economic system actually works. They can learn about community, state and national organizations by participating to the extent possible as members or as observers. Parks and other nature areas can serve as laboratories for the study of botany, biology and other ecological sciences. The democratic model has walls, but they in no way restrict or limit the pursuit of learning beyond them.

Each secondary school of the democratic model will have a character of its own. Although all will have a common core of democratic values, each will express the individuality of its students, teachers, principal, and community. Emphasis on different types of learning and aspects of the educational process will vary from school-community to school-community responding to the needs, ideals, and aspirations of those the school serves. The school will strive to represent what is finest and best in the community. It will recognize its responsibility for the educational welfare of both rich and poor, black and white, gifted and subnormal, physically handicapped and physically strong. It will be an individual school serving individuals of many kinds. It will never be an institution promulgating the interests of selfish groups or proselytizing organizations.

A school of this type must have a broad, varied, and comprehensive educational program to meet the needs of its clients. It should be large enough to offer such a program economically and efficiently. It should be well furnished, with modern educational equipment and materials as valuable aids to learning, but never as ends in themselves. The democratic model is a person-oriented school, not a machine-oriented one.

Perhaps it would be helpful to enumerate what the democratic school is not. First of all, it is not a school in which students simply read, listen, and recite. It is not a place which is dominated by the teacher. It is not a place where students are regimented, with teachers acting as drillmasters. It is not a place where students take orders and carry them out without knowing or understanding the reason behind them. Teachers do not treat students as inferiors, nor do students regard teachers as antagonists. Rules and regulations for student conduct and appearance are not handed down from on high, as ultimatums.

Teachers are not solely concerned with teaching skills and the cognitive processes, at the expense of neglecting personal and social values. They do not neglect the responsibility for examining the curriculum with regard to its relevancy, currency and appropriateness with respect to students. They do not resist change simply because it is easier to do things in the same old way. They do not expect uniform achievement among students. They do not measure their success as teachers solely by the number of merit scholarships their students receive. They do not disregard their students' homes and family backgrounds in the formulation of their goals and the progress they make toward achieving them. They are not unmindful of the stresses and strains which life places on the adolescent in a very complex and rapidly changing world.

Finally, the democratic model is a community of learners which extends beyond the walls of the school. Students and teachers alike regard themselves as learners. They learn not only from books and experimental equipment, they learn from each other. Teachers, as they work with students, learn from them about life in broken homes, in the ghetto, in the tenement and in the plush suburban homes of the wealthy. They learn about gang mores, drug pushers, juice and protection rackets, alcoholism in the home, and the problems of advantaged as well as disadvantaged students. As a result, they can teach better because they know better the individuals who are their students. Education is personalized rather than standardized or mechanized. The process of learning is more humane, more compassionate, and more effective.

The administration of the democratic school calls for the highest type of leadership. A leadership which shares with all school personnel the attitude of learning. In such a school, the principal is always willing to listen to both students and teachers, and to learn of their problems. He is not only a learner in the school, he is a learner about the community. He recognizes the community as a vast learning laboratory with innumerable educational resources in the form of people and institutions, as well as materials. It is part of his job to bring those resources into effective use in the educational process.

The principal is the leader of the secondary school community of learning. His primary duty is to facilitate learning. In order to do this he will need to share leadership with those he leads. He must recognize that by sharing leadership he can make his own leadership more effective and more comprehensive. As a fringe benefit of considerable significance, he will enable others to develop the skills and abilities of leadership.

Bibliography

Allison, Clinton B., ed. *Without Consensus: Issues in American Education.* Boston: Allyn and Bacon, 1973.

Brembeck, Cole S., ed. *Social Foundations of Education: A Reader.* New York: Wiley and Sons, 1969.

Canning, Jeremiah. *Values in an Age of Confrontation.* Columbus, Ohio: Charles E. Merrill, 1970.

Cunningham, Luvern. *Governing Schools: New Approaches to Old Issues.* Columbus, Ohio: Charles E. Merrill, 1971.

Graham, Grace. *The Public School in the New Society.* London: Harper and Row, 1969.

Hand, Harold C. *Principles of Public Secondary Education.* New York: Harcourt, Brace and Co., 1958.

O'Neill, William F., ed. *Selected Educational Heresies.* Glenview, Ill.: Scott, Foresman and Co., 1969.

Saxe, Richard W., ed. *Opening the Schools.* Berkeley: McCutchan Publishing Corp., 1972.

Selakovich, Daniel. *The Schools and American Society.* Waltham, Mass.: Blaisdell Publishing Co., 1967.

4

The Principal as a Leader

Several beliefs or assumptions are implicit in the concept of the principal as leader. One is that the secondary school principal is in a key position to improve the quality of opportunity provided to the boys and girls in his school. It is within their particular schools that principals, staff members, and students meet and work in personal, face-to-face, day-to-day encounters. Given strong leadership and a reasonable amount of freedom from constraints, the individual school system can best know its students, devise alternative plans for their education, create a school community, and provide the necessary flexibility of program and practices to meet changing needs and conditions.

Consistent with this view of the crucial position of the secondary school in education is the belief that the community the school serves will be and must be more actively involved in helping to determine school policies, not only through the members appointed or elected to serve on school boards, but also through the active, day-to-day participation of parents and other citizens. Also consistent is the belief that secondary school students themselves can and should be given the opportunity to participate actively in the decision making process.

To be sure, the secondary school does not exist separately from the other parts of the school system, nor is it immune from district-wide policies or legislative enactments or requirements. It is true that in some school systems policies are set in such minute detail by the board of education and the central administration that little latitude remains at the school level for creative leadership, flexibility, experimentation, or change. This does not mean, however, that such a pattern of administration, where it exists, needs to continue. On the contrary, strong arguments are being advanced for the decentralization of educational decision-making. A hierarchical, bureaucratic type of organization can grow ponderous, slow-footed, and unresponsive, both to changing conditions and to the people it is supposed to serve.

The New York State Commission on the Quality, Cost and Financing of Elementary and Secondary Education, which was appointed by the legislature of the state of New York, had this to say on the question

> ... we recognize that the test of the responsiveness of any organization to its clients occurs at the point where the two come in closest contact.
> There should be increased control at the school level exerted by citizens, a school's officials, parents, faculty and students, subject to strengthened measures of accountability. This means that parents, the principal, students and teachers should have substantial choices open to them, limited only when clearly necessary by policies, standards, guidelines and legislative requirements imposed by higher levels of educational hierarchy.
> To this Commission, it appears that the school principal, of all involved, has the greatest potential for improving the quality of education.[1]

Another belief implicit in the concept of the principal-as-leader is that the principalship of the American secondary school can and should be worthy of a life-long career. Too often it has been considered a transitional stage to some other position—superintendency, for example, or a line or staff position in central administration. Properly conceived, the principalship can offer psychological rewards which provide rich benefits and deep satisfaction. These rewards come, in large measure, from the opportunities to associate with and to serve youth, to provide or to help create an environment within which people may learn, discover themselves, prosper as persons, test their interests and capabilities, develop healthy self-concepts, and form trustful relationships with adults. It is an obvious cliche, but true nevertheless, that in the secondary schools are those who will determine what will be. Among the students are those who will write the books, generate the thoughts, make the discoveries, carry on the work, make the political decisions, dream the dreams, and set the tone for society as the present gives way to the ever-emerging future.

In a period when job satisfaction is a prime consideration in career choice in all types of occupations, the personal dividends of the principalship are not to be discounted. Material rewards of the principalship have also improved substantially, and salaries have become respectable both in the absolute and in relationship to income in other occupations. Because of changing salary conditions, no specific figures are mentioned here, but anyone contemplating the principalship as a career may easily verify the conclusions stated.

Much has been written about the large numbers of persons who hold

---

[1]Report of the New York State Commission on the Quality, Cost and Financing of Elementary and Secondary Education, Vol. 3, p. 11.2.

certificates which entitle them to hold principalship positions, thus creating a supply which exceeds the number of positions available. However, some who aspire to become principals have little conception of the demands and possibilities of the position. Without a substantial grasp of the social forces which are changing the nature and function of the school, many who wish to become principals do so only within the scope of "getting ahead," working their way up, securing greater financial benefits, or obtaining a place of power, status, and authority (which they mistakenly believe is assured by the mere act of assuming the role of principal). The truth is, that although many seek to become principals, there is a shortage of those who are really prepared to take on the task of leadership.

A third belief implicit in the role of the principalship, as interpreted by this book, is in the importance of the leadership role of the principal. It should be made clear that although the emphasis here is on the principal, what is written also applies to all who work in the school, because all *effective* leadership is in some degree *shared* leadership. No principal can move toward better goals for a school unless all staff members identify problems, come to share goals and purposes, and are willing to gain the insights, understandings, and skills necessary to move toward them.

We have chosen to emphasize the leadership aspects of administration rather than the management functions; however, it is recognized that the leader-administrator does have management responsibilities which must be effectively carried out, either directly or by delegation. In an organization which is more or less static, where purpose and function and operating procedures are generally agreed upon, and where the primary task is to keep the organization *as it is* running smoothly, the management function is probably paramount in importance. On the other hand, when an organization or institution is in a state of flux, when new goals and directions are called for, and when the organization or institution requires an adaptation to changing circumstances and demands, then different qualities and skills are necessary on the part of the person heading the organization or institution. This latter condition probably exists more often in public institutions than it does in the private economy, and is found more often in times of rapid social change than in stable times. The fact that an institution is public, and does not and should not have a single accepted measure of effectiveness (like a profit or loss statement, for example), adds to its complexity and places demands on its leader which are in many ways different from those demands placed on persons who hold positions of responsibility in the private sector.

Leadership is easier to talk about than it is to define or measure. We will try to describe some of its qualities. The reader will no doubt be able to add to the characteristics. Although leadership characteristics seem to vary with the situation, and different leadership styles may vary within a particular kind of enterprise, we are thinking of leadership here as it applies to the secondary school.

To be effective over a period of time, leadership must be based on knowledge. Those who lead must have a clear vision of where they want to go, and, more importantly, why they want to go there. They must know that to persuade others to go with them, they must have facts and knowledge at their command. The knowledge of the leader-principal must go far beyond the housekeeping chores of "running the school." It must extend to understanding the community served by the school, and the students in it. He must be aware of the larger society within which the school exists, not only as it is, but also as it may become as a result of the movements and ideas that influence it.

THE GOOD LEADER

Leadership is more than charisma, even though those characteristics and qualities that add up to what is called "personality" are important. The good leader inspires trust; he is not perceived as one who seeks to gain his ends by manipulating others, or by being devious. He is credible. He carries an air of confidence and self-possession, without giving the impression that he thinks himself to be infallible. He does not shrink from taking a position or expressing a conviction. Many educational administrators seem to try to maintain a low profile, that is, low visibility. At best, this may keep the administrator temporarily out of difficulty and outside of controversy. At worst, it comes close to avoidance of responsibility and is a stance more related to self-survival than to leadership.

The good leader is not inclined to blame others when things go wrong. He is ready to take responsibility for his decisions. He is not arbitrary in his judgments, but he still knows that he must arrive at decisions. Habitual indecisiveness and strong leadership are incompatible.

The good leader is also a realist. He knows that all his goals may not be reached. He is open to new evidence and is willing and able to modify his views if the evidence is compelling. He can compromise, but he also knows the fine line beyond which, in the interests of integrity and credibility, compromise is not an acceptable solution, for example in a case involving the right of due process.

In an era of change, the educational leader recognizes that he must cope with conflict. Once he accepts this, the management of conflict becomes one of the tests of leadership. Many individuals and groups have a stake in what the schools do and what functions they are to perform. A secondary school does not exist in a vacuum. Although we often talk about "the public," the truth is there are many publics. People sometimes belong to groups that are more or less permanent, and at other times they coalesce into groups that are temporary, formed around a particular issue of the moment. As often as not, the views of different groups of "publics" are opposed, or at least represent

The Principal as a Leader

certain differences. Sometimes the differences of opinion about some aspect of school policy or practice become sharp and conflicting, and differences rise to a high pitch.

Sometimes the source of conflict is internal to the school. It may surround the negotiation or bargaining process or it may evolve as an aftermath. It may evolve from differing opinions about the direction of change, about proposed innovations, or from differing opinions about relationships of teachers to pupils. Occasionally, the seeds of conflict are sown by students themselves as they present grievances, or protest some aspect of teaching or administration. (A later section will deal with some of these sources of conflict in considerable detail.)

The point made here is that leadership of the secondary school requires acceptance that conflict is inherent in the operation of the school, that it is not necessarily to be deplored, and that skill in resolving conflict is one measure of effective leadership. Basic to conflict resolution, however, is a philosophy and a set of goals derived from the philosophy which guide the efforts of the leader in conflict situations. Without certain philosophies and goals, conflict resolution is only improvised, crisis to crisis, and the conclusion of a particular conflict is then aptly referred to as "putting out the fire."

In discussing the leadership role of the principal, we referred earlier to the belief that as much decision-making as possible should be decentralized in the system to the level of the individual school.

The Bureaucratic Model

Designed to meet the needs of business and industry, the bureaucratic model was adopted early by American school systems. A few generations ago, students of school administration were accustomed to classes which compared a board of education to a corporate board of directors; the school superintendent, to the company president or chief executive officer; principals, to line officers; research persons, to staff officers; and, by implication, the teachers were compared to the ordinary day-to-day workers. Somewhere below (but not described), were, presumably, the students. Orders were supposed to go from top to bottom. Policy was made at the top and transmitted to the bottom. Staff, students, and public were expected to go through "channels." Although in the middle years of this century movements to democratize the administration of schools made headway, tacit acceptance of the essentials of the hierarchical, bureaucratic model of organization remained.

A Newer Model

Today some students of organizations are coming to the conclusion that the hierarchical arrangement is no longer suitable to the present and future, and will have to be modified or replaced. This thought is presently directed primarily to business and industrial organization.

In an article which he published in *Think* magazine, titled "The Coming Death of Bureaucracy," Warren G. Bennis, Professor of Organizational Psychology and Management, and head of the Organization Studies Group of the Alfred P. Sloan School of Management at M.I.T., comments on the bureaucratic model. Bennis' article is included in the selected readings at the end of this chapter.

Early concepts of man as a worker in an organization have been challenged by a number of social scientists who, in the past twenty-five years or so, have directed their attention to organizational and administrative theory. Many of the studies were carried on in an industrial setting, but students of school administration have adapted them to school organization. The earlier concepts considered the role of management should be to organize materials and labor to achieve the economic goals of a business or industry. The purpose of management was to direct efforts of people, thus controlling their behavior on the job as the needs of the organization dictated.

Douglass McGregor puts the case clearly in his book, *The Human Side of Enterprise*. According to McGregor, the conventional theory held that unless management actively intervened, people (workers) would be passive, possibly resistant to the needs of the organization, so, "they must therefore be persuaded, rewarded, punished, controlled—their activities must be directed."

Behind this conventional theory, McGregor states, are several beliefs which are less explicit, but widespread: "The average man is indolent—he works as little as possible. He is gullible, not very bright, the ready dupe of the charlatan and the demagogue." McGregor calls this conventional view "Theory X". He goes on to present a theory which is based upon a different set of beliefs about human nature in regard to organizations. He says that management is still responsible for organizing the elements of productive enterprise to economic ends, but the conceptions of human nature are different. This view holds that people are not naturally passive nor are they inherently resistant to the needs of an organization. If they appear so, it is because of their experiences in organizations. People have motivation, they can take responsibility, they are ready to direct behavior to the goals of the organization. Management should recognize such human characteristics and should make it possible for people to develop them.

McGregor also discusses human motivation. He stresses the fact that basic human needs must be satisfied first; that is, unless he has food, shelter, and opportunity to rest, man is not likely to be concerned with higher needs. Assuming basic needs are met, man begins to be motivated by higher needs: safety, protection against danger, threat, etc. Beyond this, social and ego needs become important. Man needs to belong, to be accepted, to give and receive friendship, to develop self-esteem and independence, to achieve, and to get recognition, appreciation, and respect from his fellows. On top of everything else, man needs self-fulfillment.[2]

Management continues to operate on the conception of man and human nature which fails to take into account the needs that lie above the physiological. However, the new task for management is to recognize the higher motivations that exist and to rearrange organizational patterns and methods so that people can reach their own goals by directing their efforts toward organizational goals.

Adaptability to Schools

One observation should be made about the application of theory drawn from industrial studies to school organizations. In industry, the elements of the economic enterprise are management, workers, labor, materials and equipment. In schools, one important element which is often overlooked is the pupils. As mentioned earlier in the analogy of school to factory, the boys and girls seem to be considered much as is the raw material in the industrial process. Of course this is not true because they are human beings, the same as their teachers and administrators. The same needs that motivate adults are present in the young. The higher needs of students—a good self-concept, the need for recognition and friendship, the desire to achieve, to be accepted, to be appreciated, and to be a participating part of the enterprise—must be taken into account in a school organization, just as such needs of teachers and administrators need to be valued. The needs of the person must be considered as well as the objectives of the organization, and the two need to be brought into congruence.

In schools, this brings us to the question of the goals and purposes of the organization. The leaders and others (teachers, counsellors, students) must continually review goals and purposes, relating practice and process to purpose. It is difficult to see how the needs of persons and the goals of the organization can be harmonized unless the goals and purposes are clear to all concerned. This, we suggest, is a more complex question than is faced by the industrial or business organization. It is also a question that is not often pursued in sufficient depth by administrator-leaders and school staffs. On the other hand, schools, by their nature and because they are service-oriented, and because they include workers who aspire to be considered professional persons, are in a more favorable position to move quickly toward newer concepts of organization than are industrial organizations. A grasp of what this means, and a desire to move in new directions of administration and organization offer exciting possibilities to the principal as leader. As we move into later discussions of the secondary school and how it may be organized effectively, we shall attempt to relate the theory to practice.

---

[2]Douglass McGregor, *The Human Side of Enterprise* (New York: McGraw-Hill, 1960).

Bibliography

Abbott, Max G. "Hierarchical Impediments to Innovation in Educational Organizations." *Change Perspectives in Educational Administration.* Edited by Abbott and Lovell. Auburn, Alabama: Auburn University, 1965.

Bennis, Warren G.; Benne, Kenneth B.; and Chin, Robert. *The Planning of Change.* New York: Holt, Rinehart and Winston, 1969.

Bennis, Warren G., and Schein, Edgar A. *Leadership and Motivations: Essays of Douglass McGregor.* Cambridge, Mass.: M.I.T. Press, 1966.

Brain, George B. "Organizational Renewal: The Superintendent's Role." *The School Administrator.* Washington, D.C.: The American Association of School Administrators, June 1972.

Cartwright, Darwin, and Zander, Alvice, eds. *Group Dynamics: Research and Theory,* 2d ed. Evanston, Illinois: Harper and Row, 1960.

Gible, Jack R. "Dynamics of Leadership." In *The Search of Leaders.* Washington, D.C.: National Education Association, 1967.

Griffiths, Daniel E. *Human Relations in School Administration.* New York: Century-Crofts, 1956.

Haskew, Lawrence. "Leadership is Personal." *The Bulletin of the National Association of Secondary School Principals,* April, 1964.

National Association of Secondary School Principals. *The Principalship: Job Specifications and Salary Consideration for the 70's.* Arlington, Virginia, 1970.

Shannon, Thomas A. *Resolving Management Conflicts Through Associations: The Administrative Team.* Arlington, Virginia: National Association of Secondary School Principals, 1972.

Thompson, Victor A. *Modern Organization.* New York: Knopf, 1961.

Selected Readings

The School as a Factory

Warner Bloomberg, Jr.

There is a growing uneasiness among teachers in American colleges and universities at the charge that our so-called "institutions of higher learning" are increasingly "education factories." The phrase conjures up an image of masses of students, identified only by IBM numbers, moving through a conveyor-belt system of standardized courses during which they view lectures video-taped by professors never seen in the flesh and then read programmed learning texts in preparation for multiple-choice exams graded by electronic devices that scan standardized answer sheets on which they have registered their new knowledge with mark-sensing pencils. This vision of a dehumanized academia is, of course, a caricature of even the schools it best describes. Nevertheless, there is enough reality in this portrayal that it clearly is not pure fantasy. We do not have to be told what kinds of institutions are being satirized. We recognize all too easily that this polemical cartoon refers to most of our schools, not just to the allegedly higher levels.

But why do such criticisms, such accusations, make us uncomfortable? We are more thoroughly committed to mass education for more people through more years than almost any other modern society. What is wrong with using the most efficient organizational techniques and artifacts of advanced technology to facilitate the achievement of this democratized participation in education? Why not honestly accept the notion that our schools constitute a massive and most important service industry that ought to be concerned about cutting costs and improving efficiency by the established techniques of standardization, more productive machinery, better quality control, and tighter organization?

I suspect that what disturbs an increasing number of professional educators is more fundamental than a cultivated disregard for costs or a romantic

---

Address prepared for Interdistrict Teachers Institute, Homewood-Flossmoor, Ill., 13 February, 1967. Reprinted by permission. The author is a professor in the Department of Urban Affairs and Extension University of Wisconsin–Milwaukee.

but reactionary resistance to technological innovations. Rather, we sense that the very process of teaching and learning undergoes critical, if not mortal, damage when cast into a mechanical mold. The process involves the growth and development of living creatures, not the manufacture or servicing of mechanical objects. Its dimensions are organic, psychological and social; these are fundamentally misinterpreted and misrepresented by analogies from physics or from chemical and electrical engineering.

Of course, living organisms can be organized as units in a system or production based on mechanical models. We have already accomplished this with industrialized agriculture, "egg factories," organic drug production, and the like. But the factory model is most completely and satisfactorily fulfilled when we can get away from organic processes altogether, as when we shift from producing drugs organically to synthesizing them by some combination of strictly chemical, electrical, and mechanical procedures. Or when we shift from human operatives to the computer control of an automated assembly line.

But what if our goal is not the production of more and more standardized objects, be they organically or synthetically produced? What if our aim is the development of increasingly complex and diversified emotional and intellectual behavior on the part of immensely intricate, living, growing, thinking, and self-conscious beings? Does it make any sense to apply mechanistic models to that activity? Most of us would answer, "No." We can imagine a factory setting up to produce tomatoes, or eggs, or antibiotics. But a "learning factory" is the concept of "education." So we are disturbed by the charge that our schools are more and more becoming "educational factories," especially when we realize that contemporary trends in this direction are simply a continuing extrapolation of what has long been the tendency in our educational system.

We are now so used to building and organizing schools on the model of the factory and its white-collar offspring, the bureaucratized office, that we forget this approach is hardly more than a century old. We disregard as irrelevant to modern educational problems the organization of teachers and students into what might best be called a "learning community," such as developed with the rise of the medieval universities in Europe and their much earlier predecessors in the Far East. And we dismiss as patently obsolete the rural school in which one classroom often contained children separated by six "grade levels" and even more years, to say nothing of diversity in genetic endowment and family background. No matter that some of the most successful persons in contemporary industrial institutions recall with high praise the education they received in country schools. We are still so involved in debunking those parochial and politically destructive myths which romanticized everything about the disappearing farmer that we usually dismiss out of hand any suggestion that the legend may not be wholly a lie.

So I will not ask that we consider the virtues that may have obtained in earlier modes of educational organization, as well as their shortcomings. But we should be willing to cease romanticizing contemporary schools and to examine the work of our own hands with that honesty, candor, and regard for facts that we claim we try to cultivate among our pupils. Recognizing that the present factory format of our schools was an inevitable concomitant of industrialization and American urbanism, rather than a product of educational necessities, will help free us to consider realistic alternatives rather than reacting with escapist utopian fantasies of the Paul Goodman variety.

As schools for the mass education of children of ordinary citizens were established in the urbanized places of the United States, their organization increasingly reflected the factory model of our rapidly developing industrialism. Where such a model obtains, the school is viewed essentially as a workplace, and learning is perceived in terms of productivity. The achievement of marketable skills, which would be only one facet of the educational goals of schools oriented to facilitating the growth of a humane and capable democratic citizenry, becomes the major and sometimes the only real objective of the school. How well the finished pupil sells to undergraduate colleges and to technical schools or to available employers is the measure of the factory-school's success. There also is substantial concern about the rate of spoilage, since pieces—that is, pupils—which cannot be processed to completion must be scrapped, dropped out from the production line, which is the most accurate definition of "dropouts." Whether this spoilage results from the use of flawed raw materials or from mistakes on the part of the craftsmen and technicians—teachers, counselors, and the like—does not alter the fact that a school-factory which accumulates too large and visible a pile of scrapped pieces, of "dropouts," is going to be under pressure from higher management and criticism from those who view themselves as stockholders or their representatives, usually taxpayers' associations.

Worker-teachers and their foremen, the principals, react like all other factory workers; they tend to do everything possible to shove pieces along the production line whether or not each piece, each pupil, meets the specifications for quality officially claimed by the company, the school system. Of course, if the products are seriously flawed too often, the customers, colleges, and employers, will reject them and may even embarrass the company's management with public complaints, possibly with calls for investigation. Worker-teachers and their foremen-principals therefore must seek a strategic balance between the number of pieces scrapped and the number which will be placed on the market with the company lable, a diploma, but will then prove faulty. This is an especially pressing problem for those factory-schools where the raw materials are of low quality to start with, the equipment old and inadequate, and the worker-teachers lower in skill and more resentful than those in the fancier, better-paying, technologically improved suburban plants. Pity the supervisors and managers in that situation, especially when the market for low-quality products has undergone a relatively sudden and severe contraction!

School officials often give speeches reiterating the pre-factory goals of public education, emphasizing the development of a competent, humanistic, liberally educated citizenry, with appropriate quotations from Jefferson, Horace Mann, and even John Dewey (If the John Birchers aren't too strong in the district). But everyone understands that such pronouncements have the same meaning and value as when the heads of industrial concerns assert that their greatest interest is in national progress rather than corporate profits. Certainly most of the pupils are not taken in for long by the facade of altruism with which the factory-school so often decorates its exterior. For they, too, are like the employees in a pre-automation factory. They, too, have production tasks to be performed in accordance with a rigid time schedule and instructions provided by a management which pays on a piece-rate basis for the stipulated products, using company script known as grades. If one earns enough of this script, it can be used to purchase privileges within the school factory, such as exemption from certain exams, entrance into certain clubs, and the like. A minimum of company script must be acquired to purchase official release from this bondservant-like situation; much more is necessary to purchase admission to college. As in pre-union factories, this pits each individual competitively against all others, and each must try to keep up with management's schedules for productivity, regardless of his individual growth rates, interests and needs.

Indeed, every element of community is systematically obliterated in the factory-style school, except that underground community of resistance that develops among some of the pupils as they grow old enough to comprehend their situations more clearly; with that increasing comprehension and their growing physical size and strength, they can react much as factory workers reacted to the same system in the days before unions. As this happens, teachers become increasingly like old-time factory foremen; more and more of their time and energy goes into distributing and supervising production assignments, trying to maintain productivity standards, making out payrolls, protecting company property, coping with worker resistance and subversion, and trying to stay on good terms with supervisors and upper management in general.

Even the time and space format for the school embodies the organizational model of the factory of early industrialism and of its offspring, the bureaucratized office: classes begin and end on a shift-change schedule and, with a few special exceptions, rooms are completely standardized. Teachers and students themselves are likely to be treated as easily replaceable and frequently even as interchangeable parts. In such a system order inevitably rests more upon authority and potential coercion than upon commitment to common values, a sense of mutuality, and developing social responsibility. As in the pre-union, pre-automation factory, a large group of low-skilled and thus poorly paid workers are especially likely to resent their fate, which often has nothing to do with their actual potentialities, and to be both more restive and more resistive to management than those who are accorded high pay and the official privileges and prestige that go with "making out" in terms of the company script of grades.

Like most workers in the old-style factory, most people do their chores without real enthusiasm or authentic involvement; the system makes it impossible for most of them to care much about the work itself most of the time, but some of them will work hard in order to increase their piece-rate bonuses and thereby acquire a better-than-average take-home pay at the end of each semester.

In general, those parts of the human personality which come into play in authentic relationships—the elements we point to when we talk about really caring, being deeply concerned, experiencing genuine involvement—remain disconnected from the overt and intellectual behavior of the worker-pupil. This schizoid pattern of conduct is not only acceptable to the typical foreman-teacher, but is usually desired; for it means that the class will remain a standardized experience and production schedules will be maintained. There will be regulated laughter at appropriate remarks, and some students may be induced to "read with feeling" during recitation in English literature. In such classes, body language is repressed, even facial expression. When students hit the halls they "come alive" in a very literal sense, and some of them become quite boisterous in releasing pent-up emotional resources that could have been linked into the learning process instead of being disconnected from overt and intellectual behavior and repressed.

As a result, most of the experiences of the classroom are internalized in only a superficial way; they do not become part of the personality system, thereby inducing change in behavior; "learning" amounts to little more than storage of information in easily accessible and easily erased or rapidly fading components in the brain's storage and retrieval system. Supposedly "learned" material passes superficially into and out of the worker-pupil's personality by way of the notebook and the test or essay, just as the factory worker quickly forgets a well memorized work assignment once that job is over and he goes on to the next.

Because of the emphasis on standardized production of oral performances and written exams, creativity is perilous for the worker-pupil and disturbing, if not threatening, to the foreman-teacher. In such a system individualizing deviations from the production schedule are not to be tolerated and challenges to the methods or conclusions of the textbook and teacher are not permitted. The creative pupil may, of course, be wrong; but rather than being encouraged to explore his proposed innovation and thereby discover and correct his error, which would be a genuine learning experience, he will instead be brought quickly back into line, whether by sarcasm and other forms of derogation or by a blunt insistence that he shape up. Art may be exempted from this demand for factory and office conformity, but even here there are still many teachers who destroy creativity by insisting that the children accept the official dictums about what is beautiful and how to draw a tree.

It is important to the operation of this old-fashioned, pre-union factory and bureaucratic office type of organization that genuine leadership not develop among the subordinates. The foremen-teachers and higher echelons of management are continuously fearful that their control over inevitably discontented and restless worker-pupils may break down. Official positions of alleged student leadership normally are attained only by those who appear to be willing to conform to the system, which normally means those who master the skills of standardized oral performance and production of acceptable exams in accord with managerial schedules, thereby becoming highly rather than poorly paid members of the work force. As in pre-union factories, they tend to be disliked, if not actually despised, by those who fail to make out; this serves the interests of management by destroying the potential solidarity of the pupil work force, but tends to induce among the lower paid pupil-workers the development of anti-management and sometimes openly rebellious leadership.

In such a system the so-called "student councils" and "student governments" operate as the crassest and most despicable forms of "company unions." They are allowed a measure of control only in those areas that the real management doesn't really care about, and may actually be used to relieve teachers and administrators of some unhappy or distracting chores, such as trying students accused of misconduct, without it in any way bringing about even a modicum of genuinely shared authority.

This whole factory-school system of organization and management tends to produce a majority of students who are at least mildly alienated, and many who are almost totally disaffected. But this also is true of teachers in all but very exceptional systems. They do not relate to one another as colleagues in a learning community. Rather, their behavior reflects the fact that most schools have yet to employ the continuous-flow organization of production now available in automated and computerized factories; teachers continue to design their programs on the model of the old-style factory in which production is broken up into well-bounded units, each performed in a different place by different craftsmen-teachers. After a unit of work on the material—the child—has been completed and that piece of material has passed or slipped by inspection, it is transferred to the workplace at which the next unit of production will occur.

One result of this ridiculous fixation on old-style factory boundaries is that the teacher-craftsmen constantly accuse those in the preceding workplaces of having not finished their component in this divided and divisive production schedule. First-grade teachers complain that the materials—the children—have not been made ready in kindergarten for the production routines of the first grade. Third-grade teachers accuse second grade teachers of passing along materials—that is, children—that do not meet the standards set for completion of production routines at the work station known as second grade. Thus teachers who talk about education in terms of continuous and subtle processes of biological and social-psychological development in fact organize teaching and learning on a mechanical model, and an obsolete one at that!

Reflecting the situation of the skilled worker in the old-style factory, teachers tend to isolate themselves as much as possible at their work stations. One of the cardinal sins of the contemporary school is to stick one's nose into another teacher's classroom problems unless invited to do so, and such an invitation rarely comes from any but the most recently hired teacher-workers. Curriculum planning also reflects the old-style factory format of simple and highly specialized units of production. It comes very close to saying that pupils cannot, indeed ought not, learn about reading in an arithmetic class or about calculations during English.

As a result, it is almost inconceivable that arithmetic and English teachers might have something useful to say to one another about each other's tasks and the potential relationships among them; one might as well ask for extensive and meaningful collaboration between a lathe operator and the worker manning a high-speed punch-press—all they have in common is employment in the same factory and work on the same materials as they are passed along the production line.

The same holds true, for, say, third grade teachers and seventh grade teachers; why should those who are just getting the ore refined at the blast furnace be expected to have anything relevant to say to the fellows in the finishing shops where the billets of steel are converted into rails, plates, and sheet metal? It is rather like a semi-automated poultry factory. One team of specialists attends to the hatchery in which the chicks emerge, another to the area where they are raised into hens, a third to the sheds in which they eat and lay eggs, and a fourth to the packing and shipping of the eggs. Each team concentrates on the jobs within its boundaries, though they may envy or derogate the work of another; those who are trying to get the hens to lay more eggs feel no need whatever to be in a continuous communication and collaboration with those who are trying to get more eggs to hatch into healthy little chicks. What the craftsmen-operatives in this type of factory set-up may require is a report-sheet of some sort that will indicate what has been done with the material at a preceding stage of production, plus warnings about any ways in which the material departs from the usual norms. Does this piece of steel have new chemicals in it or has it seemed to be brittle (though not enough to be rejected, or held back for further treatment, especially if you're worried about production records)? Has this chick been raised on a new type of feed or has it shown signs of not being as a good layer ought to be ("Number 172-05 disrupts the flock—maybe send to slaughter")? And so a cumulative file of information about the material being processed may accompany it from one work station to another. Meanwhile, conversation among workers from different machines tends to deal, not with their actual work, but with gripes about the company, or bad materials, with gossip, and with life outside the factory. I hardly need to detail the analogy to the cumulative file so many schools acquire for each pupil, in which one finds lists of grades, profiles derived from one to another nationally standardized test, and such rich portrayals of the human personality as "Needs to be drawn out—doesn't participate," or "Won't stop talking to neighbors and is a troublemaker."

Teachers most oriented to the factory model have very little interest in how the materials on which they work, the pupils, behave once they are done with them, unless there are complaints from the customers, from colleges and employers, directed specifically against their products. Although the school in theory has the purpose of enabling the children to become more effective as citizens, human beings, and workers outside of school little or nothing is done to determine if this actually happens during or after the period the child is enrolled. Rather, emphasis is almost entirely on what the material does while it is in the factory—how well it passes the various inspections. "Homework" is not work the child does at school to enhance the life of the home, but is an archaic leftover from the protofactory "putting out" system of manufacture when workers performed tasks in their cottages and brought the products to a central place for completion or for combination into lots for shipping. Little or no effort is made to determine if homework actually accomplishes anything except to reduce the time young people have for nonschool elements in their lives and thereby to extend the control of the school. Like the artisan in a putting-out situation, the child must meet a take-home production schedule, returning with so many pieces of paper that pass inspection.

Attitudes towards class composition also reflect the influence of the factory model. Gardeners, as contrasted with those engaged in the industrialized production of flowers, seek an aesthetically pleasing heterogeneity among their plants. Similarly, sophisticated leaders in human organizations know they must have diversity among members if the complex functions through which groups are sustained and accomplish their goals are to be carried out well. But mass production factory workers want to work on materials which are as standardized and constant in their characteristics as is possible. For every time the material changes, we must change production routines. The pre-factory artisan might prefer that each work assignment be, if not unique, at least somewhat different from the preceding one; the factory craftsmen and technicians prefer homogeneous grouping of materials and jobs so that their own behavior as producers can be simplified and thus easier. And so there has been a fairly steady pressure from teachers towards homogeneous grouping of materials and jobs so that their own behavior as producers can be simplified and thus easier. And so there has been a fairly steady pressure from teachers towards homogeneous grouping, not because the children learn in such a setting, but because in a classroom where pupil's ages and abilities appear very similar the teacher can feel he or she is dealing with individual children while in fact using a single behavior routine for processing the entire batch.

As I have already indicated, mechanical systems are most fully realized in efficiency terms as organic components are eliminated, when chemical synthesis replaces growth processes and when automation and computers replace human operatives. Teachers, like employees on industrial farms or in egg factories, cannot shift to synthetic production. The closest they can get to it is the highest possible standardization of activity and product using organic components. Homogeneous grouping, standardized lesson plans, standardized tests, and standardized "developmental" tasks all help to achieve this factory-model goal. But one result is to make some of the teachers' activity more subject to displacement by increasingly complex and refined machinery. The egg factory, after all, is only an automated poultry farm with many hired hands displaced by transmission belts, feedback circuitry, and a few technicians. We already have replaced the farm laborer in cotton-fields and cornfields by automatic machinery, and the computer-controlled farm is already in experimental form. We have recently learned how to displace bureaucratized office personnel with automatic machines and cybernetic control systems, but we are somewhat startled to discover that apparently much more complex work now carried on by many so-called middle management people also can be assumed by adequately sophisticated computers. The factory-model school is ripe for such technological innovation. Experimental models of mechanical and computerized teaching machines are meeting with surprising success. Teachers may protest that such machinery removes the "human element" from the classroom and thereby will undermine the teaching-learning process. However, it's clear that the teachers themselves have effectively standardized and dehumanized the factory-model classroom, so such protests will provide no more long-run resistance to the further mechanization of teaching than the riots of the Luddites prevented the mechanization of the textile industry in England several centuries ago.

The fact that the school has become an educational factory also affects the attitudes of the public toward teachers. Intuitively, the public senses that teachers are not professionals, like doctors and lawyers and clergymen, but are increasingly skilled and highly-paid craftsmen and technicians. It does not matter if teachers choose to call the organizations through which they protect and advance their occupational interests "associations", rather than "unions"—airline pilots and industrial machinists also belong to "associations." Nor does the requirement of more so-called "higher education" for licensing make the difference—sanitary engineers and certified public accountants often have to meet similar requirements. Indeed, so-called professional standards bend rather easily under the pressure of personnel shortages. When we face a scarcity of doctors, lawyers, or clergymen in some of our communities, we do not give that professional title to individuals who lack professional preparation but are willing to do the work; rather, we try to induce available professionals to work longer hours and thereby make more money or otherwise advance their careers. But where there are teacher shortages the allegedly professional standards prove rather fragile, as in the slum schools of certain large cities where superintendents must desperately try to get anyone who can somehow be called a teacher to man the classrooms and keep mayhem at a minimum by any means that work. The situation is a nice analogy to many factories during World War II labor shortages, when the peace-time standards of employment offices gave way to the sheer necessity of having a live body beside every operating machine.

Again, as is true of many crafts and technical fields, a majority of those who prepare for entry into the field either find a better-paying work opportunity elsewhere or leave the field within a few years and do not return to it. From a vocational point of view, especially for women who fail to get married or choose not to by the end of college, or who want a second income for themselves and their husbands prior to having children, teaching is patently more a convenient craft than a professional calling, especially if one can get into a rather plush suburban school system.

What lies ahead for the education industry in America? It seems to me that there are two alternate lines of possible development. The most likely is the rapid modernization of schools and school systems on the basis of the factory model. Programming of work will embody more and more continuous-flow processes. The most standardized activities of teachers will be subject to mechanization by means of the highly sophisticated hardware cybernetics makes increasingly available. Even more emphasis will go into developing school analogies to contemporary industrial management techniques with their focus on the psychological needs of workers and potential production gains from "good human relations." Efforts to reduce teaching and learning to more and more explicit and standardized routines, analogous to time-and-motion studies in industry, will increase very rapidly. Thus, schools will become more and more efficient with respect to factory-type goals and more and more pleasant places in which to be engaged in these essentially industrial modes of work and relationships.

The Coming Death of a Bureaucracy

Warren G. Bennis

Not far from the new Government Center in downtown Boston, a foreign visitor walked up to a sailor and asked why American ships were built to last only a short time. According to the tourist, "The sailor answered without hesitation that the art of navigation is making such rapid progress that the finest ship would become obsolete if it lasted beyond a few years. In these words which fell accidentally from an uneducated man, I began to recognize the general and systematic idea upon which your great people direct all their concerns."

The foreign visitor was that shrewd observer of American morals and manners, Alexis de Tocqueville, and the year was 1835. He would not recognize Scollay Square today. But he had caught the central theme of our country: its preoccupation, its *obsession* with change. One thing is, however, new since de Tocqueville's time: the *acceleration* of newness, the changing scale and scope of change itself. As Dr. Robert Oppenheimer said, " . . . the world alters as we walk in it, so that the years of man's life measure not some small growth or rearrangement or moderation of what was learned in childhood, but a great upheaval."

How will these accelerating changes in our society influence human organizations?

A short while ago, I predicted that we would, in the next 25 to 50 years, participate in the end of bureaucracy as we know it and in the rise of new social systems better suited to the 20th-century demands of industrialization. This forecast was based on the evolutionary principle that every age develops an organizational form appropriate to its genius, and that the prevailing form, known by sociologists as bureaucracy and by most businessmen as "damn bureaucracy," was out of joint with contemporary realities. I realize now that

---

Reprinted by permission from *Think* Magazine, published by IBM, copyright 1966 by International Business Machines Corporation.

77

my distant prophecy is already a distinct reality so that prediction is already foreshadowed by practice.

I should like to make clear that by bureaucracy I mean a chain of command structured on the lines of a pyramid—the typical structure which coordinates the business of almost every human organization we know of: industrial, governmental, of universities and research and development laboratories, military, religious, voluntary. I do *not* have in mind those fantasies so often dreamed up to describe complex organizations. These fantasies can be summarized in two grotesque stereotypes. The first I call "Organization as Inkblot"—an actor steals around an uncharted wasteland, growing more restive and paranoid by the hour, while he awaits orders that never come. The other specter is "Organization as Big Daddy"—the actors are square people plugged into square holes by some omniscient and omnipotent genius who can cradle in his arms the entire destiny of many by way of computer and TV. Whatever the first image owes to Kafka, the second owes to George Orwell's *Nineteen Eighty-four*.

Bureaucracy, as I refer to it here, is a useful social invention that was perfected during the industrial revolution to organize and direct the activities of a business firm. Most students of organizations would say that its anatomy consists of the following components:

- A well-defined chain of command.
- A system of procedures and rules for dealing with all contingencies relating to work activities.
- A division of labor based on specialization.
- Promotion and selection based on technical competence.
- Impersonality in human relations.

It is the pyramid arrangement we see on most organizational charts.

The bureaucratic "machine model" was developed as a reaction against the personal subjugation, nepotism and cruelty, and the capricious and subjective judgments which passed for managerial practices during the early days of the industrial revolution. Bureaucracy emerged out of the organizations' need for order and precision and the workers' demands for impartial treatment. It was an organization ideally suited to the values and demands of the Victorian era. And just as bureaucracy emerged as a creative response to a radically new age, so today new organizational shapes are surfacing before our eyes.

First I shall try to show why the conditions of our modern industrialized world will bring about the death of bureaucracy. In the second part of this article I will suggest a rough model of the organization of the future.

Four Threats

There are at least four relevant threats to bureaucracy:
  (1) Rapid and unexpected change.
  (2) Growth in size where the volume of an organization's traditional

activities is not enough to sustain growth. (A number of factors are included here, among them: bureaucratic overhead; tighter controls and impersonality due to bureaucratic sprawls; outmoded rules and organizational structures.)

(3) Complexity of modern technology where integration between activities and persons of very diverse, highly specialized competence is required.

(4) A basically psychological threat springing from a change in managerial behavior.

It might be useful to examine the extent to which these conditions exist *right now:*

(1) *Rapid and unexpected change*—Bureaucracy's strength is its capacity to efficiently manage the routine and predictable in human affairs. It is almost enough to cite the knowledge and population explosion to raise doubts about its contemporary viability. More revealing, however, are the statistics which demonstrate these overworked phrases:

- Our productivity output per man hour may now be doubling almost every 20 years rather than every 40 years, as it did before World War II.
- The Federal Government alone spent $16 billion in research and development activities in 1965; it will spend $35 billion by 1980.
- The time lag between a technical discovery and recognition of its commercial uses was: 30 years before World War I, 16 years between the Wars, and only 9 years since World War II.
- In 1946, only 42 cities in the world had populations of more than one million. Today there are 90. In 1930, there were 40 people for each square mile of the earth's land surface. Today there are 63. By 2000, it is expected, the figure will have soared to 142.

Bureaucracy, with its nicely defined chain of command, its rules and its rigidities, is ill-adapted to the rapid change the environment now demands.

(2) *Growth in size*—While, in theory, there may be no natural limit to the height of a bureaucratic pyramid, in practice the element of complexity is almost invariably introduced with great size. International operation, to cite one significant new element, is the rule rather than exception for most of our biggest corporations. Firms like Standard Oil Company (New Jersey) with over 100 foreign affiliates, Mobil Oil Corporation, The National Cash Register Company, Singer Company, Burroughs Corporation and Colgate-Palmolive Company derive more than half their income or earnings from foreign sales. Many others—such as Eastman Kodak Company, Chas. Pfizer & Company, Inc., Caterpillar Tractor Company, International Harvester Company, Corn Products Company and Minnesota Mining & Manufacturing Company—make from 30 to 50 percent of their sales abroad. General Motors Corporation sales are not only nine times those of Volkswagen, they are also bigger than the Gross National Product of the Netherlands and well over the GNP of a hundred other countries. If we have seen the sun set on the British Empire, we may never see it set on the empires of General Motors, ITT, Shell and Unilever.

Labor Boom

(3) *Increasing diversity*—*Today's activities require persons of very diverse, highly specialized competence.*

Numerous dramatic examples can be drawn from studies of labor markets and job mobility. At some point during the past decade, the U.S. became the first nation in the world ever to employ more people in service occupations than in the production of tangible goods. Examples of this trend:

- In the field of education, the *increase* in employment between 1950 and 1960 was greater than the total number employed in the steel, copper and aluminum industries.
- In the field of health, the *increase* in employment between 1950 and 1960 was greater than the total number employed in automobile manufacturing in either year.
- In financial firms, the *increase* in employment between 1950 and 1960 was greater than total employment in mining in 1960.

These changes, plus many more that are harder to demonstrate statistically, break down the old, industrial trend toward more and more people doing either simple or undifferentiated chores.

Hurried growth, rapid change and increase in specialization—pit these three factors against the five components of the pyramid structure described [earlier], and we should expect the pyramid of bureaucracy to begin crumbling.

(4) *Change in managerial behavior*—There is, I believe, a subtle but perceptible change in the philosophy underlying management behavior. Its magnitude, nature and antecedents, however, are shadowy because of the difficulty of assigning numbers. (Whatever else statistics do for us, they most certainly provide a welcome illusion of certainty.) Nevertheless, real change seems under way because of:

    a. A new concept of *man,* based on increased knowledge of his complex and shifting needs, which replaces an oversimplified, innocent, push-button idea of man.

    b. A new concept of *power,* based on collaboration and reason, which replaces a model of power based on coercion and threat.

    c. A new concept of *organizational values,* based on humanistic-democratic ideals, which replaces the depersonalized mechanistic value system of bureaucracy.

The primary cause of this shift in management philosophy stems not from the bookshelf but from the manager himself. Many of the behavioral scientists, like Douglas McGregor or Rensis Likert, have clarified and articulated—even legitimized—what managers have only half registered to themselves. I am convinced, for example, that the popularity of McGregor's book, *The Human Side of Enterprise,* was based on his rare empathy for a vast audience of managers who are wistful for an alternative to the mechanistic concept of authority, i.e., that he outlined a vivid utopia of more authentic human relationships than most organizational practices today allow. Furthermore, I suspect that the desire for relationships in business has little to do with a profit motive per se, though it is often rationalized as doing so. The real push for these changes stems from the need, not only to humanize the organization, but to use it as a crucible of personal growth and the development of self-realization.*

The core problems confronting any organization fall, I believe, into five major categories. First, let us consider the problems, then let us see how our 20th-century conditions of constant change have made the bureaucratic approach to these problems obsolete.

1. *Integration.* The problem is how to integrate individual needs and management goals. In other words, it is the inescapable conflict between individual needs (like "spending time with the family") and organizational demands (like meeting deadlines).

Under 20th-century conditions of constant change there has been an emergence of human sciences and a deeper understanding of man's complexity. Today, integration encompasses the entire range of issues concerned with incentives, rewards and motivations of the individual, and how the organization succeeds or fails in adjusting to these issues. In our society, where personal attachments play an important role, the individual is appreciated, and there is genuine concern for his well-being, not just in a veterinary-hygiene sense, but as a moral, integrated personality.

Paradoxical Twins

The problem of integration, like most human problems, has a venerable past. The modern version goes back at least 160 years and was precipitated by an historical paradox: the twin births of modern individualism and modern industrialism. The former brought about a deep concern for and a passionate interest in the individual and his personal rights. The latter brought about increased mechanization of organized activity. Competition between the two has intensified as each decade promises more freedom and hope for man and more stunning achievements for technology. I believe that our society *has* opted for more humanistic and democratic values, however unfulfilled they may be in practice. It will "buy" these values even at loss in efficiency because it feels it can now afford the loss.

2. *Social influence.* This problem is essentially one of power and how power is distributed. It is a complex issue and alive with controversy, partly

---

*Let me propose an hypothesis to explain this tendency. It rests on the assumption that man has a basic need for transcendental experiences, somewhat like the psychological rewards which William James claimed religion provided—"an assurance of safety and a temper of peace, and, in relation to others, a preponderance of loving affections." Can it be that as religion has become secularized, less transcendental, men search for substitutes such as close interpersonal relationships, psychoanalysis—even the release provided by drugs such as LSD?

because of an ethical component and partly because studies of leadership and power distribution can be interpreted in many ways, and almost always in ways which coincide with one's biases (including a cultural leaning toward democracy).

The problem of power has to be seriously reconsidered because of dramatic situational changes which make the possibility of one-man rule not necessarily "bad" but impractical. I refer to changes in top management's role.

Peter Drucker, over twelve years ago, listed 41 major responsibilities of the chief executive and declared that "90 percent of the trouble we are having with the chief executive's job is rooted in our superstition of the one-man chief." Many factors make one-man control obsolete, among them: the broadening product base of industry; impact of new technology; the scope of international operation; the separation of management from ownership; the rise of trade unions and general education. The real power of the "chief" has been eroding in most organizations even though both he and the organization cling to the older concept.

3. *Collaboration.* This is the problem of managing and resolving conflicts. Bureaucratically, it grows out of the very same social process of conflict and stereotyping that has divided nations and communities. As organizations become more complex, they fragment and divide, building tribal patterns and symbolic codes which often work to exclude others (secrets and jargon, for example) and on occasion to exploit differences for inward (and always fragile) harmony.

Recent research is shedding new light on the problem of conflict. Psychologist Robert R. Blake in his stunning experiments has shown how simple it is to induce conflict, how difficult to arrest it. Take two groups of people who have never before been together, and give them a task which will be judged by an impartial jury. In less than an hour, each group devolves into a tightly-knit band with all the symptoms of an "in group." They regard their product as a "masterwork" and the other group's as "commonplace" at best. "Other" becomes "enemy." "We are good, they are bad; we are right, they are wrong."

Rabbie's Reds and Greens

Jaap Rabbie, conducting experiments on intergroup conflict at the University of Utrecht, has been amazed by the ease with which conflict and stereotype develop. He brings into an experimental room two groups and distributes green name tags and pens to one group, red pens and tags to the other. The two groups do not compete; they do not even interact. They are only in sight of each other while they silently complete a questionnaire. Only 10 minutes are needed to activate defensiveness and fear, reflected in the hostile and irrational perceptions of both "reds" and "greens."

4. *Adaptation.* This problem is caused by our turbulent environment. The pyramid structure of bureaucracy, where power is concentrated at the top, seems the perfect way to "run a railroad." And for the routine tasks of

the 19th and early 20th centuries, bureaucracy was (in some respects it still is) a suitable social arrangement. However, rather than a placid and predictable environment, what predominates today is a dynamic and uncertain one where there is a deepening interdependence among economic, scientific, educational, social and political factors in the society.

5. *Revitalization.* This is the problem of growth and decay. As Alfred North Whitehead has said: "The art of free society consists first in the maintenance of the symbolic code, and secondly, in the fearlessness of revision.... Those societies which cannot combine reverence to their symbols with freedom of revision must ultimately decay...."

Growth and decay emerge as the penultimate conditions of contemporary society. Organizations, as well as societies, must be concerned with those social structures that engender buoyancy, resilience and a "fearlessness of revision."

I introduce the term "revitalization" to embrace all the social mechanisms that stagnate and regenerate, as well as the process of this cycle. The elements of revitalization are:

1. An ability to learn from experience and to codify, store and retrieve the relevant knowledge.

2. An ability to "learn how to learn," that is, to develop methods for improving the learning process.

3. An ability to acquire and use feedback mechanisms on performance, in short, to be self-analytical.

4. An ability to direct one's own destiny.

These qualities have a good deal in common with what John Gardner calls "self-renewal." For the organization, it means conscious attention to its own evolution. Without a planned methodology and explicit direction, the enterprise will not realize its potential.

Integration, distribution of power, collaboration, adaptation and *revitalization*—these are the major human problems of the next 25 years. How organizations cope with and manage these tasks will undoubtedly determine the viability of the enterprise.

Against this background I should like to set forth some of the conditions that will dictate organizational life in the next two or three decades.

1. *The environment.* Rapid technological change and diversification will lead to more and more partnerships between government and business. It will be a truly mixed economy. Because of the immensity and expense of the projects, there will be fewer identical units competing in the same markets and organizations will become more interdependent.

The four main features of this environment are:

- Interdependence rather than competition.
- Turbulence and uncertainty rather than readiness and certainty.
- Large-scale rather than small-scale enterprises.
- Complex and multinational rather than simple national enterprises.

"Nice"—and Necessary

2. *Population characteristics.* The most distinctive characteristic of our society is education. It will become even more so. Within 15 years, two thirds of our population living in metropolitan areas will have attended college. Adult education is growing even faster, probably because of the rate of professional obsolescence. The Killian report showed that the average engineer required further education only 10 years after getting his degree. It will be almost routine for the experienced physician, engineer and executive to go back to school for advanced training every two or three years. All of this education is not just "nice." It is necessary.

One other characteristic of the population which will aid our understanding of organizations of the future is increasing job mobility. The ease of transportation, coupled with the needs of a dynamic environment, change drastically the idea of "owning" a job—or "having roots." Already 20 percent of our population change their mailing address at least once a year.

3. *Work values.* The increased level of education and mobility will change the values we place on work. People will be more intellectually committed to their jobs and will probably require more involvement, participation and autonomy.

Also, people will be more "other-oriented," taking cues for their norms and values from their immediate environment rather than tradition.

4. *Tasks and goals.* The tasks of the organization will be more technical, complicated and unprogrammed. They will rely on intellect instead of muscle. And they will be too complicated for one person to comprehend, to say nothing of control. Essentially, they will call for the collaboration of specialists in a project or a team-form of organization.

There will be a complication of goals. Business will increasingly concern itself with its adaptive or innovative-creative capacity. In addition, supragoals will have to be articulated, goals which shape and provide the foundation for the goal structure. For example, one might be a system for detecting new and changing goals; another could be a system for deciding priorities among goals.

Finally, there will be more conflict and contradiction among diverse standards for organizational effectiveness. This is because professionals tend to identify more with the goals of their profession than with those of their immediate employer. University professors can be used as a case in point. Their inside work may be a conflict between teaching and research, while more of their income is derived from outside sources, such as foundations and consultant work. They tend not to be good "company men" because they divide their loyalty between their professional values and organizational goals.

Key Word: "Temporary"

5. *Organization.* The social structure of organizations of the future will have some unique characteristics. The key word will be "temporary." There

will be adaptive, rapidly changing *temporary* systems. These will be task forces organized around problems-to-be-solved by groups of relative strangers with diverse professional skills. The group will be arranged on an organic rather than mechanical model; they will evolve in response to a problem rather than to programmed role expectations. The executive thus becomes a coordinator or "linking pin" between various task forces. He must be a man who can speak the polyglot jargon of research, with skills to relay information and to mediate between groups. People will be evaluated not vertically according to rank and status, but flexibly and functionally according to skill and professional training. Organizational charts will consist of project groups rather than stratified functional groups. (This trend is already visible in the aerospace and construction industries, as well as many professional and consulting firms.)

Adaptive, problem-solving, temporary systems of diverse specialists, linked together by coordinating and task-evaluating executive specialists in an organic flux—this is the organization form that will gradually replace bureaucracy as we know it. As no catchy phrase comes to mind, I call this an organic-adaptive structure. Organizational arrangements of this sort may not only reduce the intergroup conflicts mentioned earlier; it may also induce honest-to-goodness creative collaboration.

6. *Motivation.* The organic-adaptive structure should increase motivation and thereby effectiveness, because it enhances satisfactions intrinsic to the task. There is a harmony between the educated individual's need for tasks that are meaningful, satisfactory and creative and a flexible organizational structure.

There will also be, however, reduced commitment to work groups, for these groups will be, as I have already mentioned, transient structures. I would predict that in the organic-adaptive system, people will learn to develop quick and intense relationships on the job, and learn to bear the loss of more enduring work relationships. Because of the added ambiguity of roles, time will have to be spent on continual rediscovery of the appropriate organizational mix.

I think that the future I describe is not necessarily a "happy" one. Coping with rapid change, living in temporary work systems, developing meaningful relations and then breaking them—all augur social strains and psychological tensions. Teaching how to live with ambiguity, to identify with the adaptive process, to make a virtue out of contingency, and to be self-directing—these will be the tasks of education, the goals of maturity, and the achievement of the successful individual.

No Delightful Marriages

In these new organizations of the future, participants will be called upon to use their minds more than at any other time in history. Fantasy, imagination and creativity will be legitimate in ways that today seem strange. Social structures will no longer be instruments of psychic repression but will increasingly promote play and freedom on behalf of curiosity and thought.

One final word: While I forecast the structure and value coordinates for organizations of the future and contend that they are inevitable, this should not bar any of us from giving the inevitable a little push. The French moralist may be right in saying that there are no delightful marriages, just good ones; It is possible that if managers and scientists continue to get their heads together in organizational revitalization, they *might* develop delightful organizations—just possibly.

I started with a quote from de Tocqueville and I think it would be fitting to end with one: "I am tempted to believe that what we call necessary institutions are often no more than institutions to which we have grown accustomed. In matters of social constitution, the field of possibilities is much more extensive than men living in their various societies are ready to imagine."

The School Principal: Key Man in Educational Change

Kenneth A. Tye

It goes without saying that the role of the school principal is changing. New pressures are being applied every day. State legislatures are calling for more accountability on the part of both the principal and his staff; the community is asking for parity in decision making; teachers are demanding more power; and, above all, everyone seems to be suggesting that we decentralize.

The principal can and should be the key agent for change in his school. This concept runs counter to the notion that he is a "manager" who holds teachers accountable for results spelled out in a negotiated contract. It also runs counter to the notion that he must be a master teacher. What it does mean is that the principal performs a leadership role. In American education we have neither the financial nor the human resources to develop new change agents who are "added on" to existing institutions such as schools. We should concentrate therefore, upon the development of the personnel we already have to fill the leadership role, and I feel that the principal is the most obvious person for that job.

ORGANIZING FOR CHANGE

Unfortunately, most of us in this room have been trained as administrators rather than as leaders. The distinction, while subtle, is significant if we are to meet the demands of contemporary society. The role of the administrator is to accomplish established goals through the utilization of established means. The principal who can be judged as the best administrator is the one who can follow established policy and procedure and make others do likewise.

Taken from *NASSP Bulletin*, May 1972, pp. 77–84. Reprinted by permission. Kenneth A. Tye is a program officer in the Research Division of the Institute for Development of Educational Activities (IDEA).

On the other hand, the role of the leader is to find and initiate new means to reach established goals or to formulate with the staff new goals for the school. How does the principal organize himself and his school for planned change? The behaviorists, the technocrats, the systems advocates—and they hold sway today—will tell you that the key lies in planning. The way to heaven (used synonymously with planned change) is in preparing large charts with lots of boxes. In each box is listed something to do, an event. Each event, of course, is put in a time perspective. By going from one box to the next, one can easily see how we reach our goal, whether it be the completion of the SST, the Rolls-Royce aircraft engine, the rocket that will take us to Mars, or an improved school. The only problem with this approach is that people somehow have a way of wiggling out of boxes.

THE "PEOPLE APPROACH" TO CHANGE

Let me suggest another way of organizing the planned change. For lack of a better term, let me call it the "People Approach" or better yet, "Happiness is what you do *with* other human beings, not *to* them."

Self-understanding. Perhaps the most important place for a principal to begin organizing for planned change is with himself. Give yourself a short true-false test on the following statements:

____ 1. People need to be inspired or pushed or driven.
____ 2. People need to be told, shown or trained in proper methods of work.
____ 3. People naturally resist change; they prefer to stay as they are.
____ 4. People need to be released and encouraged and assisted.
____ 5. People who understand and care about what they are doing can devise and improve their own methods of doing work.
____ 6. People naturally tire of monotonous routine and enjoy new experiences; everyone is creative.

Perhaps the answers to these questions are obvious. Perhaps they are not. If you answered false to the first three statements and true to the last three, you are probably a leader whom Douglas McGregor would refer to as a "Y."[1] That is, you believe that if people (in our case, teachers, parents, and children) are treated as responsible, independent, understanding, goal-achieving, growing, and creative, they will become so.

The point of the quiz, of course, is not whether you had the right or wrong answers. It is, rather, that you know where you stand with regard to

---

[1] Douglas McGregor, *The Human Side of Enterprise* (New York: McGraw-Hill, 1961).

those with whom you work. Further, it is that you attempt to make your behavior or "style" consistent with what you believe. "Know thyself" is a good maxim with which to start the process of planned change.

Climate. Once the principal knows himself, he can move to establish a climate within his school. (1) He can be formal and impersonal with those with whom he works. In this case, policies and regulations become important. (2) He can emphasize goal attainment. In this case he sets direction and lets others know what is expected of them. (3) He can be an example. In this case, he works hard himself and assumes that others will follow his example. (4) He can develop an esprit within the staff. In this case, he is very "human" and attempts to meet as many staff needs as possible.[2] (5) He can be any combination of these things, as appropriate, utilizing policies and regulations, setting direction, being an example, and working for esprit, all as conditions or needs dictate.

The point, of course, is not that the principal is authoritarian, democratic, or laissez-faire. The point is, rather, that he knows his people and his circumstances and, subsequently, determines and sets the climate that best allows those with whom he works the opportunity to perform their tasks.

There are those behavioral scientists who suggest that the main purpose of any organization is to provide good work for those it employs. While I might not go that far, I would suggest that in those schools where the climate is open and where the principal balances his initiation and consideration behavior, more school improvement does occur.

Communication. A major contributing factor to an open climate within an organization is the pattern of communications established by its leader. We have found that good communications are open, face-to-face, and two-way whenever possible, particularly when important matters are involved. Unimportant matters can be relegated to memoranda. Listening, of course, is an important part of communication. The effective leader is, above all, a good listener.

More communication takes place through informal channels than through formal ones. The alert principal should plan to get feedback through such channels—for example, in the coffee room or in the hall.

Communications with parents is of special importance in changing schools. Sanctions from advisory councils or PTA boards are helpful. Tours, coffee klatches, explanatory meetings, opinion surveys, evaluation reports, and newsletters are all means which, when used during initial stages of change, reap great benefits during later stages, particularly if trouble arises.

We communicate ourselves to others through our words and our nonverbal behaviors. Others perceive us as behaving in certain ways. Often how

---

[2]Andrew W. Halpin and Don B. Croft, *The Organizational Climate of Schools* (Chicago, Illinois: Midwest Administration Center, The University of Chicago, 1963).

we perceive ourselves and how others perceive us are not the same thing. To keep communications open it is often valuable to check such perceptions. Instruments such as the Leader Behavior Description Questionnaire[3] and the Dialogue, Decision-Making, and Action Communications Rating Scales,[4] can be of value in testing perceptions and communication patterns within schools.

Conflict Management. Often, schools which attempt to change find themselves involved in various kinds of intergroup conflict. Most frequently, such conflict arises from unclear role and task accomplishment definitions. This is often true where team teaching is being tried, because such teaching sharply alters role definitions. To avoid unnecessary conflict, principals should assist teachers in clearly defining roles well in advance of actual trial of any new venture, including, of course, his own role.

Conflict most often arises because of differences in values, philosophies, or perceptions. The typical administrator tends to suppress or avoid such conflict, assuming that it will go away. Suppressing conflict, however, usually results in some type of confrontation at a later date. Often, such confrontations, in turn, result in irreparable damage to the organization. The alert leader will sense such conflict early or even potential conflict before it occurs. If he moves in early and assists others to talk through their differences, he more often than not heads off damaging confrontations.

Conflict of ideas is healthy in a changing organization, for it frequently leads to new and better ideas. In a communicative school climate, the principal and others are able to deal with differences in points of view, while still maintaining a common purpose.

Decision Making. Griffiths suggests that the effectiveness of a leader is inversely proportional to the number of decisions which he must personally make concerning the affairs of the organization.[5] Principals can come to believe that teachers should make *all* instructional decisions, since they are the ones who have the appropriate data about pupils. Such decisions include those about self, instructional objectives, learning opportunities, materials, time, space, and classroom organization.

As a leader, the principal has a three-fold responsibility in decision making. He monitors instructional decisions made by teachers, he serves as a facilitator for their decision making, and he acts as a transactional agent between and among levels of decision making.

---

[3]Ralph M. Stogdill, *Manual for the Leader Behavior Description Questionnaire: Form XII* (Columbus, O.: Bureau of Business Education Research, Ohio State University, 1963).

[4]*Dialogue, Decision-Making and Action Rating Scales,* An instrument developed by Research Division, Institute for Development of Educational Activities, Los Angeles, Calif., 1969–1971.

[5]Daniel E. Griffiths, *Administrative Theory* (New York: Appleton-Century-Crofts, 1959).

Selected Readings

As a monitor, the principal sets forth procedures which will assist teachers. For example, if teachers wish to organize into an instructional team, the principal might advise them to:

1. read what scholars and informed practitioners have written on the subject,
2. seek his advice,
3. become familiar with the experiences of other schools,
4. develop a long-range plan, and
5. pilot-test aspects of the plan.

As a facilitator of decisions, the principal provides the time, space, and atmosphere wherein instructional decisions can be made. He also serves as a resource person by knowing what information is available, which consultants are appropriate, where visits can be made, and so forth.

As a transactional agent, the principal transacts among instructional personnel or teams in such matters as time, space, materials, and paraprofessional personnel. He involves community members and interprets the school program to them. He informs teachers of policy decisions and institutional decisions of boards and districts that influence their instructional decisions. Conversely, he informs the district of teachers' decisions.

It is perhaps within such decision-making structures and processes that professionalism and appropriate modes of decentralization and accountability actually reside.

Stages of Planned Change. Let me describe briefly the various stages of behavior that ultimately lead people to the adoption of an innovation. By being aware of these stages, by knowing where individual staff members are in terms of these stages, and by knowing what activities he himself can engage in as a facilitator, the principal can continue to move innovations forward and avoid resistance.

Awareness is the initial stage. The principal can create such awareness or promote it with an article, book, film, speaker, or other stimulus.

When an individual or group moves from awareness to active interest and information-seeking, the principal can provide more information. At this stage, a teacher from another school where the idea has been utilized can be a valuable resource.

Once people have gathered sufficient information, they begin in their own minds to evaluate the utility of the new idea for themselves. It is at this point that visits to successful programs nearby can be of most value.

After an idea has been evaluated and found to be worthwhile, the next stage is testing. It is at this point that the principal must provide appropriate inservice training through the utilization of appropriate resource personnel.

After an innovation has been adopted and integrated into the ongoing program, the principal will continue to assist by providing necessary services such as time, space, materials, and personnel. He will also give encouragement and serve as a transactional agent, translating the new program to parents, the district, and other staff members.[6]

Such stages, while not rigidly prescribed, are important. Most of our change efforts that fail, and these are numerous, result from efforts to try something new without consideration of the human necessity to become aware, to become interested, and to evaluate.

Problem Solving. Earlier in this paper, I poked fun at the "systems types" and their boxes. Actually, rational problem-solving procedures are necessary. The danger is that in many situations change is planned at the top level and then imposed downward, although common sense indicates that people change more easily when such change solves problems that are real to them. The principal should encourage his staff to use rational problem-solving procedures, generally utilizing the following kinds of procedures:

1. Identifying a problem that has real relevance for the group
2. Defining the problem, its scope and its implications
3. Considering a number of alternatives for solving the problem
4. Selecting one alternative for testing
5. Testing the alternative; keeping records of its results
6. Evaluating the results of the test in terms of its success in solving the problem
7. Recycling.

Usually such a procedure is not employed by those of us in education. In reality, we tend to change by selecting one new alternative. Then we install it, whether it be a new instructional practice, new curriculum, or new organizational pattern. In many instances it fails. Although there are many possible reasons for such failure, one significant reason is our inability to use a scientific approach.

Problem solving is a difficult, often intense, and time-consuming activity that most educators have not truly been involved in. The principal who wishes to create an atmosphere of scientific problem solving in his school should start by helping to identify problems that are real to the group, that are as nonthreatening as possible, and that are as well-defined as possible.

---

[6]Everett M. Rogers, *Diffusion of Innovation* (New York: The Free Press of Glencoe, 1962).

Selected Readings 93

The staff which can utilize rational problem-solving procedures need have no fear of such things as accountability, PPBS, decentralization, or planned change.

CONCLUSIONS

This decade well may be the *decade of the principal.* Bureaucratic district structures and state and federal intervention have not markedly changed American education. The single school with its principal as leader *is* the setting for effecting significant educational change.

Well over 80 percent of the resources of education are vested in human beings. The principal who invests his efforts in human activities such as self-understanding, setting an open climate, building communication structures, managing conflict, clarifying decision-making roles, paying attention to each individual's capacity for change, and implementing problem solving procedures will be a successful leader.

As John Gardner says about our capacity for growth and change: "Unlike the jailbird, we don't know that we've been imprisoned until we've broken out."[7]

[7] John W. Gardner, *Excellence: Can We Be Excellent and Equal, Too?* (New York: Harper and Row, 1961).

Freedom Must be Taught

Walter Cronkite

In our time, nations have fallen under dictatorial rule because of conquest or a will of the majority to surrender its liberties—or because of intellectual indolence leading through political sloth to governmental disaster.

The threat to our liberties has not reached such a critical stage that we can even begin to compare the danger to that which overcame modern Germany or Italy or today threatens Chile.

But there are warning signs, and we would be making the mistake that other peoples have made to their deep regret if we did not heed them.

We have been in our recent years through a traumatic time—assassination, civil riots and disobedience, a divisive war, crime in the streets, a narcotics epidemic, apparently runaway welfare costs amid rising prices and severely crippling inflation.

It has been a time of crises—an overlapping of one crisis upon another—and a certain bewildered hopelessness has crept into our national being. We know not what specifically can be done about each problem but, in our frustration, we are inclined to grasp at apparently easy solutions.

If the dissenters get too obstreperous, jail them; if you suspect conspiracy, tap their wires; if you suspect narcotics, don't knock but break in the door; if the *press* gets too inquisitive, cut off their sources, and if any citizen dares protest all this, classify him a possible subversive and put him in the unforgetting government computers.

All of this has happened in the last few years or is still happening under various government orders. Most of it is under court review and some of it under legislative examination.

The fact that such rules and actions should have been promulgated in the first place is disturbing enough, but more—perhaps most—disturbing is that

---

Address given to the American Association of School Administrators at its 105th Annual Convention, Atlantic City, N.J., February 25, 1973. Used with permission.

the American people, as understandably worried and concerned as they are, have acquiesced in all this with slightly a murmur.

We are bred and steeped in liberty, we love a form of government that can only exist with individual freedom, yet we stand silently by while those freedoms are diluted, one by one.

There are various reasons for our passivity: The end justifies the means, is only one unfortunate rationale—"things are so bad, we've got to do *something*," we say, and "if you haven't done anything wrong, you have nothing to fear."

But what about the Constitution, someone might ask. "Ah," we answer, "the Constitution was never meant to protect the kind of people we've got running around loose today."

Well, you and I know better. As Lyndon Johnson used to say: "That dog won't hunt." But unfortunately, that dog's out there flushing a lot of frightened civil libertarian rabbits right now.

The danger, of course, is that, in seeking solutions to clearly serious and pressing problems that themselves impinge upon our individual liberties, we permit the imposition of measures which chip away at the very foundation of our democracy.

It is not that our people love liberty less. It is that they *understand* it less. In a highly organized, crowded, and complex society, freedom must be taught. And this is where we come in—you and I, the teacher and the journalist.

As an example of our problem, let me note a CBS News poll, taken a couple of years ago, that put to a scientifically-selected cross-section of our populace some questions about the Bill of Rights.

The pollsters did not say that the query concerned the Constitution and its guarantees. Instead, they put specific questions. The results were discouraging, indicating that a majority of the population, no matter what the lip service rendered, doesn't fully believe in freedom of speech, press and assembly.

They were asked: "As long as there appears to be no clear danger of violence, do you think any group, no matter how extreme, should be allowed to organize protests against the government?" Seventy-six percent said "no."

Another: "Do you think everyone should have the right to criticize the government, even if the criticism is damaging to our national interest?" No, fifty-four percent. There were similar percentages against freedom of press, double jeopardy, habeas corpus.

I hope you will excuse me, and not think me ungrateful for the honor you have paid me tonight, if I suggest that this clear contradiction, this serious misunderstanding of our Bill of Rights, must indicate that somewhere the education process has broken down. I would not presume to tell you your jobs—although I should note we have so many teachers in my family that the Thanksgiving table looks like a PTA dinner—so I have expertise through kinship and everyone knows that is the worst kind.

We must redouble our efforts to inculcate a clear understanding in each of our future citizens of the real meaning behind our Constitution and its Bill of Rights—the history and development of that magnificent document—and, although I dislike the over-use of the word, permit me to say its *relevance* today.

The contradictions between the theoretical acceptance of the Bill of Rights by rote and a full understanding of its meaning must be wiped out—and the job is yours.

We ought to teach *how* to live under our Constitution, how to get the most out of freedom. We can gain the greatest *respect* for our Constitution by learning how to use it, how to exercise our rights, how to petition for redress of grievances, how to organize, how to dissent.

These things should be taught in the measured exposition of the classroom so that they are not learned, imperfectly, in the passionate oratory of the streets.

We are living right now in one of the most exciting periods of history—the great scientific-technological revolution that almost certainly will outstrip the industrial revolution in its sociological, political and cultural effect.

In the life span of the youngest member of this audience we have plunged into three eras—the atomic age, the computer age, the space age—and now we stand on the threshold of the most revolutionary of them all, the DNA age—the discovery of the genetic key which unlocks the very secret of life, of what makes us what we are.

We will soon have the *frightening* knowledge of how to make man any way we want him—smart or stupid, tall or short, black or white.

In the next thirty years the transplant of human organs will be commonplace, the birthrate must be controlled, we will be exploring and perhaps colonizing the ocean floor.

Can anyone deny that a revolution in our way of life will accompany that *scientific* revolution?

We have the future in our power. The twenty-first century will not burst upon us in full flower. We can mold it to be what man wants it to be.

But to do *that* we must know *what* we want, and we must examine our institutions to determine whether they stand up to the challenges of the century ahead.

We so desperately need to promote in our schools, and among us, the adults, the study of our institutions so that we can intelligently and with open minds *make them work*—or change them.

It will be a tragedy of overwhelming proportions, fatal perhaps even to the existence of life on this planet, if we do not—through education—pull our socks up so that the next generation can cope with the revolution in a spirit of scholarly discourse and tolerance.

In the turmoil of the last fifteen years, only the most strident voices have seemed to come through the cacophony. The fanatics of the left have

Selected Readings

maintained that there is no salvation in our system and therefore the system must come down. The fanatics of the right have tried to protect the status quo by branding as subversive the mere questioning of our institutions and their efficiency.

The imperfections of the system are many and are worthy of our deepest concern, but to suggest that reform is impossible within the system is to fly into the face of incontrovertible history. It is the worst form of demagoguery on the left, but it is so patently and demonstrably wrong that it is not the greater danger.

More insidious is the defense mechanism of the fanatic right. The worst form of its demagoguery is the impugning of the motives of those who would dare to raise questions about our institutions and their custodians.

The intellectual community of which you are the leaders naturally is the ultimate enemy of this form of no-nothingism. At the moment the particular target is the news media.

In the attacks upon us, they have touched a sensitive public nerve.

There *is* a certain public discontent with the media, particularly television. Some of the public, at least, feel that we tell only the bad news, and they transfer to us, the messengers, their displeasure over the message.

Politicians—and they are of both parties—have cynically played upon this. Since they clearly would be better off if *their* errors, *their* failures, and *their* incompetence were not exposed to public gaze by the diligent press, they attempt to neutralize the news media by casting doubt on our ability and our motives.

Now we certainly are not beyond criticism. We are a long way from being perfect. There are things we do that we could do better—or, in some cases, perhaps should not do at all.

It is *most* important that the public not believe everything it reads in a single newspaper or hears on a single broadcast. All of us journalists make errors, sometimes factual, sometimes in our judgment of what is news and what is not.

There is no mathematical formula by which either can be eliminated and since the danger is present, it is well that everyone read and watch and listen with a healthy skepticism that sends him on to other sources for corroborating or perhaps, contradictory evidence.

There should be courses in every high school to teach how to read the newspaper, how to watch television and listen to the radio, and with such a critical public thus created, the newspapers and news broadcasts would be better than ever.

But with this same questioning attitude, the public should analyze the criticism that self-serving politicians level against the media—the media that, it should be remembered, are the *only* monitor on *their* performance as public servants.

It is regrettable that this administration, in attempting to raise its own credibility by dragging down that of the press, has so politicized the issue of the press' performance that rational discussion is difficult. It is not too hard to believe that, indeed, that may have been one of the aims of the clever managers of this anti-press campaign. For, indeed, to defend itself against their charges now appears self-serving on the press' part. To stand up and defend freedom of speech and press is to appear anti-Nixon, and to so appear is only to speed the merry-go-round of mutual suspicion.

It is sad, and a mystery, that the administration should dull its considerable accomplishments with such petty and churlish tactics.

Churlish, perhaps, but dangerous. In the atmosphere it has created, the press is under such attack as rarely in our history. The Supreme Court has stripped it of the privilege to protect its sources, and without such protection a free press cannot survive. Congress is studying remedial legislation now, and it would be well if those who understand the basics of our freedoms let their congressmen know of their concern.

And in this atmosphere the administration seeks to bring the network news programs to heel by making them responsive to the local stations, where it has licensing authority and thus can bring political and financial pressures to bear.

It is strange that they cannot see that the power with which they would invest themselves today they might have to pass on to another political party tomorrow. Or, perhaps, do they believe that with such power over a cowed and intimidated press that is not a serious possibility?

I do not really think that is going to happen. I am at heart an optimist. I believe in this country. We've got it all right here. I think we are going to put it all together again and march into the twenty-first century with a life that again will be the envy of and the example to the world.

And I believe that most Americans still hold that dream. But our dream depends on our getting back to some fundamental values.

What promise this nation will realize when we all believe, without hint of doubt, that the words of the Constitution and the Bill of Rights mean precisely what they say, and apply equally to every man of us, rich or poor, black or white, northerner or southerner, no matter how contemptible or untidy either his thoughts or his appearance.

That lesson will not come through osmosis. It must be taught, fearlessly, without favor to misguided patriots or heckling malcontents. The place for that is the classroom. The ball is in your court.

Part Two

The Secondary School Student

5

The Youth Revolution

Have fundamental changes taken place among youth, transcending that which has been characteristic of prior generations? A good deal of opinion concludes that this is indeed so. Other opinion holds that the activities of the youth of the seventies are simply the antics of former generations cast in a different form. Whether the observable changes in the life-style of the present youth generation are transitory, temporary abberations, or whether they represent a more permanent phenomenon, only time will tell. In any event, those who teach and associate with the adolescent in the secondary school should have some idea of the nature of what has been described as the youth revolution that characterized the latter part of the decade of the 1960s.

Dr. William Dalrymple, director of University Health Services at Princeton University, addressed himself in the Winter 1972 issue of the *Princeton Quarterly* to the topic of the new generation. His article was titled "The Youth Revolution is Over: How It Changed Us."

According to Dalrymple, the youth revolution began in 1964 when the Beatles landed in America and the student uprisings in Berkeley occurred, and it ended in 1970 with the strikes provoked by the United States intervention in Cambodia. Dalrymple asserts that the revolution "had its roots in earlier developments . . . including the black civil rights movement of the previous decade, the Sputnik episode, and even in the changes which occurred as an aftermath of World War II." But he also says that "while like most revolutions it was only partially successful, it brought in a very short time the momentous changes characteristic of a revolution, and life in America will never be the same again."[1]

Dalrymple believes that beneath the surface of the youth revolution—the violent confrontations, the strikes, the protests, experimentation with drugs—

---

[1]William Dalrymple, "The Revolution is Over: How It Changed Us," *University: A Princeton Quarterly*, Winter 1972 (Princeton, N.J.: Princeton University Press), p. 1.

fundamental changes were taking place. These changes included an increased tolerance for diversity, a questioning of the status quo, variety in political opinion, the acceptance of feeling as being of equal importance to reason and intellect, a greater informality in living patterns, a rejection of certain secondary values or rules of the pre-1964 period, such as acceptance of the American political system as being invariably right, the assumption that all things illegal are also immoral and undesirable, and the acceptance of the general forms of the American economic system as being unquestionably desirable. Other secondary assumptions questioned are that rules produce morality, and that the American system of government is always, invariably right.

Dalrymple's article concludes that a final characteristic of the post-revolutionary period is the feeling that society is now strongly influenced by its young; that we have a "prefigurative society" in which the youth culture is "autonomous from the main stream of its adult culture." In further explanation, Dalrymple writes:

> ... the emphasis of middle class Americans on developing children's minds and ability for independent judgments at an early age, encouraged the development of an independent, relatively self-sufficient youth, much less dependent than their predecessors on the approval and support of their elders, and indeed ready to reject those elders when they feel them to be misinformed or superficial. Appeals to these young people have to be made much more in terms of the situation and the hard facts than in terms of 'I will like you more if you do such and such.' The youth culture has achieved an ability to realize many of its own goals and impose many of its patterns on the rest of society. To this extent the revolution has given us a prefigurative society.[2]

THE WORLD-WIDE NATURE OF STUDENT UNREST

In Partnership with Youth is a booklet published by UNESCO. Excerpts taken from an article in *UNESCO Courier* which is based on the booklet, appear in the Selected Readings which follow Part Two. The article asserts that at times youth feel they are being "manipulated," which is in part a reaction against attempts of teachers, social and educational institutions, and business and political parties to direct or influence them. Because they remain out of the working society for such a long time, and are under separate conditions, they are isolated from the larger society. They then take on the status of a distinct community of their own, and since this is their own community—and in a sense their only one—youth are determined to win from society the esteem to which they believe themselves and their community to be entitled.

---

[2]*Ibid.*, p. 32.

Charles Reich, in his book *The Greening of America,* speaks of the crisis of contemporary life, and develops the theme that the youth of America are developing a new consciousness, labeled by him as Consciousness III, which addresses itself to how man may remain human in a technological age:

> The great question of these times is how to live in and with a technological society; what mind and what way of life can preserve man's humanity and his very existence against the dominance of the forces he has created. This question is at the root of the American Crisis, beneath all the immediate issues of lawlessness, poverty, meaninglessness, and war. It is this question to which America's new generation is beginning to discover an answer, an answer based on a renewal of life that carries the hope of restoring us to our sources and ourselves.[3]

The youth revolution Reich sees is not ideological or political in the usual meaning of these words. It is instead a whole new set of beliefs, understandings, ways of perceiving, and new values and value choices that govern thoughts and actions. It is a rejection of many of the values of the Corporate State, of the producing-consuming society, of obsessive materialism.

Although Alvin Toffler's book *Future Shock* is not primarily concerned with education or the youth revolution, it has implications for secondary schools as well as for all forms of education, formal and informal, and does have a good deal to say about youth in modern society:

> We are creating a new society. Not a changed society. Not an extended, larger-than-life version of our present society. But a new society.
> This simple premise has not yet begun to tincture our consciousness. Yet unless we understand this, we shall destroy ourselves in trying to cope with tomorrow.
> A revolution shatters institutions and power relationships. This is precisely what is happening today in all the high-technology nations. Students in Berlin and New York, in Turin and Tokyo, capture their deans and chancellors, bring great clanking educational factories to a grinding halt, and even threaten to topple governments. Police stand aside in the ghettos of New York, Washington and Chicago as ancient property laws are openly violated. Sexual standards are overthrown. Great cities are paralyzed by strikes, power failures, riots. International power alliances are shaken. Financial and political leaders secretly tremble—not out of fear that communist (or capitalist) revolutionaries will oust them, but that the entire system is somehow flying out of control. These are indisputable signs of a sick social structure, a society that can no longer perform its most basic functions in the accustomed ways. It is a society caught in the agony of revolutionary change.

---

[3]Charles A. Reich, *The Greening of America.* (New York: Random House, 1970), p. 16.

In the 1920's and 1930's, communists used to speak of the "general crisis of capitalism." It is now clear that they were thinking small. What is occurring now is not a crisis of capitalism, but of industrial society itself, regardless of its political form. . . .

Reaching deep into our personal lives, the enormous changes ahead will transform traditional family structures and sexual attitudes. They will smash conventional relationships between old and young. They will overthrow our values with respect to money and success. They will alter work, play and education beyond recognition. And they will do all this in a context of spectacular, elegant, yet frightening scientific advance.[4]

The theme of Tofler's book is that through education, a large scale effort in which there is the widest possible participation must be made to direct human thought to the future, to assess in advance the possibilities and probabilities, and in so doing, must consciously control the dimensions and directions of change. Otherwise, change will disorient the individual, will result in a psychosis of the social order.

The widest possible participation in thinking of the future must include the young. Otherwise, Tofler says, young people forced into prolonged adolescence and deprived of the right to participate in social decision-making will grow more unstable and will threaten the system. He reiterates a maxim which appears throughout this book, that goals set without the participation of those affected will be increasingly hard to execute.

The youth revolution that characterized the decade of the 1960s changed the way young people viewed themselves, and how they perceived society and their roles as members of society. It was as if an entire generation began to think and behave differently. Values once accepted were examined; the gap between rhetoric and deeds of political leaders and social institutions was exposed; the earnest quest for meanings in life called to account some of the principles which older generations had accepted without question. The young were involved personally or emotionally in the civil rights movement, and it was the young who first questioned the morality of the involvement of the United States in the war in Southeast Asia. Added to these was the shock created by a growing awareness that the very environment that sustained life itself was endangered by pollution of the rivers and seas and air, and that life on the planet was also threatened by overpopulation. Excessive materialism, which was a by-product of technological advance, and which had come to govern so many of the life choices people made, was held up to scrutiny—and was found wanting.

STUDENT DISSENT

One measure of the capacity and desire to be an educational leader in the secondary school is the response a principal makes to student unrest, dissent,

---

[4]Alvin Toffler, *Future Shock*. (New York: Random House, 1970), pp. 185–6.

and protest. The period 1968–1970 witnessed widespread difficulties in schools. Although the critical period was followed by a period of relative quiet (some say by student apathy), the basic causes for the most part remain. Student activism could surface again, perhaps sporadically, perhaps generally. The principal must not only be conscious about evidence of student unrest in his own school, but equally important, he should also be familiar with the considerable literature on the subject which indicates that student questioning of time-honored practices is endemic not only to the United States, but is also found elsewhere in the world.

It is not enough for the principal alone to be well-informed. The causes of student disaffection are pervasive. All of the school staff—the administrative and supervisory personnel, guidance counselors, and, most important of all, the teachers—need to recognize the symptoms as matters of concern. It is the principal, however, who must take the lead.

In considering the topic of student unrest the reader will have to make a conscious effort to put aside some common excuses which schools offer for avoiding self-examination when student unrest, dissent, or protest occur or are under discussion. Some of these excuses include:

1. Trouble inside the school is caused by "outsiders." These (it is often alleged) are older troublemakers who stir up their younger friends; or they are outside organizations that foment disruption to advance their own objectives; or they are unnamed subversive groups using the schools to further their own purposes. *The evidence shows that only rarely—and this primarily in big cities—have outside persons or groups played any significant role in what occurred within the schools.*

2. The cause of student unrest is only a reflection of the larger society, and is thus outside the control of the school. *While it cannot be denied that what goes on outside, in the home, the community, the nation, and the world affects how adolescents think and feel, the evidence indicates that student unrest is almost always directed toward the school itself.*

3. Disruptions in schools are almost always racially motivated. *This theory does not hold up either, under examination. Some of the more highly publicized disruptions have involved clashes between black and white students, but even in these instances much of the underlying tension grew out of real or imagined grievances having to do with school policies, staff attitudes, claims of unequal treatment, and the like.*

4. Student unrest as revealed in overt dissent and protest is but an example of waywardness and misbehavior, and is to be treated as such and put down as quickly and forcibly as possible. *This is a great oversimplification. Some student dissidence may be laid at this door. Again evidence indicates that much more is based on justifiable causes and is more mature and discerning than many school officials are willing to concede.*

A principal may rationalize student unrest on any one of a combination of the above reasons; many have done so. Others, however, have engaged in self-examination and in examination of school concepts and practices, and have persuaded a sometimes reluctant faculty to likewise observe the symptoms of student malaise in an effort to find the cause and seek remedies.

A survey by the National Association of Secondary School Principals on the extent of student activism in the secondary schools of the United States was reported in 1969.

The NASSP Survey

Based on a sampling of one of every fifteen secondary school principals in the nation, an NASSP survey conducted in 1969, showed that more than half of all schools reported some kind of activism or protest.[5] Tables 5-1 and 5-2 reveal student disaffection in both large and small schools, in urban and rural communities, and in junior and senior high schools. In addition, many principals who reported no activism said they expected to experience it in the future.

Responses from principals showed that student protests covered a wide range of issues. Dress and grooming codes, general discontent with school rules and regulations, smoking restrictions, problems associated with the cafeteria, the need for new student organizations, demands for a greater voice in rule-making, and open versus closed campus election of cheerleaders are examples. Racial tensions gave rise to some form of student activism in approximately one-fourth of the schools surveyed.

Responses by principals to the NASSP questionnaire illustrate divergent attitudes. One principal stated:

> Forces are afoot which will destroy education as it has been known here, and it is doubtful that, like the Phoenix, it could rise again from its ashes.

Table 5-1

Percentage of Schools Reporting Student Activism

	Large (Over 2000)	Medium (801–2000)	Small (801 or less)	All
Urban	74	62	60	67
Suburban	81	72	56	67
Rural	67	67	50	53

Source: The NASSP Bulletin 52, (May 1969). Used with permission.

---

[5]*The Bulletin of the National Association of Secondary School Principals* 52, (May 1969), pp. 150–58.

Table 5-2

Percentages of Junior and Senior High Schools with Student Activism

	Junior High	Senior High
Urban	59	63
Suburban	61	69
Rural	48	53
All	56	59

Source: The NASSP Bulletin 52, (May 1969). Used with permission.

Another said:

> Accord respect to *responsible* protest—they might just be right. The students, to our utter despair, are exhibiting—at long last—the very kinds of behavior that we say we want to encourage, nourish and develop as responsible educators, the requirements for (and agonies of) change are on our doorsteps more so than on theirs. We must change—or foster total revolution in our schools—public or private.

Significantly, almost half the schools surveyed by NASSP reported discontent with their educational programs. Dissatisfaction was due to the quality of teachers and teaching; teachers who did not like their jobs or their students; unsuitable curriculum content; lack of freedom of students to choose teachers; unfair class grouping; poor scheduling; homework; and the grading and examination system.

In an address based on the NASSP survey, J. Lloyd Trump, associate secretary of the organization, reflected on the meanings to be found in student discontent:

> Schools must use both immediate and long range programs to attack the dilemmas that student unrest produces. We dare not ignore student extremists. We must analyze their demands even though ultimatums are met. Above all, we need to talk with them to establish dialogs. I am equally certain that we must not be lulled into complacency by the often bland opinions of student council members and the 'good' students that provide a comfortable impression that everything is fine in schools. The two foregoing extremes are separated by the great majority of student opinions, ranging on a continuum that at times produces student support for one extreme or the other.
>
> What causes the school revolt? Many high school students today know enough to lack confidence in the judgment of their elders. True, 'a little learning is a dangerous thing.' However, when the kids become creative in dress, dance, social relationships, and the like, they find themselves copied by their parents and other oldsters who try to outdo them, often becoming ridiculous in the process. The apparent adult interest in war rather than peace, in profits rather than service,

in wheeling and dealing rather than legal methods, and so on, mirrors a hypocrisy that young idealists abhor. The schools contain similar unreasonable procedures, including especially their systems of reward and punishment, their overportrayals of certain ideals, their organizational rigidity, and their willingness to accept and perpetuate adult mores that seem unreal to youth.[6]

Special Report: Education U.S.A.

In 1969, the National School Public Relations Association devoted an entire issue of its publication, *Education U.S.A.* to a special report, entitled "High School Student Unrest." "Bubbling like super-charged soda," the report began, "student unrest in 1968 exploded and sprayed the high school landscape with boycotts, demonstrations, sit-ins, picketing, vandalism, and violence." In addition to repeating the findings of the NASSP survey, the report called attention to a subsequent study by Alan F. Westin, the director of the Center for Research and Education in American Liberties at Columbia University. Westin reported that 318 high schools in 38 states had undergone some form of disruption between November 1968 and February 1969, and that an additional 239 schools had suffered "serious" episodes. By May 25, 1969, Westin reported that the total number of protests was around 2,000.[7]

The *Education U.S.A.* survey showed a tendency among schools to blame the student unrest on someone or some organization outside the school. This is what the survey report had to say about that theory:

> Despite the widespread wish to pin the blame on some conspiratorial plot hatched off-campus, the facts don't usually bear out this theory. For example, only 5 percent of the principals in the NASSP survey reported SDS (Students for a Democratic Society) involvement in their schools. The Lemberg Center for the Study of Violence investigated the school disorders of 1968 and could find no evidence of outside plotters. Other knowledgeable observers agree. The unrest, it seems, is largely homegrown in the schools themselves—and it is there the answers must be found.[8]

Civic Education: An Alternative

A twenty-one-month project funded by the Bureau of Comprehensive and Vocational Education Research of the United States Office of Education was completed in 1970. A summary of the research findings was published under the title, *Civic Education in a Crisis Age: An Alternative to Repression and Revolution.* Principal investigators were Alan F. Westin, Professor of public

---

[6]"Antidote for Student Unrest in American High Schools." Address by J. Lloyd Trump.

[7]Alan F. Westin et. al., "Civic Education in a Crisis Age: An Alternative to Repression and Revolution" (Columbia University and Teachers College: Center for Research and Education in American Liberties, 1970), p. 3.

[8]National School Public Relations Association, *High School Student Unrest: Education U.S.A.* (Washington, D.C., 1969), p. 3.

The Youth Revolution

law and government at Columbia University, John P. De Cecco, Professor of psychology and education at San Francisco State College, and Arlene Richard, of New York University. The overall goal of the project was to develop behavioral objectives and guidelines for effective civic participation in the 1970s. Recognizing the basic commitment of American democratic theory and law to the concept of citizen participation in society's major social institutions (churches, unions, business, universities, community institutions, and government), the investigators determined to find out whether students in secondary schools shared the concerns of society at large. They were especially interested in the implications of student responses in this area to questions dealing with curriculum, teacher-student relations, student-administration relations, and the relation of schools to the local community.

Data were collected by questionnaires from approximately 7,000 junior and senior high school students in the greater New York City and Philadelphia areas. The questionnaire was open-ended. It asked students to describe a crisis in democracy with which they had personal experience—an occurrence in their own lives in which they had had difficulty deciding the democratic thing to do, and in which there seemed to be at least two alternative solutions. Analysis of the questionnaire responses gave a picture of democratic expectations by students, and it revealed the daily operational realities in the schools as the students felt they had experienced them.

What were the results and conclusions?

> The principal findings of the survey are that a large majority of the students feel they are regularly subjected to undemocratic decisions. These are seen as unilateral actions by teachers and administrators that deny fundamental rights of persons to equality, dissent, or due process, and of members of an institution to some meaningful share in its rule-making processes. Students feel that the results of the dilemma situations are bad, and report increased levels of dissatisfaction, tension, frustration, and anger with school as a result of the outcomes. Because they cannot see ways to resolve their dilemmas through the use of alternative means, they register strong feelings of powerlessness. Taken as a whole, the survey finds that a majority of these students perceive their schools to be essentially undemocratic institutions. . . .
>
> We hope that the implications of this survey and our project will be considered carefully by educators, key civic groups, public officials who shape educational policy, and students themselves. Some observers may have been inclined to brush aside recent secondary school demonstrations and protests as the work of a few radical agitators, or an imitative reflection of college trends. *But our survey suggests that the great majority of students in secondary schools—the supposedly silent majority—is becoming increasingly frustrated and alienated by school. They do not believe that they receive individual justice or enjoy the right to dissent, or share in critical rule-making that affects their lives.*
>
> If this is true, then our schools may be turning out millions of

students who are not forming a strong and reasoned allegiance to a democratic political system, because they receive no meaningful experience with such a democratically-oriented system in their daily lives in school. For them, we should remember, public school is the governmental institution which represents the adult society in its most direct and controlling aspect. If we do not teach the viability of democratic modes of conflict-resolution, and win respect for these as just and effective processes, we will lose more and more potential democrats. If we mean to alter this, we had better look with painful attention at what our children are saying about their perceptions of schools, for it is these perceptions, and not our wishful thinking about what schools should or might be, that are fundamental in the citizenship education now taking place in American secondary education.

One answer to the results of our survey might well be that schools are not meant to be democratic institutions, and that young people from 12 to 18 years of age are not yet ready either to participate in making some of the rules of their institutions or to receive rights of citizens in the adult society. Of course, schools do deal with young people in the process of forming themselves, and of course we do not expect school decisions and secondary education to be a rigid reproduction of adult political society. Yet recognizing these realities does not mean that schools can ignore the growing insistence on clearer citizen rights and more meaningful participation that have marked our society during the past decade. These demands have been given legitimacy and sanction by many court rulings, legislative acts, governmental programs, and intraorganizational reforms. *We believe it is the challenge of civic education in our schools to find ways to conduct learning, teaching, and administration within such a deepened democratic context, and that it is the task of students, teachers, administrators, parents, and community leaders to create schools for the 1970's in which such experimentation can take place.*[9] (Italics added)

The Underground Newspaper

An illuminating reflection of student opinion and student unrest is contained in "underground" newspapers which are written and circulated in secondary schools. The label "underground" has been given to the publications because they are produced outside the provisions made in the school for journalistic enterprise. They are in part in competition with the authorized school paper, in part a protest against what the underground writers consider to be the administrative and faculty control over the regular school newspaper; but more than that, they are a mirror of what the students who write for the underground find objectionable in their schools. Generally, the editors and writers for the underground papers are among the more capable students. This corresponds to various studies of student activism which indicate that the activists come from the ranks of the more able students. This is not, of course, to say that all of the capable students are activists or necessarily write for, or support, the underground press. Like other forms of dissent, the

---

[9]*Ibid.*

The Youth Revolution

underground newspaper may provide valuable insights for the principal and faculty who wish to understand the issues that motivate the activist, protesting, dissenting student.

Underground newspapers have been generally frowned upon by school authorities. Some papers have contained four-letter words ordinarily not used in newspapers in general. Others, however, have been sources of annoyance because they were critical of school boards or individual school administrators and teachers, or because they challenged in-school institutions such as the student council or the regular newspaper, or because they were critical of school rules, regulations, or the quality of teaching.

School Dropouts

Another form of student protest, often not recognized as such, is that made silently by the boys and girls who drop out of school. These are not ordinarily the signers of petitions, the class boycotters, the marchers, the writers for the underground press. But in their own way many dropouts are making the ultimate form of protest.

Leaving school is not, of course, a recent phenomenon. Most of the reports on secondary education since 1890 have recorded the dropout. Today, however, all the powers of persuasion are used to prevent students from leaving high school before graduation. From radio and television, from the United States Employment Service, and from the Advertising Council comes the message "Stay in School." Guidance counselors and principals issue frequent warnings against leaving. And in truth, the choice today for most young persons is school or the streets. Yet in spite of the pressures to remain, in 1970–71, 530,000 boys and girls chose to leave rather than remain.

Indications point to the fact that student dissatisfaction is not something that is confined to in-school bickering. Candidates for the Board of Education of the Princeton, New Jersey Regional School District answered questions posed by the local League of Women Voters. One of the student-related parts of its questions and answers, which were printed in the *Princeton Packet* in its 19 January 1972 issue, follows:

> *Question: Why do you think there have been tensions within and among teachers, students and administrators at Princeton High School?*
>
> There is a great fear when change takes place, as it inevitably is new and will also be in the future. I feel that many of these changes that are positive have to take place to insure reaching all of our children with a greater education.
>
> Schools are for students, operation of our modern school system must be a truly shared responsibility. Participation and involvement must be carried out with sincerity and integrity. Students, as well as

teachers and parents, must be involved in a continuing review and evaluation of the total school program for diversity, integrity, flexibility and relevance.

To eliminate tensions at the high school, more student participation is needed in structuring committees: on school government, services, cultural activities, and (self)discipline. Student involvement in decision-making at the high school level and effective communication would not disrupt the educational process but would tend to make the student feel that he is needed, wanted, respected, and valued.

We do have tensions being caused by many things, including racial conflicts, lack of confidence, rumors, curriculum changes and administrative decisions, etc. There, too, our young people are examining the role of school in society. They are also questioning our value system. These things make many adults defensive.

There are many factors that have contributed to the tensions at Princeton High School. While no single incident, group, or individual is fully responsible, many problems combine to create dissatisfaction.

There is a great need for students, faculty, administrators, and parents to work together toward common goals. They should also have a voice in defining the objectives and must recognize and work with honest differences.

I would also hope to see more involvement of parents, teachers and students in policy-making decisions as well as in the resolution of specific problems.[10]

Expressions such as those noted above are certainly not common among citizens who aspire to membership on boards of education or to citizens in general. However, it would be a mistake to assume that what students are saying and the dissatisfactions they express are not known at home and elsewhere in the community. A sizable number of adults is not unsympathetic with what adolescent boys and girls are trying to say to older generations.

Youth and Education as a Career

Youth and Careers in Education is a report which was prepared by the National Center for Careers in Education, a research organization supported by grants from the United States Office of Education. The purpose of the study was to discover attitudes of high school and college students toward education as a career choice. Some of the findings are pertinent to the general theme of this chapter.

Responses to questionnaires were received from 6,821 high school students in 20 high schools, including 3,402 from sophomores and 3,419 from seniors; college students accounted for 3,064 of the respondents. The high schools represented all geographical regions, and urban, suburban, rural,

---

[10]The *Princeton Packet,* p. 5. Used with permission.

The Youth Revolution

small, medium, and large schools. Public, private, and parochial schools were all surveyed.

Of the 6,821 high school students, only 7.6 percent expected to start their careers in education. Broken down by sex, 4.8 percent of the boys and 12.9 percent of the girls thought education would be a career choice, either at secondary school or college level.

A total of 400 personal interviews were held with a sampling of those who responded to the questionnaires, from both high schools and colleges. Selected excerpts from the interviews reveal data relating to the kind of questions contained in this chapter:

> Many of the young ... made it very clear that in thinking of future careers they inevitably think in terms of changes that need to be made in society, because they are so disturbed by what they see as hypocrisy in the older generation.[11]
>
> Most ... are optimistic about the ability of their generation, in time, to bring about changes in society, largely because they place so much faith in the job values they expect to bring with them to their future careers.[12]

When those interviewed related their responses to education specifically, they valued education as a way of bringing about a better way of life. Although they generally spoke favorably of their teachers, when they were critical it was because teachers seemed out of step with the times, or did not apparently have time to take a personal interest in students. The major criticisms expressed by the students were directed to the educational system as a whole. They were opposed to the system because of its "cold, impersonal nature" and they felt that the system's administrators stifled creativity and innovation. Students were also bothered about the difference they saw between the potential of education, and its performance.

> A number of students make it clear that if they could be convinced that education were indeed an effective vehicle for bringing about changes in society and for building a new social order, they might seriously consider the field. For this to happen, they need to see signs of greater innovation in the schools, greater freedom and flexibility, and a greater sensitivity and concern on the part of the education....[13]
>
> When it comes to recruiting young people to careers in education, it seems that for many of the young—particularly those who are bright and creative—education in some ways becomes its own worst

---

[11]The National Center for Careers in Education, *Youth and Careers in Education.* (New York: Hill and Knowlton, 1971), p. 44.

[12]*Ibid.,* p. 46.

[13]*Ibid.,* p. 81.

enemy. Many students are seemingly turned off from education because of the image they get of the field at first hand as recipients of the educational process. Put simply, they don't like what they see close up.[14]

Bibliography

"The Authority Crisis in our Schools." *The Bulletin of the National Association of Secondary School Principals,* (February 1971).

Bachman, J. G. et al. *Youth in Transition,* vol. 1. Ann Arbor, Mich.: University of Michigan Institute for Social Research, 1970.

"Campus Unrest: Today's Education." *The Journal of the National Education Association,* November 1969.

Dobbins, C. G. "Alienation: A Time for the Long View." *Educational Record* vol. 51, 1970.

Dolee, Carl J. "A Sensible Assessment of Student Rights and Responsibilities." *The School Administrator,* September 1971. The American Association of School Administrators, Washington, D.C.

Halleck, S. L. "Hypotheses About Student Unrest." *Today's Education,* September 1968.

Hendrick, Irving G., and Reginald L. Jones. *Student Dissent in the Schools.* Boston, Mass.: Houghton Mifflin Company, 1972.

Pennsylvania Department of Education. *Student Unrest: Pennsylvania Education.* September, 1969.

---

[14]*Ibid.,* p. 115.

6

Student Rights

INTRODUCTION

In the evolutionary process which characterizes our society, laws typically follow the course of social change, occasionally accompany it, but seldom precede it. Law performs a very useful function in providing guidelines for acceptable human behavior, and assessing penalties against those who refuse to observe such guidelines. However, it is important to remember that as social attitudes and values change, so must the law change if we are to have an orderly and responsible society.

In our country, the basic law, that is, the Federal Constitution, sets forth in the Bill of Rights those rights which are the heritage of every citizen of the country. The interpretation of those rights, and their application with respect to the individual, are determined by the courts, the ultimate decision resting with the United States Supreme Court. The interpretation and application of Constitutional provisions change with the changing society. For example, until 1954 the courts accepted the principle of "separate but equal" schools. In that year, a socially-conscious Supreme Court reflected the moral commitment of a substantial part of our society, and, in the historic *Brown v. Topeka* decision, reversed the rulings of over a century and declared that "separate" was not "equal." The history of the Court has been a record of legal interpretations reflecting a changing social order. Strict constructionists have gone so far as to say that the Supreme Court *makes* law instead of merely interpreting it. On the other hand, those who interpret the Constitution liberally see it as an instrument designed to protect human rights in a changing social atmosphere, and by its very nature flexible enough to serve this purpose. It is this latter view which has dominated the Court in recent years, and it is difficult to foresee any radical change in this trend.

While amending the Constitution is provided for in the document itself, the process of amendment is a long and laborious one, and so far no serious attempt has been made to amend the Bill of Rights provisions. Therefore, it appears logical that the broad and generalized guarantees of human rights will change only in their interpretation and not in substance. History has shown that this process has operated successfully in preserving human rights as well as in accommodating the changing social situation. It is testimony to the soundness of the Bill of Rights and to the foresight of the founding fathers.

The interpretations of the constitutional statement of individual rights have tended not only to enhance those rights but to enlarge the scope of their application. This tendency is reflected in the extension of rights to minority groups such as blacks and the youth of the country. It is this latter group with which we are primarily concerned in this book.

Today's youth have ready access to a broad spectrum of information which was relatively unknown to the youth of several decades ago. Because of the vastly improved communication media, many aspects of life which were relatively unknown to yesterday's high school students are common knowledge today. The television cameraman brings the horrors and inhumanity of war right into the family living room. The life styles of the affluent as well as those of the ghetto dwellers are revealed for all to see. We see man walking on the moon, and we can observe first-hand, via satellite, the reception of a President of the United States in a country ten-thousand miles away. Today youth, as never before, have an awareness of social conflict, social injustice, economic deprivation and political acitivities of many kinds. Televised sessions of congressional hearings, political campaign speech-making, and press interviews give both the young and the old a picture of politics and government which was never revealed in the civics textbooks.

Thus, awareness has made youth more active participants in the social scene, and this awareness has naturally been reflected in their school lives. In one notable instance, high school students asserted their right to symbolize a protest against the Vietnam war despite school regulations, and they maintained that right in the courts. The lowering of the voting age to eighteen years in national elections has had a significant impact on the development of social as well as political activity of youth.

The high school student of today is much more sophisticated than his counterpart of twenty years ago. As a result of the forces at work in our society and the technological advances in communication, he has become aware at a relatively early age of what life is all about. By and large, he is no longer willing to accept his elders as necessarily truthful, honest, and reasonable simply because they are older. He questions accepted values, traditions and customs. He raises reasonable doubts. He is often unwilling to accept the dictates of his elders, and particularly so when they vitally affect his own life. This attitude asserted itself in the lives of thousands of young men who

Student Rights

refused induction into the armed forces, left the country, or deserted after being inducted. They perceived the traditional call to duty, to country, to national defense, and to the defense of liberty as outworn cliches without logical meaning. They refused to equate defense of their country with going 9,000 miles away to fight on foreign soil.

Youth was in the forefront of the movement in opposition to the involvement of the country in the Vietnam war. High school graduates and college students raised their voices in protest on college campuses across the breadth of the land. These protests appeared for the most part to be honest, socially-motivated objections to national policy. Of course, there was the natural objection of the male youth to risking life and limb in military action. But essentially the protest appeared to rise out of a newly-acquired social consciousness, especially since young women were as much involved as young men.

Youth who only a decade ago were staging panty-raids and still further back were swallowing gold fish are now concerning themselves with social, moral, and political issues. Annoying as this may be to those who insist on the traditional values of our culture as established and maintained by the elders of the society, it offers great promise for the rejuvenation of that society. The trend is quite clear. Youth are moving rapidly toward greater social involvement. They are having and will continue to have a significant influence on the course of national policy and on the resolution of social and economic issues.

The parallel evolution of our national society and the development of the individual youth have now converged upon the secondary school as well as the colleges and universities. Students at all levels are insisting on their rights as citizens and as integral parts of the social order. They are quick to recognize any sign of exploitation, and they are not reluctant to exercise power. On one occasion, a large midwestern university decided to fire its football coach in mid-season. Shortly after the athletic director made known the discharge action, the members of the team met and agreed that they would not play unless the coach was retained for the remainder of the season. Prompted by visions of an empty stadium and the loss of hundreds of thousands of dollars, the discharge order was quietly rescinded. This incident illustrates an exercise of power undreamed of by college athletes of the past.

Thus, the modern secondary school faces a situation in its relationship with students which is unprecedented. Today's youth have a social awareness, a desire to be heard, an insistence on the rights of citizenship, and the ability, in many instances, to wield considerable power. Furthermore, the courts have rendered and are continuing to render decisions which protect and in some cases amplify these rights and privileges and powers. This chapter will deal with the rights of students and with implications these rights have for the secondary schools.

FOUR BASIC AREAS OF STUDENT RIGHTS

Student rights, as stated in constitutional law and adjudicated in the courts, may be generally divided into four areas. They are freedom of expression, freedom of assembly, freedom of personal appearance, and freedom of religion. These rights, in the case of minors, have only recently been fully protected by the extension of the right of procedural due process to juveniles in the more serious types of cases.[1]

Early in the century juvenile courts were created for the express purpose of protecting the rights of youths. However, such protection was based on the benevolence of the juvenile court judge, rather than on any constitutional guarantees. The primary goal of these courts was to protect children from exploitation and corruption by adults. The achievement of this goal was to be realized by individual treatment administered through informal proceedings largely at the discretion of the judge. The fact that the work of the court was characterized by clinical considerations, humanitarianism, compassion, and a sort of kindly paternalism made it antiprocedural in nature.

Until the mid-sixties, the actions of school authorities in ignoring procedural requirements in dealing with students were rather consistently upheld by the courts. Only in cases where their actions were proven arbitrary, capricious, misinformed, or had involved conspiracy have the courts intervened on behalf of the student.

This posture was based on the age old concept of "in loco parentis" which freely translated means "in place of the parent." Since compulsory attendance laws compelled children to leave their parents and be placed under the control of school authorities it then followed that the school must temporarily assume the role of the parents for the protection and welfare of the child. Thus, the courts naturally presumed that as parents, in effect, school authorities could exercise control over students and could mete out punishments without regard to procedural rights, as long as such actions were school-related and fell within the limitations which ordinarily applied to parents.

Now we find that the concept of in loco parentis has seriously eroded. From challenges in the courts, to the authority exercised by the school and its almost total neglect of procedural requirements in even the most serious discipline cases, a significant change has taken place. Secondary school students are rapidly being accorded full rights of citizenship. The courts have acknowledged that Section One of the Fourteenth Amendment of the United States Constitution applies to youth as well as other minority groups. That section reads as follows:

> All persons born or naturalized in the United States, and subject to the jurisdiction thereof, are citizens of the United States and of the

---
[1] In re Gault, 387 U.S. 1 (1967).

State wherein they reside. No State shall make or enforce any law which shall abridge the privileges or immunities of citizens of the United States; nor shall any State deprive any person of life, liberty, or property, without due process of law; nor deny to any person within its jurisdiction the equal protection of the laws.

Procedural rights are most frequently involved when punishment is being meted out for infractions of school rules and regulations, usually involving expression or conduct which is regarded as harmful to the welfare of the school. The type of punishment most frequently used for the graver offenses is suspension or expulsion. The former term is applied to a short and usually temporary exclusion from school, and the latter to a more extended exclusion, ordinarily for the remainder of the school year. It is in this context that the issue is most sharply drawn. It represents a conflict between the right of the student to remain in school and the obligation of the school to insure that the educational process is not disrupted nor the rights of others jeopardized. The exclusion of students from school, no matter what the offense, represents a deprivation of a right or privilege in which case the courts are inclined to insist on the most careful adherence to procedural requirements of due process. As far back as 1943, the U.S. Supreme Court said "it is clear that the student does not leave his constitutional rights at the schoolhouse door."[2]

Procedural rights of students, in this case college students, were first specifically set forth in the case of *Dixon* v. *Alabama* in 1961.[3] Although the case involved college students and an institution of higher learning, it is equally applicable to students in tax-supported public high schools. The court in this case specifically stated that any student faced with expulsion must be afforded adequate notice of the charges preferred against him, a fair hearing, sworn testimony, confrontation with his accuser or accusers, and full opportunity to present his defense against the charges.

The importance of the courts' recognition of procedural rights in the case of juveniles, even within limitations, can hardly be overestimated in connection with the administration of the secondary school. The rights of citizenship so conferred should be directly reflected in the student-school relationships. Student rights as discussed in the succeeding sections of this chapter are largely implemented through the procedural requirements established by the courts.

Freedom of Expression

The exercise of freedom of expression by students presents problems to educators which are manifest and manifold. The issue, briefly stated, is "to what extent may the school restrict freedom of expression on the part of students in order to maintain an effective learning situation?" Or, put in

---

[2]West Virginia State Board of Education v. Barnette, 319 U.S. 642 (1943)
[3]Dixon v. Alabama State Board of Education, 368 U.S. 930 (1961).

another way, the issue is the right of the individual student to express himself versus the society's interest in an orderly learning atmosphere. It is the age-old issue of individual rights versus the common welfare.

Freedom of expression involves both the spoken and written word as well as symbolic forms of expression. As indicated in the previous section of this chapter, students are to be treated as citizens and therefore have rights of free expression which are not susceptible to unreasonable infringement by the school. As citizens, they are protected by the First Amendment, which reads:

> Congress shall make no law respecting an establishment of religion, or prohibiting an establishment of religion, or prohibiting the free exercise thereof; or abridging the freedom of speech, or of the press; or the right of the people peaceably to assemble, and to petition the Government for a redress of grievances.

In 1943, in the case of *West Virginia* v. *Barnette,* the Supreme Court established in general terms that First Amendment rights applied to students. Unfortunately, the nature, extent, and circumstances of their application were not spelled out. Furthermore, the issue was somewhat clouded by the religious aspects of the case and the fact that students were carrying out the wishes of their parents.

It was not until 1969 that the courts asserted clearly and specifically the nature of students' rights to express themselves. In the case of *Tinker* v. *Des Moines,*[4] high school students planned to wear black armbands as an expression of their opposition to the Vietnam War and their grief over the deaths which that conflict occasioned. School officials learned of the proposed expression of protest and dissent, and passed a regulation specifically forbidding the wearing of armbands on the school premises. The students disregarded the rule and wore the armbands as originally planned, and a number of them were suspended from school for violation of the regulation. Three of the suspended students petitioned a federal district court for a restraining order preventing the school from disciplining students because of their disregard of a school regulation which violated their right of free expression. Thus the issue was clearly drawn: "Could the school enforce a regulation which forbade student expression on a public issue?" In this case the expression was symbolic, but this did not affect the basic issue.

Although the *Tinker* v. *Des Moines* case originated in 1965, it did not reach final adjudication until 1969, when the U.S. Supreme Court rendered its decision overruling lower courts which had held for the school district. During the course of the litigation it was made quite clear that school authorities did not approve of the sentiments expressed by the students. They apparently felt that whatever government policy might be, the school was

---

[4]Tinker v. Des Moines Independent Community School District, 393 U.S. 503 (Iowa, 1969).

Student Rights 121

obligated, as a state institution, to support it. No disruption of the school was shown, and the Court brushed aside the concept of school authorities that there should be no organized expression of dissent from governmental policy. The Court said:

> School authorities do not possess absolute authority over their students. Students in schools as well as out of school are persons under our Constitution. They are possessed of fundamental rights which the state must respect, just as they themselves must respect their obligations to the state. In our system, students may not be regarded as closed circuit recipients of only that which the state chooses to communicate. They may not be confined to the expression of those sentiments that are officially approved. In the absence of a specific showing of constitutionally valid reasons to regulate their speech, students are entitled to freedom of expression of their views.
> A student's rights ... do not merely embrace the classroom hours. When he is in the cafeteria, or on the playing field, or on the campus during authorized hours, he may express his opinions on controversial subjects.

The Court then proceeded to draw the boundaries to which free speech, symbolic or otherwise, might go before encountering restriction. It observed that:

> Conduct by the student, in class or out of it, which for any reasons ... materially disrupts classroom works or involves substantial disorder or invasion of the rights of others is, ... not immunized by the ... guarantee of freedom of speech.

Thus, the Court has delineated the extent to which the student can exercise freedom of expression, or, conversely, under what conditions such expression is curtailed. Particular attention is called to the words *"materially"* in connection with the term "disrupting," and *"substantial"* as a modifier of "disorder." This means that trivial, isolated or perfunctory disruptions may not be used as excuses for curtailing free speech. The disruption must be material and substantial to justify suppression. Clearly, the intention of the Court is to permit full freedom of expression which does not cause a degree of disruption which precludes the normal functioning of the educational process. The invasion of the rights of others would, of course, be disruptive as well as unlawful.

An interesting question which logically follows is whether these restrictions apply if the disruption is caused by the reaction of others to students who express themselves. Suppose, for example, those students wearing black armbands were assailed by other students motivated by a misguided sense of patriotism, thus "materially" disrupting the order of the school. Would restrictions on the armband wearers then be justified? The Court did not pursue this question so it is left to speculation. However, it would seem logical and consistent with previous court rulings that the assailants would be held to be at fault rather than the armband wearers, since it would be they who actually caused the disruption As long as the protestors were peaceful, and the disruption originated with the other students it appears logical to assume that it would be they who would be subject to discipline—not those who exercised their constitutional right of free speech. If the courts ruled otherwise, it would make possible the suppression of free speech at any time there were those who disagreed and took unlawful action to disrupt the school. The court would in such case be condoning unlawful acts—which constitute an invasion of rights guaranteed by the Constitution.

Freedom of expression by means of student publications has been the subject of a number of recent court cases. Probably the case of *Scoville* v. *Board of Education of Joliet Township High School*[5] is the best guide to judicial ruling. It was appealed to the U.S. Supreme Court, which declined to hear the case and thus let the ruling of the appellate court stand, thereby, in effect, upholding that ruling.

In this case, two high school students were expelled in early 1968, for publishing and selling a school magazine which contained an editorial sharply critical of the school administration. The magazine, *Grass High,* was published off school property but was sold in school. The students brought suit in district court seeking readmission to school. The court ruled against the students saying that they had advocated what amounted to a disregard for established school administrative procedures, thus inciting disruption of the school. The Court of Appeals affirmed the judgment but later granted a rehearing of the case.

On closer examination, and after a more exhaustive hearing, the court found that no evidence had been submitted to show any disruption of the school due to the magazine, but had implicitly applied the concept of "clear and present danger" of such disruption. The appeals court then ruled that there was no reasonable basis for anticipating disruption in the school, and in fact there had been no disruption in consequence of the sale of the first three issues. Since the freedom of expression of the students had been restricted, the Board had the obligation to show that the disciplinary action was taken upon the basis of a reasonable forecast of disruption. The evidence indicated no such reasonable basis existed, and the appeals court reversed its earlier ruling in favor of the Board. In so doing, it said the Board had failed to balance the rights of students to express themselves against the right of the administration to maintain order.

In making its decision, the appellate court relied heavily upon the *Tinker* v. *Des Moines* case since that case was decided by the Supreme Court. The expulsion of the students was based solely on the grounds of the objection-

---

[5]Scoville v. Board of Education of Joliet Township High School District 204, 425F 2nd 10 (Illinois, 1970).

Student Rights 123

able nature of the material published. The material in question was critical of some administrative practices which the students considered arbitrary, unnecessary, and unduly restrictive. Such criticism might even have been regarded as constructive by an impartial observer. In view of its nature, when the court applied the *Tinker* concept of *material* disruption and *substantial* disorder, the jurists could discern no threat in the magazine material.

Thus, the general conclusion can be drawn that the rights of students to publish materials critical of teachers and administrators must be balanced against the interest of good order in the school. In disciplining students for such publication, the burden of proof rests upon the administration. This case, which may be considered a ruling one in this area, is another straw in the wind showing the trend in the courts to uphold citizen rights for students as long as their exercise does not disrupt the normal activities and procedures of education. Like adults, they have the right, within reasonable limits, to criticize those in authority over them. The difference lies in the greater limitation imposed by the fact that students are intimately involved in a process, education, which is essential to the preservation of the state, and any disruption would adversely affect the social welfare.

It should be noted, however, that in a case[6] where a teacher published a letter which was severely critical of his board of education, his right of free expression was upheld despite the board's claim that not only were members defamed but that it was "detrimental to the efficient operation and administration of the schools of the district." Lower courts, including the Illinois Supreme Court, found that the latter claim was supported by substantial evidence, and therefore ruled in favor of the board.

The letter in question was an attack on the board's handling of school finances, and after a hearing in which the board showed, to the satisfaction of the lower courts, that the letter was "detrimental to the best interests of the school," the courts ruled in favor of the board. The Supreme Court, in holding for the teacher, said:

> In sum we hold that, in a case such as this, absent proof of false statements knowingly or recklessly made by him, a teacher's exercise of his rights to speak on issues of public importance may not furnish the basis for his dismissal [7]

This case is an interesting parallel to the *Scoville* case, with the major difference being that in the one case the plaintiff was a student and in the other, a teacher. Despite the fact that there are certain other differences, the essential factors are quite comparable. An analysis of the two cases would tend to indicate a judicial trend toward moving the balance toward the

---

[6]Pickering v. Board of Education of Township High School District 205, 391 v. 563 (1968).

[7]Pickering v. Board of Education, 391 v. 563 (1968).

protection of constitutional rights of free expression of both adults and youth.

Two other recent cases tend to go along with the *Scoville* ruling. They are the cases of *Eisner* v. *Stamford Board of Education*[8] and *Sullivan* v. *Houston School District*.[9] In the former, high school students distributed a student newspaper on schoolgrounds without prior approval of school authorities. The question at issue was whether the school administration had the right to require that the content of each issue of the paper be submitted to school authorities for approval before distribution. The court ruled against the board's use of blanket prior restraint on the publication. The court, however, indicated that in "carefully restricted circumstances" the board might require prior submission of materials if there was reason to believe that reasonable regulations governing student publications were being violated.

In the *Sullivan* case, two high school seniors were instrumental in the production and distribution of a newspaper which criticized school authorities and were expelled. The administration contended that the newspaper created disruption in the operation of the school and caused "turmoil" among students. It was also charged that the publication incited a disregard of school administrative procedures among students. After hearing the evidence the court decided that disorder and "turmoil" created by the newspaper were neither substantial or "materially" disruptive. The jurists also found the criticism of school authorities mature, intelligent, and constructive, and not the type which would tend to incite insubordination. The court, in ruling for the students, stated that in the absence of precise, clear, and reasonable regulations regarding student publications, the sole criterion of legality was their effect upon the normal order and activities of the school. And in order to legally restrict or deny such publication, material and substantial disruption must be shown.

It is well to note, however, that the courts will not condone the use of profanity and vulgarity in secondary student publications under the guise of free expression. In the case of *Baker* v. *Downey City Board of Education*,[10] two students were suspended for distributing to other students a publication containing both profanity and vulgarity. Relying on the *Tinker* case they brought suit saying that the publication was not disruptive and that they were punished for exercising free expression. They also asserted that the terms "profane" and "vulgar" were too vague to be applied in their case.

Some twenty-five teachers had reported that the publication had been a distracting factor in their classes. Aside from this evidence, however, the court ruled that the right to free expression does not, at least on the part of high school students, include the right to use vulgarity and profanity. Thus, in

---

[8]Eisner v. Stamford Board of Education, 314F. Supp. 832 (1970).
[9]Sullivan v. Houston Independent School District, 307F. Supp. 1328 (1969).
[10]Baker v. Downey City Board of Education, 307F. Supp. 517 (1969).

effect, the court held that the denial of the use of indecency in expression was not the denial of free expression.

Freedom of Assembly

The protests and demonstrations characterizing student dissent against war, military conscription, ecological pollution and the "establishment" in general, while greatest on college campuses, have also been present in high schools. Protests based on racial issues and the rights of minorities have not been uncommon. Marching, chanting, congregating, and picketing frequently obstruct and disrupt the educational process. Not infrequently, aggressive student bodies express opposition to school policies or disciplinary acts by these means. A U.S. Office of Education report[11] stated that three out of five high school principals reported student protests in their schools during the 1968-69 school year.

Cases involving the rights of students to peacefully assemble have usually been associated with symbolic expression such as the wearing of buttons or other insignia symbolizing a protest of some kind. In the case of *Blackwell* vs. *Issaquena*,[12] high school students wearing buttons depicting a handclasp between blacks and whites congregated in the halls and on the playground. Although the demonstrators claimed their right to assemble peaceably in a protest action and to express, as a group, their feelings, the court ruled against them on the evidence presented that their actions caused an "unusual degree of commotion," thus substantially disrupting the order of the school.

A contrary ruling was made in the case of *Burnside* vs. *Byars*,[13] in which school officials banned the wearing of "freedom buttons." The reason for the ban, as given by school officials, was that the distribution and group discussion of these buttons and what they symbolized was a disruptive factor. The court held that no disruption was shown, even though there was a concerted participation of a group of about thirty students. In upholding the students, the court said, "Where the exercise of such rights in the school . . . does not materially interfere with the requirements of appropriate discipline in the operation of the school," they cannot be proscribed.

Student protests and demonstrations carried out by means of picketing, boycotts, walkouts, and physical obstruction are generally self-evident disruptions of the school, whether conducted on the schoolgrounds or nearby. In such case, the school administration has not only the right but the duty to take appropriate action to restore order, always observing due process.

The essential test, as in freedom of expression, is, "Does the act materially and substantially disrupt the order of the school?" Unless the evidence

---

[11] U.S. Office of Education. Report of Subcommittee on Easing Tensions in Education. 1969.
[12] Blackwell v. Issaquena County Board of Education, 363F. 2nd 749 (1966).
[13] Burnside v. Byars, 383F. 2nd 744 (1966).

supports an affirmative answer, any restraint constitutes a denial of the right of peaceable assembly and protest. However, it should be noted that the very fact that a group of students assembles during school hours, constitutes strong presumptive evidence that some disruption is taking place. The question, then, is whether that disruption is material and substantial. Here school authorities must exercise their own judgment and must be prepared to present proper evidence if court action is brought. When protest demonstrations and informational picketing takes place after school hours and at places other than school premises the evidence of its disruptive effect is certainly more difficult—but not impossible—to establish.

Freedom of Personal Appearance

There has been a multiplicity of cases involving the school's right to control the personal appearance of pupils. Most of the cases involve male high school students and are centered around the length of the hair. This is no doubt due to the increasing popularity of the fashion among males of wearing long hair, elongated sideburns, and other hirsute adornment such as moustaches and beards. In cases involving girls, the typical issue is concerned with the length of skirts.

While these issues may appear trivial (on several occasions the Supreme Court refused to consider them), they have occasioned a large number of litigations. These cases have usually been suits brought against boards of education and have dealt with school policies regarding attire which were deemed an infringement of constitutional rights. In most cases the student was disciplined, suspended, or expelled for violating a school dress code or regulation. Most such dress codes require that students dress neatly, modestly, and appropriately, and give careful attention to personal cleanliness. Some, however, quite explicitly designate the exact length of hair permitted and the type of haircut allowed. In the case of girls' dresses, the permissible distance from knee to hem of skirt is often designated.

In dealing with such cases, the federal courts (as might be supposed) have rendered divergent decisions. Some of the apparent reasons for the divergence lies in the interpretation of the codes and policies. What was immodest and inappropriate a few years ago may now be modest and appropriate. Fashions and styles change with the times, and youth characteristically are in the forefront of change. Although a definite trend in court decisions is not clearly defined at this time, it would appear that the scales are tipping in favor of the student's right to control his personal appearance within quite liberal limits.

One of the earliest cases of wide significance involved a high school student, a professional musician, who was told by his principal that he would be excluded from school unless his hair was cut to conform to school standards.[14] The student brought suit but the court sustained the principal, ruling that the hair style was disruptive as claimed.

---

[14] Leonard v. School Committee of Attleboro, 212 N.E. 2nd 468 (1965).

Student Rights

In the case of *Davis v. Firment*[15] a student was dismissed for the same reason. He sought preliminary injunction in the federal district court and cited violation of constitutional rights. The Court held for the school authorities and said that long hair is not a symbolic expression and that free choice in grooming is not a student right.

In 1969, in the case of *Breen v. Kahl,* the court made a break from the previous pattern of decisions and ruled in favor of a high school student who had been expelled for failure to cut his hair to the length specifically required in the school regulation. The reasoning of the defendant was that the school had the power to regulate hair length because the plaintiff was a student and a minor. The court disagreed, saying:

> An effort to use the power of the state to impair this freedom (to present one's self as he chooses) must bear a substantial burden of justification whether the justification be in terms of health, physical danger to others, obscenity or distraction to others. For the state to impair this freedom, the absence of a compelling subordinating interest in doing so, would offend a widely shared concept of human dignity—it would deprive a man or woman of liberty without due process of law in violation of the Fourteenth Amendment.[16]

The 1969 case of *Griffin v. Tatum*[17] followed the same line of reasoning. In *Richards v. Thurston* in the same year, the court said:

> The personal liberty of a minor as well as an adult has a high order of importance and the state cannot arbitrarily infringe upon it without a strong showing of need.[18]

The late 1969 case of *Miller v. Gillis,*[19] the 1970 case of *Sims v. Colfax,*[20] and subsequent cases generally uphold students' rights to appear as they please, as long as they do not interfere with the orderly conduct of the school, impair their own health or that of others, or infringe on the rights of others.

Early decisions with regard to the exclusion of students from extracurricular activities, particularly athletics, followed the same pattern. Students were forced to conform to uniform codes requiring short hair, no moustaches, and similar restrictions. However, in 1970, in a Vermont case[21] involving high school tennis players, the federal court ruled an athletic dress code requiring a special hair length was unconstitutional. The court based its decision on the

---

[15]Davis v. Firment, 269F. Supp. 524 (1967).
[16]Breen v. Kahl, 296F. Supp. 702 (1969).
[17]Griffin v. Tatum, 300F. Supp. 60 (1969).
[18]Richards v. Thurston, 304F. Supp. 449 (1969).
[19]Miller v. Gillis, 315F. Supp. 94 (1969).
[20]Sims v. Colfax Community School District, 307F. Supp. 485 (1970).
[21]Dunham v. Pulsifier, 312F. Supp. 411 (1970).

equal protection provision of the Constitution observing that those whose hair length conformed were allowed to participate in athletics while those not so conforming were denied access to tax-supported school programs.

A careful analysis of court decisions regarding personal appearance of students both in the academic program and on the athletic field leads to a number of conclusions. First and basic is the fact that the courts recognize that styles and fashions of dress and grooming change with a constantly changing society. Therefore the unacceptable in dress and grooming of one era becomes fashionable and therefore socially acceptable in a subsequent one. If a particular mode of dress or grooming finds general acceptance in a community, the school in that community will find it legally difficult—if not impossible—to proscribe such dress among students.

The courts recognize the power of the school to establish and maintain dress codes. However, they will not uphold such codes if they simply represent an exercise of authority of the administration over students. In other words, there must be valid reasons for the limitations which are put on student dress. A principal is not free to impose his personal standards of dress upon his students. Students are not to be treated in an arbitrary or capricious manner. They are persons and as such possess rights which are guaranteed in the constitution. In ruling on any given dress code, the courts balance the interests of the school against the interests of the individual. If a specific dress or grooming style is not detrimental to the learning process it will ordinarily be found acceptable by the courts. If, on the other hand, the evidence shows that such dress distracts students from their work or otherwise disrupts the order of the school, a dress code prohibition will be upheld.

A common test of the legality of a dress code applied by the courts is that of vagueness or ambiguity. If the code is ambiguous or so vague that it is not readily and clearly understandable, it will not be upheld. If a dress code is to be enforced by disciplinary action, the courts will require that it be written in clear and definite terms which are uniform in application and not susceptible to misunderstanding or misinterpretation.

In the case of the student athlete, his eligibility to compete shall not be denied because of his hair length and style unless it interferes with the activity which is involved. Pleas by a coach that there must be uniformity of appearance among members of a team, or that dissension may arise because of the uniqueness of one or two individuals, are of no avail. However, if a hazard to the individual himself or to others can be clearly shown, restrictive measures will be upheld.

Finally, if restrictions on dress and grooming are to be imposed by school authorities, they would be well advised to be sure that demonstrable justification exists. For the court to accept such restrictions there must be sound evidence, real or presumptive, that distraction, disruption, or danger results or will result from the dress-style or grooming if it is permitted.

Student Rights

Somewhat related to the right of personal appearance is the claim to privacy which has been raised on a number of occasions with regard to school lockers and school records. Such claims to privacy may conflict with the educational welfare of the student and the maintenance of order and safety in the school. The courts have held that when search of lockers, desks, and similar places are made in the best interests of the student and the school, such search is proper. Although provided for the use of students, lockers and desks are the property of the school. In the case of school records, likewise school property, the same rationale applies; however, it must always be kept in mind that the revelation of privacy for one purpose does not give license to use the information for another purpose or under a different set of circumstances.

Freedom of Religion

Freedom of worship is one of the oldest freedoms of this nation. It was a natural result of the past, since many of the early settlers in America were fugitives from religious persecution. Freedom of religion has been zealously guarded as a constitutional right since early colonial times. It is firmly imbedded in the Constitution of the United States and is reflected in hundreds of court decisions.

Freedom of religion for students in school was established much earlier than were the other student rights discussed in this chapter. The issue took the form of questioning the rights of the school to promote or allow religious instruction or religion-oriented devotional exercises thus exposing the student to a religious atmosphere even though he was not forced to take part. In 1948, the Supreme Court ruled that the school did not have such rights and declared unconstitutional a program of released time religious instruction *in the school on school time* even though students were not required to attend.[22] The fact that lower courts, including the Illinois Supreme Court, had affirmed the board's right to maintain the program reveals the landmark nature of the Court's ruling. From that time on, the rulings of the courts have enhanced the right of students to be free of religious influence while in the public school. Conversely, the powers of school authorities to impose any form of religion or devotional exercise upon students have been gradually diminished and have finally been dissipated. The more recent rulings in *Engel v. Vitale*[23] and *Abington v. Schempp*[24] denied the right of the state to impose a state-wide prescribed prayer upon students, or to require or permit the recitation of the Lord's Prayer or the reading of the Bible (even without comment).

---

[22]McCollum v. Board of Education, 333 U.S. 203 (1948).
[23]Engel v. Vitale, 370 U.S. 421 (1962).
[24]School District of Abington v. Schempp, and Murray v. Curlett, 377 U.S. 203 (1963).

Thus, the courts have made clear that students are to be free of any religious activity which, whether so designed or not, might invade their right to freedom of religion. The Court said its rulings should not be interpreted as antireligious but rather that education, being a function of the state, must maintain the separateness provided in the Constitution. The Supreme Court espouses no religion and disparages none. The right of the school to offer religion, and the student to study religion and its impact on society was not in question.

Patriotic exercises such as singing the national anthem, pledging allegiance, and saluting the flag have been challenged on religious grounds as well as those of free expression. In general, the courts hold that the requirement of such exercises is permissible, but that students who have religious, moral, or political objections shall not be compelled to participate.

The right of the school administration to ban voluntary religious activities in the school on the part of students has been affirmed. However, the question as to whether such activities may be permitted has not been brought to the courts. Although this may be evidence of the lack of interest of students in religion, it might just as easily be credited to their good judgment. If students did wish to engage in voluntary religious activities on school time in school facilities, with permission but without the sponsorship of the school, would it be legal? In other words, do they have the right (with school permission) to engage in religious exercises in school? The weight of the evidence is in the negative, as the Supreme Court has zealously maintained the concept of separation between church and state. Although strenuous attempts have been made to secure public funds for parochial school support, the wall of separation has not yet been seriously breached.

IMPLICATIONS FOR SECONDARY SCHOOL ADMINISTRATION

The courts in the late sixties and early seventies have clearly and repeatedly voiced the fundamental conept that *students are citizens,* and as such they have constitutional rights which cannot legally be denied them. They are protected by the Bill of Rights. They are members of a great society of free men and women. They are living in and enjoying the benefits of a democratic society. Their individual rights are to be respected, and, as individuals in a democracy, they should have the right to participate in the making of decisions which affect them.

The implications of these court rulings for secondary school administration are very significant. It might be simply stated that the courts have pointed the way to better school administration and more functional secondary schools. At first glance, such a statement might appear to have little basis in fact. How could those whose training and experience has been in the interpretation and the adjudication of the law provide any insights in educational administration? What relationships, if any, exists between the profession of law and that of school administration? Is not the function of the court merely to tell us within what legal limits we may operate the school?

The answer is that the courts are making rulings that reflect the social morality of America today. Society, through an evolutionary process discussed earlier, has arrived at the point where the rights of all minorities—blacks, Indians, Mexican Americans, and youth—are a matter of genuine concern. The courts speak the conscience of a better informed, a better educated, and hopefully, a more just society. Their interpretations of the Constitution today are in every way consistent with the democratic form of government to which we are committed as a people. Their rulings are expanding the meaning of democracy to encompass not only a political concept, but also a way of life. The school administrator who ignores this call to change and the social basis which underlies it fails in his essential responsibility. He not only fails his students, his school, and his community; he fails himself as a member of the educational profession.

To the administrator with vision, the implications of this change in the social outlook—and in some respects the very structure of our society—presents a challenge rather than a roadblock; an opportunity, rather than an obstacle. To the imaginative administrator, the concept of the school as a democratic society in and of itself is truly inspiring. Regardless of the difficulties which he may encounter in breaking out of the traditional pattern of secondary school administration when and wherever it exists, his responsibility for educational leadership leaves him no realistic alternative. He faces a real challenge to his leadership in creating a harmonious and effective relationship among students, teachers, and administrators for the achievement of the desired goal—a democratic school. The rewards of his efforts can be of immeasurable benefit and will be reflected in the lives of both students and teachers.

With this type of leadership, the school can become an institution where democracy is practiced as well as taught. The concept of respect for individual rights could be exemplified in the relationship between teacher and student and among students. Each would respect the personality of others and their right to be different, to voice opinions, and to criticize and be criticized in a constructive fashion. Students would be encouraged to participate in the development of school policies which affect them. Paralleling participation should be the responsibility which accompanies such participation. Just as the democratic national society is organized for the pursuit of political, economic, and social goals which meet the needs of individuals, so would the school, as an institutional unit within the larger structure, be organized for the pursuit of educational goals which meet the needs of students. In such pursuit, each individual would necessarily assume the responsibility of sharing in the common effort, and any failure to do so would result in the loss of privileges or even the exaction of penalties in the school, just as it would in the larger society.

The school would become a laboratory of democracy, where authority would be balanced by responsibility, and both would operate within the framework of institutional goals. Responsible free expression would not only be allowed but would be encouraged, both at the student and the adult level. Responsible free assembly would be not only encouraged but provided for in the school program. Respect for the individual would be the keystone of policy in all the relationships involved in the educational process. Need for restrictive rules of dress or grooming would tend to disappear in any atmosphere of mutual respect and toleration. Time devoted to interpreting and enforcing dress codes could be utilized in discussing school policies. Efforts in determining whether an individual hair styling met the required width of two fingers between hairline and eyebrows might be more usefully directed toward determining how well the school curriculum was meeting educational needs of students.

Nothing in the foregoing should be interpreted to mean that rules of conduct and dress must be summarily eliminated. It is suggested, however, that as long as such rules are required, those who are affected should participate in their formulation. If restrictions of this nature are necessary to the good order, safety, and health of those in the school, then the problem should be shared with the students. Their ingenuity and good sense would be tested by challenging them to provide reasonable solutions. If this procedure is followed there is little likelihood of rules being promulgated simply as an excuse to exercise authority. However, in the long run, a truly democratic school will have need for few rules as an atmosphere of mutual trust, toleration, and respect is developed and as students and teachers alike work toward common goals. Perhaps one rule would suffice, "Do unto others as you would have others do unto you."

As can be surmised, student government would have a significant role in such a school. Students would, as a matter of course, participate in the work of curriculum committees. They would have an input with regard to the nature, organization, administration, and extent of extracurricular or cocurricular activities. They would have membership on athletic boards and similar policy-making bodies. They would be consulted on matters of communication between school and home, such as that represented by report cards. They would in effect be active members in the educational enterprise.

Students can be a very significant force in the development of good relations between the school and the community. They can represent the school in a very effective fashion in its relationship to the community. They can, for example, contact executives of industry, public officials, directors of art galleries, and others to arrange for field trips and laboratory learning situations outside the walls of the school but within the boundaries of the community of which the school is a part. They can help in securing lawyers, businessmen, public officials, and other members of the community to serve as vocational guidance counselors on Saturdays, after working hours, or at such other times as would be convenient for both students and citizen-counselors. These kinds of efforts would not only add to the strength of the secondary program but would give the student valuable experience in dealing with the adult world.

Students under the sponsorship of the school could organize forums and debates on local, state, and even national issues to be held in the school auditorium and be open to the public. Such discussions might involve knowledgeable local persons and experts in appropriate fields as well as students themselves. The experience of initiating, organizing, and providing such presentations would provide extremely valuable experience for students and would augment the adult education program of the school. In sponsoring such discussions, the role of the school would be to provide information and opportunity for discussion—*not* to promote any given point-of-view. In fact, impartiality and objectivity would be essential to the success of such a project.

The teacher in such a school is not simply one who imparts information but one who identifies with the common effort as a guide, a counselor, an adviser, and above all as an individual committed to the concept of democracy as a way of life. Such a teacher will not only strive to improve her teaching but also to improve her relationship with students, which in the final analysis is most likely to make her teaching truly effective in contributing to student growth and development.

In brief, the public secondary school is a public enterprise, and as such, needs the cooperation of citizens of the community to be most effective. Students are citizens, and, in the case of the school, they are the citizens most directly concerned. It follows in our society that they should actively participate in the policy-making and the administration of that enterprise. Such participation, properly guided, is bound to result in more relevent and more effective learning, as well as a more democratic institution.

Bibliography

"Constitutional Law: Right to Counsel." *New York University Law Review* 42, November 1967, p. 961.

Edwards, Newton. *The Courts and the Public Schools.* Chicago, Ill.: The University of Chicago Press, 1971.

Hazard, William R. *Education and the Law.* New York: The Free Press, 1971.

"Legal Aspects of Student-Institutional Relationships: A Conference." *Denver Law Journal* 45 (Special) 1968, p. 497.

Morgan, Warren. "A Look at the Law of Pupil Management." *Pennsylvania Bar Association Quarterly* 39, October 1967, p. 101.

Peterson, Leroy; Rossmiller, Richard A.; and Volz, Marlin M. *The Law and Public School Operation.* Evanston, Ill.: Harper and Row, 1969.

Plasco, Marvin R. "School Student Dress and Appearance Regulations." *Cleveland-Marshall Law Review* 18, January 1969, p. 143.

Ray, Montfort S. "Constitutional Law: A Student's Right to Govern his Personal Appearance." *Journal of Public Law* 17, 1968, p. 151.

Turner, Larry S. "Schools—Rules and Regulations Affecting Married Students—Reasonableness and Validity." *Western Reserve Law Review* 16, May 1965, p. 792.

Ware, Martha L., editor. *Law of Guidance and Counseling.* Cincinnati, Ohio: The W. H. Anderson Company, 1964.

Selected Readings

Wanted: A Humane Education

The Montgomery County Student Alliance

PART I—PRESENT SITUATION

Stated Educational Goals vs. Reality in County Schools

Montgomery County Public School Students who examine the public utterances and public relations rhetoric of county school officials are struck by how far removed they are from the administrative priorities and expediencies which are, in fact, shaping the experience of being educated in county schools. This gap, and its serious and often humanly catastrophic consequences, must be confronted and dealt with.

> The biggest mistake we could make would be to prepare children for today's world ... our job is to teach people to be adaptable to change.
> —Dr. Homer Elseroad
> Superintendent Montgomery County Public Schools

> While preparation for college may be a legitimate goal for a student, it cannot be justified as a goal of public education.
> Dr. James C. Craig
> Assistant Superintendant for Instructional and Pupil Services, Montgomery County Public Schools

> For many years it was generally assumed that the whole class could be taught as a unit and that it was the responsibility of the individual pupil to keep 'up with the class.' We know enough about

---

Full title: *A Study Report on the Montgomery County Public School System— Wanted: A Humane Education. An Urgent Call for Reconciliation between Rhetoric and Reality.* Issued by the Montgomery County Student Alliance, 4927 Cordell Ave., Bethesda, Maryland, February 11, 1969.

learning and psychology now to realize that this is a faulty assumption and that a class of students is a collection of individuals that must be taught, in part at least, as individuals if they are to gain the most from their school experience.
—Kenneth K. Muir
Information Director, Montgomery County Public Schools

At this point, it is appropriate to make note of an observation made by Terry Borton ("Reach, Touch, and Teach," *Saturday Review,* January 18, 1969), former co-director of the Affective Education Research Project in the Philadelphia public schools, which appears to be all too applicable to the situation in Montgomery County Public Schools:

> There are two sections to almost every school's statement of educational objectives—one for real, and one for show. The first, the real one, talks about academic excellence, subject mastery, and getting into college or a job. The other discusses the human purpose of school—values, feelings, personal growth, the full and happy life. It is imcluded because everyone knows that it is important, and that it ought to be central to the life of every school. But it is only for show. Everyone knows how little schools have done about it.

What the School System Has Done to Students

Some of the county school system's announced goals are being met. County students on the whole are equipped with certain skills and facts, and test scores and grades show that the school system has by and large prepared them for college. Despite the disavowals of Dr. Elseroad and Dr. Craig, however, the inevitable conclusion after looking at the school system on an operational level is that the county schools are basically keyed to fulfilling requirements and developing attitudes that are necessary for admittance and academic success in college and success in today's society.

The most significant effect of this emphasis on measurable, "acceptable" performance has been to subordinate greatly other basic goals of a desirable educational climate—goals which are less tangible but which, we feel and the county school system says (rhetorically) it agrees, are of far greater and more lasting importance. It is these latter goals that have, practically speaking, been almost totally ignored by the county school system and the way it operates. Feedback to see whether these much more vital aims are being fulfilled has just not been sought by school officials; to our knowledge the county schools have shown little willingness to confront these questions and bring about the fundamental changes in attitude and organization that are necessary.

From what we know to be true as full-time students and researchers of the county school system (as well as from every attempt we know of to survey student attitudes in the county), it is quite safe to say that the public schools have critically negative and absolutely destructive effects on human beings and their curiosity, natural desire to learn, confidence, individuality, creativity, freedom of thought and self-respect.

More specifically, the county public schools have the following effects which are absolutely fundamental and crucial:

1. Fear—The school system is based upon fear. Students are taught from the outset that they should be afraid of having certain things happen to them; bad grades, punishment from authorities, humiliation, ostracism, "failure," antagonizing teachers and administrators—are all things that terrify students as they enter first grade. These fears, which school officials use as a lever from elementary school through high school to establish and maintain order and obedience, have horribly destructive effects: they may be reflected in extreme nervousness, terror, paranoia, resentment, withdrawal, alienation; they may be viable, they may be submerged, but in either case these effects should be of utmost concern to those who value the human mind and spirit.

2. Dishonesty—Schools compel students to be dishonest. In order to be as "successful" as possible (the school system loses no time in providing the definition), students must learn to suppress and deny feelings, emotions, thoughts that they get the idea will not be acceptable. In the place of these honest feelings, emotions and thoughts, students are taught that to "succeed" other exteriors—dishonest though they may be—have to be substituted. The clearly defined rewards and punishments of the school system have an instructional effect on an impressionable child, and the message is clear throughout elementary school, junior high school and senior high school: "unacceptable" honesty will be punished, whether with grades, disciplinary action or a bad "permanent record"; "acceptable" responses, however dishonest, are—in the eyes of the school system and therefore according to the values it instills—simply that: "acceptable."

3. Approach to problems—It is soon clear to students what types of responses are likely to be successful at playing the high school game. And so, before too long a student's approach to questions and problems undergoes a basic change. It becomes quickly clear that approaching a question on a test by saying "What is my own honest response to this question?" is risky indeed, and totally unwise if one covets the highest grade possible (and the school system teaches the student that he should). Rather, the real question is clear to any student who knows anything about how schools work: "What is the answer the teacher wants me to give? What can I write that will please the teacher?"

4. Destruction of eagerness to learn—the school system takes young people who are interested in the things around them and destroys this natural joy in discovering and learning. Genuine, honest reasons for wanting to learn are quashed and replaced with an immediate set of rewards (which educators say are not ends in themselves but which nevertheless become just that). Real

reasons for wanting to learn—the students' own reasons—are not treated as though they were valid. As George Leonard points out in his new book *Education and Ecstasy,* and as everyone who has gone through the public schools knows, our school systems smash the natural joy in learning and make what we know as an "education" into a painful, degrading experience.

5. Alienation—With its dishonesty and premium on dutiful obedience, the school system causes feelings of resentment and alienation, whether these feelings are expressed or (as is usually the case) hidden and submerged.

6. Premium on conformity, blind obedience to authority—The school system's values and priorities *as they are practiced* ultimately become those of its students. Students—keenly aware of the rewards and punishments that can affect them—are made aware of what the school system wants most from its students on an operational basis—an actual day-by-day basis. The fact that the county school system as it presently operates puts a very large premium on conformity and "knee-jerk" obedience is, we feel, indisputable; students simply know this to be true as a fact of school life survival.

7. Stifling self-expression, honest reaction—The fact that students who "step out of line" are likely to be punished for it is not lost on students, and this provides students with a basic object lesson on how to "succeed" in the public school. Once again, this overpowering sense of rewards and punishments, which has been artificially created by the school system, has a very negative effect on the development of students.

8. Narrowing scope of ideas—The range of ideas students are exposed to by the school system is pitifully narrow, especially in the earlier grades; through use of textbooks which give only limited perspective, and through use of curriculum and teacher attitudes that are confining, students' minds are conditioned to accept what they are familiar with and reject what seems foreign.

9. Prejudice—By insisting that the schools remain pretty much isolated from ideas and cultures that do not blend in with those of the immediate community, school officials have the effect of solidifying and perpetuating local prejudices. Only with the free exchange of all kinds of different ideas and life-styles can students gain a broad outlook.

10. Self-hate—Perhaps most tragic is what the school system does to the emotional and mental attitudes and subconscious of its students. The system, for instance, is willing to and does label students as a "failure" at age eight, twelve or seventeen. In addition to the fact that this often acts as a self-fulfilling prophecy, this has a cruelly damaging and degrading effect on students, and is inexcusable. Further, tension has been shown to be an integral part of the school experience, with very damaging effects. The self-hate which results can be directed inward or at others, but whatever the

case it is extremely unhealthy; a community which says it cares about human emotions and feelings should not permit this to go on.

These are the realities that students in county schools know. Their complaints about the public schools are confirmed by the findings of the leading educators in America. As Terry Borton explained in *Saturday Review:*

> The new critics do not simply attack the schools for their academic incompetence, as did the Rickovers of a decade ago. They are equally concerned with the schools' basic lack of understanding that students are human beings with feelings as well as intellects. Jonathan Kozol has given a gripping sense of the destruction of the hearts and minds of Negro children in his *Death at an Early Age*. In *How Children Fail*, John Holt has shown that even in the best progressive schools children live in constant fear which inhibits their learning, and in Paul Goodman's *Compulsory Mis-Education* there is a powerful case for the contention that the present school system is leading straight to 1984. The intuitive warnings of these 'romantic critics' have been backed up by statistical evidence from the largest survey of education ever conducted, James Coleman's *Equality of Educational Opportunity*. This survey correlates academic achievement with attitudes such as a student's self concept, sense of control over his fate, and interest in school. The study concludes that these attitudes and feelings are more highly correlated with how well a student achieves academically than a combination of many of the factors which educators have usually thought were crucial, such as class size, salary of teachers, facilities and curriculum.

Lack of Feedback

The extent to which school officials appear unaware or unconcerned about how students feel and the effects of the schools is frightening and disturbing. Top county school administrators' discussion of the need for relevance, sensitivity to human needs and feelings, student rights and freedom of expression and exchange of ideas seems to have little connection with the policies and priorities the administrators and teachers at the individual schools are pursuing. As for many principals and teachers, they quite often are just not concerned; their concept of the school system is that its job is to mold the behavior and attitudes of its students, and those students who balk at being molded are viewed as undisciplined annoyances, to be dealt with accordingly. The feedback in the form of grades, scores and college admissions is apparently considered adequate to prove the merit of the system; all else, it seems, must take a back seat.

The Student Alliance plans to collect feedback in these neglected but crucial human areas. It is inexcusable that the Montgomery County School System has not made a real effort to seek this kind of feedback and enter it into the policy and organizational decision-making.

Inability to Make Desired Changes

Perhaps most frustrating is the fact that leading school officials in Rockville have criticized the schools and their inability and/or unwillingness to view and treat students as individual human beings.

The grading system is a good example, and extremely vital. Dr. James C. Craig, Assistant Superintendent for instructional and Pupil Services, told a MCPS seminar on human relations in August, 1968: "Any school system which participates in, or suffers to continue a system of grading which by its very nature is demeaning of the human spirit, is cruel, inhumane—which approves and accepts the bright—which disapproves of and rejects those not so bright—such a school system is not worthy to be entrusted with any concerns involving differences among human beings...." Yet no one has been willing to make the basic changes that would be necessary to stop this "demeaning, cruel, inhumane" system from continuing to take its toll on the minds and spirits of 120,000 Montgomery County Public School students.

What it appears to come down to is a lack of a sense of urgency about these kinds of issues. If a school's heating system is found not to be working, it is quickly repaired. But say that the schools are destroying the minds and morale of its students, and administrators—perhaps even agreeing theoretically—will give you a dozen reasons why corrective action cannot be taken.

If the county school system really believes what it says about its goals, then it must devote itself to bringing the actual situation in line with these aims. If the goal of allowing students to develop as free-thinking individuals is really basic to a desirable educational setup, then it is not enough to merely say, "It would be nice ... "

A disturbing example of this approach is revealed in a quote attributed to Supt. Homer O. Elseroad in the January 16, 1969 issue of *The Montgomery County Sentinel:* "There is some truth in their [the Student Alliance's] statement that the schools ought to do a better job in fostering creativity. But I don't know of any way to make some of these changes by proclamation."

We are going to have to do better than that. It is obvious that a multitude of practices and policies in the county schools are the result of "proclamations." If only we could give the same priority to making the schools humane and relevant that we now give to keeping computerized attendance cross-check cards and catching and punishing students who skip classes.

Who and What Represents Student Attitudes

It is important to realize what effect all this has had on students and what their resulting responses have been.

Just about every student in Montgomery County feels the oppressiveness of the school system. Their responses, however, differ widely.

Only a fraction of the students are oriented to organizing groups, developing analyses and recommendations and approaching school officials.

Some students drop out—for varying reasons, but increasingly because school is not relevant to what they are interested in doing. (A number of county high school students have dropped out of public school to attend a "New Educational Project" founded by unhappy students from Montgomery County along with several college graduates, including an Antioch intern who taught history at Montgomery Blair for the 1967-68 school year. Other students attend the school on a part-time basis.)

Other students cut classes or skip school entirely on a consistent basis—not an intellectualized reaction, but merely an immediate, logical response: despite the attempt at "sledgehammer" motivation through grades and threat of punishment, what is going on in the classrooms is simply not worth getting involved with. These students, thousands of them, are punished; they are providing feedback that the school system does not care for.

Even for students who are not able to maintain passing grades (or who are not interested in doing so)—and "fail" or even "flunk out," it is apparent that the schools are failing by being unable to meet a wide range of needs.

But for most students, the sad results is that they take it, in fact they learn to adapt to the system and do the best they can "to succeed"—they accept (though many of them will tell you they do so reluctantly) the idea of working for the goals that have been dreamed up for them by the school system—and they learn the most successful way to play the game. The goals—high test scores, high grades—have taken on an enormous importance. And, inevitably, in pursuing these goals, students learn the usefullness—indeed the necessity—of dishonesty, conformity and yesman-ship.

But the system's impersonal and authoritarian way of dealing with these students has taken its toll; submerged though the effects may be, the system has caused resentment, lack of self-respect and self-confidence, extreme nervousness, and/or behavior to compensate for such serious anxieties.

> When we talk about 'drop-outs' in school we are talking about how long (in time) a student has stayed in school. We are not talking about how well he is educated. For example, we view with alarm a student's decision to quit school after the eleventh grade (no matter what the reason) and yet we drop more than six thousand out at the end of the twelfth grade and lose no sleep over it. In neither case do we assess what the schooling has done for the child."
>
> —Dr. Craig

Lack of Relevance

> Our educational system in the United States is by and large totally irrelevant, except for vocational education. For the most part, it is confusing, intellectually dishonest, even depressing . . . Teachers still view the cranium as an empty vessel to be stuffed with facts. If you do it right, the right moral and ethical decisions will come out. This is baloney. The bright human being is saying No, No, I don't want this. . . .

—Albert Leas
Supervisor of Social Studies for elementary schools
Montgomery County Public Schools

The public school as an institution for educating children is rapidly becoming obsolete. For the most part its programs are dull and boring, intellectually sterile, and almost totally unrelated to the real concerns of youth, or to the concerns of society outside of school. . . .

—Dr. Craig

It is becoming almost a cliché to say that the public schools are not relevant, yet very little positive action has been taken to do anything about it. Every student has things that interest him; but the sad fact is that the school system very rarely gives him an opportunity to explore these interests. In many cases the student is actually hindered by the pressures and restrictions of the school system. There is no provision for giving students the chance to explore different areas of interest and follow wherever this exploration may lead them.

Knowledge is very much inter-related—math, science, history, literature and psychology, for instance, all have a great deal to do with one another, and the ways in which they have interacted have been fundamental to the development of man. Yet the school system insists on compartmentalizing these topics and creates artificial boundaries around each area. This makes learning seem narrow and confining; there is no need for it to be anything of the kind.

By the time a student reaches high school, attending school often seems to be a dull, boring and irrational experience that is viewed as something that simply has to be tolerated. This state of affairs should not exist.

Very importantly, the individual student himself, who he is, what he feels, his concerns are ignored. How does he fit into all this? What is important to him? What does this mean to him and to his life? These questions do not fit into the school system's equation. Assisted by experience and efficiency, the county public school's operational equation seems simple: raw material (students) plus conditioning (classes, teachers, textbooks, discipline) equals products (graduates equipped to fill the necessary slots in society). The complexities of the individual developing human mind are passed over; the system is "successful," and, we are told, is among the best in the nation.

Instead of the system's being built around the needs of the students, the students are being built around the needs of the system.

Student Freedom and Civil Liberties

If you see any copies of the Washington Free Press in possession of a student, confiscate it immediately. Any questions from the student regarding this confiscation should be referred to the administration. If you see a student selling or distributing this paper, refer them [sic] to an administrator and they will be suspended.

—Memorandum to Staff from the Principal,

tration. If you see a student selling or distributing this paper, refer them [sic] to an administrator and they will be suspended.
—Memorandum to Staff from the Principal,
Gaithersburg High School, February 4, 1969

I don't want to hear anything about Constitutional rights, student rights, human rights or any other rights.
—Wheaton Principal to students guilty of
possession of the Washington Free Press
in the school library, February 7, 1969

The situation that exists with regard to student freedom of expression and civil liberties is a disturbing reflection of the school system's operational priorities. Students at one secondary school or another in the county are constantly being suspended, disciplined or threatened for trying to distribute "unauthorized" student publications or statements or for being a threat to student "discipline." This has the effect of penalizing students who insist on their right to express their opinions.

The school system responds to such charges by saying that students are free to express themselves as long as they get whatever they have to say "approved" by going through proper channels. But "going through proper channels" with unpopular opinions still involves many risks, on top of the fact that administrators are free not to authorize whatever they don't like for whatever reasons. (There is still the case of the Bethesda high school where, even after approaching the county school officials as well as the principal, students putting out an underground newspaper have not been allowed to distribute their publication on school grounds. The administration-sanctioned newspaper, however, is permitted to collect money for its publication and sale on school grounds.) Counselors, principals and teachers, sometimes not even bothering to be subtle, make it clear to students they consider "troublemakers" that they have control over college recommendations and "permanent record files."

In the way of a few examples: One student who insisted that he would protest against the Vietnam War in front of the school was told by a vice-principal that if the student persisted the school official would see to it that he could not get into college . . . Another high school student, a National Merit Scholarship Finalist as it happened, was told by his counselor that he would get a bad recommendation for college because he was a "nihilist." He had been arguing with her over the value of the county school system . . . The last few weeks several disciplinary actions have been taken against high school students for passing out leaflets, distributing personal statements protesting actions taken against other students or merely possessing "unauthorized" leaflets. One girl caught in "possession" of leaflets was threatened with suspension if she tried to distribute them . . . A student at another school was called to the office and received a lecture from a vice-principal who admonished her for her political beliefs.

Interestingly, administrators at individual schools sometimes allude to "county regulations" in justifying their actions which county officials say do not exist.

Although the county school system says it does not approve of such practices, they are still going on, and they are usually very difficult to pin down. Apparently, the county's position on such goings-on has not been fully or forcefully communicated sufficiently to teachers, counselors and administrators. Very importantly, there has been no attempt to provide a means for having such cases recognized and rooted out; this would have to mean the establishment of a county office with the aim of eliminating practices which the county school system has said it does not approve of.

The announced county policy regarding censorship of student newspapers is too ambiguous in that it allows sponsors and principals to make totally subjective evaluations of the "suitability" or "taste" or "appropriateness" of what students want to write. The ACLU statement on this matter is relevant.

Due Process

The average student is unaware that he has any rights, and administrators wishing to dispatch with "difficulties" as smoothly and efficiently as possible do nothing to change this feeling. The typical student feels himself to be at the mercy of school administrators, and in practice indeed he is.

The school system must not be afraid to directly inform every student of his rights, and must recognize the unhealthy effects keeping students "off balance" by failing to assure them of their fundamental protective rights. Students must be able to know where they stand, and the fact that they do not has the effect mentioned earlier.

Dress Codes

Dress codes in high schools appear to be on the way out, and this is a healthy development. There are still some high schools, especially in the upper part of Montgomery County, where rigid dress regulations are still being enforced, and it would seem unfair to have this unnecessary regulation still imposed on these students.

Rigid dress codes—often bordering on the absurd—are very common in the county's junior high schools, no doubt owing to the fact that these students have very little power to determine or even voice opinions about the regulations that affect them.

We feel it would be a healthy development if the School Board would vote to eliminate dress codes at all Montgomery County secondary schools.

Innovation and Teachers

Being an innovative teacher in county schools appears to be something of a risky business. There are some, to be sure, in the system who do what they can and still remain within the confines of the schools and their regulations.

But all too often the school system poses all sorts of obstacles for teachers and students who wish to make their classes into relevant, meaningful experiences. The school system should have provisions which aid and encourage flexibility and innovation. Yet many teachers say it is extremely difficult to "go through the proper channels" and get permission to try new programs, approaches or techniques. More specifically, some teachers tell students they are bound by the requirement that letter grades be given for each course every six weeks; these teachers say they want to innovate but are confined. In addition, a required "curve" for the distribution of different letter grades is still in use.

But there is evidence that innovative teachers are reprimanded by principals. One glaring example is the case of the four Antioch interns who came to county high schools in the fall of 1967, full of progressive approaches to education. Joel Denker, who taught history at Blair, displeased the administration and undoubtedly would not have been allowed to return for the 1968-69 school year. But Denker was extremely critical of the way the schools are run and, together with unhappy county high school students, has set up the New Educational Project mentioned earlier.

Two of the Antioch interns taught at Wheaton High School during the 1967-68 school year. They were popular and students said they were responsible for challenging students to think for themselves. Neither of the two returned to Wheaton this year. One of the pair was transferred to Kennedy, the county's token "progressive" high school.

As for the second teacher, the following story appeared in the Wheaton student newspaper, the *Open Door:*

> Mr. Jay Rung, a history teacher here last year, has temporarily left the teaching profession to continue studies at Antioch College. Mr. Rung has not been informed why, but he will not be able to teach in Montgomery County Public Schools again ... Mr. Rung believes that human beings are 'naturally positive and curious.' He feels that education should not be a punishment ... The present system does not encourage student creativity and searching for ideas as much as the unstructured system Mr. Rung would like to see. He feels that maybe people's immediate reaction to this freedom might not be entirely good, but that after awhile people, being usually positive, would adjust and use greater freedom advantageously....
>
> Mr. Rung feels dissatisfied with the system to the point where he's inclined to give up.

Experimental Efforts

Kennedy High School has existed for four-and-a-half years. The only high school in the county with any sort of significant flexibility, Kennedy is without a doubt successful in the eyes of its students, though many note that it sometimes takes a while to be able to shake off the bad effects of previous years in the school system. So, the obvious question to county school officials: Why aren't all the secondary schools like Kennedy?

The system is proud of the "Experiment in Free Form Education" scheduled to last a week at Whitman High School in March. It is a hopeful development. We can only wonder about the 17 other high schools, scores of junior highs and—at Whitman—about the other 35 weeks of the school year.

All over the country, school systems are trying new programs and developing schools which do not restrict student development as much as orthodox schools; Newton High School in Massachusetts is a good example.

The Montgomery County school system must learn to measure the "success" of an educational setup differently than it apparently does at present. It must start getting—and using—feedback dealing with how the school system helps the student develop individually, what effects its form and structure have on his self concept and whether it gives him confidence, stimulates him and helps him to learn for the reasons that are most important to him.

Discipline and Tension

County public schools are places of tension. The fact that many students seem to have adapted to this situation merely provides a cover for a horrible reality—the discipline and pressures created by the schools and imposed on students destroy and warp them in a magnitude that far overshadows any benefits that could have been imagined. A school system which causes its students to feel insecure, tense and open to punishment for a multitude of petty infractions cannot claim to be meeting the most vital needs of its students.

Basis Upon Which Decisions Are Made

It is all too clear that the most fundamental operational priority of individual school administrators is order and keeping everything running smoothly. The fact that this often means mistreating, manipulating, scaring, threatening and destroying students in the process seems to make no difference. Students are treated collectively like cattle—it makes for easier handling.

Priorities

County education officials are often willing in many cases to concede the extremely harmful effects of the school system outlined in this report. The fact that comprehensive corrective action has not been taken, and that in the meantime thousands of county students continue to be emotionally assaulted by the school system, can only be regarded as indications of tragic insensitivity of the most fundamental and vital of human needs.

PART II—WHAT NEEDS TO BE DONE

A Program for Change

1. Establishment of an ombudsman office, responsible directly to the Board of Education, to investigate and resolve complaints from students.

If the goals and realities of the school system are ever to be brought into line with one another, it is essential that a procedure be developed to deal with instances of questionable treatment of students. Every student in county schools should be informed of the existence and purpose of the ombudsman office, and they should be made to feel free to make use of it without any fear of retaliation. It is important that the ombudsman office not be in the position of having to be defensive about the actions of school administrators and teachers. Ombudsman officials, independent of any such pressures or biases, must take a stance of neutrality and work vigorously to correct the thousands of injustices which occur every year to students who presently have no way of seeking redress.

2. The school system must put an end to intimidation of students through abuse of college recommendations, grades, secret files and "permanent record files" by school officials.

These incidents are often hard to pin down, but students are definitely being blackmailed and intimidated—with varying degrees of subtlety—through use of these documents. Students must be given access to their own files, and must have control over who can and cannot see them. The Board of Education should issue a firm memo to all teachers, administrators and counselors in the county schools emphasizing the Board's disapproval of intimidation and anything short of straightforward dealings with students in these areas. In addition, the ombudsman office for students should work to uncover and eliminate misuse of these files and documents.

3. Students must have an important role in the shaping and implementation of courses. They are also in an excellent position to provide meaningful feedback by providing continuous evaluation of the effectiveness, strengths and weaknesses of their classes.

The school system has "proclaimed" many policies and has made them stick. Teachers should be told that it is essential to have students discuss how courses and classes should be designed and operated. This continual re-evaluation will see to it that classes and courses of study are constantly improved and updated. County school officials determining courses of study must be willing to permit much more flexibility and originality than is presently allowed. Departmental faculty meetings, it should be made clear, are open to participation and input from students. On the individual class level, the successes and failures of the class can be continually evaluated by students and teachers working together and planning together.

4. Student input in teacher evaluations.

Being a good teacher involves many characteristics beyond the ability to keep accurate records, complete forms neatly, "control classes" and receive degrees from graduate school. Whether a teacher is stimulating, creates enthusiasm, is responsive to individual needs and problems of his students, can relate to students (and vice versa) and treats students with respect for their human dignity is all extremely important. Students are in the best position to provide very valuable information in these areas, and it would seem logical to construct a regular system for obtaining such feedback from students.

5. Tension and rigidity must be eliminated from the schools. Administrators must be made to stop constantly threatening students with arbitrary, almost whimsical disciplinary actions.

This implies a change in attitude; an elimination of the approach which says that to have students expressing themselves, verbally and through interaction, can pose a threat to the "authority" and "order" of the school system. Students are being pressured, threatened and suspended for skipping classes, being in the halls without passes or even possession and/or distribution of literature. A system which has an elaborate policing-system network for keeping students out of the halls and for catching students who chose not to attend classes is perpetuating tension which is absolutely unnecessary, damaging to morale and totally out of place in an institution which says it seeks to encourage learning and exploration.

6. Hiring of educators and researchers to deeply examine what effect the school system has on a student's self concept, creativity, and desire to explore and learn.

Much of the evidence and research in this area, we feel, has already been developed (and is presently being ignored—no doubt because the findings are so very unpleasant). The study mentioned earlier, James Coleman's Equality of Educational Opportunity, shows that self concept and sense of control over one's own destiny is much more significant in the development of a child than the many other factors school administrators spend all their time worrying about. The forces which presently destroy a student's self concept and feeling of control over his own fate must be eliminated immediately. We feel it is clear that this is going to have to mean elimination of the disciplinary threats and punishments prevailing throughout the school system, of the clockworklike class schedules and tension created by school administrators and teachers who have been encouraged to emphasize and flaunt their authority.

7. Elimination of letter grades.

This is extremely important. The use of letter grades as the basis upon which the school system is operated sets the tone and patterns of the public school experience. Its destructive effects have already been noted.

In elementary and junior high schools, grades should be abolished immediately and replaced with written evaluations by the teacher. In high school, students should simply receive credit or not receive credit for each course he has taken. In order for the students to get feedback as to how they are progressing, teachers should provide students with written and/or oral evaluations as often as necessary. Students should receive a copy of all written evaluations; a copy could be entered in students' files, but should not be released to colleges without student-parent consent.

Transition may seem rather difficult at first. But the benefits will be both immediate and increasingly apparent as students make the adjustment and begin to shake off the bad attitudes and effects of the old system. The natural joy in learning will re-emerge, and hopefully for those starting out in the system it would never be squashed in the first place.

If a complete change is made for all the schools in the county, colleges will have no choice but to consider each applicant from the county on their individual merits; they would be forced to do without grades and class rank in evaluating applicants (there are many other methods of evaluation), especially in view of the reputation Montgomery County enjoys nationally as a school system of unquestionable academic quality.

There are ways if there is the will.

8. Teachers must be encouraged and allowed to respond to the individual needs of their students. This will have to mean fewer regulatory restrictions, more flexibility.

9. Students must be given the ability to exercise control over what happens to them in school. Specifics: The right to transfer out of a course that is not satisfactory; the right to go on independent study at any time; the right to formulate their own goals and how they can best go about achieving them.

10. Rigid periods now being used in county secondary schools must be replaced with shorter and more flexible modules.

Kennedy High School's use of modules—short blocks of time—make the school more flexible and open to different kinds of activities. There are now no provisions for spontaneous activities; in fact, they are absolutely prohibited. Periods which last 50 minutes or an hour are confining and should be eliminated. Elimination of bells would be a healthy development.

11. Students must have a right to print and distribute their own publications, and restrictions should not be set up to impose obstacles—as has been the case—but rather to provide students with an orderly means of distribution, such as tables in the halls, near doors or in the cafeteria. These requirements should apply equally to all student publications. (The fact that money is involved has been used as an argument against allowing "underground" or unsanctioned papers, but money is always also involved with sanctioned, official student newspapers.)

12. Students have the right to have the freedom to decide what they want to print in student newspapers, literary magazines and yearbooks. Censorship by sponsors or principals, whatever the degree of subtlety, must not be allowed.

13. Outside speakers must be given a chance to speak to students without favoritism or discrimination.

Military recruiters, for example, address assemblies at each county high school every year, but the same right has been refused to groups presenting different or opposing viewpoints. Students must make the decisions to invite speakers and arrange assemblies.

14. The providing of the names and addresses of senior boys to the armed forces must be ended.

The county school system makes a point of its desire to protect students from businesses who get hold of mailing lists of students, yet it provides the names and addresses of senior boys in county high schools to the military. Peace and pacifist groups have been refused the same privilege. The lists should either be available to groups which disagree with the military or should not be released at all.

15. Relevant courses must be developed to meet student interest.

Students should be surveyed as to what courses they would like to see offered, and the results should play a determining role in the direction of course offerings. Racism, urban life, suburban life, drugs, human relations, foreign policy, police-youth relations and civil liberties are a few topics in great need of curriculum development.

16. Students should be free to arrange voluntary seminars to be held during the school day.

If schools are really to become relevant, students must be allowed—indeed encouraged—to set up discussions, hold workshops and seminars, hear speakers who are well-informed about the subjects that interest students. The students should be free to invite speakers and outside authorities to come in and give their views, without the obstacles which presently exist. Schools must come alive. The concept behind the "Experiment in Free Form Education" being tried at Whitman for one week must be integrated into the everyday functioning of the schools. With schools becoming much more individualized, students should be given the flexibility of attending seminars of interest during the school day.

17. Expansion of the range of resources.

Diversified paperback books giving different perspectives could play an important part in widening the scope of thought and exposure in the schools. Textbooks alone are just too limited in coverage and perspective.

18. Informing students of their rights.

The school system should take the responsibility of informing each student of his rights in dealing with administrators and teachers. If the School Board agrees that students do have rights, then it must be willing to make these rights directly known to each student.

19. Restrictions having to do with student dress must be eliminated throughout the county.

20. County seminars in human relations, racism and progressive teaching methods should be held for teachers.

An excellent week of seminars was held by the Montgomery County Public Schools last August for about 100 county administrators. It would be

Selected Readings 153

very good if the same sort of program could be set up for the county's teachers.

21. Material thoroughly exploring Negro history must be integrated into classes such as U.S. History and Problems of the 20th Century. Special training should be provided to teachers in order to make them qualified to deal with this very important aspect of American history and society.

22. The School Board should launch an investigation of illegal searches of lockers in secondary schools for drugs and the recruiting by school officials of students to become narcotics informers.

School officials have been known to actively seek and encourage students to become drug informers. The unhealthy atmosphere which such a situation creates should be a matter of concern. We feel the School Board would agree that it is not a desirable situation to have students promoted to act as spies on other students in school. Such activities have no place in an institution of learning.

23. School Board hearings for students.

It is important that school officials come into contact with the concerns of students. The Board could schedule hearings every two weeks at which time students would be invited to testify and voice complaints and suggestions.

24. Student voice on School Board.

The School Board would do well to include representation of students. Every semester the School Board could supervise the election of student representatives from among county high school students, printing a special bulletin for each high school student which would give the positions of each of the students who had volunteered to run for the positions.

In Partnership With Youth

At times, youth feel they are being "manipulated," and make no bones about expressing resentment. This is a way of reacting against attempts not only by teachers but by social and cultural institutions, political parties, and businessmen to direct or influence them. Institutions, customs, and economic conditions have altered, and most young people of today start working at a later age than their parents did. No doubt this is an improvement, but such a long wait tends to isolate youth in society. It keeps them in a situation where they are denied the rights and responsibilities of adulthood because of the very fact that they are unbound by its main obligations.

But there is probably nothing that has influenced youth more deeply than the impact of scientific and technological development on society, the crisis of our tentacular cities and the revolution in our modern ways of life and high speed communications.

These factors have disturbed, bewildered, and disrupted the lives of the young, but at the same time they have given youth unique opportunities for assertion. The role of young people in the modern world has thus taken on extraordinary new *dimensions,* not only because of their sheer strength of numbers but also because of the specific part they can play in the changes implied by modern development.

Youth have now achieved the status of a distinct community. This has led to the most basic conflict of all: it stems from youth's determination to win from society the status and esteem they deem to be their right. It is endemic in universities and schools, in factories and villages, and certainly in institutions designed for youth but usually run by adults.

Reprinted from the UNESCO Courier, April 1969, distributed in the U.S. by Unipub, Inc., 650 First Avenue, New York, N.Y. 10016. Also published as a booklet under the title *In Partnership with Youth.* © UNESCO, 1969.

These demands often clash with the adult world's tendency to regard youth as awaiting admission into society. Until the young have crossed the barrier, adults believe they have no claim on all the rights denied them—even though this does not prevent society from demanding youth's contribution when necessary.

Then there is an intellectual and moral conflict that widens the gap between youth and adults with every passing day. Modern information media familiarize youth with different cultures while ignoring frontiers. On a world scale, a sort of international "youth culture" seems to have sprung up. It clashes head-on with an adult culture still fenced in by tradition.

This leads to conflicts of opinions, customs, and behavior and ethical principles that affect the very foundations of modern society. It raises problems whose gravity is keenly felt on all sides. These may be the hardest problems of all to solve under present circumstances.

Even when adults accept children as personalities, they often refuse to admit that children can exist as a community by and among themselves. Instead of aiding the creation of a youthful society, adults fight it in different ways: discipline, punishments, competition, appeals to pride, and other methods that try to force the child to conform to adult society.

Certain young people even see "manipulation" in efforts to "cultivate" them before they are old enough to put up a fight against the prestige and the pitfalls of a ready-made culture. They can also rebel against other efforts to lead them into "participation" or "dialogues" in exchange for reforms that they consider of no importance.

They insist on changes in the content of university education to make it pay more heed to youth's real concerns in all fields whether cultural, personal, social, political, or professional. They start by criticizing the university; in many cases, they end with the idea of a "critical university." Finally, they seek to change the style of life in the universities themselves.

In other words, a growing proportion of modern youth feels a malaise whether they are college or secondary school students, young workers or rural youth. They want "freer, franker, and warmer human relations than what they get from us." They are afraid that "the national and international system into which they are being driven contains grave injustices to which they do not want to be party."

Many young people refuse to participate in public life—but many more insist on their rights to do so. This demand derives not only from an interest in public life but also because they regard it as a prerequisite for winning the rights, still the privilege of adults, that will enable them to break away from their status as minors.

At other times, they refuse to participate even when given the chance. They are afraid that if they "sold out" to the Establishment they would lose their dynamism and their influence as a protest group.

It is true that a permanent dialogue is needed with youth—but it is also true that such a dialogue can be fruitful only if it influences decision-making bodies. Youth occasionally feel that willingness to talk conceals a total lack of willingness to share the power of decision-making.

More and more often, secondary school children above a certain age and especially college students insist on participating in the formulation of curricula. Youth want to lend a hand to the shaping of new university structures and in devising new ways to give examinations and select students.

Even student extremists do not seem to be trying to take the reins of authority away from the teachers but simply to find a common ground for discussion, using simpler and more human forms of communication. This is conscious and responsible participation; it is spreading student government beyond classrooms into the lunchrooms, dormitories, and general disciplinary machinery of secondary schools.

At one extreme of public opinion, there is an attitude that just about affirms that the whole youth crisis is "artificial" and that their revolt is simply dictated from within by their own status and hopes.

Another attitude consists of considering the youth movement as isolated with its own laws and outside our overall social context. This does not fit the evidence of recent years that have seen youth like adults refuse to remain on the same side all the time.

They can oppose their own social group, yet conform to it. They can seek and find allies or strongholds in another social group, then adopt its mode of behavior. Youth and adults still seem permanently linked, and, despite superficial appearances, no one can describe the present situation in terms of "father-and-son struggles."

In many respects, youth's new ways of action are healthy ways. They help give new forms of expression to the reaction against outdated social and political structures. In particular, the adult world realizes that educational systems can be reformed and renovated only with the participation of youth.

One must face facts, however; in its present form, this appeal to the generosity of the young often tends to use them, to mobilize them as involuntary "volunteers". Ideally, it should be based on civic spirit or solidarity and it certainly should give youth a say in the process of development which, after all, will determine their future.

It is equally obvious that youth can play such a role only in a system that enables them to take a hand both in the preparation and the execution of plans as full-fledged participants.

Three Court Cases

ORDWAY v. HARGRAVES

Pregnant Unmarried Student Cannot Be Excluded from School Attendance

CAFFREY, DISTRICT JUDGE. This is a civil action brought on behalf of an 18-year-old pregnant, unmarried, senior at the North Middlesex Regional High School, Townsend, Massachusetts. The respondents are the Principal of the High School, Robert Hargraves, the seven individual members of the North Middlesex Regional High School Committee, and the School Committees of Pepperell and Townsend. The cause of action is alleged to arise under the Civil Rights Act, 42 U.S.C.A. 1983, and jurisdiction of this court is invoked under 28 U.S.C.A. 1343. The matter came before the court for hearing on plaintiff's application for preliminary injunctive relief in the nature of an order requiring respondents to re-admit her to the Regional High School on a full-time, regular-class-hour, basis.

At the hearing, eight witnesses testified. On the basis of the credible evidence adduced at the hearing, I find that the minor plaintiff, Fay Ordway, resides at East Pepperell, Massachusetts, and is presently enrolled as a senior in the North Middlesex Regional High School; and that plaintiff informed Mr. Hargraves, approximately January 28, 1971, that she was pregnant and expected to give birth to a baby in June 1971. There is outstanding a rule of the Regional school committee, numbered Rule 821, which provides: "Whenever an unmarried girl enrolled in North Middlesex Regional High School shall be known to be pregnant, her membership in the school shall be immediately terminated." Because of the imminence of certain examinations and the fact that school vacation was beginning on February 12, Mr. Hargraves informed

United States District Court, D. Massachusetts, 1971. 323 F.Supp. 1155.

plaintiff that she was to stop attending regular classes at the high school as of the close of school on February 12. This instruction was confirmed in writing by a letter from Mr. Hargraves to plaintiff's mother, Mrs. Iona Ordway, dated February 22, 1971, in which Mr. Hargraves stated that the following conditions would govern Fay Ordway's relations with the school for the remainder of the school year:

1. Fay will absent herself from school during regular school hours.
2. Fay will be allowed to make use of all school facilities such as library, guidance, administrative, teaching, etc., on any school day after the normal dismissal time of 2:16 P.M.
3. Fay will be allowed to attend all school function such as games, dances, plays, etc.
4. Participation in senior activities such as class trip, reception, etc.
5. Seek extra help from her teachers during after school help sessions when needed.
6. Tutoring at no cost if necessary; such tutors to be approved by the administration.
7. Her name will remain on the school register for the remainder of the 1970–71 school year (to terminate on graduation day—tentatively scheduled for June 11, 1971).
8. Examinations will be taken periodically based upon mutual agreement between Fay and the respective teacher.

Thereafter, plaintiff retained counsel, a hearing was requested, and was held by the school committee on March 3, 1971. The school committee approved the instructions and proposed schedule set out in Mr. Hargraves' letter of February 22, and a complaint was filed in this court on March 8.

It is well-established that in order to obtain a preliminary injunction, the plaintiff must satisfy two requirements, (1) that denial of the injunction will cause certain and irreparable injury to the plaintiff, Celebrity, Inc. v. Trina, Inc., 264 F.2d 956 (1 Cir. 1959), and (2) "that there is a reasonable probability that (she) will ultimately prevail in the litigation." Cuneo Press of N.E., Inc. v. Watson, 293 F. Supp. 112 (D.Mass.1968).

At the hearing, Dr. F. Woodward Lewis testified that he is plaintiff's attending physician and that she is in excellent health to attend school. He expressed the opinion that the dangers in attending school are no worse for her than for a non-pregnant girl student, and that she can participate in all ordinary school activities with the exception of violent calisthenics. An affidavit of Dr. Charles R. Goyette, plaintiff's attending obstetrician, was admitted in evidence, in which Dr. Goyette corroborated the opinions of Dr.

Lewis and added his opinion that "there is no reason that Miss Ordway could not continue to attend school until immediately before delivery."

Dr. Dorothy Jane Worth, a medical doctor, employed as Director of Family Health Services, Massachusetts Department of Public Health, testified that in her opinion exclusion of plaintiff will cause plaintiff mental anguish which will affect the course of her pregnancy. She further testified that policies relating to allowing or forbidding pregnant girls to attend high school are now widely varying within the state and throughout the United States. She testified that both Boston and New York now allow attendance of unmarried pregnant students in their high schools. She further testified that she was not aware of any reason why any health problems which arose during the day at school could not be handled by the registered nurse on duty at the high school.

Dr. Mary Jane England, a medical-doctor and psychiatrist attached to the staff of St. Elizabeth's Hospital, expressed the opinion that young girls in plaintiff's position who are required to absent themselves from school become depressed, and that the depression of the mother has an adverse effect on the child, who frequently is born depressed and lethargic. She further testified that from a psychiatric point of view it is desirable to keep a person in the position of plaintiff in as much contact with her friends and peer group as possible, and that they should not be treated as having a malady or disease.

Mrs. Janice Montague, holder of a Master's degree in social work from Simmons Graduate School, testified that on the basis of her eleven years experience working with Crittenton House, she has learned that the consensus among social workers who specialize in working with pregnant unwed girls is to give to the individual the choice of whether to remain in class or to have private instruction after regular class hours.

Plaintiff testified that her most recent grades were an A, a B-plus, and two C-pluses, and that she strongly desires to attend school with her class during regular school hours. She testified that she has not been subjected to any embarrassment by her classmates, nor has she been involved in any disruptive incidents of any kind. She further testified that she has not been aware of any resentment or any other change of attitude on the part of the other students in the school. This opinion of plaintiff as to her continuing to enjoy a good relationship with her fellow students was corroborated by the school librarian, Laura J. Connolly.

The remaining witness for plaintiff was Dr. Norman A. Sprinthall, Chairman of the Guidance Program, Harvard Graduate School of Education, who testified that in his opinion the type of program spelled out in Mr. Hargraves' letter of February 22, for after-hours instruction, was not educationally the equal of regular class attendance and participation.

It is clear, from the hearing, that no attempt is being made to stigmatize or punish plaintiff by the school principal or, for that matter, by the school committees. It is equally clear that were plaintiff married, she would be allowed to remain in class during regular school hours despite her pregnancy. Mr. Hargraves made it clear that the decision to exclude plaintiff was not his personal decision, but was a decision he felt required to make in view of the policy of the school committee which he is required to enforce as part of his duties as principal. In response to questioning, Mr. Hargraves could not state any educational purpose to be served by excluding plaintiff from regular class hours, and he conceded that plaintiff's pregnant condition has not occasioned any disruptive incident nor has it otherwise interfered with school activities. Cf. Tinker v. Des Moines Independent Community School District, 393 U.S. 503, 514, 89 S.Ct. 733, 740, 21 L.Ed.2d 731 (1969), where the Supreme Court limited school officials' curtailment of claimed rights of students to situations involving "substantial disruption of or material interference with school activities."

Mr. Hargraves did imply, however, his opinion is that the policy of the school committee might well be keyed to a desire on the part of the school committee not to appear to condone conduct on the part of unmarried students of a nature to cause pregnancy. The thrust of his testimony seems to be: the regional school has both junior and senior high school students in its student population; he finds the twelve-to-fourteen age group to be still flexible in their attitudes; they might be led to believe that the school authorities are condoning premarital relations if they were to allow girl students in plaintiff's situation to remain in school.

It should be noted that if concerns of this nature were a valid ground for the school committee regulation, the contents of paragraph b), c) and d) of Mr. Hargarves' letter of February 22 to plaintiff's mother substantially undercut those considerations.

In summary, no danger to petitioner's physical or mental health resultant from her attending classes during regular school hours has been shown; no likelihood that her presence will cause any disruption of or interference with school activities or pose a threat of harm to others has been shown; and no valid educational or other reason to justify her segregation and to require her to receive a type of educational treatment which is not the equal of that given to all others in her class has been shown.

It would seem beyond argument that the right to receive a public school education is a basic personal right or liberty. Consequently, the burden of justifying any school rule or regulation limiting or terminating that right is on the school authorities. Cf. Richards v. Thurston, 424 F.2d 1281, at 1286 (1 Cir. 1970), where the court ruled:

> In the absence of an inherent, self-evident justification on the face of the rule, we conclude that the burden was on the defendant.

On the record before me, respondents have failed to carry this burden. Accordingly, it is ordered:

Selected Readings

1. Respondents are to re-admit plaintiff to regular attendance at North Middlesex Regional High School until further order of this court.
2. This order will be effective as of the opening of school, at 8:00 A.M., Monday, March 15, 1971.

TINKER v. DES MOINES INDEPENDENT COMMUNITY
SCHOOL DISTRICT

Armband Regulation Denies Students Right of Free Speech

MR. JUSTICE FORTAS delivered the opinion of the Court.

Petitioner John F. Tinker, 15 years old, and petitioner Christopher Eckhardt, 16 years old, attended high schools in Des Moines, Iowa. Petitioner Mary Beth Tinker, John's sister, was a 13-year-old student in junior high school.

In December 1965, a group of adults and students in Des Moines held a meeting at the Eckhardt home. The group determined to publicize their objections to the hostilities in Vietnam and their support for a truce by wearing black armbands during the holiday season and by fasting on December 16 and New Year's Eve. Petitioners and their parents had previously engaged in similar activities, and they decided to participate in the program.

The principals of the Des Moines schools became aware of the plan to wear armbands. On December 14, 1965, they met and adopted a policy that any student wearing an armband to school would be asked to remove it, and if he refused he would be suspended until he returned without the armband. Petitioners were aware of the regulation that the school authorities adopted.

On December 16, Mary Beth and Christopher wore black armbands to their schools. John Tinker wore his armband the next day. They were all sent home and suspended from school until they would come back without their armbands. They did not return to school until after the planned period for wearing armbands had expired—that is, until after New Year's Day.

This complaint was filed in the United States District Court by petitioners, through their fathers, under § 1983 of Title 42 of the United States Code. It prayed for an injunction restraining the respondent school officials and the respondent members of the board of directors of the school district from disciplining the petitioners, and it sought nominal damages. After an evidentiary hearing the District Court dismissed the complaint. It upheld the constitutionality of the school authorities' action on the ground that it was reasonable in order to prevent disturbance of school discipline. 258 F.Supp. 971 (1966). The court referred to but expressly declined to follow the Fifth Circuit's holding in a similar case that the wearing of symbols like the

---

Supreme Court of the United States, 1969. 393 U.S. 503, 89 S.Ct. 733.

armbands cannot be prohibited unless it "materially and substantially interfere[s] with the requirements of appropriate discipline in the operation of the school." Burnside v. Byars, 363 F.2d 744, 749 (1966).

On appeal, the Court of Appeals for the Eighth Circuit considered the case *en banc.* The court was equally divided, and the District Court's decision was accordingly affirmed, without opinion. 383 F.2d 988 (1967). We granted certiorari. 390 U.S. 942, 88 S.Ct. 1050, 19 L.Ed.2d 1130 (1968).

The District Court recognized that the wearing of an armband for the purpose of expressing certain views is the type of symbolic act that is within the Free Speech Clause of the First Amendment. See West Virginia v. Barnette, 319 U.S. 624, 63 S.Ct. 1178, 87 L.Ed. 1628 (1943); Stromberg v. California, 283 U.S. 359, 51 S.Ct. 532, 75 L.Ed. 1117 (1931). Cf. Thornhill v. Alabama, 310 U.S. 88, 60 S.Ct. 736, 84 L.Ed. 1093 (1940); Edwards v. South Carolina, 372 U.S. 229, 83 S.Ct. 680, 9 L.Ed.2d 697 (1963); Brown v. Louisiana, 383 U.S. 131, 86 S.Ct. 719, 15 L.Ed.2d 637 (1966). As we shall discuss, the wearing of armbands in the circumstances of this case was entirely divorced from actually or potentially disruptive conduct by those participating in it. It was closely akin to "pure speech" which, we have repeatedly held, is entitled to comprehensive protection under the First Amendment. Cf. Cox v. Louisiana, 379 U.S. 536, 555, 85 S.Ct. 453, 464, 13 L.Ed.2d 471 (1965); Adderley v. Florida, 385 U.S. 39, 87 S.Ct. 242, 17 L.Ed.2d 149 (1966).

First Amendment rights, applied in light of the special characteristics of the school environment, are available to teachers and students. It can hardly be argued that either students or teachers shed their constitutional rights to freedom of speech or expression at the schoolhouse gate. This has been the unmistakable holding of this Court for almost 50 years.

The school officials banned and sought to punish petitioners for a silent, passive expression of opinion, unaccompanied by any disorder or disturbance on the part of petitioners. There is here no evidence whatever of petitioners' interference, actual or nascent, with the schools' work or of collision with the rights of other students to be secure and to be let alone. Accordingly, this case does not concern speech or action that intrudes upon the work of the schools or the rights of other students.

Only a few of the 18,000 students in the school system wore the black armbands. Only five students were suspended for wearing them. There is no indication that the work of the schools or any class was disrupted. Outside the classrooms, a few students made hostile remarks to the children wearing armbands, but there were no threats or acts of violence on school premises.

The District Court concluded that the action of the school authorities was reasonable because it was based upon their fear of a disturbance from the wearing of the armbands. But, in our system, undifferentiated fear or apprehension of disturbance is not enough to overcome the right to freedom of expression. Any departure from absolute regimentation may cause trouble.

Any variation from the majority's opinion may inspire fear. Any word spoken, in class, in the lunchroom, or on the campus, that deviates from the views of another person may start an argument or cause a disturbance. But our Constitution says we must take this risk, Terminiello v. Chicago, 337 U.S. 1, 69 S.Ct. 894, 93 L.Ed. 1131 (1949); and our history says that it is this sort of hazardous freedom—this kind of openness—that is the basis of our national strength and of the independence and vigor of Americans who grow up and live in this relatively permissive, often disputatious, society.

In order for the State in the person of school officials to justify prohibition of a particular expression of opinion, it must be able to show that its action was caused by something more than a mere desire to avoid the discomfort and unpleasantness that always accompany an unpopular viewpoint. Certainly where there is no finding and no showing that engaging in the forbidden conduct would "materially and substantially interfere with the requirements of appropriate discipline in the operation of the school," the prohibition cannot be sustained. Burnside v. Byars, supra, 363 F.2d at 749.

In the present case, the District Court made no such finding, and our independent examination of the record fails to yield evidence that the school authorities had reason to anticipate that the wearing of the armbands would substantially interfere with the work of the school or impinge upon the rights of other students. Even an official memorandum prepared after the suspension that listed the reasons for the ban on wearing the armbands made no reference to the anticipation of such disruption.

On the contrary, the action of the school authorities appears to have been based upon an urgent wish to avoid the controversy which might result from the expression, even by the silent symbol of armbands, of opposition to this Nation's part in the conflagration in Vietnam. It is revealing, in this respect, that the meeting at which the school principals decided to issue the contested regulation was called in response to a student's statement to the journalism teacher in one of the schools that he wanted to write an article on Vietnam and have it published in the school paper. (The student was dissuaded.)

It is also relevant that the school authorities did not purport to prohibit the wearing of all symbols of political or controversial significance. The record shows that students in some of the schools wore buttons relating to national political campaigns, and some even wore the Iron Cross, traditionally a symbol of Nazism. The order prohibiting the wearing of armbands did not extend to these. Instead, a particular symbol—black armbands worn to exhibit opposition to this Nation's involvement in Vietnam—was singled out for prohibition. Clearly, the prohibition of expression of one particular opinion, at least without evidence that it is necessary to avoid material and substantial interference with schoolwork or discipline, is not constitutionally permissible.

In our system, state-operated schools may not be enclaves of totalitarianism. School officials do not possess absolute authority over their students.

Students in school as well as out of school are "persons" under our Constitution. They are possessed of fundamental rights which the State must respect, just as they themselves must respect their obligations to the State. In our system, students may not be regarded as closed-circuit recipients of only that which the State chooses to communicate. They may not be confined to the expression of those sentiments that are officially approved. In the absence of a specific showing of constitutionally valid reasons to regulate their speech, students are entitled to freedom of expression of their views. As Judge Gewin, speaking for the Fifth Circuit, said, school officials cannot suppress "expressions of feelings with which they do not wish to contend." Burnside v. Byars, supra, 363 F.2d at 749.

If a regulation were adopted by school officials forbidding discussion of the Vietnam conflict, or the expression by any student of opposition to it anywhere on school property except as part of a prescribed classroom exercise, it would be obvious that the regulation would violate the constitutional rights of students, at least if it could not be justified by a showing that the students' activities would materially and substantially disrupt the work and discipline of the school. Cf. Hammond v. South Carolina State College, 272 F.Supp. 947 (D.C. S.C.1967) (orderly protest meeting on state college campus); Dickey v. Alabama State Board of Education, 273 F.Supp. 613 (D.C.M.D.Ala. 1967) (expulsion of student editor of college newspaper). In the circumstances of the present case, the prohibition of the silent, passive "witness of the armbands," as one of the children called it, is no less offensive to the Constitution's guarantees.

As we have discussed, the record does not demonstrate any facts which might reasonably have led school authorities to forecast substantial disruption of or material interference with school activities, and no disturbances or disorders on the school premises in fact occurred. These petitioners merely went about their ordained rounds in school. Their deviation consisted only in wearing on their sleeve a band of black cloth, not more than two inches wide. They wore it to exhibit their disapproval of the Vietnam hostilities and their advocacy of a truce, to make their views known, and, by their example, to influence others to adopt them. They neither interrupted school activities nor sought to intrude in the school affairs or the lives of others. They caused discussion outside of the classrooms, but no interference with work and no disorder. In the circumstances, our Constitution does not permit officials of the State to deny their form of expression.

We express no opinion as to the form of relief which should be granted, this being a matter for the lower courts to determine. We reverse and remand for further proceedings consistent with this opinion.

Reversed and remanded.

RICHARDS v. THURSTON

Haircut Rule Violates Substantive Due Process

COFFIN, CIRCUIT JUDGE. Plaintiff, a seventeen-year-old boy, was suspended from school at the beginning of his senior year because he refused to cut his hair, which a local newspaper story introduced into evidence described as "falling loosely about the shoulders". Defendant, the principal of the high school in Marlboro, Massachusetts, admits that there was no written school regulation governing hair length or style but contends that students and parents were aware that "unusually long hair" was not permitted.

On these sparse facts the parties submitted the case posed by plaintiff's request for injunctive relief against the deprivation of his rights under 42 U.S.C. § 1983. Each relied on the failure of the other to sustain his burden of proof, plaintiff claiming that he should prevail in the absence of evidence that his appearance had caused any disciplinary problems, and defendant maintaining that plaintiff had failed to carry his burden of showing either that a fundamental right had been infringed or that defendant had not been motivated by a legitimate school concern. The district court granted plaintiff's request for a permanent injunction and ordered plaintiff reinstated. Richards v. Thurston, 304 F.Supp. 449 (D.Mass.1969).

Plaintiff, too, advances a narrow argument for prevailing—the lack of any specific regulation authorizing suspension for unusual hair styles. We do not accept the opportunity. We take as given defendant's allegation in his answer that parents and students—including plaintiff—were aware that unusually long hair was not permitted. Moreover, we would not wish to see school officials unable to take appropriate action in facing a problem of discipline or distraction simply because there was no preexisting rule on the books.

Coming to the merits, we are aware of a thicket of recent cases concerning a student's wearing of long hair in a public high school. While several of the decisions holding against the student have relied on the prior occurrence of disruptions caused by unusual hair styles, we think it fair to say that many of those courts would hold against the student on a barren record such as ours, on the grounds that the student had not demonstrated the importance of the right he asserts. On the other hand, in few of the cases holding for the student was there any evidence of prior disruptions caused by hair styles. Despite the obvious disagreement over the proper analytical framework, each of the "pro-hair" courts held explicitly or implicitly that the school authorities failed to carry their burden of justifying the regulation against long hair.

What appears superficially as a dispute over which side has the burden of persuasion is, however, a very fundamental dispute over the extent to which the Constitution protects such uniquely personal aspects of one's life as the length of his hair, for the view one takes of the constitutional basis—if

---

United States Court of Appeals, First Circuit, 1970. 424 F.2d 1281.

any—for the right asserted may foreshadow both the placement and weight of the evidentiary burden which he imposes on the parties before him. For this reason, we resist the understandable temptation, when one is not the final arbiter of so basic a constitutional issue, to proceed directly to an application of the constitutional doctrine without attempting to ascertain its source as precisely as possible.

It is perhaps an easier task to say what theories we think do *not* apply here. We recognize that there may be an element of expression and speech involved in one's choice of hair length and style, if only the expression of disdain for conventionality. However, we reject the notion that plaintiff's hair length is of a sufficiently communicative character to warrant the full protection of the First Amendment. That protection extends to a broad panoply of methods of expression, but as the non-verbal message becomes less distinct, the justification for the substantial protections of the First Amendment becomes more remote.

Our rejection of those constitutional protections in this case is not intended to denigrate the understandable desire of people to be let alone in the governance of those activities which may be deemed uniquely personal. As we discuss below, we believe that the Due Process Clause of the Fourteenth Amendment establishes a sphere of personal liberty for every individual, subject to reasonable intrusions by the state in furtherance of legitimate state interests.

The idea that there are substantive rights protected by the "liberty" assurance of the Due Process Clause is almost too well established to require discussion. Many of the cases have involved rights expressly guaranteed by one or more of the first eight Amendments. But it is clear that the enumeration of certain rights in the Bill of Rights has not been construed by the Court to preclude the existence of other substantive rights implicit in the "liberty" assurance of the Due Process Clause.

We do not say that the governance of the length and style of one's hair is necessarily so fundamental as those substantive rights already found implicit in the "liberty" assurance of the Due Process Clause, requiring a "compelling" showing by the state before it may be impaired. Yet "liberty" seems to us an incomplete protection if it encompasses only the right to do momentous acts, leaving the state free to interfere with those personal aspects of our lives which have no direct bearing on the ability of others to enjoy their liberty. The Founding Fathers wrote an amendment for speech and assembly; even they did not deem it necessary to write an amendment for personal appearance. We conclude that within the commodious concept of liberty, embracing freedoms great and small, is the right to wear one's hair as he wishes.

Determining that a personal liberty is involved answers only the first of two questions. The second is whether there is an outweighing state interest justifying the intrusion. The answer to this question must take into account the nature of the liberty asserted, the context in which it is asserted, and the extent to which the intrusion is confined to the legitimate public interest to be served. For example, the right to appear au naturel at home is relinquished when one sets foot on a public sidewalk. Equally obvious, the very nature of public school education requires limitations on one's personal liberty in order for the learning process to proceed. Finally, a school rule which forbids skirts shorter than a certain length while on school grounds would require less justification than one requiring hair to be cut, which affects the student twenty-four hours a day, seven days a week, nine months a year. See Westley v. Rossi, 305 F.Supp. at 713–714.

Once the personal liberty is shown, the countervailing interest must either be self-evident or be affirmatively shown. We see no inherent reason why decency, decorum, or good conduct requires a boy to wear his hair short. Certainly eccentric hair styling is no longer a reliable signal of perverse behavior. We do not believe that mere unattractiveness in the eyes of some parents, teachers, or students, short of uncleanliness, can justify the proscription. Nor, finally, does such compelled conformity to conventional standards of appearance seem a justifiable part of the educational process.

In the absence of an inherent, self-evident justification on the face of the rule, we conclude that the burden was on the defendant. Since he offered no justification, the judgment of the district court must be affirmed.

Affirmed.

Part Three

The Student and the School

7

The Curriculum

Although our own conception of the curriculum is broad, embracing all the learning experiences in classes, clubs, student government, assemblies, student press, and informal encounters of students with teachers, principal, counsellors and the like, we shall confine ourselves here to that part of the curriculum contained in the formal arrangement of teacher and class.

It would be simple if we could dismiss all questions of the curriculum with a decision about what subjects to teach. But no sooner is that done, than other, more difficult questions arise. Assuming we agree on the subjects, we are faced with the problem of content. That leads to the question of selection, for in no subject can all available "content" be included, the extent of knowledge being almost unlimited and constantly expanding. For example, an older teacher of United States history who began teaching in 1932, discovers that over forty years of history have been added since he began teaching. The Great Depression, World War II, Korea, Vietnam, the full or partial administrations of six presidents, the invention and use of television, the moon landings, and hundreds of other significant events have occurred since he began his teaching career.

The school life of a high school student is short and not all that is known can be taught. Yet many harried teachers in all fields of study rush madly on in an attempt to "cover" the material. The curriculum of the secondary school resembles the household effects of the family that for generations has been accumulating but could never bear to throw away.

If we agree on the subjects, we have found a partial answer to the matter of content. Then we have to ask ourselves how the time should be allotted, and, at that point, we are up against the problem of scheduling. Traditionally, since the beginning of the century we have allocated time on a forty- to sixty-minute daily block per subject, repeated five times a week, usually for a full school year. We have parcelled the time this way regardless of differing needs of individual students. When critics talk about a lock-step curriculum, this is in part what they are talking about.

Having wrestled with the questions of *what* (subjects and subject content) and *when* (the time allocation), it might seem that the troublesome problems have been met and solved. But if we are perceptive we have even more fundamental questions to ponder. One of these is related to the question *why*; at this point we are up against the hard task of relating process to purpose on the one hand, and justification on the other.

School principals and teachers are familiar with the students who ask why they are expected to learn this or that subject or bit of information. Now the same kind of inquiry is coming from outside the school. Earlier we made reference to the book *Future Shock*. Alvin Toffler, the author, could hardly be considered to be among the "radical" school reformers. Former associate editor of *Fortune,* once a Visiting Scholar at The Russel Sage Foundation, he is among an increasing band of men and women who are peering into what will be a rapidly changing future. He advocates the creation of Councils of the Future in every school and community to project "assumed futures" and define "coherent educational responses to them by opening these alternatives to active public debate." The Councils, he said, should not be monopolized by any one group. Even though specialists are needed, the Councils should not be

> captured by professional educators, planners, or any unrepresentative elite. Thus students must be involved from the very start—and not merely as co-opted rubber stamps for adult notions. Young people must help lead, if not, in fact initiate these councils so that 'assumed futures' can be formulated and debated by those who will presumably invent and inhabit the future.[1]

As for the curriculum, he goes on to say

> ... The Councils of the Future, instead of assuming that every subject taught today is taught for a reason, should begin from the reverse premise: nothing should be included in a required curriculum unless it can be strongly justified in terms of the future. If this means scrapping a substantial part of the formal curriculum so be it.[2]

Not all search for justification will be answered as the Futurists would answer, but there must be valid reasons in any event. Even if we can answer with sufficient reason the question of why or whether something should be taught, still a further perplexing question presents itself. This is the question *how,* and the answer to that leads us to ponder the teaching act and the nature of learning. Is what is in the course outline what is taught? Is what is

---
[1] Alvin Toffler, *Future Shock* (New York: Random House, 1970), p. 409.
[2] *Ibid.*

taught that which is *learned?* For example, does the teaching of literature lead to a desire on the part of the person being taught to read ever more widely and eagerly on his own, to enjoy reading, to make books an important part of his life? Or does it result in a distaste for books and the intention to read no further after the class demands have been met? Does the extensive and often repetitive teaching of English grammar result in better writing and lead to the habit of writing as one of life's activities? Are we more interested in right answers than in right questions? Can we relate subject matter to the legitimate needs and concerns of students? A large part of the answers to such questions are related to the *how* of the curriculum. Relevance, though perhaps an overused word, is nevertheless not *ir*relevant. It is associated with the questions of *why* and *how*.

Even after arriving at tentative answers to the questions above, it should be recognized that to a large degree the individual teacher makes the curriculum. Regardless of syllabus, textbook, and teaching guide, the teacher chooses what is really taught, how it is taught, and to whom it is taught. Some teach the class, some teach the individual students in the class. Once in the classroom, alone with the students, the teacher is the key person who brings curriculum and student together. For this reason, the principal's work with teachers, individually, in small groups, and as an entire faculty, is central to improving the kind of educational opportunity afforded each student. This is more important than selecting materials, preparing curriculum guides, and scheduling classes. It is the teaching act itself, with its degree of artistry, sensitivity, and awareness that influences learning. The curriculum is inert; only good teaching brings it alive and turns it to productive use by the learner.

Examined closely, the question of the curriculum is not as simple as it is sometimes made to appear. Nor can the matter of curriculum be neatly compartmentalized, and separated from other aspects and activities of the school. If you talk about discipline, then in large part you are talking about the boys and girls who are sent from class because of misbehaviors in the places in which they confront the curriculum—the classroom. Guidance? How much of the work of guidance is concerned with grades (a product of the curriculum), or failure (in the curriculum)? The dropouts? It is the curriculum they have left behind.

THE PRINCIPAL AND THE CURRICULUM

This brings us to the principal and his leadership and administrative roles in relation to the curriculum. Studies of how principals spend their time show that a disproportionate amount is spent doing things which have almost nothing to do with the educational program. Many principals shut themselves off from curriculum questions because they are uncomfortable about their own knowledge and wisdom. Others have not attempted to lead in the curriculum area because of a false notion of what constitutes expertise. An argument often advanced for closing the principal out of curriculum leadership runs like this: no principal can possibly know, in depth, subject matter fields taught in secondary schools. He doesn't know French, or calculus, or the intricacies of mechanical drafting, or machine shop. Therefore, he must leave decisions about these and other subjects (the curriculum, in short) to those who have expert knowledge of the field—teachers of the subjects, and department chairmen. This argument has some merit to it, but not a great deal. As we pointed out, the questions associated with the curriculum are much broader than the subjects to be taught and the content to be included, and are quite within the leadership role of the principal. In fact, if he avoids this aspect of his responsibility, he is abrogating the largest part of his duty as educational leader. A good school is much more than the sum of the individual teaching acts performed. We will try to illustrate this and put curriculum responsibilities in perspective in the sections which follow.

SCHOOL CLIMATE AND THE CURRICULUM

Earlier an analogy was drawn between school and factory. Where the factory analog exists, it is the result of attitudes and a set of beliefs about the curriculum and learning, and the resulting relationship of teachers and principals to students. In the book *High School Students Speak Out,* a report of a study of eight high schools carried out under the direction of David Mallery, Esther Rauschenbush (a former president of Sarah Lawrence College), made a pertinent observation. She said:

> We can monkey all we want to with devices and curriculum changes, debate about what is a good size for a school, or whether college bound and non-college bound students belong together, or how advanced placement classes should be handled, but what counts is the climate of the institution and the values it has, or instills, not by a program, but by its existence. Programs help, obviously, but these are consequences of a climate, not the primary causes of it. I think it is healthy to deal with this fact: what gives a school the kind of influence over its students that some of these schools have is the conviction the people who make the school have about education and about students.[3]

Anyone with experience in schools can identify one type of climate. Teachers and students are essentially adversaries. The curriculum is uniform,

---

[3] David Mallery, *High School Students Speak Out* (New York: Harper and Besthers, 1962), p. 154.

inflexible; its rationale is seldom examined or explained. Marks, grades, and rank in class are used as leverage to control behavior. Teaching is primarily telling, learning is primarily listening. The textbook is sacred, and progress is measured by ability to recall pieces of information. The evaluation process is arranged so that large numbers will fail or receive such small recognition that the effect is as damaging as failure. Teachers and students play a cat-and-mouse game. Rules and regulations proliferate, and principals and teachers develop an elaborate system of penalties for those who violate them. Students who learn how to play the game, figure out how to pass the tests and get the marks. Learning becomes equated with grade-getting. If uniformity characterizes the learning and evaluation process, conformity becomes the acceptable code of behavior. In such schools it is not only the students who are joyless or passively or openly antagonistic; for teachers, too, the daily routine of keeping order, seeking out wrongdoers, cajoling, holding over the heads of students the threat of failure and the prospects of a dim future makes teaching a tiring, unrewarding chore. It is remarkable that principals and teachers in such a situation do not seem to be able to identify the sources of their discontent. Such a climate need not be. If the school leadership and faculty wish it to be otherwise, a quite different kind of climate for learning may be created.

THE SCHOOL CAN BE A MODEL DEMOCRATIC COMMUNITY

For the school as a factory is substituted the school as a democratic community, or the school as a good family. Such a concept does not violate the idea of the school as a place for learning. On the contrary, it can provide the environment within which the psychological bases for learning can be established and within which learning can be freed from the pedantic, dry, sterile restrictions which have encompassed so much that has passed for education.

The school as a community is in part a state of mind, a series of convictions, a climate that is the result of what a school believes in and what it stands for. It is in part a result of a conscious, sustained effort to reduce or eliminate, where possible, those practices, procedures, forms of organization, and methods of administration that perpetuate the model of school as a factory. Let us assume that a school is to be a place where adults form the kind of association with adolescents that produces warm, helpful relationships based upon mutual respect. The adults are learners as well as teachers. They are studying and learning about the boys and girls in the school—who they are, where they come from, what they want to do with their lives. The adults are also seeking all the ways possible to help individual boys and girls learn what they need to learn. They throw away the crutches on which they have been taught to lean—the threats of failing grade, the menace of the trip to the office, the tracking, the grouping, the thinly disguised weapon concealed in the words "you'll never make it to college." In a school community, students help other students. Let us suppose that we substitute one mode of speech for quite another kind. The first is characterized by saying to a boy or girl, in effect, "you can't," "you won't," or "you shouldn't."

"You can't serve on the Student Council unless you bring up your grades."

"You won't do your homework" or "you won't listen to the teacher" or "you won't get to school on time."

Or, "you shouldn't chew gum," or "you shouldn't talk back."

The second kind of talk is characterized by questions such as "What do you want us to do to help you?" "Where has the school fallen short, in your judgment, in its efforts to bring meaning to your school life and to the tasks you are asked to perform?" "What do you have on your mind?" "What is bothering you?" "What in school has caused you to have feelings of inadequacy?" "Where in your school experience are you gaining self-satisfaction?"

The good family recognizes that there are differences among the children, but the differences are valued and not used as a base of invidious comparison. Mary is not valued less because she is different from John. The individuality of each child in the family is acknowledged and cherished.

In the good community a wide variety of accomplishments is respected and praised. If our car stalls on a cold winter day, we are thankful for the competent mechanic. If we are sick, we are grateful that a good doctor is available, and if we are in the hospital, our gratitude goes to the efficient, caring nurse. In the good community even the unfortunate are encouraged and assisted to rehabilitate themselves. We have the people who help the alcoholic, the mentally ill, the infirm, and the drug user, without passing judgment. Wide differences in opinion, life style, preferences, and tastes are tolerated and respected. In our own communities, we are frequently astonished at what others know that we do not, and at the kinds of learning pursued, on their own, by different people—the skillful amateur photographer, the antique collector, the geneology enthusiast, the local history buff, the furniture refinisher, the coin or stamp collector, the weekend painter. The list is almost endless. Why, then, should the school not take into account and value these same intriguing differences, possibilities, and individual variations as it organizes its learning program?

Before a school decides upon what it is going to teach, how it is going to be taught, and how boys and girls are going to be appraised, it must first come to grips with what kind of school it wants to become, whether its definition of learning is to be narrow and restricted or broadly encompassing, whether the path to school success is a single one or whether many roads lead to Rome.

Innovation

During the past decade the word innovation has been invoked frequently in educational discussions. No meeting of educators has been complete without at least one reference to it. That different approaches to schooling are required if secondary schools are to meet the demands made on them by the needs of a student body that now includes almost all boys and girls of secondary school age cannot be denied. Yet it is also undeniably true that many practices heralded as innovative have appeared, attracted attention for awhile, and disappeared.

An innovation is defined as something new or contrary to custom; to innovate is to make changes, to alter by introducing something new. An innovator is one who initiates or makes changes. Although we subscribe to the belief that outworn customs must be displaced and that significant changes need to be made in secondary education, we offer several observations about how the concept of innovation has been used and abused.

Our first observation is that among the innovators are those who advocate changes for the sake of change. Discouraged by what they believe to be the slow response schools make to new conditions, the change advocates propose that anything that is new or different should be tried on the theory that the act of change itself creates a favorable environment for experimentation, is stimulating, and leads to other changes. There may be some substance to such reasoning, but it falls short of the thoughtful response we believe is necessary if new ideas and programs are to survive and be incorporated into school practice.

Secondly, schools have often "bought" innovations proposed from outside the school, such as those proposed by foundations, government agencies, universities, and commercial firms, and have tried to graft them onto existing school programs. The innovation has then become an end in itself instead of a means to an end that is consistent with the overall goals of the school which have been clearly identified and accepted by the administration and teachers. The innovation becomes an appendage instead of an integral part of a carefully devised plan.

An example of an innovative practice which received wide publicity in the 1960s was team teaching. It was the product of what was known as the Staff Utilization Studies of the National Association of Secondary School Principals. The objective of the committee appointed to make the studies was to explore better ways of using staff during a period of acute shortage of teachers. In order to finance the studies, the committee applied for assistance to the Fund for the Advancement of Education of the Ford Foundation. Apparently as a condition for receiving the grant, implicit or explicit, the committee accepted for promulgation among secondary school principals several innovations which had earlier been put forth by the Graduate School of Education of Harvard. One of these was team teaching. The idea was to select a team of teachers in a subject field who would work and plan together for the instruction of a large group of students. Three teachers might be responsible for ninety students in history, for example. One of the three might be an experienced, or master teacher. The others might be less experienced. As the plan was conceived it was stylized. It was centered around large group—small group instruction. The master teacher would prepare a lecture for the group of ninety. The large group would then be broken up into smaller groups, with each of the three teachers working with one of the small groups, the objective being to further explain and clarify the content of the lecture. Actually, the plan was similar to that used in many universities where a professor lectured to a large class, and teaching assistants worked with small sections of the class.

As described, and as actually used in many secondary schools, the plan was simply a different way of trying to get students through a prescribed, prepared block of subject matter, and hence was consistent with the view of the curriculum as a prearranged, rather inflexible and uniform subject-centered learning experience.

The innovation as defined in practice might not be suitable for a school which espoused a different concept of teaching and learning. The general proposition that teachers need to work and plan together to avoid the fragmentation of learning that plagues so many efforts to make learning a whole, integrated experience is sound. How the team planning and working together are used, and to what ends, is the central question, the answer to which depends upon what the school believes in, its attitudes toward the teacher-student relationship, and its concepts of learning.

Our third observation on the use of innovation is that sometimes an innovative practice has been imposed on a school more or less by administrative edict. The reasons for this are various. One seems to be the desire by an administrator to appear forward looking before community and colleagues. Some administrators have sought reputations as innovators by convincing a board of education or a superintendent of schools that they have an arsenal of new ideas which will revolutionize the school. After a brief stay, they move on and the innovations they have brought with them die, never having taken sufficient root in the school or the community to sustain themselves after the innovator has left.

The points made here are reinforced by the experience of the Ford Foundation. A report titled "A Foundation Goes to School," issued in December, 1972, was a summation of the $30 million worth of grants spent for innovative projects over a decade by the Foundation's Comprehensive School Improvement Program.

The principal innovations were team teaching, flexible schedules, programmed instruction using teaching machines, various curriculum revisions, independent study, nongraded schools, and the use of teacher aides. The hope of the Foundation was that districts receiving grants for a particular innovation would be lighthouses to which other districts would turn and which they would imitate. Apparently that did not occur to any significant degree. Leadership in innovative districts was not stable and had high turnover. The projects were carried out in financially able suburbs and there was no carry-over to less affluent systems. The Foundation report pointed to conservative attitudes of staff and public as a principal reason for lack of success of the innovations.

A statement by Edward J. Meade, Jr., the Ford Foundation Program Officer in charge of public education, gets to the core of the problem of change: "There is almost no way that educational innovations to improve learning in schools can succeed without the active participation of the instructional team."[4]

This leads us to some assumptions about what is needed to make changes last. When a school sets out in new directions, the entire fabric of attitudes and behaviors of teachers and administrators needs to be examined and usually modified. Short of a coercive conditioning process, the only ones who can change attitudes and behaviors are the ones whose attitudes and behaviors are subject to change. If teachers have an image of teaching as being the practice of purveying information by lecturing, covering a textbook, and testing recall of facts lectured and covered, and if they continue to act in accord with that image, nothing important will be accomplished by an innovation based upon a different set of beliefs and attitudes. If a school staff is so obsessed with the marking and grading system that grades are more important than learning and teacher-student relationships, no innovation is going to be successful unless it corresponds with those particular attitudes and behaviors.

If principals and teachers look upon secondary school students as too immature to be responsible persons, and if order and regimentation are the *sine qua non* of the good school, it is doubtful that innovations such as independent study or open classrooms will succeed. To reiterate, unless a school staff proceeds from a base of willingness to change attitudes and behavior, nothing significant is likely to follow. Unless a staff is convinced of the need for change and is willing and ready to make the deep commitments necessary, not much of fundamental importance will come about.

Academic Freedom and Controversial Issues

Differences of opinion often arise in a community about teaching in areas of controversy. Since freedom of inquiry is essential in education, the school should be protected by a clear statement of policies governing academic freedom and the teaching of controversial issues. If there are no such statements, the principal should take the initiative, along with the staff, in urging their development. The superintendent of schools should also be

---

[4] Edward Meade, Jr., "A Foundation Goes to School," *Today's Education 62* (March 1973), p. 22.

involved, and through the superintendent recommendations should be made to the board of education for adoption of the necessary policies. They will, of course, be subject to a vote of the board in public session and should be subject to open discussion before adoption.

The following statements, adopted by the Board of Education of District #333, Oak Park, Illinois, are exemplary, and are similar to policies adopted by boards of education elsewhere.

Academic Freedom. Freedom of inquiry and discussion is essential to the educational process: All areas of human behavior and activity are proper subjects for classroom examination; Children must be afforded the opportunity to discuss controversial subjects so that they may learn to understand and respect valid opposing viewpoints and to reconcile differences; Teachers have the right to initiate as well as to permit such discussion; concomitant with the right of teachers to present their personal viewpoints in such discussions is their obligation to identify their views and to avoid the presentation of opinion as fact.

Controversial issues. The ... schools are unequivocally dedicated to the perpetuation of the democratic values and institutions which have created the American way of life. If these democratic values and institutions are to survive, an enlightened citizenry is essential in order to resolve issues through rational, independent thought. The schools have a responsibility for passing on from generation to generation an understanding of the basic nature of freedom of thought and inquiry. At the same time, the curriculum should provide adequate instruction concerning major social forces and trends of the present time.

A controversial issue involves a problem for which society has not found a solution that can be universally accepted. Because the social studies are concerned with the study of man and his society, controversial issues arise more frequently in this area of the curriculum. Other areas of the curriculum also deal with topics or problems that are at least potentially controversial.

The ... schools affirm the following positions expressed by the Office of the Superintendent of Public Instruction. In this document (the Illinois Curriculum Program, "Teaching the Social Studies in Grades K-Nine," January, 1962, p. 126, Springfield, Illinois, Office of the Superintendent of Public Instruction), four rights of pupils in the study of controversial issues have been recognized.

The right to study any controversial issue which has political, economic, or social significance, concerning which he is capable of forming an intelligent opinion (and which is appropriate to his level of maturity).

The right to have free access to all available relevant information.

The right to study under competent instruction in an atmosphere free from bias and prejudice.

The right to form and express his own opinions on controversial issues.

In order to give pupils the opportunity to exercise these rights, the Board of Education and the administration expect the teacher to retain responsible objectivity in the classroom. The teacher makes no attempt to convert the individual child to the beliefs and opinions which he holds, but conducts the classroom as a forum and acts as a discussion leader. The teacher is free to express his personal opinions when they are appropriate. He helps to create a climate of free and open discussion within which the student can clarify, refine, and extend the range of his own understanding of the topic. In this manner, students can learn that there are very few absolutes and that most of the ideas and "truths" of our civilization are subject to condition, qualification, and opinion. While an individual student may arrive at a conclusion which meets his need for a tentative stand, the teacher does not attempt to present a single solution. The topic remains in the realm of the controversial.

The Board of Education and the administration firmly support the teachers of the. . . schools so long as they strive for objectivity, to be fair, and to use tact and good judgment as they seek to develop critical thinking in the young.[5]

Domination of the Curriculum by College and University

A reading of the reports on secondary education in the period 1913–1944 as described in the opening section of this book reveals a recurring theme. This theme is the undue influence on secondary curriculum imposed by the colleges and universities. The reports repeatedly assert that the secondary school has a mission of its own, and that it should be free to pursue that mission without unreasonable restriction from higher education. This is not to say that some articulation between the secondary school and the college is not necessary or desirable, but that articulation calls for accommodation on the part of both institutions—a condition seldom apparent to the secondary school. Articulation for the most part becomes a one-way street. The so-called college preparatory curriculum in secondary schools is made up of subject requirements and unit requirements dictated by college admission policies. Much of the over-testing to which secondary students are subjected is likewise the result of college demands made in an effort to simplify the work of admissions. In fairness to colleges, two observations should be made. First, the heavy reliance on the use of test scores for admissions administered by the American College Testing Service and by the SAT administered by the Educational Testing Service is in part the product of the large number of applications received by colleges in the past decade. The supply of places in colleges and universities has been exceeded by the demand for places. This has been compounded by the practice of multiple applications whereby an anxious secondary student applies to admission to more than one college (with five to ten applications not being uncommon). With declining numbers

---

[5]Reprinted by permission.

in the college age group in the next decade, this kind of pressure may be reduced.

Secondly, schools have not really tested the willingness of admissions directors to accept students whose patterns of courses in the secondary school have departed from standard or to disregard the outdated practice of measuring standards for admission in units and time spent per subject. However, there are limitations on the efforts of individual schools in securing a large measure of relief from college dictates. One of the responsibilities of the associations of secondary school principals, on both state and national levels, is to work to remove the barriers that prevent the secondary school from asserting the integrity of its own purposes. Until a secondary school is no longer judged exclusively by its success in getting boys and girls into college, experimentation with programs aimed at improving the experience of students in secondary schools, including those going on to advanced education, is not likely to get very far. By and large, state and national organizations of secondary school principals have not come to grips with the important question of the relation of school to college—yet it should be given high priority.

One place to begin is to abandon the practice of calculating, using, and publishing ranks in class. It is impossible to make such fine discriminations as determining whether a student should be number five or number eight. The sooner schools face up to this, the better. If colleges continue to require some form of class distribution based on grades, the most that should be promised colleges is a report by quarters or fifths.

Other means of identifying to colleges the truly exceptional student whose future academic promise seems beyond question are available and would serve student and college better than rank in class. One such means is a personal letter describing the high potential of the student.

ALTERNATIVE SCHOOLS

One of the interesting and challenging developments in secondary education in the past several years is the increase in the number of schools created as alternatives to conventional schools. Most of these are within the framework of the school system, carried on with the support and encouragement of school officials. Others have been organized apart from the school system by parents, students, and teachers who wish to provide an educational program that is different from those in conventional systems.

Whether a part of a system or privately controlled, the existence of alternative schools reflects a degree of dissatisfaction on the part of some parents, students, and teachers with the traditional model that characterizes most public secondary schools.

It is not intended here to describe in detail the alternative schools, to choose some over others, or to recommend those which might be adopted as exemplary by schools looking for guidance. Some now in existence will no doubt disappear. Others will probably be modified as experience dictates. It is not beyond speculation that the ideas behind the alternative schools may be incorporated into conventional programs, altering these to the extent that the present sharp differences between alternative and conventional models will be blurred.

Before discussing the movement toward alternatives within the established school system, we here comment briefly on the phenomenon of the "new" private schools which grew out of a desire for something different from what was offered in the public schools. Beginning in the late 1960s and continuing into the 1970s, the move to establish a different kind of school spread fairly widely. The National Directory of Alternative Schools (private) published in 1971, estimated an enrollment of 15,000 in 450–500 schools, with schools located in 37 states and the District of Columbia. The totals included both elementary and secondary schools. The "new" schools had a national newsletter and a network of regional education switchboards designed to serve as "coordinating and information centers for free schools and other 'alternatives in education' activities in their local area; they list schools, give advice and help to people who want to start schools, help to find jobs for teachers, help to find teachers for schools and many other useful things," according to the National Directory. The "new" schools have been influenced heavily by such writers as Dennison, Friedenberg, Goodman, Holt, Kohl, Kozal and Neill. Unfortunately, practical problems such as financing, housing, and obtaining and retaining teachers create difficulties for many of the new private schools, which casts some doubt upon their permanence on the educational scene.

Since we are concerned with public education, we shall comment at more length on the "alternative" schools within the public system. Enough of these had been established by 1972 to warrant a publication of the Educational Research Service of the American Association of School Administrators and the NEA Research Division. Its title was *Alternative High Schools: Some Pioneer Programs.* Based on inquiries to all school systems enrolling 12,000 or more pupils, the ERA study gave descriptions of 47 alternative schools in 38 school systems. Most of these had been established since 1971. The criteria established for including a description were as follows

1. The school would have to be one in which students voluntarily enroll as an option to regular high school programs available in their district.
2. Dropout centers and schools for pregnant students were not included.
3. The school must provide an alternative approach to teaching and learning in core subjects, rather than options in the area of enrichment or elective courses.

Of more than passing interest is the summary of replies from State Departments of Education, regional accrediting agencies and colleges about recognition and approval of alternative school programs. State departments of education on the whole provided more flexibility than is ordinarily supposed. Regional accrediting agencies also looked with favor on experimental efforts. Three school systems had queried colleges and universities about accepting graduates of alternative schools. The responses were not negative, and generally expressed willingness to forego grade point averages and rank in class, but asked for scholastic aptitude test scores and descriptions of a student's activities.

The *Curriculum Report* of the Curriculum Service Center of NASSP in March, 1973, stated

> The rapid increase in the number and variety of alternative schools . . . and the continuing expansion that seems certain to take place in the next five years both suggest that this is a movement all principals need to examine closely. This is the case whether you *are thinking about opening your own alternative school or are wondering what you and your associates* can learn *from the experiences of alternative schools* to improve your own or *are simply trying to keep abreast of major developments* affecting American secondary education.[6]

The *Report* gives ways in which alternative schools can be distinguished from "conventional" or "regular" schools. Alternative schools are (1) significantly different in curriculum and instructional practices; (2) strive for greater involvement of staff and students in decision-making; (3) are more flexible, and, therefore more responsive to evaluation and change; (4) tend to make more extensive use of community resources and facilities; (5) usually have a commitment to be more responsive to some community need or needs; and (6) are most often comparatively small schools, with student bodies ranging from 30 to 400.[7]

The NASSP estimated that at the time of their report more than 3,000 alternative schools were in operation, including both elementary and secondary, and referred to one projection which forecast 20,000 by 1976. In the opinion of those who prepared the NASSP report, the alternative schools are not just another educational fad. Society is moving toward alternatives of all sorts, and a "temporary" society faced with continuing change probably requires small autonomous units that can respond quickly to pervasive change. Most alternative schools are "open" systems that can survive change and pressure by making minor or major corrections of course, without undue strain. Finally, the idea of smaller and quite different schools as options is not

---

[6]National Association of Secondary School Principals, Curriculum Service Center, *Curriculum Report* (Washington D. C., March 1973), p. 1, et seq.

[7]*Ibid.*

new; it is an old practice that is now gaining new strength. So our best guess is that alternative schools—perhaps under some other name—will be around for some time to come.

Other NASSP observations include

>Cost—about the same level as for larger conventional schools
>
>Selection of students—varied
>
>Location—no one location best. Some are in part of existing school; some, in annexes to existing schools; some are separate.
>
>Staff—wider variety, including part-time teachers, community volunteers with special skills and abilities, people from nearby colleges, and their own students. Less use of "specialists" as part of staff.
>
>Organization—minimal administrative staff.
>
>Reporting system—varied choices offered.

The report points out that alternative schools have about the same number of problems as conventional schools but with the difference that the problems are more likely to be real and to affect real people; they seem more easily solved; there is more concern for solving problems by cooperative effort.

REPORTING PUPIL PROGRESS

Few practices in American schools have been so entrenched over so long a period of time as methods of grading and reporting pupil progress. From the early years of the century the report card has been sanctified, and efforts to modify it or to clarify what it is assumed to measure have not met with a great deal of success. Earlier report cards presented to student and parent an estimate of success expressed in a percentage, subject by subject. The percentage grade yielded to criticism and to studies which attacked its reliability, and it was gradually replaced by a letter system, the A, B, C, D, and E symbols characteristic of most secondary school grading systems in use today.

The letter system itself is proving to be unsatisfactory if one may judge from the many studies carried on by schools over the country to improve reporting practices. One major organization, the National Council of Teachers of English, in 1971 adopted a policy which rejected the failing grade. This was in line with considerable sentiment in favor of "schools without failure," stemming in part from the writings of William Glasser, a psychiatrist with the Los Angeles school system and author of a widely discussed book, *Schools Without Failure.*

Policy on Grading

In 1971 the Board of Directors of the National Council of Teachers of English adopted the following five propositions as statements of policy and urges that NCTE seek means to put these statements on policy into action:

1. Reporting of a child's progress in the early years should be done through methods other than the assignment of a letter or numerical grade. Rather, the reporting of a child's progress should be through regular conferences based upon anecdotal records, comparative samples of a child's growth in skills, and his growth toward achieving other goals that the community and the school might have set.
2. After the early years, at all educational levels, only passing grades (Pass or A-B-C or any other symbols distinguishing levels of passing performance) should be recorded on a student's permanent record.
3. If a student has progressed in a course, but has not completed it when the calendar indicates the term is over, he may either withdraw without penalty or request a temporary mark of Incomplete, subject to his later completing the work by a date agreed upon by the student and the instructor.
4. An instructor should not be required to record grades A-B-C or any other symbols distinguishing levels of passing performance if the course has been taken by the student on a Pass basis.
5. The institution will maintain no second set of books, no secret file in which instructors report the "actual" performance of the students in terms or symbols other than Pass or A-B-C or any other symbols distinguishing levels of passing performance.

A teacher opinion poll, reported in the NEA Research Bulletin for October, 1971, indicated that there is no general agreement on methods of grading and reporting. The report revealed differences among teachers both as to what they do and what they would prefer to do. The results of the poll are shown in Tables 7-1 and 7-2.

Table 7-1

Method of Reporting Used*	Percent
Teacher-parents conferences	54.4
Classified scale of letters	79.4
Formal letter or written paragraph to parents	21.1
Descriptive word grade	10.1
Percentage grade	13.7
Pass-fail	9.3
Classified scale of numbers	7.8
Dual marking system	4.9
Other	2.4

Source: NEA Research Bulletin, October 1971. Used with permission.

Table 7-2

Teacher Opinion of Best Method of Reporting	Percent
Teacher-parent conferences	42.8
Classified scale of letters	19.0
Formal letter or written paragraph to parents	9.7
Descriptive word grade	11.4
Pass-fail	10.5
Percentage grades	2.6
Dual marking system	2.0
Classified scale of numbers	1.0
Other	1.0

Source: NEA Research Bulletin, October 1971. Used with permission.

The National Public Relations Association in 1972 surveyed a sampling of school systems and issued a report, *Grading and Reporting Current Trends in School Policies and Programs.*[8] As might be expected, replies represented mixed opinion. The trend, according to the report, is for more schools to adopt some new form of reporting practice. On the other hand were those who believed the child should "experience failure," and that traditional grades are important to guidance counsellors and college admissions officers.

From the sampling of opinions, the following conclusions can be drawn about the success, or lack of success in traditional grading

1. If the purpose is to give the school administrative office a convenient way to sort out those students who should receive promotions, honors, scholarships and valedictories—grading works well.

2. If the purpose is to decide who should go to college, and to help college admissions officers select candidates for their freshmen classes—grading also works well.

3. If the purpose is to communicate with the parent, giving information about the child's progress and asking for help in overcoming problems—grading could stand improvement.

4. If the purpose is to motivate the student toward intensive learning—grading often doesn't work well at all.

We wish to comment on the argument that children should experience failure, which can be translated to mean children should be given failing grades. All people, children included, find that they are not successful at something they try to do. The cook occasionally burns the dinner; the fisherman does not always catch any fish; the cancer researcher sometimes finds himself at a dead end; in spite of his best efforts, the school principal knows the faculty meeting did not come off well; some boys cannot put the basketball in the basket; some children cannot solve quadratic equations; the

---
[8]*Grading and Reporting: Current Trends in School Policies and Programs* (Arlington, Va.: National Public School Relations Association, 1972), p. 9.

lead in the school play forgets her lines; some men lose their jobs or do not get promoted. But very seldom, outside of academic institutions, is a person regularly and consistently branded failure, total and complete. Of course when a teacher gives failing grades, he does not intend to brand a student a total failure. But so much importance is attached to grades, that the effect on the person who fails is translated by the recipient as failure as a person—total failure. We do not make it clear to parents, or even to ourselves, that a grade is only an effort to measure, in an imperfect, imprecise manner, how well a student performed in certain specific tasks, and nothing more.

Research has determined that judgment of performance is also often colored by subjective things like good behavior, regular attendance, compliance, and sex. It has been reasoned that girls in secondary schools, on the whole, receive better grades not because they are superior in intelligence, but because they are outwardly more docile, more willing to work to please. Hopefully, this will change as the role of women is redefined.

No psychologist, to our knowledge, has recommended constant failure as a spur to effect success. On the contrary, it is success that nurtures success, and even the least likely student can have his real successes, if his efforts are measured against himself and are not related to some norm, to a group, or to the bell curve which, like other relics, is still used by pedants to distribute measures of success or failure.

A principal who wishes to test a theory about grades might well examine teacher-made tests, for these are the stuff that grades are made of. Following are questions taken from a final examination in world history. The answers are in parentheses.

1. The rulers of Egypt wore _____ crowns. (double)
2. Queen Nefertititi was famous for her _____. (beauty)
3. It took _____ kings to build the temple. (twenty-one)
4. There are four things the Egyptians used to make their toys realistic. (a. movable jaws, b. crystal eyes, c. metal teeth, d. real hair)
5. The plant from which the Egyptians got nail polish _____. (henna)
6. The Rosetta stone was discovered in _____. (1799)
7. Tyrian dye comes from _____. (shellfish)
8. Define: Ziggurat
9. Who discovered how to read hieroglyphics? (Champellion)
10. Who were the first to smelt iron? (The Hittites)

Out of such slender threads are the web of grades so often woven.

Some schools, trying to find a way out of the traditional grading system, are experimenting with reports on specific behavioral objectives. This has some promise but is subject to the same kind of analysis and cautions described in the following section on behavioral objectives.

The Curriculum 189

A further indication of dissatisfaction with grading systems, the use to which they are put, and the interpretative problem associated with grading is apparent in the review currently in progress in colleges and universities. In May, 1973, a report on grading was adopted by the Educational Policy Committee of the Faculty Senate of the University of Illinois, Champaign-Urbana campus, after several months of study by an ad hoc Senate committee.

Section III of the report, "Deleterious effects of grades," is included here since many of the points made about university grading apply perhaps even more severely to secondary schools.

Deleterious Effects of Grades

All grading systems suffer from some major or minor defects. The rationale for grading must recognize certain potential abuses, generally *unintentional,* which may result from the system. It is not sufficient to justify the necessity for grading as "preparation for the real world." The world outside academe is surely competitive and selective, but the criteria used for evaluation and advancement in the "real" world are sufficiently different from those within the university that any academic grading scheme must be self-justifying for its academic relevance. Similarly, its potential abuses must be evaluated for their impact on the academic process.

The following are a sample of too-frequent abuses of grades:

1. Perversion of the *learning* process: Too frequently, students adapt their study habits to maximize their grade in a course, not their knowledge or mastery of the course material. Students sometimes select instructors by their performance as graders, not as teachers. In this way, long-range objectives may be subverted by short-range goals.

2. Distortion of the *teaching* process: Instructors too often stress those subjects which can be quantitatively evaluated in examinations to the exclusion of more subtle topics which are difficult to measure but may be more important to the total education of a student. Some courses, 'cram sessions,' etc. are directed solely toward improving performance on examinations with little relevance to long-range goals.

3. Inconsistent grades: The meaning of grades and the scales used by different colleges, departments, and even instructors in the same course, tends to be highly variable. A grade of C in one course given by one instructor may be worth an A in a comparable (or even the same) course with a different instructor. Thus grades tend to be an imprecise measure of the quality and degree of mastery of any individual student.

4. The 'halo' effect: Students' reputations may precede them into a grading session. 'Good' students may be graded higher than 'poor' students for the same level of accomplishment.

5. Enforcement of consistent behavior: Grades are sometimes used as rewards for conformity, not as a measure of academic achievement.
6. Imprecision of averages: Any overall grade average, which lumps grades in "hard" courses with those in "easy" courses and those given by "tough" instructors with those given by "nice" instructors, may well be a highly imprecise measure of a student's overall level of accomplishment.
7. Over-penalization: A single poor or failing grade of record, even in a non-required course, can preclude a student's acceptance to graduate or professional school and affect his entire career. Thus, a student carrying 20 hours who received 4 A's and a C, D, or E may appear a poor risk compared to a student who carried only 15 hours but received all A's.
8. Extrapolation to extracurricular life: Grades can create intense personal anxiety in students, which often affects performance in class and on examinations. A student's concern with academic success may restrict his participation in many social, cultural, and professional opportunities offered within the University community that could well be as valuable in preparation for living as his academic performance.[9]

SCHEDULING

For most of this century, secondary schools have been locked into a class schedule dictated by the Carnegie Unit. As described earlier, this is a method of equating learning with a quantitative measure of time spent in studying a subject. The measurement of learning history, for example, was a time space made up of classes meeting five days a week, from forty-five to sixty minutes per day over the course of a school year. This resulted in a uniform schedule by which a school day might, for example, contain six "periods." A student taking four subjects in addition to physical education would be in classes twenty-three periods a week. Since the total number of periods in a week totaled thirty, the student would have seven "free" periods during the week in which he would usually be assigned to a study hall. Variations might include double periods for laboratory work in the sciences, home economics, industrial arts, or vocational subjects. Sometimes an activity period was included in the schedule, and the periods rotated during the week so that the activity period and other classes fell at different times on different days.

In the past ten years, many schools have questioned the virtues of the traditional schedule. Why should a class meet every day? Why should time allotments for various learning activities be the same? Why should there not be flexibility in time spans and in frequency of sessions?

---
[9]Senate Committee on Educational Policy, (Champaign-Urbana: University of Illinois, May, 1973).

The Curriculum

As principals and staffs tried to answer such questions, it became clear to many that custom alone had locked the schools into an inflexible schedule. With ingenuity, any school could vary its schedule in almost any way it wished—if it were believed educational advantages could be gained by doing so.

One variation which has been tried is the flexible modular schedule, which gained a number of supporters during the 1960s and which is in use in numbers of schools at present. The schedule, for example, might contain twenty (or some other number) twenty-minute periods, or modules. The modules may be combined to provide varying lengths of time for various classes or other activities. The time combination might differ from day to day throughout the week. Four modules totaling eighty minutes might be given to one class or activity, or two, or three, or five—hence the name flexible modular schedule. Many schools trying out this kind of scheduling arrangement contracted with computer firms to place students in classes in the modular schedule after the school had prepared a master schedule and received individual student requests. Since what comes out of a computer is no better than what the human beings put into it, some unfortunate experiences have been reported with computer scheduling.

The point we want to make here is not that one type of flexible schedule should be adopted simply because some neighboring school may be using a stylized version of scheduling—models for which can be bought on the open market. The real point is that an imaginative principal and staff, considering their own school, can build almost any kind of schedule to meet their needs as they see them. They can experiment until they find the combination that works. Only lethargy—or the fear of temporary confusion, perhaps—stands in the way.

To illustrate how far a school may depart from a traditional schedule, we describe briefly one put into operation in a private school, Gill-St. Bernards, located in New Jersey. A report on the Gill Plan appeared in the February 1972 issue of the *Independent School Bulletin,* and is reproduced in part in the readings section following Part Three.

All students in grades nine through twelve take only one course at a time over a five-week period. The year is divided into six five-week blocks, two each in the fall, winter, and spring, with two optional possibilities added in a summer session. The advantages claimed for the plan are (1) students can become immersed in the subject; (2) a new kind of student-teacher relationship develops, requiring new methods and goals; (3) because of the opportunity to know students over a longer span of time, teachers place less reliance on testing to obtain information about a student's learning; (4) students see teachers from a different vantage point, and vice versa; (5) the plan provides flexibility for field trips, laboratory, library work, and the use of guest lecturers; (6) teachers bring more variety into their teaching; (7) teachers are forced to team with other teachers; and (8) with a school day running from 8:30 to 2:30 for the five-hour block for academic subjects, the time from 2:30 to 3:10, when the school is dismissed, is used for physical education, extracurricular activities, meetings of student government organizations, student-faculty committees, class meetings, and faculty meetings.

Inquiries made to colleges and universities to which students generally apply for admission resulted in favorable responses. In the case of Gill-St. Bernards, radical departure from traditional scheduling was no handicap to college admission.

TRACKING AND GROUPING

Whenever more than one student is taught, some form of grouping occurs. In the one-room country school of the past, the school group was all children from the six-year-old beginner to the eighteen-year-old youth. The teacher knew nothing of "grades" or "groups." She taught different combinations of students which varied as the situation and maturity of the students required. As schools grew in size, the grade division was established, the first grade, second grade, and so on in the elementary schools, and the seventh, eighth, ninth grades, and so on in the secondary schools. Within the grades, assuming a large enough number, classes were established, three classes of tenth grade English, for example, or three classes of world history intended for students, say, in the ninth grade. The grades were intended for boys and girls in the same age group, but the age span within the grade became less than uniform, since some were held back in the grade. Some did not "pass."

Having established the graded school, and having divided the grade into classes, the question arose as to how students would be chosen for a particular class. Although the basis of grouping (in classes) by ability would be found in a few schools in the last century, the real impetus for ability grouping occurred in the decade 1920–1930, spurred by the widespread use of intelligence tests in the schools. On the basis of results on paper and pencil tests which were supposed to measure I.Q., or intelligence, or by a combination of I.Q. tests, teacher opinion, and achievement tests, students were sorted and classified and placed in classes according to measurements of ability.

The ability grouping movement fell into disfavor in the 1930s and 1940s, but surfaced with renewed force in the 1950s, with a particularly strong resurgence after Sputnik. One survey reported that 81 percent of "large" high schools in 1960 reported an increase in ability grouping in the preceding five years.

At the same time that ability grouping came into favor, secondary schools adopted rather generally a tracking system which, in a way, was associated with the ability grouping movement. Four common tracks were "college preparatory," "vocational," "commercial," and "general."

In practice, the low ability students, as measured by tests, were shunted to the vocational and general tracks, students of varying ability into the commercial tracks, and the brightest and best (according to the tests) into the college preparatory track. Once on a track, few opportunities were given to switch to another. Although an anachronism in education today, many secondary schools still cling to a tracking classification.

James Conant, in *The American High School Today,* leveled criticism at the tracking system in one of his Recommendations:

> It should be the policy of the school that every student has an individualized program; there would be no classification of students according to clearly defined and labelled programs and tracks such as "college preparatory," "vocational," "commercial."[10]

Ability grouping in secondary schools has strong support from teachers, despite lack of any evidence that it accomplishes what teachers seem to think it does.

In his book *Classroom Grouping for Teachability,* Herbert Thelen reviews the many studies which have been made of the effects of homogeneous or ability grouping. In addition, he reports on an international conference held at the UNESCO Institute for Education in Hamburg, Germany, in 1964. At this conference the most notable researchers into the effects of homogeneous grouping drawn from this country and foreign countries examined forty-eight studies and their own investigations in order to review what was known about grouping, primarily by ability, and to find possible improvements that could be made concerning the various grouping practices.

The findings as reported by Thelen are

1. Grouping either homogeneously or heterogeneously produces almost the same result. When it comes to school achievement in the various subjects as measured usually by tests, the evidence fails to support the hypothesis that children will learn more when they are separated by ability.
2. When it comes to non-cognitive outcomes, such as self-perception, mental health, etc., the evidence is scantier except in England where the *unstreamed* [heterogeneous] classes are consistently superior.[11]

Grouping does seem to stratify students on a socioeconomic basis, which may explain in part why parents of those who fall into the upper groups join with teachers in supporting ability grouping. Parents of lower socioeconomic groups are far less likely to be heard on the subject. In any event, principals

---
[10] James B. Conant, *The American High School Today* (New York: McGraw Hill, 1959), p. 15.
[11] Herbert A. Thelen, *Classroom Grouping for Teachability* (New York: John Wiley and Sons, 1967), p. 29.

who organize their classes on some kind of homogeneous grouping based on intelligence and achievement test results cannot, it would appear, fall back on the argument that children learn best when grouped as a justification for grouping.

A good deal of the education in secondary school falls into the category of general education and is designed to help boys and girls understand the political system in which they live, to develop those understandings that make them more intelligent consumers and more effective members of the family, to develop a sense of the aesthetic, to enjoy art, music and literature simply as persons, not as producers, and to explore the questions, who am I? What is the world like? What shall I do with my life? Certainly no justification for ability grouping may be defended for the achievement of these ends.

For the specialized courses—physics, trigonometry, advanced language classes, for example—boys and girls of secondary age have had enough experience to group themselves, so to speak. We learn of our own accord whether specialized science, mathematics, and language are among our interests and special talents, and we come to choose accordingly. A world of difference exists between a choice or lack of choice based on a predetermined placement in an ability group or on a track and a free choice based upon a person's own assessment of his capabilities in a special field of study.

Since homogeneous grouping has no positive effect on learning, principals may profitably consider the virtues of heterogeneous assignment to class groups. In a democratic society it is to the advantage of all boys and girls of different backgrounds, talents, interests and ambitions to come to know and understand each other by *exploring* in common the problems they will *face* in common in adult society. Out of the schools will emerge leaders in government, business, and civic affairs. Others will follow those who know how to lead. No leader can succeed unless he knows the nature and thoughts of those he hopes will follow. No followers can be expected to follow blindly those they do not know, trust, and understand. Only in totalitarian states can such a condition exist for long.

In his book referred to earlier, Thelen advocates grouping for what he calls *teachability*. A teacher works well with one child, less effectively with another. A student relates well and learns with one teacher, less effectively with another. Why not attempt to match teachers and students in classes according to whether particular students thrive under a particular teacher? The idea has merit. Anyone with experience in secondary schools knows the student who "can't get along" with Mr. Jones, but likes and "gets along fine" with Miss Smith. An experienced administrator also knows of the resistance that frequently occurs when it is suggested a student transfer from one teacher to another. Somehow it seems to be an unfavorable reflection upon the teacher whose class the student is permitted to leave. The belief that once assigned, no recourse is available is one of the many shibboleths which govern school decision-making. Matching student and teacher on the basis of teaching and learning rapport is a promising concept. Students of administration who wish to explore the concept further and acquaint themselves with research and experimentation on the subject may read with profit the Thelen book.

Forty years ago the Commission on the Relation of School and College of the Progressive Education Association had this to say about the secondary school principal of that era

> Only here and there did the Commission find principals who conceived of their work in terms of democratic leadership of the community, teachers, and students. Usually, the principal was a benevolent aristocrat or a 'good fellow,' letting each teacher do as he pleased as long as neither parents or pupils complained. Most principals were constantly busy just 'running the machine.' They seldom stopped long enough to ask themselves, why are we doing this or that? What are we driving at? Where are we going?[12]

These are the kinds of questions the principal must ask himself as he thinks of the curriculum. He will be confronted with curriculum neatly packaged and for sale in almost every area. He will be confronted with demands from many sources. Career education, mini-courses, drug abuse education, education for the pregnant, unwed teenager, consumer education, international education, and other education under a variety of labels will crowd in on him. In a period notably lacking in a consistent, unified curriculum theory, the principal must find the unity in the definition of purpose for his school. What is the curriculum intended to do? How is what is taught related to the present and future needs of the students in his school? Among the many alternatives, how does one choose?

ACCOUNTABILITY

The predisposition expressed in this book toward the humane school and toward the school as a model democratic community is obvious. We would be remiss, however, if we did not point out again, as we have in other sections, that cross currents run beneath the surface of discussions and proposals about what schools should be, and how they should be organized, administered, and taught. Caught in the cross currents, principals may find themselves unwittingly espousing practices which are incompatible with the goals they seek.

We referred earlier to the current application of the word *accountability* to schools. At the outset it should be made clear that accountability, in the sense of being responsible or liable, is a legitimate concept. The idea that a school should be responsible for what it says it is trying to do or that individual teachers will stand responsible for what they say they are trying to

---

[12]Wilford M. Aiken, *The Story of the Eight-Year Study* (New York: Harper and Brothers, 1942), pp. 9-10.

do is not inconsistent with the points of view or the kinds of goals implicit in this book. It is also true that some applications of the accountability concept currently proposed run counter to the goals of a student-centered school which focuses on individuals, with human considerations paramount.

Principals will have to confront the growing interest in accountability as they think of the curriculum and the evaluation process. The recent attention on the part of economists, business leaders, and state and federal governments for holding the schools accountable for the dollars invested in them is generating an enlarging controversy.

To the economist or business executive who is familiar with industrial and business organizations, it is convenient to speak of inputs and outputs. In a manufacturing industry, the inputs are management, labor, capital, and raw materials. The outputs are finished products, the worth of which is measured by their marketability, price, and the profits which can be realized from their sale. Transferring this concept to the schools, those who draw the parallel between industry and schools argue that large sums of money (capital), the efforts of large numbers of workers (teachers, administrators, and others) are invested by the public in the education of millions of boys and girls. What, they ask, are the outputs, the measurable benefits (in the language of the economist, the cost-benefits) derived from the investment? Schools, so the thinking runs, have no good answers to questions about their effectiveness. They can make no assurance of their "productivity."

Some of this concern with productivity grew out of studies made of the results of large federal expenditures designed to improve the education of children from impoverished homes. Many of the children were black, Mexican-American, or Indian. Some were the children of poverty-ridden whites. The results of many of the studies were disappointing. In spite of large expenditures, school achievement levels, as measured by standardized tests of reading and arithmetic, did not improve appreciably. It is true that a fairly large number of children, whatever the reason, do not acquire the minimum basic skills in reading and numbers to perform effectively in modern society. This cannot be overlooked in any discussion of curriculum, and the secondary school is not exempt from the responsibility to do all possible to remedy the situation.

One by-product of the findings growing out of the studies is a tendency to equate all measures of accountability to a few objectives—improvement in reading and arithmetic, for example. Some state governments, pursuing this kind of objective as a definition of accountability, have mandated state-wide tests of achievement. The importance attached to such mandated tests has several unfortunate results. One is to create the impression that the sole legitimate objective of the schools is to secure better performance on the tests. Another, concomitant to the first, is to encourage schools to teach for the tests, since the public is led to believe test results are the single measure of the schools' effectiveness, and of the effectiveness of individual teachers.

The Curriculum

Another example of testing that is imposed from outside the school, designed, presumably, to measure the extent of accountability, is the National Assessment of Educational Progress. Its origins are illuminating. In his budget request for 1965–66 Francis Keppel, then United States Commissioner of Education, revealed that he had encouraged the Carnegie Corporation to initiate the assessment program, and that the results of such an assessment were needed in order to determine how well schools were accomplishing their purposes and how effectively students were learning the subjects they were generally taught. The Office, he said, was "interested in encouraging the [Carnegie] Corporation and allied agencies in the development of tests and procedures."

When news of the intention of the Commissioner and of the work done by the Carnegie Corporation and allied agencies became generally known, school officials and others raised serious objections. A testing program financed and managed by the federal government would go a long way toward furthering federal control of education. Allowing programs of private organizations such as the Carnegie Corporation would be tantamount to placing the possibility of considerable control of education in the hands of groups who were publicly accountable to no one. A spirited controversy arose, which was resolved when it was agreed by all parties that the assessment program would continue but would be placed under the aegis of the Education Commission of the States, a quasi-educational, quasi-political entity created by the various state legislature under an interstate compact.

By and large, as shown in the illustrations given above, neither those who work in the schools nor the public which supports them have had much part in considering and stating the goals or in participating in the development of standards by which the accomplishment of agreed upon goals will be measured.

The NEA Board of Directors, at its meeting in February, 1973, took sharp issue with what it termed "simplistic approaches to accountability in America's schools." An account of the meeting at which the declaration on accountability was approved included a statement by the NEA president. She noted that "compulsion about accountability has reached crisis proportion in at least thirty states and is spreading fast to all fifty. Teachers nationwide will respond happily to accountability when they become autonomous enough to have part in shaping standards for certification and in determining curriculum. We will be accountable when our knowledge about the needs of youngsters in school becomes a part of planning the total educational structure.... students and teachers will no longer be victimized by a simplistic approach that has caught the public fancy."

The chairman of the NEA's Committee on Educational Accountability said, "Dollars in and a visible and measurable product out are the criteria of many of the accountability measures being placed on schools today. These may be appropriate for an industry that produces paper clips or cans of soup, but are hardly responsible measuring devices for determining the effects of schooling on students."

The NEA's declaration calls for (1) a state-by-state analysis of "hard data" to identify where the dangers now exist; (2) coordination among NEA state and local affiliates to develop an action plan at all levels with positive implications that will place teachers in the leadership role; (3) investigation of possibilities for initiating legal action challenging misguided accountability rules; and (4) modification of national and state legislation leading to positive programs of accountability for quality education.

What is at issue, then, is not whether teachers, schools, and school systems should be responsible for what they do. It is whether, in response to demands for accountability, the goals set for the schools are to be broad and inclusive or narrow and exclusive; it is whether those who have the responsibility for meeting the goals will have a significant role in setting them and in determining how it will be determined if goals are met, partially or completely. It is at this point that a principal should be clear about the rhetoric he uses. He might be held responsible for what he says and what he says might not be compatible with the development of a school attuned to the last quarter of the century.

PLANNING, PROGRAMMING, AND BUDGET SYSTEMS

We are not going into detail about the current interest in planning, programming, and budget systems. Its origin is often ascribed to the Rand Corporation. The system was put into operation in the Department of Defense in the early 1960s, at the direction of Secretary McNamara. It spread to other departments of the Federal government and was early espoused by the United States Office of Education and advocated for local school systems.

In its simplest form, a program budget, as applied to a school system, substitutes cost accounting based upon programs for the traditional budgeting method emphasizing such categories of expenditure as administration, instruction, auxiliary services, supplies, equipment, transportation, operation of plant, maintenance of plant, capital outlay, and debt service. Under a program budget, costs are rearranged to reflect programs such as languages, mathematics, home economics, art, driver education, and the like.

Although experience at the Federal level has not shown the remarkable results claimed by some of the more ardent program budget advocates, the program budget for school systems does have advantages over the traditional budget. It is possible to see comparative costs of various programs and thus to provide some basis for choice among programs determined by the cost information. Cost data do not, of course, remove the need to make judgments. Breaking out the cost of offering a fourth year of a foreign language in a secondary school with small enrollment may reveal that the expenditure per pupil is very high. Whether to continue to offer the fourth year of the language remains a matter of judgment based upon a number of variables such as expectations of the community, overall financial stringencies, and characteristics of the student body.

Since an increasing number of states are mandating program budgeting, it is likely that this method of accounting will continue to expand among school systems. Like any other so-called "management tool," it is in and of itself neutral and neither provides a panacea nor does its adoption lessen the necessity for professional judgment. On the contrary, its use may require more, rather than less, educational statesmanship.

An example of the contrast between a traditional budget and a program budget is shown in Table 7-3.

When planning and evaluation are added to the program budget, additional elements are introduced. Many proponents of PPBS or PPBES (Planning, Programming, Budget and Evaluation Systems) link the program budget to the establishment of behavioral objectives. Thus we are led, in considering PPBS, to the important and central question of the purposes and goals of the secondary school. It is at the point of establishing goals and attempting to assess progress toward the attainment of stated goals that basic questions of

Table 7-3

A Comparison of the Traditional Budget and the Program Budget

Traditional Budget		Program Budget	
Administration	$ 135,713	Art	$ 128,458
Instruction	2,047,160	Business Education	95,493
Coordinate Activities	68,617	Child Study Center	226,240
Libraries	43,043	Coordination (includes classroom administration)	238,702
Transportation of Pupils	94,400		
Recreational Activities	7,000	Driver Education	11,936
Auxiliary Agencies	453,500	Foreign Language	54,324
Operation of School Plant	371,692	Home Economics	59,683
		Industrial Arts	60,309
Maintenance of School Plant	45,116	Kindergarten	89,509
		Language Arts	1,029,052
Capital Outlay	11,100	Learning Resource Centers	46,435
Federal Programs	98,000	Mathematics	351,009
		Music	123,520
		Physical Education	170,581
		Science and Health	315,951
		Social Studies	310,947
		Student Activities (Sports, etc.)	51,246
		Vocational Agriculture	11,936
	$3,375,341		$3,375,341

Source: Harry J. Hartley, "PPBS in Local Schools: A Status Report," *The Bulletin of the National Association of Secondary School Principals* 56 (October 1972), p. 15. Used with permission.

belief and philosophy surface, or should. It is at this point that the leadership role of the principal should be asserted. Hartley states

> In PPBS literature, a distinction is made between goals and objectives. A goal is defined as a statement of broad intent that is timeless, and thus *not* concerned with a particular, measurable achievement within a specified time period. Goals provide the basic direction and mission of all activities in an organization . . . they serve as a guide to preparing more limited objectives for the immediate future. In order to bring the planning process to a level where decisions can be made, alternatives considered, actions taken, resourses allocated, and results evaluated, objectives must be prepared.[13]

At this point, in our judgment, dichotomies often appear between general goals and immediate objectives. Let us take, for example, some of the goals implicit or explicit, underlying the principles expressed in this book. We believe the school should reflect the highest ideals of democracy, respect the worth of each student as a person, encourage participation in decision-making, foster a relevant program of student activities, encourage independent thinking, inquiry and study, forge vital links between school and community, recognize unique talents, develop skills of leadership, nurture student-teacher relationships based on mutual trust and respect, provide activities that encourage and prepare for wise use of leisure, be concerned in a systematic way with problems of the environment, and should teach consumer education, family life, the world of work, and the world of government and politics. In addition to these goals, we would add the goals of efficiency in reading at a level to function effectively as worker, citizen, consumer, and parent; likewise the ability to use computational skills at the same functional level; the ability to write simply and clearly in relation to the same functions; the ability to listen and to speak to the point on controversial issues. The list is, of course, illustrative and not exhaustive.

One point we want to make is that progress toward the attainment of some of the goals may be more easily broken down into shorter term objectives than it can be for others. Setting up short-term objectives for reading and compuitation is relatively simple, and evaluation of progress toward reaching the objectives is not difficult. The goal of creating a school which reflects in its daily operation the ideals of democracy can be broken into shorter term objectives, too, but evaluation of progress toward the objective does not lend itself to something that may be measured by "counting" or quantifying and is therefore more difficult.

This leads to a second point, which is that schools may easily fall into the trap of working only toward those goals and objectives which are subject to relatively easy assessment and may gradually lose sight of goals and objectives which do not yield so easily to quantitative measurement. This same danger is pointed out in the discussion of accountability.

---

[13]*Ibid.*, p. 7.

The Curriculum

Some of the cautions to be observed in moving into PPBS are as follows:

1. There is no single approach to PPBS that is adaptable to all schools or school systems.
2. It can, if applied unwisely, result in more inflexibility of program rather than less.
3. If it is tied too closely to narrow behavioral objectives, teachers will tend to lose sight of student needs and will teach only for the objectives.
4. The use of PPBS may be used in ways that run counter to the humanistic curriculum and the humane school (although this is not necessarily so).
5. The principal's role of educational leadership in his school may be weakened by central office specification of goals and objectives.
6. Specification of too many short-term objectives, too specifically stated, may reduce teaching to technician status.
7. At best, PPBS is no complete answer to educational planning. It offers possibilities, but as in any educational endeavor, the tools must not be allowed to dictate how they shall be used.

PPBS, as we have said, is likely to spread among an increasing number of school systems. In the use of PPBS as in all other matters, much depends upon the knowledge, beliefs, insights, philosophy, and goals of the principal. His leadership can determine to what uses a planning, programming, budgeting system can be put, consistent with the kind of school the principal and staff wish to have.

BEHAVIORAL OBJECTIVES

Accountability, the use of PPBS, and behavioral objectives are all related. All received stimulus from the federal government during the 1960s when interest on the part of federal officials in programmed instruction and the use of educational technology was high, and when the federal government was financing various curricular "packages." Emphasis was on costs and educational benefits deriving from large expenditures.

Leon Lessinger, a former U. S. Associate Commissioner of Education, was a frequent spokesman for "educational engineering" theories and the scientific management theory of education. He called for data on children in the nation's schools which would show specific educational gains which followed specific sequences of teaching. Once we measure learning in specific ways, he argued, we can then tell what it costs to produce a given output. His oversimplified approach rested on his belief in the value of sets of highly specific learning sequences and objectives which lend themselves to quantifiable measurement.

Even though the bright promise forecast by the advocates of programmed instruction and the use of teaching machines failed to materialize, the movement to establish behavioral objectives gained considerable momentum. The term *behavioral objectives,* as used here, refers to the statement of innumerable specific objectives covering almost all aspects of the curriculum. They are highly specific, and are to be distinguished from general goals and purposes which have been listed from time to time in educational literature.

The specific kind of objectives are based upon the theories of the behaviorist school of psychology, the leading spokesman of which is B. F. Skinner, and the school of curriculum planners, whose work is based on behaviorist principles. Skinner states that becoming competent in any endeavor requires that learning be divided into small steps. Reinforcement rests upon the mastery of each of these steps. The curriculum workers, including behavioral psychologists who have entered the field, have responded by developing extensive lists of objectives, running into the thousands.

One predictable result of the emphasis on specific objectives is the pressure on teachers to develop their own tests of specifics for all aspects of their instruction. Understandably, some teachers under pressure to conform have simply borrowed from an increasing number of tests of objectives published by those who pass as experts in the formulation of behavioral objectives.

Not everyone is in agreement with the behavioral objectives movement. It is argued that their use presupposes a highly mechanistic view of learning, and results in more of the rote learning and memorization which has plagued education for centuries. Daniel Tanner, in his book *Using Behavioral Objectives in the Classroom,* provides an excellent analysis. He asserts that many of the efforts in the area of behavioral objectives "have been guided by an ultra operational rationale, with the result that the specificity demanded of the learner has led educators to concentrate mainly on the lower cognitive skills."[14] He maintains that higher cognitive processes have as a consequence been neglected, and collateral learning has been almost completely ignored. Also overlooked in the development and use of the hundreds of specific learning objectives is *affective learning,* and the impossibility of separating cognitive learning from affective learning in almost any learning situation.

Tanner echoes a belief held by many others when he states "Humans are not yet so standardized and mechanical that their behaviors can be shaped, predicted, and assessed in accordance with a catalogue of quantifiable specifications."[15]

---

[14]Daniel Tanner, *Using Behavioral Objectives in the Classroom* (New York: MacMillan Co., 1972), p. V.

[15]*Ibid.,* p. 27.

The Curriculum

While we agree that for some learning, the statement of specific objectives may be useful, we would reject the theory that all learning should be so based, and the notion that any learning that matters can be easily and immediately quantified. A school predicated on such principles and based upon the implied beliefs that students are objects to be conditioned on theories of animal psychology is antithetical to the purposes of the secondary school as we describe them, presently and for the future.

Bibliography

Academic Freedom in the Secondary School. New York: American Civil Liberties Union, 1968.

American Association of School Administrators. *Curriculum Handbook for School Executives.* Arlington, Virginia, 1973.

Comer, James P. *The Circle Game in School Tracking: Inequality in Education.* Harvard University, Center for Law and Education, July 1972.

Common Sense Priorities for the Seventies. Selected speeches from the 1971 NASSP Convention. *The Bulletin of the National Association of Secondary School Principals* (May 1971). Washington, D.C.

Glasser, William. *Schools Without Failure.* New York: Harper and Row, 1969.

National Association of Secondary School Principals. *More Options: Alternatives to Conventional Schools.* Curriculum Report Vol. 2, March 1973.

Purpel, David and Belanger, David. *Curriculum and the Cultural Revolution.* Berkeley, California: McCutchen Publishing Corporation, 1972.

Rogers, Carl. *Freedom to Learn: A View of What Education Might Become.* Columbus, Ohio: Charles E. Merrill, 1969.

Sabine, Gordon A. *How Students Rate Their Schools and Teachers.* Washington, D.C.: National Association of Secondary School Principals, 1971.

Sciara, Frank J. and Jantz, Richard K. *Accountability in American Education.* Boston: Allyn and Bacon, 1972.

The National Association of Secondary School Principals. *How Students Rate Their Schools and Teachers.* Washington, D.C., 1971.

"The Principal and PPBS." *The Bulletin of the National Association of Secondary School Principals.* Washington, D.C., 1972.

"The Subject is Curriculum." *The Bulletin of the National Association of Secondary School Principals* (November 1969). Washington, D.C.

Thomas, James H. "Some Thoughts on Accountability." *The School Administrator* (May 1972). Washington, D.C.

8

Student Activities

INTRODUCTION

Today it would be hard to imagine a secondary school without a varied program of student activities. Intramural sports, organized athletics, clubs, newspapers, yearbooks, service organizations, bands, orchestras, choruses, student government organizations—all operate for the most part outside the formal curriculum, but are an integral part of secondary school life. If there were not officially sanctioned activities, students would invent them, as indeed they did for generations before the schools decided they should become a part of their official responsibilities.

The scope of activities is so great that their proper supervision and the development of policies under which they are carried on becomes one of the major responsibilities of the principal. Having said that, it must be added that the principal must arrange the administration of the activities program so that it does not consume an unreasonable amount of his time. Two responsibilities which the principal must carry out, however, are (1) overseeing the development of an overall policy for the student activities program and policies governing specific activities, and (2) clearly delegating responsibility and authority for the various activities. The principal cannot and should not attempt to develop policies by himself. Both faculty and students should be involved in policy formulation. All policy statements should contain built-in provisions for review and modifications.

Delegation of responsibility to staff members is in part a question of assignment and in part a matter of compensation. In the past ten years, compensation for major assignments to student activities has more often than not become a matter of collective bargaining agreements, with pay for particular services set in detail. Extra compensation for coaching, advising student newspapers, yearbooks, and the like is sometimes a flat sum amount, and sometimes is related to additional steps on a teacher salary schedule. All faculty should be expected to take some responsibility for student activities, and it is usually only those activities which take very considerable time and effort over a continuing period, over and above what is reasonably expected of a teacher, that qualify for additional compensation. It would be unfortunate, indeed, if teachers come to consider their teaching duties to be the only responsibility they have to students or to the school.

The nature of some student activities has been changing during the past several years, as will be shown in some of the sections which follow. In some schools principals have indicated a lessening of interest on the part of faculty in sponsoring activities. In others, principals report a shift in focus of interest of students away from some of the more traditional types of activities. The extent of interest on the part of students, the degree of staff support, and the shift in the nature of activities varies from school to school, and no generalizations apply to all schools. Overall, however, there are no signs that student activities are becoming a less important part of the school program.

COSTS OF PARTICIPATION

Various studies, beginning with those made by Harold Hand in the 1930s, have called attention to the considerable amount of expense to secondary school students caused by out-of-class activities. Club and class dues, subscriptions to school newspaper and yearbook, admission to athletic events, cheerleading expense, and so on require considerable annual outlay. In many schools such expenses, on top of those required for lunches, laboratory fees, purchase of class materials, and costs of graduation, are beyond the capacity of some students. No good answer has been found to this problem. Certainly ways should be found to see that no student is barred from participation in student activities because of lack of ability to pay. If such activities are to be considered a part of the school program, the Board of Education could be persuaded to provide a subsidy to the principal to be used in cases of real need. In some districts, Boards of Education have made direct appropriations to Student Councils, a part of which, presumably, might be allocated for this purpose. The amount required would be small, but the benefit of seeing that no one is excluded from activities for financial reasons would be great.

Safeguarding Funds

Money collected from the various student activities, and expenditures made from the funds amount to a good-sized business operation in any school, large or small. Funds should be safeguarded and expenditures accounted for in accordance with sound business practices. The accounts should be in such form that they may be subject to audit by outside auditors. This aspect of the principal's obligations will be more fully described in Part Four.

IT'S WHERE THEY "COME ALIVE"

Anyone familiar with secondary schools knows that it is in the activities program that students "come alive." In the documentary motion picture *High School*, for example, this was apparent in the program put on by the students in the Space Club. Through sports, clubs, service organizations, and student newspapers, boys and girls bring to reality the claim that high school is life, and that learning and living can be the same. It is either hypocrisy or ignorance of the real world of the secondary school that leads critics to relegate to a position of little importance the range of activities that are in truth the cement of the adolescent community of the school.

The Student Press

Although we will be concerned primarily with student newspapers, both officially sponsored and "underground," we are also aware that in an increasing number of schools students also have access to other communications media, such as licensed FM radio, closed circuit television, bulletin boards, and even certain types of assembly programs.

The day of the faculty-controlled, antiseptic student newspaper—sterilized, innocuous and strictly noncontroversial—is passing. Its demise has brought new problems, but more important, it has presented new opportunities. The foreshadowing of change came with the widespread resort to "underground" papers, accompanied by the series of related court decisions referred to in an earlier section.

Attempts on the part of students to enlarge the concept of student expression brought considerable discomfort to principals and staff who were unaccustomed to critical comments or pointed inquiry from student writers. The Supreme Court made note of this in the case of *Tinker* v. *Des Moines Independent School District* involving the wearing of black arm bands (see the selected readings for Part Two). Although this was not a case involving rights of the press directly, it did bear on the rights of expression. A summary of one of the points made in the decision appeared in the publication of the NASSP titled *The Reasonable Exercise of Authority*. The summary stated:

> Any departure from absolute regimentation in school may cause trouble, but undifferentiated fear or apprehension of disturbance is not enough to overcome the right of freedom of expression. Any deviation from the majority's opinion may inspire fear or cause a disturbance, but our Constitution says we must take this risk.
> To justify prohibition of a particular expression of opinion in the schools there must be more than a mere desire to avoid the discomfort and unpleasantness that accompanies an unpopular viewpoint. Where there is no finding or showing that engaging in the forbidden conduct would materially and substantially interfere with the require-

ments of appropriate discipline in the operation of the school, the prohibition cannot be sustained.[1]

A principal will be less than delighted when he reads something like the following excerpt from a student "underground" paper distributed in a suburban high school. The writers were among the more academically able students. They also described themselves as "activists." The names of staff, and the name of the school have been deleted.

> On January 9 and 10 a few of us were distributing leaflets in the halls of _____ for a January 20 anti-war march. The second day of leafleting, four of us were rewarded with a trip to the dean's office. While we were talking with Mr. _____ the point was made that the leaflet was neither obscene or slanderous and therefore legal. Mr. _____ agreed that the leaflet was legal. A lengthy discussion followed, which determined only that we would be allowed to continue leafleting, provided the classes were not disrupted in any manner.
>
> The following Monday, January 15, Mr. _____ informed us that the principal had decided we could no longer distribute the leaflet; and to make sure the leafleting was stopped, Mr. _____ confiscated the leaflets. Specifically, he said anything distributed in the school was to be submitted to the principal in advance.
>
> We paid the principal a visit Monday afternoon. In answer to our inquiries as to how he could order us to discontinue our leafleting, he stated that in his opinion it was disruptive to the school activities. We were certain we had in no way disrupted school activities. We had remained in the corridor by the foyer and did not block the passage of any people.... We asked the principal how he would prove in court, that we disrupted the proceedings of the school. He added that the superintendent had delegated him the power to approve or disapprove leaflets. Plus he mentioned that district policy was for him to make the decision. After further discussion we ascertained that no actual policy exists on the matter of leaflets, only a "practice." After some further discussion the principal said he would not approve the leaflet because he didn't wish to get involved in politics. We also learned two additional things while we were talking. First, if we continued the leaflet, disciplinary action would be taken. Secondly, the only manner in which we could press our argument was to take the case to court.
>
> The administration is not showing any respect to students as people, only something which must be kept in passive order. We are (apparently) not supposed to have or communicate ideas that the administrators do not agree with. Evidently the principal is a fine example of pseudoliberal. One who puts on a fake front of progressiveness, only to hide any repressive actions he sees fit to take. Restricting our legal right to leaflet can most assuredly be considered repressive.

---

[1] Robert L. Ackerly et al., *The Reasonable Exercise of Authority* (Washington, D. C.: National Association of Secondary School Principals, 1969), pp. 27-28.

If the administration attempts to prohibit the publication of this paper it will be a further example of repression of ideas which conflict with the ideas of the administration.

It is not the intention here to pass judgment on the incident reported by the students, nor on the ensuing report in the "underground" paper, nor on the decision of the principal. However, an analysis does reveal the need for schools to examine policies and practices respecting rights of expression by students. The place to begin is with what the courts have ruled. This is taken into account in a resolution adopted by vote of the membership of the American Association of School Administrators at their annual convention in 1973. The resolution follows:

Students' Rights and Involvement

Administrators must respect the Constitutional rights of students. Any limitation on those rights—such as freedom of speech and inquiry or due process—may be imposed only when the administration can show an overriding public purpose which can be served in no other way. That is, factual evidence (not opinion) must show that substantial disruption has occurred or is likely to occur; or that there is an invasion of the Constitutional rights of others; or that there exists a clear and present danger to students or others. Courts are delineating these rights with increasing clarity. Justice must be accorded students consonant with their share in the rights the Constitution guarantees all citizens. . . .

So far as student expression is concerned, the Courts have not condoned obscenity. Also, of course, libel laws apply to students as well as to others. However, it should be observed that in the case of *New York Times* v. *Sullivan* the Supreme Court rules that "courts will not protect a newspaper that has been proven to defame someone with 'knowledge that was false or with reckless disregard of whether it was false or not.' " The ruling on the other hand held that public officials could be criticized openly, and if the criticism was without malice, it would not be considered actionable libel. The definition of public official may well include school principals, in which case the principal under criticism would have to fall back for defense on whether the criticism threatened to or did in fact materially and substantially interfere with the operation of the school.

Emphasis on student rights frequently brings the response "What about student responsibilities?" That is a fair question. It is assumed that citizens whose basic rights are guaranteed also are obligated to carry the responsibilities that the exercise of rights entails. Yet one learns to be responsible by having the opportunity to function in situations where responsibility is learned. As in all learning, this carries with it the possibility of making mistakes or appearing to others to do so.

Perhaps it would be more productive in considering the widening freedom of the student press to think about the opportunities this expanding freedom provides. First of all, it provides the opportunity for student writers to report on and editorialize on matters of importance. Under this purview would come all aspects of school experience: the curriculum, the student government, other student activities, the governance of the school, and the policies in effect or under consideration. Why should student reporters not cover faculty meetings, except perhaps when specific matters involving personnel are under consideration? Secondly, it gives student writers the opportunity to report on and editorialize on other matters not directly related to the internal operation of the school, but of concern to young citizens. A number of organizations, the League of Women Voters, for example, query those who are running for membership on boards of education, and publish the replies. Is this not a legitimate kind of activity for the student press? Certainly students have a large stake in the quality of board membership and in the points of view of prospective members. An emerging trend is for a board of education to officially welcome student advisory members to meetings of the board. Is it not reasonable that reporters from the student press also attend? Thirdly, since older adolescents are close to the age of full voting rights and to the age when they are entitled, in some states, to run for certain offices and serve on juries, broader societal issues of concern to students may be proper topics for reporting and editorializing. Questions about the future quality of life, including ecology, pollution of air and water, overpopulation, and any number of other issues are particularly important to the young. Finally, the student press should not be closed to letters and opinions of administration and faculty.

As in all other student activities, a policy governing the student press should be developed, preferably jointly by students, faculty, and administration. The policy should include provisions for an editorial review board made up of students selected in a manner to be representative. A faculty adviser should be assigned to serve as ex officio member of the board of review. The faculty adviser should not impose his or her views, arbitrarily serve as censor, or have an absolute veto.

The following statement by the chief counsel of the NASSP may serve as a general guideline for policy development and as a help in defining the role of adviser.

School-sponsored publications should be free from policy restrictions outside of the normal rules for responsible journalism. These publications should be as free as other newspapers in the community to report the news and to editorialize.

Students who are not on the newspaper staff should also have access to its pages. Conditions governing such access should be established and be in writing, and material submitted should be subject to evaluation by the editorial board and, if need be, a faculty review board. These same general principles apply to access to other school publications.[2]

Because students of junior high school age are less mature and less experienced, somewhat more supervision of the production of a newspaper and somewhat more guidance about standards of responsible journalism are needed than at the senior high school level. Even at the junior high school level, however, broadening the scope of content is desirable and affords a good learning experience.

Finally, we think it is a fair assumption that students, having been accorded the right of free expression, will learn to use this right responsibly. The offensive use of four-letter words in some of the underground papers was intended to shock adult readers into attention. They added little to the arguments being advanced. If the need to shock is removed, one may believe that good writing will supersede the use of the meaningless obscenities.

Is it just because courts have ruled in favor of freedom of speech and press for students that schools, many grudgingly, are beginning to accord these rights? Certainly there must be educational reasons which persuade schools to welcome freer student expression. How else, in a democracy, is the search for truth to go forward, if not by the clash of opinion, the opportunity to have an argument in an open forum? How else does one learn to respect the right of another to his point of view unless that point of view may gain expression? These reasons, and not the weight of court rulings alone, should impel schools to welcome and further free discussion and to refrain from putting obstacles in its way.

Student Government Councils

Two generalizations may fairly be made about student councils in secondary schools: (1) They have not fulfilled the expectations of their advocates, and (2) conditions may now be right for these possibilities to be realized. Neither students nor administration and faculty are satisfied with student government as it operates in most schools. Student government has lacked the vitality which usually characterizes other student activities. One reason for this is that student government suffers from a lack of credibility. Experience has revealed to students that its representatives on the council are not given responsibilities for anything of much importance. Deciding on the date for a dance or how the gymnasium will be decorated hardly seem to be matters of overriding concern. As a consequence of its relative ineffectiveness, students elected to office come to consider election merely as one more item to add to their extracurricular records, or as an honorary position carrying the prestige of being "big man (or woman) in school." Lacking any significant responsibilities, council meetings tend to become exercises in parliamentary maneuver-

[2]*Ibid.*, p. 17.

ing punctuated by frequent cautions from the faculty advisor about the limitations placed on the council by the legal authority carried by the school principal or by school rules and regulations that inhibit council decisions. It is the inability to make decisions about things that matter that lies at the heart of the dilemma of student government. Thus, we have a paradox: student government that cannot govern. We suggest that the pretense of governing be abandoned. It is true that final decisions in many areas of concern to students cannot in fact be made by student representatives on a council. The council cannot, by itself, decide to have an open campus, go to a pass-fail system of grading, rearrange lunch schedules, or change vacation dates. If, then, it is agreed that student councils cannot make final decisions and get things done by deciding, what are proper and real functions which the student council can perform?

This brings us to the opportunities that lie at hand. Although students cannot make final decisions, they may certainly participate in and influence decision-making. Discussion of and recommendations concerning a wide variety of school policies and practices should not run up against the warnings of faculty advisers that the council has no final authority or that it cannot make binding restrictions on the principal or faculty. Thus, freed from stifling impediments to discussion, the council may debate freely any item under discussion, arrive at any position on a particular issue, publicize the debate and the resolution of the issue, and recommend what in its judgment is a proper and desirable policy.

Nothing in the school need be out of bounds for examination. The curriculum, the conduct of student activities, the grading system, teaching, and the rules and regulations under which the school operates are all legitimate questions for discussion and recommendation. Given the opportunity to raise issues, debate and discuss them, and arrive at recommendations, members of the council will find it necessary to keep in close touch with the members of the student body. This requires seeking out the under-represented boys and girls—the ones someone has called the Silent Majority—and probing their feelings and soliciting their ideas. On occasion, as necessary, the council can hold open meetings to which all are invited and at which any who wish may speak. The council acts, then, as the voice of the student body. One may ask how this procedure becomes anything more than a debating society, with nothing happening except the flow of words. The belief is that the actions of the council, and its resolutions and recommendations will have an important bearing on ultimate decisions. To believe otherwise is to suggest that the school principal intends at all costs to have his opinions prevail and that the faculty at all costs will not take into account student opinion as expressed through the official representatives of the student body. This might be the case in some schools, in which the whole idea of student council had better be abandoned in the interest of intellectual honesty. We do not believe it would be the case in the majority of schools.

The underlying purpose of student representatives sitting on a council is to provide opportunities for the young citizen to gain experience in the democratic process. As such, it is worth the time and effort spent by principal, faculty, and students. Students will learn, as adults in the larger society come to know, that instant change is the exception rather than the rule, and that resolving differing points of view and interests is a delicate, time-consuming activity, requiring patience and skill. Administration and faculty will learn that no one group, not even theirs, has a patent on good ideas, and that the voice of students is not necessarily strident but rather may be an expression to which principal and teachers may listen with profit to themselves and the school. The result may be a growing mutual respect.

Aside from being a forum for ideas, the council may legitimately be given responsibilities quite within their capacity to perform. Some of these lie within the area of student activities themselves. The chartering of clubs (within a general policy), the scheduling of activities, responsibilities for budgeting certain expenditures, and guidelines for student conduct at public events are examples of duties which may be placed on the council.

Imaginative principals aided by staff and students can devise their own variations in the ways student councils can be chosen and organized, and the responsibilities they can be given. The question is whether there is sufficient commitment on the part of the school to make student councils meaningful and effective. Like anything else worth doing, time is required both from faculty who serve as advisers, and from the principal, who must take the results of the council's deliberations seriously, meet with the council as required, and act in some way on the council's recommendations. Time will also be required of students who run for office, are elected, and serve. With work that has real meaning to it, student leadership takes on new dimensions. Gone will be the perfunctory meetings and the cynical attitude toward council service and toward the council itself. In its place will be more effort, and consequently more psychic rewards for effort expended.

One final comment may have implications for the student council movement. As discussed in another section, schools are responding to the desire of students for more involvement in policy-making and decision-making by creating a variety of student advisory committees on curriculum, grievances, and biracial problems, or by creating student-faculty councils to consider a range of questions. The future relation of student councils to these emerging student advisory groups is not clear, but given a new structure and mission there is no reason why council and student advisory groups may not be compatible and complementary rather than competitive.

Interscholastic Athletics

The question here is not whether interscholastic athletics should be a part of the student activities of a secondary school, but within what set of standards they should be carried on. A sports program has benefits; it can also be abused.

For the participants, who are mostly (but not exclusively) the boys in the secondary school, interscholastic sports can be a form of enjoyment and a healthy release of energy. There is a thrill in competition for those well-enough endowed athletically to take part. How many have this opportunity depends upon the variety of sports offered. While the public interest seems to be centered around football and basketball, many schools offer a much wider choice. Track and field, wrestling, tennis, and swimming are frequently offered where facilities are available. The school teams generate a school spirit and *espirit de corps* beyond that arising from most other kinds of activities.

A prospective principal being interviewed by a board of education was asked his opinion of interscholastic athletics. He replied that the tail should not be allowed to wag the dog, but that on the other hand the dog should have a tail to wag. How to keep such a nice balance is one of the major tasks of the principal. In addition to the positive benefits of the sports program, he must keep in mind the possible abuses, some of which are explicated in the following:

1. Under no circumstances should the participants in a sport be exploited. Thorough physical examinations before a boy is permitted to compete, and refusal to play an injured player are basic requirements. A coach who is tacitly encouraged or who feels impelled to drive boys beyond the limits of physical and emotional endurance is guilty of exploitation. Insofar as is practical, a school should protect the superior athlete and his parents from over zealous recruiting by college coaches.

Signs adorning a locker room reading "Winning isn't everything. It is the only thing" convey a message of doubtful truth or value. Winning isn't the only thing, either in athletics or in life, and such a philosophy is not worthy of a place in an educational institution. No team can win all the time and sometimes a team in a particular year will not win much of the time. Just as good students make a good school, so do good athletes make a winning team. The supply of both vary from time to time and from school to school.

2. The public has a legitimate interest in the sports program, and is entitled to the enjoyment of watching spirited contests. But this interest sometimes extends beyond healthy bounds. Overly enthusiastic booster clubs can distort the purposes of the athletic program, bring pressures to bear on coaches and players, and can, if unchecked, result in the tail-wagging-the-dog kind of overemphasis. This overenthusiastic response can cause a principal difficulties, which is one reason, among others, why a clearly stated policy on interscholastic athletics should be formulated and adopted by the board of education.

In some communities, most often in the larger cities, crowd control is a problem. The schools have the obligation to take whatever measures necessary to prevent rowdyism, fights, and vandalism by spectators, who, more often than not, are persons not enrolled in the school. The use of police to assure proper security is sometimes supplemented by parent volunteers. In any event, whatever measures are required should be taken to preserve a proper atmosphere of good, fair competition free from spectator disruption.

3. The principal must not abrogate his responsibility to represent his school in regional and state athletic associations. High school athletic programs are usually carried on in relation to policies, rules and regulations, and guidelines governing eligibility, tournaments, officiating, spectator conduct and the like which are developed by a state athletic association made up of the secondary schools in the state. The principal is usually the official representative and voting member of the state association. In practice, attendance at meetings of state and regional associations is sometimes made up of coaches to whom school representation is delegated. This is acceptable, with the strong proviso that the principal must keep himself informed on all issues and must make it clear that his representative speaks for the school and not for himself. When important matters of policy are up for decision, the principal should personally attend, speak, and vote. He should also initiate questions of policy at any time he feels that decisions about athletics are veering away from sound educational policy.

4. The principal must see to it that the facilities provided for sports, games and recreation are not monopolized by the interscholastic sports program. Boys who do not participate in interscholastic competition nevertheless enjoy playing competitive games. Girls, too, get the same pleasure and benefit from sports activities. Opportunities on a broad scale should be made available through an intramural program. Such a program cannot succeed, however, unless some reasonable use of playing fields, gymnasiums and swimming pools is provided, and unless faculty supervision for intramural sports is arranged.

An article in the NASSP *Bulletin,* written by Wayne Dannehl and Joele Razor, members of the Department of Physical Education for Men at the University of Illinois and both athletic officials, touches on the above issues. It is summarized below.

> ... Athletics can be of great value to the educational, psychological, and social growth of students, but moderation is the key to that value. Competition on the athletic field tends to lose its educational value when victory is the ultimate goal.
>
> The solution to the problem of exploiting athletics and thus not realizing their educational potential lies in the attitude of the school community. Many communities take so much pride in the winning record of their teams that coaches must win or be dismissed. A coach in this situation is, of course, likely to submit his players to many ... abuses. It is the function, therefore, of the school board, school administrators, and the community, as well as the athletic staff to ensure that the educational values inherent in athletics are not perverted by an over-emphasis on winning.

> Like all educational programs, athletics can be defended only to the extent to which they contribute to established goals. When school people, especially coaches, consider winning a concomitant result of athletic competition, athletics will have an excellent opportunity to achieve desired outcomes.
>
> The values of athletics are many and inherent within the activity, but exploitation through ill-conceived goals and improper administration is common and on the increase. Only through careful philosophical inquiry and practical application can the values be realized.[3]

Court rulings have held that athletics are part of the school program and that students may not be excluded for arbitrary reasons. This means that the same requirements that apply to participation in other student activities apply to athletics, but no arbitrary reasons outside general policies may be used as a basis for exclusion.

Courts have also ruled that girls may compete with boys in noncontact athletics, such as tennis, golf, and swimming, as team members, provided no such competition is available to girls.

It is the latter proviso that is stimulating schools to develop interscholastic programs for girls, with women coaches and officials. The Illinois High School Association in 1973 endorsed an extensive interscholastic sports program for girls, including among the approved sports tennis, golf, swimming, archery, bowling, track and field, volleyball, table tennis, and badminton. Most of these sports require relatively little in the way of facilities, but they do require some field and gymnasium space and time for use. Along with the desirable goal of increasing intramural programs, additional strain is placed on facilities and equipment, demanding more careful planning and scheduling and some additional funds.

Interscholastic sports programs in the junior high school present special problems. While some competition with other schools can be supported, the schedule of games should be shortened from that of the senior high school. The use of the junior high school as a training ground for senior high school athletics cannot be supported on educational grounds and carries the real possibility of exploitation of the younger players.

Cheerleaders

Probably as much trauma results in the selection of cheerleaders as in the selection of the starting five for the basketball team, but with far less justification. In most schools, elaborate tryouts and eliminations are held before the winning combination is finally put together. In many instances, judgments about who will become cheerleaders rests with members of the faculty, including physical education teachers and coaches themselves.

---

[3]Wayne E. Dannehl and Joele E. Razor, "The Values of Athletics: A Critical Inquiry," *The Bulletin of the National Association of Secondary School Principals* (September 1971), p. 65.

Since cheerleading is not parallel with the competitive athletic team selection, it is difficult to defend the method used or results obtained in almost all schools to choose *the* official cheerleaders. At least, this is an activity where those selected might best be judged by their peers. At best, one may question why several squads of cheerleaders might not be selected. After all, there are many athletic events during the course of a year and there is no good reason why the number of girls and boys who wish to take part in this activity cannot be expanded. It's all in fun; the prestige of the school does not *really* hang in the balance, and no principle of education dictates that there must be only one squad of cheerleaders. In some schools bitter feelings are aroused because of alleged racial discrimination in selection of cheerleaders. Where such feeling exists, every precaution needs to be taken to see that such discrimination does not in fact occur.

Clubs and Service Organizations

Changes in student motivation and interests are being reflected in new kinds of clubs and service activities. Unfortunately, research into trends in this aspect of the student activities program is scanty, but some directions may be discerned in a study conducted by Robert L. Buser in cooperation with the officers of the NASSP and reported in part in the NASSP *Bulletin* for September, 1971.

The study was based on a select sample of schools nominated by officers of state principals' associations as having developed outstanding activity programs. Subject area clubs and hobby clubs were among those reported most frequently dropped from the activities program. Among club activities added were those associated with societal problems and issues. Illustrative are ecology and antipollution clubs, foreign affairs clubs, women's liberation clubs, and peace clubs. Others reported as having been added grew out of ethnic interests and included such organizations as the Afro-American club, the Jewish Educational League and the Italian-American Club.

Seminars on topics of student interest with such names as life discussion seminar, world affairs seminar, and drug seminar, were reported. Leisure interest activities are reflected in such names as riding, skydiving, out-of-doors, folk music, skiing, scuba diving and weight training clubs. School-community service organizations seem to be increasing in number and type, examples of which are service to homes for the aged, voter registration activities, antipollution and cleanup days, and tutoring services.

Time provisions for club and service activities included meetings during evening hours in private homes, replacement of the home room period with an activities period, and the use of a rotating schedule including an activities period. Many organizations, of course, continue to meet in the school building after school hours. One aspect of the study referred to was the response to the question of what is most likely to reduce the effectiveness of the student activities program. In order of importance the principals reported the following: lack of (1) faculty commitment, (2) relevant activities, (3) student interest, (4) administrative support.

We mentioned earlier the need for an overall policy governing all student activities. For clubs and service organizations, specific policies within the general policy are required. These include the conditions under which a club or organization may be chartered, and the procedures to be followed by students who wish to organize a club and secure a charter for it.

Music, Speech and Dramatics Activities

A uniformed band is an asset to a school. Public appearances of orchestras and choral groups and presentations of dramatic productions not only provide valuable learning experiences to the students who participate in them but also serve to form a link between school and community.

These activities are not always carried on exclusively outside the formal curriculum, nor should they be. The creative and performing arts should be as much of a part of the curricular offerings as science, mathematics, or language. Even where this is so, however, performing groups use time outside of school for practicing and performing.

Questions arise about the time that should be used for such purposes. Excesses need to be avoided. For example, the requests for appearance of the school band for all kinds of civic and ceremonial purposes can easily get out of bounds. If all such requests are granted, unreasonable demands on students' time may be made which may also infringe on school time required for other purposes. Also, long distance travel for bands, orchestras, and choral groups, occasionally including out-of-state trips and even excursions to foreign countries may not be in the best interests of either student or school.

Competitive activities, primarily involving music groups but also including speech contests, are open to question. These activities are often carried on under the umbrella of a state high school activities association which includes interscholastic athletics in addition to music, speech, and debating competition. Faced with regional and state competition, an inordinate amount of time in practicing, rehearsal, and travel to centers where the competition is carried on can be spent preparing for and taking part in the competition. Costs connected with this kind of activity can also be excessive. The desire to "win" may abort other more desirable outcomes.

Contests

Few high schools escape requests from organizations for students to compete in contests of various kinds for assorted prizes, ranging from cash awards to plaques or certificates. Essay and poster contests head the list. Some contests originate locally, usually with the best of motives. A local service club, casting about for some way to be helpful, might decide that it would be good if less litter were thrown in the streets. How to bring this to people's attention? Obviously, a high school essay contest is the answer. The club appropriates

$100 from its treasury for first, second, and third-place prizes. The topic and length of essay and the time limits for the contest are agreed upon. The principal is approached, the proposed plan is presented, and cooperation is requested. Unless the school has a policy, the principal is hard pressed to refuse. He knows, of course, that this is one of several requests that will come his way. He knows that essay contests have relatively little educational value. Yet he does not want to offend the service club which has only the best intentions. To take another example, the local Womens Club has as its project the beautification of a local park. How dramatize this interest? The art department of the high school comes instantly to mind. A poster contest is what is needed. Again, the theme, the prizes, the request to the principal.

Local requests for essays and posters present special difficulties simply because of the association of school and community. They may be discouraged by a candid but friendly statement that such contests really do not inspire either better writing or better art, and that there are preferable ways for secondary school students and community groups to work together on desirable projects.

National contests present another problem with different dimensions of difficulty. An almost limitless number of organizations, businesses, and special interest groups would like to have access to the captive audience of adolescents in secondary schools. The aims range from selling a product to selling an idea. One helpful screening is that done by the Committee on National Contests and Activities of the NASSP. For more than thirty years the Committee has compiled an Advisory List, a copy of which is sent to all members of the organization. This is helpful in that so far as is possible, sponsors with ulterior motives have been screened out. The list that remains is still quite extensive, leaving many judgments to be made by the local school as to which organizations, if any, to endorse.

Fund Raising Activities

In many communities, householders seldom go a week without greeting a caller from some organization in the high school either soliciting contributions outright for a student activity or offering for sale some item, from candy to Christmas wreath. Younger boys and girls of junior high school age are often driven by car, the mother waiting while the traveling mendicant knocks on each door in the block. Older students do the whole thing on their own. A plethora of such fund raising activities does not benefit the student and most surely does not endear the school to the community. Better ways to support student activities must be found. One way to reduce the need for what amounts to begging is for the board of education to appropriate a fixed sum to aid in the support of activities. In one district, the high school faculty and parents have annually written, produced, and presented a variety show which attracts a sell-out audience who attend because the entertainment is good. The proceeds go into the student fund. With a little imagination, the

Student Activities

nuisance type of fund raising may be avoided. With proper budgeting of resources, no approved activity need go unfinanced.

Bibliography

Divoky, Diane, ed. *How Old Will You Be in 1984? Expressions of Student Outrage From the High School Free Press.* New York: Avon Books, 1969.

Keith, Kent M. *The Silent Majority: The Problem of Apathy and the Student.* Washington, D. C.: Council of the National Association of Secondary School Principals, 1971.

_____. *The Silent Revolution in the Seventies.* Washington, D. C.: National Association of Secondary School Principals, 1972.

Kvaraceus, William C. "Working with Youth: Some Operational Principles and Youth Values." *The Bulletin of the National Association of Secondary School Principals* (December 1969), pp. 62-71.

"Non-Athletic Activities Program." *The Bulletin of the National Association of Secondary School Principals* (October 1963), pp. 20-22.

Van Pool, Gerald. "Student Council Crises." *Momentum* (April 1970), pp. 56-59.

Zeigler, Earle F. "A Philosophical Analysis of Amateurism, Semiprofessionalism and Professionalism in Competitive Sports." *School Activities* (March 1964), pp. 199-20.

9

Student Personnel Services

The acceptance of the democratic model described in Chapter 3 has implications for the administration of a school's pupil personnel service departments. It is our intent to discuss, at the outset of this chapter, the broad implications of this model—that is, those that apply to all pupil personnel service areas—before discussing the implications for the implementation of particular service functions.

GENERAL PRINCIPLES

There are a number of pupil personnel services that every school must provide, such as personal counseling, course selection assistance, vocational counseling, testing, health services, and provision for dealing with antisocial student behavior. It is the responsibility of the principal to see to it that an organizational plan which is suited to the school's unique needs and resources and that will enable the various service areas to function efficiently is developed. Acceptance of the democratic model necessitates that organization and efficiency be viewed as means to an end rather than as ends in themselves. The ultimate aim must be service to the school community which in some way facilitates the optimum development of students' intellectual, emotional, social, and occupational capacities rather than the efficient processing of students. It will take a high order to leadership on the part of the principal to develop a common understanding and recognition of this aim among all pupil personnel staff members and to see that operational decisions are based on these aims rather than on considerations of administrative efficiency.

As has been stated in several preceding chapters, one of the basic tenets of the democratic ideal is respect and concern for the rights of the individual

Student Personnel Service

and for his worth and dignity. Thus, in a democratic school the focus of the pupil personnel services departments must be on providing services to individuals—services that will help individual students to better understand themselves, to achieve better interpersonal relationships, to live in harmony in the school community, to make effective choices, and to maintain good health. The factory approach, in which students are treated as numbers to be sorted, categorized, and processed, often in the name of efficiency, must be avoided, and doing so may not be as simple as one might suppose.

The principal should lead in helping all members of the pupil personnel staff to recognize the potential ramifications of the "processing" approach to their tasks. He can help them understand some of the forces which make it difficult for schools to avoid slipping into an impersonal approach. In a mass society which places a high value on technological development, such tools as the computer and data processing technology may result in a "processing mentality," with efficiency as the only goal. This is not to say that schools should not use computers, or that computerizing certain services inevitably results in impersonalization, but it can happen if a conscious effort is not made to avoid it. If used wisely, technology can probably increase the amount of time that pupil personnel service staff members have available for direct contact with students.

Another factor which contributes to the tendency of schools to adopt the "processing" approach to pupil personnel services is size. For a variety of reasons (expanding enrollments, the unavailability of land in metropolitan areas, inadequate provision for financing school construction, consolidation) many junior and senior high schools are quite large, and more than a few are overcrowded. Size has certain advantages, particularly the potential scope of the curriculum that it necessitates, but one of its undesirable effects is that the school may almost unconsciously adopt the factory model. The size of the scheduling, counseling, disciplining, and record-keeping tasks often makes the assembly-line processing of students appear to be a necessity to the pupil personnel service departments. Add to these factors the pressure on schools from business and political leaders to eliminate frills and to adopt industrial efficiency concepts, corporate management practices, and accountability systems designed for profit-oriented enterprises, and one can readily understand the need for vigilance in order to avoid slipping into the assembly-line approach.

It was suggested earlier that a historical overview of the development of secondary schools will provide the administrator with a valuable perspective. Some historical perspective of the kind of pressures mentioned in the preceding paragraph should be a part of that overview. Callahan's *The Cult of Efficiency in Education* provides knowledge of the way "efficiency" concepts have been forced on schools in the past. Reading it may well equip the principal with the kind of perspective that will help him avoid fulfilling Santayana's prophecy.

The principal must help the pupil personnel services staff members determine their role in the school on the basis of students' needs and the schools's educational philosophy rather than on the basis of the demands of current pressure groups. This is not to say that the school should be deaf to the demands of the larger society or of the local community regarding pupil personnel services, but there will always be conflicting demands about which services the school should provide and the extent to which they should be provided. The principal must be able to evaluate conflicting demands, identify vested interests, and help his staff put them in perspective.

Once the school community has arrived at consensus as to the aims and objectives of pupil personnel services, the principal must use his leadership to develop in all pupil personnel staff members a sense of commitment to the idea of service. Clerks, receptionists, and paraprofessionals, as well as the professional staff, should be committed to the idea that their occupational *raison d'etre* is to serve the school community. This implies that students should be treated with consideration rather than as second-class citizens to be sorted, shuffled off to one place or another, ordered around, or ignored. If students or parents are treated rudely by receptionists or secretaries, the effectiveness of the professional staff will be impaired.

The statement in the preceding paragraph that the role of the pupil personnel service staff is to serve the school community is a conscious one. Although its primary function is to help students, it has a broader contribution to make. The pupil personnel staff members, particularly those engaged in counseling, are in a unique position to provide valuable feedback to teachers, administrators, and curriculum planners about many aspects of the school. If the staff is rendering the kind of comprehensive services suggested, they will be in constant contact with the four main elements of the school community—students, teachers, administrators, and parents. Their close personal contact with individuals in each of these elements should enable them to gain knowledge of students' needs that are not being met and valuable insights into each element's perceptions of, and attitude towards, the other elements—insights which should be particularly useful to the principal and his administrative staff as well as to other members of the professional staff. In order to facilitate broad participation in the feedback process the principal will have to strive to develop an attitude of openness and receptivity to criticism and new ideas on the part of all members of the pupil personnel staff as well as the administrative staff. The authoritarian hierarchical organization model (with students at the bottom of the hierarchy), traditionally employed in schools, does not facilitate this kind of two-way communication, and many members of the staff may have to be "won over" before they can profit from the feedback provided by the pupil personnel services staff.

The use of the term *services* indicates that someone is to be served, and in this case it is primarily, although not exclusively, students who are the recipients of the various services. Throughout this book student participation in the decision-making process has been stressed, with the full realization that structuring meaningful participation is not easy. Students are not in the habit of participating in the decision-making process in schools; thus, it is hardly surprising that they sometimes appear apathetic in their response to initial invitations to participate, or inept at their first efforts at participation. In addition, too often when students have been asked to participate they have experienced token participation—participation which paternalistic administrators have attempted to use to give an appearance of democratic consensus to decisions that have really been made unilaterally. However, the pupil personnel services area would appear to be one that can provide a good avenue for an initial effort to involve students in the decisions that affect them. Students can readily evaluate the extent to which counseling and health services are accessible to them, whether such services are helpful, and whether students are treated with consideration. They are equipped to make suggestions, based on their perceptions and experiences, for the improvement of various services. Such input can help a staff that is open to constructive criticism to improve the services they offer students, and can point the way to services that need to be expanded or reduced, added or eliminated. Nearly every student is interested in the rules and regulations governing pupil behavior; thus, student participation in the formulation of pupil personnel policies should be easy to obtain.

A latent feature of student participation in these areas may be a greater understanding on the part of students of some of the problems and constraints faced by the pupil personnel services staff. Students are usually reasonable if given the chance, but too often schools have taken the attitude that since they are "only students" the administration and teaching staff has no obligation to explain or justify rules, practices, or decisions to them, and that there is no need for them to understand the reasons behind the way in which the school is operated nor to have any voice in determining how the school shall operate. The relationship between this attitude and some of the events described in the chapter on student dissent seems obvious.

An effective student government could develop committees to work with pupil personnel service staffs and the administrative coordinator. In addition to providing valuable input to the decision-making process, such committees can serve as a communications link between the study body and the staff. Not only can they forward student suggestions, complaints, and perceptions to the staff, but they can interpret staff problems and concerns to the student body. They may also help to communicate to other students information regarding ways to make better use of available services.

Similarly, the personnel services area would seem a natural area in which to bring parents into the decision-making process. Course selection, vocational counseling, discipline, and health care are all services that greatly involve parents and about which parents frequently have concerns. They too are being served, and in a democratic school they will have a voice in deciding how they and their children are to be served.

We now turn to a discussion of the specific pupil personnel service areas and their functions. Schools vary in the scope and extent of the pupil personnel services they provide, both because of resource limitations and because of legitimate differences of opinion regarding the school's responsibility to provide certain types of services. The latter is particularly true in respect to psychological and health services. The principal functions—those that are common to nearly every junior and senior high school—are included in this discussion.

Finally, a few words about the location and internal organization of the pupil personnel service departments. Whenever possible, the departments responsible for performing nearly all of the functions described should be located where the students are, and not off in some remote corner of the building. The one exception to this general statement may be the school psychologist. It may be advantageous for him to be located so that students can come and go unobtrusively. Students frequently must make appointments to see counselors, deans, and other staff members between class periods or in the few minutes between the time their bus arrives and their first class begins. They often do not have, or will not take, the time to go to a remote corner of the building to make such appointments. Further, staff members are better able to interact with students informally and to develop a "feel" for the prevailing student attitudes and concerns and the general school atmosphere if they are in the midst of the action. The principal should make every effort to see that they are easily accessible to students and parents in every way.

The administrative organization of the pupil personnel departments will be to some extent dependent on the size of the school; but even in a large school there should be only a limited number of departments—possibly no more than three: a guidance department, a staff of deans, and a health service. Creating many highly specialized pupil personnel service departments is likely to result in poor coordination and unnecessary disputes regarding jurisdiction and responsibility. In smaller schools, one coordinator can probably administer all of the pupil personnel functions. However, in large schools it may be necessary to have heads or chairmen for the various service departments, with the responsibility for overall coordination assigned to an assistant principal.

THE GUIDANCE DEPARTMENT

The guidance department is usually the largest of the pupil personnel service departments, and frequently nearly all such services, except health services, are included in its responsibilities. However, this traditional name for the department responsible for counseling, vocational information, testing, and so forth, has an unfortunate connotation—one that belies its true function. It is not the function of any school staff members to "guide" students or to attempt to "guide" them.

Counseling

Counseling is a legitimate pupil personnel service function. We view counseling as providing information, helping interpret information, providing empathetic understanding and support, helping develop self-awareness, and providing help in developing satisfying human relationships. These are all activities designed to help students make informed, effective choices. The counselor's function is *not* to *tell* students what courses they should select or to suggest what college they should attend, nor is it to *guide* them into a particular vocation.

Although the title applied to the department responsible for counseling, achievement testing, and interpretation of tests is not in itself important, it is important that the principal and the staff understand this distinction, since it has been but a few years since many schools were involved in a massive effort to guide or channel students. In hindsight, the post-Sputnik effort to guide or channel the most talented high school students into mathematics, science, and engineering fields in order to assist in our effort to "win" the technology race with the Russians appears ludicrous at best and immoral at worst. The rejection of the idea of "guiding" students implies that the school, through its counselors, should not serve as a manpower recruiter in order to serve the needs of the government, the military establishment, or corporate enterprise. This does not mean that students should not be provided with information regarding job availability, job requirements, pay scales, and potential fringe benefits; but providing information which will help a student make an informed, effective choice and channeling him into a vocation are two far different things. A democratic society is based on confidence in the individual's capacity to make choices. Providing opportunities to develop and practice this capacity should be a conscious goal of the guidance department.

One of the results of post-Sputnik emphasis on the early identification and channeling of talented students, and of the crush for limited college space, has been a tendency on the part of some counselors to press students to make career choices at a rather early age—frequently at the time they enter high school. The student is seldom equipped to make an intelligent choice at this stage of his development. He has not had sufficient opportunity to explore various interests and to become aware of his strengths and weaknesses, nor is his decision-making capability likely to be adequate to the task. The result of forcing him to commit himself to a career choice at too early an age is likely to be commitment to an unrealistic goal, or to one that reflects his parents' interests and aspirations rather than his own. The psychological damage to students that can result from feelings of guilt that develop from his failure to attain goals to which he is publicly committed is described in every psychology text. Counselors should blunt rather than reinforce parental pressure on students to make early career commitments. That it is unrealistic to expect high school freshmen to know the precise vocation they wish to pursue after high school, or what area in which they wish to major in college, is clear from studies that reveal that many people change jobs frequently in their early working years and that a large portion of college students change their major at least once after entering college. In helping students select their program of courses, counselors should stress the acquisition of basic skills, the investigation of interests, and the development of career options with the idea that the student will gradually focus in on a post-high school career choice.

Another function of the counseling staff is to help students adjust to their environment—particularly their human environment. Helping the student to adjust and cope must not be confused with fostering conformance. It is not the function of the counselor, or any other member of the school staff, to attempt to force the student who "marches to a different drummer" to conform to the norms of the prevailing majority group or the expectancies of the school establishment. For too long schools have attempted to adjust every student to fit the mode of the existing educational system. The resulting suppression of individual creativity, expression, and interest has been a principle target of critics such as Goodman and Friedenburg. Often the pressure for student conformity has originated with the school administration. Administrative pressure on counselors to help attain student conformity to administrative expectations has, in fact, resulted in a general distrust of administrators by many counselors. Erickson and Smith, in their book *Organization and Administration of Guidance Services,* state that "once the guidance program identifies itself with administrative authority, it is likely to become a tool for the administrator and the nemesis of pupils."[1] The principal must understand that it is not the function of counselors to serve as an extension of his administrative authority. Helping a student to adjust and cope will in many instances involve helping him to develop new attitudes and perceptions and to modify his behavior, but in others it may mean changing some aspect of the school. It should be a function of the counseling staff to provide feedback from students and parents that will enable the school to adapt to the needs of individual students.

An important function of the guidance department is to provide students with information concerning post-secondary educational and vocational possibilities and to help them interpret and use this information effectively in the process of making career decisions. It may be that the vocational aspect of counseling, particularly in large schools, can best be handled by one or more

---

[1]C. E. Erickson and G. E. Smith, *Organization and Administration of Guidance Services* (New York: McGraw-Hill, 1957), p. 8.

staff members specifically trained for vocational counseling. The information needs are so great, and require such constant updating, that it is probably unrealistic to expect every counselor to be equipped to provide comprehensive vocational counseling. Offering specialized vocational counseling would be more appropriate. Most counselors are much more familiar with college entrance requirements, procedures, and curriculums, since that is the route they have taken, than they are with vocations outside the field of education.

There are a number of sources of assistance to the vocational counseling program. Among these are the various vocational information retrieval systems that have been developed in recent years. For example, the *Computerized Vocational Information System* (CVIS), which was developed under the auspices of the Illinois Board of Vocational Education, is a system that has been operational for several years and that appears to be effective. (An excellent film and a brochure describing the system is available from Project CVIS, 1250 S. Ardmore Avenue, Villa Park, Illinois.) In addition, there are usually resources available in the community. Resource persons from a wide range of vocations, as well as from colleges and universities, can be brought into the school to talk with students and parents. Such programs should probably involve informal communication as well as lectures and demonstrations and the distribution of literature. Counselors, particularly those engaged in vocational counseling, should be encouraged to periodically update their knowledge of vocational possibilities in businesses, industrial concerns, and other sources by observing their operation and talking with their personnel staff. The school can also arrange for students to go out into the community to seek vocational information. Counselors should encourage students to do so. The success of such programs will depend on a flexible, adaptive principal who provides support rather than roadblocks.

One of the major problems faced by the principal is likely to be a lack of agreement among counselors, teachers, students, parents, and administrators regarding the role of counselor. Teachers frequently believe that the counselor's function is to "handle" difficult students, tutor students who are experiencing academic difficulties, solve attendance and tardiness problems, and see to it that students register for their courses. As mentioned earlier, some principals tend to believe that counselors are employed to help them run an orderly, efficient school, which usually means performing clerical tasks and disciplining students. Some students and parents view the counselor as their personal advocate in their battles with various divisions of the school establishment, while others expect them to be glorified baby-sitters who see to it that their children sign up for the ACT or SAT test and send in their college applications before the deadline. The professionally trained counselor, on the other hand, may feel that all of his time should be spent helping students solve their human relations problems and that any and all clerical tasks are beneath his professional dignity.

The principal must develop a clear conception of the role counselors are to perform in the school, and the formation of this concept should be influenced by input from teachers, students, and parents regarding their needs, as well as the opinions of professional counselors regarding the needs of the school community and possible ways they can help meet them. Once a consensus is reached and the counselor's role is defined, the principal and his staff must attempt to develop a common perception of the counselor's role among all members of the school community. The first step is to achieve common understanding among the administrative and pupil personnel services staffs. Through faculty meetings, parent meetings, newsletters, etc., this role definition can be communicated to teachers, parents, and students. It can also be communicated directly by counselors, for when counselors have a clear conception of their role, it will be obvious in their direct interactions with students, parents, and teachers.

Although the counselor role that evolves may differ from school to school in order to meet local needs, it will undoubtedly be a professional one that demands highly trained counselors who are particularly gifted at, and interested in, working with young people. If so, it becomes the principal's responsibility to see that the pupil personnel services area is organized in such a way that counselors are not so burdened with clerical chores that they cannot perform their professional functions. Further, since clerks can be employed at considerably less cost than professional counselors, it is obviously economically unsound to use counselor time for routine clerical tasks. However, the principal may also have to convince counselors and other professional staff personnel members that it will probably never be possible to relieve them of the necessity of performing some clerical tasks. It is doubtful that any single school staff member, including the principal, can avoid all paper handling.

THE TESTING PROGRAM

Another pupil personnel service function is the design and administration of the school's testing program. In most schools the responsibility for the testing program is usually assigned to the guidance department. In some large school systems large scale testing is the responsibility of a district level research and/or evaluation department, particularly when the purpose of the testing is to evaluate the effectiveness of some aspect of the school's program. Tests of an individual nature, such as interest inventories and specialized aptitude tests, are nearly always administered by the guidance department. Which department administers which tests is not as important as ensuring that only the most dependable tests are used, that they are properly administered, and, most important, that the personnel who have access to the test results use them judiciously. The potential for the misuse of test results is enormous in a society which bases so many decisions that have a significant effect on the lives of individuals on the results of tests. An eminent sociologist's view of the pervasive use of tests in our society is expressed in the following passage from an article entitled "Testomania," written by Pitirim Sorokin and published in the *Harvard Educational Review.*

> At the present time in the Western countries almost every individual is tested from the cradle to the grave, and before and after every important event in his life. He is given a battery of tests after his birth, in his nursery school and kindergarten, in his elementary, high school, and college, before and after his draft into the armed forces, before and during his marriage, before and after his gainful employment, and so on, up to the tests preceding and following death. His life career is largely determined by these tests. Beginning with intelligence tests and ending with the tests of loyalty and subversity, various testers have replaced the old-fashioned angel-guardians that supposedly guided the life-course of each person. We are living in an age of testocracy. By their tests of our intelligence, emotional stability, character, aptitude, unconscious drives, and other characteristics of our personality, the testocrats largely decide our vocation and occupation. They play an important role in our promotions or demotions, successes and failures, in our social position, reputation, and influence. They determine our normality or abnormality, our superior intelligence or hopeless stupidity, our loyalty or subversity. By all this they are largely responsible for our happiness or despair and, finally, for our long life or premature death.[2]

Unfortunately, most parents and students are unable to interpret test results and do not understand the limitations of the various tests. They are almost totally dependent on school personnel to interpret test results for them, but the school personnel disseminating test results are frequently not much more knowledgeable. The outcome is often blind faith in the results based on the claims of the testing company. The apparent faith of school personnel in tests coupled with the fact that test results are usually represented in a neat package of finite numbers, even though they allegedly represent such subjective factors as personality traits and interests, too often leads students and parents to conclude that the student's personality, interests, and abilities, are indeed what the test results say they are. In his 1973 presidential address to the American Educational Research Association, Robert L. Ebel stated that among other current measurement problems, "there is the problem of proper interpretation of test scores, and of the inadequacy of many professionally trained educators to make such interpretations. There is the problem of public attitudes toward testing, which seems to gravitate to the extremes of uncritical acceptance of disdainful rejection. There are the problems of needless duplication, of invasion of privacy and of self-fulfilling prophecies."

---

[2]Pitirim A. Sorokin, "Testomania," *Harvard Educational Review* 25, 1955, p. 199.

In order to avoid some of these problems, a pupil personnel staff member well-trained in the areas of tests and measurement and statistics would be a valuable addition to the school. Such a person could supervise the selection of tests and could help other staff members learn to use test results intelligently. If the school does not have an adquately qualified person on the staff, a consultant should be employed to help the pupil personnel services staff review the testing program and, above all else, to instruct them in the proper use of test results. Such a review should begin with an examination of the objectives of the testing program.

In a democratic school there is little reason for developing a testing program solely for the purpose of comparing the school with other schools, comparing students with other students, or for sorting and categorizing students. Testing should be conducted for the purpose of helping the school improve its instructional program and for helping individual students make effective choices. The use of objective tests for sorting, classifying, and pigeon-holing students is characteristic of a school based on the factory model rather than one which subscribes to the democratic ideal of concern for the worth and dignity of the individual.

A further comment concerning the use of the results of standardized tests is appropriate. More than a few school administrators, particularly those located in affluent suburbs, have in the past used the results of such tests as the National Merit Scholarship Examination for public relations purposes in a manner that comes close to being unethical. For an administrator to infer that the high scores earned on such tests by a small percentage of the school's students is the result of the superior instruction offered in the school is to indicate that he is either lacking in knowledge of such tests or is dishonest. Aside from ignoring the fact that such tests measure only one type of achievement—a type that may not be nearly as important as some of the other potential outcomes of schooling described earlier in this book—such claims reveal a lack of familiarity with what knowledge of school effectiveness that we do have. The findings of Coleman, Levin, Bowles, and others seem to clearly indicate that it is much more likely that the superior family background and innate ability of these students is the reason for their high test scores than the instruction they have received in school. Similarly, citing the high percentile rank of the scores earned by a school's students on a standardized achievement test battery as evidence that the school is providing "quality education" is dishonest unless there has been some effort to statistically control family background factors, student ability, and student interest and motivation.

In addition to the doubtful ethics, the misuse of such data can backfire on the school administrator. When the socioeconomic composition of the community changes or a few intellectually superior families move out of the community, or the tests begin to measure skills and knowledge not included in the school's curriculum, he may be hard pressed to explain why the school is no longer producing a large number of National Merit Scholars or why achievement test score means are below the 50th percentile. The public's conclusion may well be that the school has "slipped." In the long run, unfounded claims of this nature can only result in a lack of public confidence in the school and its administration.

STUDENT RECORDS

A problem common to all of the pupil personnel service departments will be how to handle student records. Ensuring the confidentiality and security of student records is a problem that has received considerable attention lately. Over the past few years, numerous professional organizations, private foundations, and state departments of education have studied the problem and issued reports and guidelines. This attention has probably resulted from a general laxness on the part of schools toward the problem. Too often the only people who have been denied access to a student's school records have been the student and his parents.

The school should not grant access to student information for commercial purposes or for any form of solicitation. Nor should they give out information to any agency, governmental or otherwise, over the telephone. Deciding how much information teachers, students, and parents should have access to, and under what conditions, and when parent or student consent must be obtained before information can be released is a complicated task, but one that the school must face.

After conducting a study of student record keeping in public schools in the United States, Vivien Stewart of the Carnegie Corporation concluded that many schools accomplish this task in a way that is unsystematic and frequently ambiguous. Further, it was her observation that the bad record-keeping and even worse systems for information dissemination common in public schools result in the frequent violation of the right of students to privacy.

In order to protect students' rights to privacy, the principal committed to the democratic model should consider the application of the following principles to the school's system for collecting, storing, and disseminating student data:

1. No information should be collected without the informed consent of parents, and in some cases student consent should also be required.
2. Student personnel data should be separated into several categories of confidentiality, with access to each category clearly defined.
3. The access of professional personnel to various categories of data should be based on professional need.

4. Parents should have access to their children's school records.
5. Parents should have the right to challenge their children's school records.
6. No agency or individual outside the school should have access to student records without parental consent, and in some cases students consent should also be required.
7. Every attempt should be made to verify the information pertaining to students that is collected. Unverified information should be destroyed rather than stored.

Each school or school system should have a written policy regarding student records which specifies, at least, the following:

1. What information can be collected and by whom.
2. A system of categorizing the information collected that will facilitate differential access to various levels of information.
3. Who shall have access to each category of information, and under what conditions.
4. Who shall be directly responsible for the maintenance and security of student records.
5. Security regulations.
6. How long each type of information should be retained.
7. How information should be disposed of when the retention period has expired.

Schools that use computer data banks for the storage of student records and data have a particular problem and will have to design special precautions to prevent unauthorized persons from obtaining confidential information from the data bank and for removing outdated information from storage. That the potential for invasion of privacy is increased by the use of computer data banks for the storage of personal data has been documented by numerous writers in the past few years—thus there is no excuse for schools being unaware of these dangers and failing to take the precautions necessary to ensure security and confidentiality.

The principal must recognize that the implementation of a system that ensures the confidentiality of student records may increase the cost of collecting, maintaining, and disseminating student data. Obtaining consent from parents and/or students for data collection and dissemination will probably require additional clerical time and some additional expenditure for printing and mailing. The supervision of data collection and storage and the implementation of security measures will require additional administrative time. Many schools attempt to save on clerical help by using student help in various offices, but security and confidentiality should preclude the use of student help for filing student records, posting grades, recording test scores, and so on.

The principal should have no problem justifying the additional cost and effort required to implement a system that ensures confidentiality. Boards of education and intelligent citizens are capable of understanding that preserving the rights of an individual in a democratic society often causes inconvenience to governmental agencies and frequently results in some loss of efficiency in terms of time and money. However, the principal may occasionally need to remind them that in a democracy the preservation of the rights of the individual is a higher order value than efficiency. In addition to fulfilling the ethical and legal obligation that the school has to its students, the effort to protect the rights of its students by implementing a student record policy that ensures confidentiality should contribute to increased parent and student confidence in their school.

For a school attempting to develop a set of comprehensive guidelines to govern the collection, dissemination, and disposal of student personal data, the 1972 Report of the Russell Sage Foundation Conference on the legal and ethical aspects of school record-keeping entitled *Guidelines for the Maintenance and Dissemination of School Records* is an excellent resource.

SCHOOL-COLLEGE RELATIONS

Articulation between the high school and colleges and universities can be another important function of the guidance department. High school personnel have been reluctant to take initiative in this area. They usually wait for the colleges or universities to summon them to articulation conferences which turn out to be forums for their administrators or admissions officers to explain what information the high school *must* provide them if its students are to be admitted to their university. But counselors can acquire information that will be helpful to their students, and frequently they can obtain useful feedback from former pupils enrolled in the university hosting the conference. Although it may be difficult for an individual school staff to change this one-way pattern of "articulation," concerted efforts through professional associations of counselors and principals may prove effective. As has been documented earlier in this book, high schools have for too long sat idly by and allowed the colleges and universities to determine the nature of secondary education.

In many schools, the guidance department is assigned the task of conducting follow-up studies of former students (the term "former students" is used here rather than graduates because we believe that follow-up studies should be concerned with dropouts as well as graduates). In large school systems, responsibility for this function may be assigned to a district-level research bureau, but in most schools the guidance department will have to secure and provide much of the data, no matter who designs and coordinates the study. Such studies should be encouraged, if not initiated, by the principal. They can provide valuable information regarding the adequacy and relevance of the school's curriculum and can offer indications of the immediate post-high school and long-term educational needs of the student population. Too often schools employ only short-term evaluative procedures while emphasizing to students the idea of delayed gratification.

PSYCHOLOGICAL SERVICE

Providing for students with complex or severe psychological problems is another problem the principal and his staff face. Most experts agree that the high school counselor should not attempt to treat severely disturbed or maladjusted students; however, some provision for helping such students must be made. If the school is large enough and has the financial resources, a qualified clinical psychologist or psychiatrist can be employed. If this is impossible, some arrangement should be worked for referring students to an adequately staffed community agency or a private psychologist who will handle school referrals on a fee basis. If the school employs one or more psychologists, they should either be a part of the guidance department or organized in a way that will facilitate close cooperation with all other professional pupil personnel service staff members.

The principal will need to consider the procedure for referring students to a psychologist. It would seem wise to avoid referrals being made directly by teachers. Teachers should probably deal primarily with counselors who in turn can talk with students and parents and suggest the possibility of psychological help. Students and parents should also be able to initiate the request for psychological counseling, either through a counselor or by going directly to the psychologist.

It will be the responsibility of the principal to see that procedures for securing prior parental permission for psychological testing and treatment are established and followed, and for determining a policy regarding the confidentiality of information obtained about and from students by the psychologist. The statements on confidentiality and professional ethics published by the various professional psychological associations can provide valuable help in developing a policy that serves the best interests of the individual and the school community.

BEHAVIORAL PROBLEMS

Dealing with instances of antisocial behavior on the part of students is commonly recognized as a pupil personnel services function, but the principal may find that there is considerable disagreement among members of the pupil personnel services staff regarding who should be assigned this responsibility. In some schools, counselors are assigned this responsibility in addition to their counseling duties. This puts them in the position of having to judge and mete out punishment to the same students with whom they are attempting to develop a trusting interpersonal relationship. C. H. Patterson states in *An Introduction to Counseling in the School* that

> A counselor may be able to develop a counseling relationship with a student who is guilty of an infraction of rules and subject to discipline, as long as the counselor is not charged with judging the case and meting out punishment. It is more difficult, and perhaps unlikely, that he can be judge and counselor at the same time.[3]

The acceptance of this position does not imply that the counselor should not be concerned with his counselees' antisocial behavior. He can and should attempt to help them understand their antisocial behavior and attempt to eliminate its causes. He can explain the potentially damaging effects of such behavior to the individual and the school community and the need for consideration and cooperation in any community of men. He may be involved in soliciting parental cooperation in the effort to solve discipline problems, particularly when truancy and tardiness are involved. The counselor's primary effort, however, should be directed toward helping the student understand and solve his own behavior problems and helping the rest of the school staff understand and contribute to the solution of student behavior problems. For him to attempt to solve such problems through the imposition of punishment or constant intervention in the student's behalf would be both inappropriate and self-defeating.

There are additional reasons why discipline problems—particularly those which may necessitate suspension or expulsion—should be handled by an assistant principal or dean rather than by counselors. The revocation of the right to attend school, even for a few days or class periods, is a serious matter. Such punishment should be administered with consistency and fairness and in strict accordance with the school's pupil personnel policy guidelines. It would seem that consistency and fairness could be achieved more easily if such authority was vested in a limited number of staff members rather than the entire counseling staff. In addition to being unfair, the inconsistent administration of pupil personnel policies is certain to result in conflict between parents and students and the school. Also, serious discipline problems should be handled by a staff member with knowledge of school law, including recent court decisions in the area of student rights. It would be unrealistic to expect all counselors to acquire and maintain knowledge in this area in addition to their professional training in counseling.

---
[3]C. H. Patterson, *An Introduction to Counseling in the School* (New York: Harper & Row, 1971), p. 30.

A more satisfactory arrangement might be for the principal to appoint a high level administrator, possibly an assistant principal, to deal with student behavior problems, or, in the case of large schools, to supervise a staff of deans assigned this task. Irrespective of the title of the staff member exercising this responsibility, he should possess mature judgment, be committed to the philosophy of the school, and should have proven ability to deal with difficult students fairly and effectively. Fairness and flexibility seem likely prerequisites for effectiveness. A rigid, authoritarian person or one insensitive to the feelings of students and parents can have a disastrous effect on the atmosphere of the school and on school-community relations.

In a democratic school the principal has an obligation to ensure that rules and regulations have a direct relationship to the educational process. He is also obliged to ensure that students are accorded all of their legal rights whenever disciplinary action is taken. As mentioned in the chapter of student rights, in recent years the courts have increasingly taken the position that students have all the constitutional rights of citizens. In particular, the courts have held that the student has a right to due process of law whenever the school institutes disciplinary action that might involve substantial punishment. In many states the legislature or state department of education has mandated guidelines for disciplinary procedures in order to ensure that schools live up to the due process clause of the fourteenth amendment to the constitution. If the legislature or state department has not developed such procedures, the local school should take the initiative to safeguard the rights of students rather than wait until they are forced to extend them by court action.

HEALTH AND SAFETY

Another important pupil personnel services function is to provide for the health and safety of students while they are at school. A health services department staffed by one or more registered nurses is just about mandatory in schools of moderate to large size and is desirable even in small schools. The health service department should be prepared and equipped to treat minor injuries, to provide first aid in emergencies, and to identify illnesses that require immediate medical attention. The possibility of a cooperative arrangement with the police or fire department emergency squad or an ambulance service for providing more extensive emergency aid and immediate ambulance service to a nearby hospital should be investigated. Such an arrangement can provide an important supplement to the school's health service facilities.

Irrespective of the size of the health service staff or facility, the principal should work to develop an attitude of sensitivity to students' feelings on the part of all staff personnel, from receptionists or secretaries to nurses. Students are often sensitive about health problems, or even such health-related statistics such as height and weight, and every care should be taken to avoid embarrassing them. The function of the staff is to provide help, not to conduct an inquisition or obtain information for the school's gossip mill.

Comprehensive health records for each pupil should be maintained. Precautions must be taken to ensure the confidentiality and security of such records. Parent telephone numbers (both home and work numbers) should be on file and readily available so that parents can be notified immediately in case of serious illness or injury. Whenever possible, parental consent should be obtained before any treatment is administered or before a student is taken to a doctor or hospital.

Health records should include information concerning any health problem, particularly hearing or vision impairment, that might hinder the student's performance in the classroom or other school activity. It is probably best if vision and hearing testing is done periodically by the school. However, the principal should allow the health service staff to conduct such tests only if a fully qualified staff member is available; if not, qualified personnel should be employed on a part-time basis. It is essential that such testing be done accurately in order to avoid alarming students and parents unnecessarily. However, the health service should notify parents of health problems that need attention and, when appropriate, suggest that parents consult their family physician or dentist.

In the case of students with health problems or physical impairments that restrict their ability to function in class or participate in certain activities, individual teachers should be notified. Teachers should be made aware of potential emergency situations and of special provisions they may make to help compensate for certain impairments. Exactly how much to tell teachers and other staff members regarding an individual student's health is a delicate question and one that the principal and health service staff should consider carefully.

The health service staff can also help the principal monitor the school to ensure that students are not asked or allowed to engage in activities which tend to result in an excessive number of injuries. Overzealous physical education teachers, and coaches in particular, sometimes have to be reminded that not all students have the physical maturity and capability to perform certain activities and that some activities are too inherently dangerous to be included in the school's program. It is not so much that such teachers are not concerned for the welfare of their students, but rather that in their eagerness for their students to achieve they do not carefully evaluate the risks involved for some students. In addition, they are usually endowed with natural athletic ability and in excellent physical condition themselves and thus may not realize the danger involved in some activities for physically immature students, students lacking in athletic ability, and students who are simply "not in shape."

Bibliography

Arbuckle, D. S. *Pupil Personnel Services in American Schools.* Boston: Allyn and Bacon, 1962.

Blair, G. M. and Jones, R. S. *Psychology of Adolescence for Teachers.* New York: The Macmillan Co., 1964.

Butler, H. E., Moran, K. D., and Vanderpool, F. A. *The Legal Aspects of Student Records.* Topeka, Kansas: Nolpe, 1973.

Dreikurs, Rudolf and Gray, Loren. *Logical Consequences: A New Approach to Discipline.* New York: Meredith Press, 1968.

Ebel, Robert L. "The Future of the Management of Abilities II." *Educational Researcher* (March 1973), pp. 5-12.

Governor's Commission on Schools Business Management Task Force. *Survey and Recommendations.* Springfield, Ill.: The Public Education Management and Survey, 1972.

Harris, JoAnn. *Computer-Assisted Guidance Systems: A Report to Counselors and Administrators.* Washington, D. C.: American Personnel and Guidance Association, 1972.

Lazarus, Richard S. *Patterns of Adjustment and Human Effectiveness.* New York: McGraw-Hill, 1969.

Zaccaria, Joseph. *Approaches to Guidance in Contemporary Education.* Scranton, Pa.: International Textbook Co., 1969.

Selected Readings

An Educational Imperative: The Human Dimension

Arthur W. Combs

Since people are human at birth, it would seem the problem of humanization ought to be no more difficult than strengthening and encouraging the tendencies with which people are born. Unfortunately, it is not that simple. In our search for the better life we have created a world which surrounds us with "things" undreamed of in previous generations. We have achieved unbelievable mastery of the processes of production only to find they have immensely increased our "people" problems. Instead of helping people to become more humane, we have created an incredible number of barriers in all our institutions, including education, that make the growth and development of humaneness a difficult task for students.

In the earlier chapters of this volume some of the forces which contribute to the processes of dehumanization and alienation have been described. Among these have been pointed out the technological revolution, the problems of urbanization, and the explosion of information in the world. To these I would add a fourth, the fetish of objectivity, which possesses us everywhere.

The veneration of objectivity is part of our mores. It is one of those "goods" which almost no one ever stops to question. It is part of our way of life, deeply rooted in American philosophy, as sacrosanct as religion. There are good reasons for this, of course. After all, we developed as a nation originally by learning to deal with the things of our world. We tore down the forests, pushed back the frontiers, and built a nation out of the wilderness. We applied the same objectivity to the production of goods and services and so developed our industrial might. We are proud of our productivity and our successes in the manufacture of things. Small wonder that we are impressed

---

Reprinted with permission of the Association for Supervision and Curriculum Development and Arthur W. Combs. © 1971 by the Association for Supervision and Curriculum Development.

with the industrial model and try to apply it to other problems of our society.

The principles we learned in the wilderness and industry tend to be further corroborated by our unquestioning worship of science, the sacred cow of the modern world. Objectivity is the method of science, and its marvelous products are all around us. Small wonder that we have become enamored of the objective approach to the solution of human problems. It is part of our blood. Applied to the problems of things, it has led us to fine solutions. Applied to people problems, however, the effect has been far less salutary. As a matter of fact, its unquestioning application to the problems of human beings has contributed greatly to the very problems of depersonalization and alienation with which we are now so concerned.

What makes people human are matters of feeling, belief, values, attitudes, understandings. Without these things a man is nothing. These are the qualities which make people human. They are also the qualities which, in our zeal to be objective, we have carefully eliminated from much of what goes on in our public schools. The problem of dehumanization is no accident. We brought it on ourselves. We have created a Frankenstein's monster which has broken loose to run amok among us.

Everyone starts life with the capacity to become a good human being. People are not born bad or inhuman. The qualities we describe as human are "warm" qualities of compassion, understanding, fulfillment, love, caring, justice, and the like, while the qualities we describe as inhuman, on the other hand, are "cold" ones, generally the reverse of these. We speak of a man as "a good human being." By that we refer to his uniqueness and value as a person, his sensitivity and compassion for others, and his capacity to interact effectively in his world. Elsewhere in this book, these traits have been called "humane." They are also the characteristics of self-actualizing persons as they are described by psychologists who have studied such people.

What kind of person an individual becomes is dependent in very large measure upon the kind of world we create for him to grow up in. As Earl Kelley tells us, "Whenever we get to worrying about the younger generation we need to remind ourselves that they were all right when we got them." After birth everyone becomes more or less human as a consequence of his experience. We learn who we are and what we are from the nature of our interactions, especially those with the significant people in our lives.

One would think, offhand, that teachers ought to be among the most significant people in the lives of children but, alas, this does not seem to be so. Quite the contrary, the attempt to tell a teacher how important he is almost certainly will bring upon you a dissertation on his insignificance. Everyone, he will tell you, is much more important in the life of a child than he is. There is little or nothing a teacher can do, he says, because "they" won't let him. The children in his classes have already been shaped by the people who had them before, and there is little or nothing left which he can hope to do. When teachers are asked the reasons for the failure of schooling, research shows that 80 percent to 90 percent of the reasons they give for not being successful have their origins in the child, the parents, or the community, almost anything but the teacher himself. Teachers on the whole simply do not feel they are significant people.

Despite all this, the psychologists continue to tell us that a child is the product of his interactions with the people in his world.

How does it happen, then, that we have gotten into this bind? I do not believe it is because we are stupid, evil-hearted, or vicious; I believe it has happened because of our preoccupation with the wrong goals for education, on the one hand, and faulty assumptions about how to help people, on the other. In the remainder of this chapter I would like to outline some of the things we need to do if our schools are truly to meet their responsibilities in the release of human potential.

A COMMITMENT TO HUMANISM

Several generations ago, Sigmund Freud told us we never do anything unless we would rather. It is a sound psychological principle that people do only what they think is important. We need but examine our own behavior to discover how true this principle is. If schools are to move toward humanism, then humanism must become important to all of us, students, teachers, administrators, and the general public.

Even deciding that humanism is important, however, is still not enough. Humanism is like motherhood. Everybody is in favor of it, but not everyone is committed to it, not by any means. There is a vast difference between an intellectual acceptance of an idea and the belief that it is truly important enough to warrant *acting* upon it. Everyone believes that peace is important, but not important enough to stop wars. For a long time people have believed that civil rights and the elimination of poverty are important, but nobody did very much about these ideas for years and years. It is not enough for us to decide that humanism is important to schools. As the children put it, "You need to put your money where your mouth is."

A commitment to the importance of humanism is not always easy in a world of things. Things can be seen, manipulated, forcibly changed, directed, and made to do and be what we wish. Human qualities of thinking, feeling, believing, and valuing, on the other hand, are matters that happen inside people and, hence, are not so readily apparent. They do not give us the comfortable feedback we get from successes with things. A commitment to humanism also calls for a shift in thinking from self to learner. It means we have to be less concerned with what *we* do and much more concerned with what happens in the hearts and minds of those we do things to.

A concern for humanism calls for the development of deep sensitivity on the part of teachers, supervisors, and administrators so that they may become aware of the consequences of their behavior in the internal life of students.

With all the pressures currently bombarding our public schools, a decision for the importance of humanism becomes more important than ever. A man who has not determined what is truly important is like a ship without a rudder, at the mercy of every fad, fancy, or force which may be exerted upon him. When a person does not know *what* is important, then *everything* is important. When everything seems important, one must *do* everything. Other people seeing us do everything then come to *expect* us to do everything, and this, of course, keeps us so busy we do not have time to think about what is important.

The only hope of escape from such a vicious circle is some kind of decision as to what is truly important. Without such a commitment, it is never possible to say "no"! A commitment to humanism can stop this merry-go-round and provide stability and direction, a frame of reference in terms of which to make our vital decisions. Once having made a commitment to humanism, moreover, it is fascinating to see how some problems which currently loom immovably in our path are reduced to insignificance; some of our age-old problems even become absurd.

THE IMPORTANCE OF HUMAN MEANING

Learning always has two phases: (a) the acquisition of new knowledge or experience, on the one hand, and (b) the discovery of its meaning, on the other. Learning may fail for lack of information or because the student has never discovered the meaning of information provided him. Effective learning requires *both* halves of this learning equation but, alas, our schools are spellbound over information. Attempts at curriculum reform are almost exclusively "hung up" on the information side of the learning equation. Whenever we want to improve education, we come up with the same old answers—let us have more! Let us have more science, more math, more languages in the elementary schools, more homework, more physical education, more driver education, a longer school year, and a longer school day.

Now with our lovely new hardware we have brand new ways to give students information. So we must now have more television, more teaching machines, more programmed instruction, more movies, overhead projectors, tape recorders, and computerized gadgetry of every form and description.

And where has all this brought us? To schools that often do not matter, to deep feelings of alienation. To dropouts, cop-outs, and a dozen forms of protest aimed at achieving personal human goals no matter what the cost in the violation of human values.

It is a naive assumption that the acquisition of facts alone will make a difference in human behavior. All we need do is examine ourselves to be quickly aware of how false this assumption may be. Most of us know what we *ought* to eat, but we do not eat that. We know how we *ought* to drive, but we do not drive that way. We know we ought not to be prejudiced, but we are. Few misbehave because they do not know any better. The dropout in school is not a dropout because he was not told. He *was* told! The problem is, he never discovered what it meant. The information half of the learning equation is the impersonal side. The meaning half is the human side but, unhappily, most of our educational effort is preoccupied with the information half of the equation. If schools are really to be made more humane, it will be necessary to redress this imbalance and devote far more time and energy to the personal meaning aspects of learning. Among other things this will require, at a very minimum, changes like the following:

1. Deemphasizing information and objectivity. Our exclusive preoccupation with these matters simply will not do.

2. Valuing meaning. The meaning of information for the learner must lie at the very heart of the school's effort. This calls for a far greater acceptance and encouragement of the subjective than currently exists in most places.

3. Developing sensitivity to student meanings. A program emphasizing personal meaning will require of teachers and administrators the capacity to see the world through the student's eyes. Since meanings exist inside of people they are not open to direct observation but have to be interpreted from observed behavior.

4. Accepting students. Since new meanings in human beings develop from those they already have, schooling must begin from where people are. This calls for schools which do not demand of students that they be what they are not or try to mold them in preconceived fashion, but accepts students where they are and helps them to become what they may be.

5. Encouraging personal exploration. The discovery of meaning is a highly personal matter occurring in a particular individual through his own explorations. If this principle is to be put into operation, then schools must become far more flexible than they currently are, must really make a commitment to individualizing instruction, and must set students free to move far more in their own directions than has previously been true.

6. Testing, evaluating, and rewarding meaning. If meaning is to become the crux of the issue, then it is meaning which needs to be the focus of evaluation and testing. If humanism is truly important, then students must be evaluated and rewarded, not so much for what they know as for what they are.

7. Teachers, too, must be evaluated and rewarded for humanism. Since teachers, like everyone else, do only what seems important, superior performance in the production of humane students must become a major objective of teaching, and teachers who do it well must be recognized and rewarded for it.

REMOVING BARRIERS TO HUMANISM

If humanism is to take its place as a prime objective of education, that fact must be spelled out in our procedures and practices. It makes a great deal of difference through what pair of glasses one looks at the schools. If one looks through the pair marked "Providing Information," the schools look very good. Common practices and procedures are clearly related to those goals and make a great deal of sense. Looked at through the glasses marked "Valuing Humanism," schools look decidedly different. In fact, some of the very procedures required for the business of giving information get in the way of achieving humanism. As one of my good friends put it, "What you make on the bananas you lose on the oranges!"

If humanism is to be given the kind of central position this volume calls for, then a careful, systematic search of our goals and practices is needed to weed out those whose effects are destructive to human values. The person who embarks upon such a search, however, must be prepared for a most dismaying prospect. One is almost forced to the conclusion that had we set out consciously and purposely to create dehumanizing conditions we could hardly have done a better job. Earlier chapters of this volume have described in considerable detail some of the forces in our society leading us to this dilemma and some of the practices in our educational structure which continue to exaggerate the processes of dehumanization. Many of these were described in the ASCD 1962 Yearbook, *Perceiving, Behaving, Becoming: A New Focus in Education.*

More recently the members of the ASCD Commission on Humanism in Education compiled another list of dehumanizing practices and conditions. In this list were the following:

1. The marking system and
   a. The competition it inspires
   b. The comparisons it makes
   c. The pressure it creates
   d. Failure
2. Corporal punishment
3. Overcrowding and resulting
   a. Class loads
   b. Easy anonymity
   c. Shallow teacher-pupil relationships
   d. Loss of privacy

4. Curricular tracking and
   a. The caste system it nurtures
5. Inflexible and non-variable time schedules
6. The scarcity of legitimate postgraduate options and
   a. Pressure to attend college
7. The "single text" approach and
   a. The conformity it demands
   b. The boredom it creates
8. The grade-level lock-step which ignores what we know about the ways in which unique selves develop and
   a. Accompanying imposition of single scope and sequence schemes
9. Misuse and misinterpretation of intelligence, achievement, and aptitude tests
10. Testing instead of evaluating
11. Teacher evaluation of students
12. Failure to reflect teacher responsibility for grade or mark "achieved" by student
13. The "objectivity model" which prevents meaningful relationships from developing between teachers and pupils
14. The ignoring of the principle of "feedback readiness"
15. The "right" answer syndrome
16. Misuse of cumulative records
17. Demonstrated distrust instead of demonstrated faith.

Almost anyone familiar with teaching will recognize that this is only a limited list. One needs but to ask himself "What kinds of things have I seen occurring in schools which have destructive effects on humanness?" and in a very few moments he could add considerably to the list above. When one considers that the public schools are our primary social institution for the production of future citizens, the fact that such a list can be made so easily is shocking indeed.

THE NEED FOR HUMANISTIC PSYCHOLOGY

Since people behave in terms of what they believe is so, the kind of psychology adopted by educators plays a vital role in determining the kinds of schools and schooling we construct. For several generations the predominant frame of reference for psychological thought in this country has been some form of stimulus-response psychology. There are many variations and theories of learning arising from this orthodox understanding of behavior, but all of them see the matter of learning as one of properly manipulating the stimuli to arrive at a desired result.

Looked at in this way curriculum design becomes, almost exclusively, a question of deciding what people "should" know, then gathering information for them and teaching it to them. Motivation becomes a matter of applying rewards and punishments. Learning, seen from this frame of reference, becomes quite logically and naturally a preoccupation with the manipulation of information and an exclusive concern with events outside the learner.

There is nothing really wrong with using stimulus-response psychology as long as our major interest is concentrated on highly controlled behavior, on rote learning, on memory, and on the acquisition of information. All these, however, are essentially depersonalized functions. If we are truly concerned about human beings or the behavior of people when they are no longer operating in our sphere of influence, we need a different approach. If it is intelligent, self directing, responsible, knowledgeable people we seek, then a different psychology is called for.

We need, not a psychology of stimulus-response, but a psychology of human meaning, a psychology which helps us to deal not only with what goes on outside the learner but with what happens inside him in the human discovery of meaning. A humanized curriculum needs a humanistic psychology. If we start from a mechanistic psychology, it should not surprise us if we come out with mechanistic answers. We need a psychology capable of dealing with man's experience, a psychology interpretive of students' feelings, values, beliefs, and understandings, and personal meanings.

Fortunately, this kind of understanding of the problem of learning is at hand in the humanistic frame of reference basic to many new approaches to psychological thought. Psychologists working in this new frame of reference call themselves by a variety of names: Personalists, Self Psychologists, Phenomenologists, Perceptualists, Existentialists, and Interactionalists, to name but a few. By whatever name they may be called, however, they are all concerned with the question of what goes on inside the learner.

These new humanistic approaches to the nature of behavior hold the keys for educators to the practices needed in the effective development of humane capacities in students and teachers alike. In recent years these approaches have already brought us understanding of the self concept, new concepts of human potential and self actualization, new insights into motivation and learning. For teachers concerned about human values and the development of human potential, humanistic psychological thought provides criteria and points directions to far more effective solutions, and we have only scratched the surface of what it may eventually do for us.

HUMANISM AS PART OF THE CURRICULUM

If we would prepare youth properly for the human world they must live in and for the human problems they must solve, the curriculum of our schools must provide students opportunities to explore human questions. Vital questions of values, beliefs, feelings, emotions, and human interrelationships in all forms must be integral parts of the curriculum. To achieve this end, it is not enough that we simply teach the humanities. Instruction in English, social studies, art, music, and drama is not enough. Humanism and the humanities are by no means synonymous. As a matter of fact, such subjects are often taught in the most inhuman fashion. It is a fascinating thing that the human qualities of love, compassion, concern, caring, responsibility, honor, indignation, and the like are largely left to accident in our schools.

The qualities that make us human are feelings, attitudes, beliefs, values, and understandings, but much of the curriculum eschews these factors as inappropriate for study in school. They make teachers uneasy. We feel as though we are wasting time talking about them, or we are fearful the Russians may beat us by training more people in science and math than we do. Here, however, is a quotation from Urie Bronfenbrenner's introduction to A. S. Makarenko's book, *The Collective Family*. Makarenko is Russia's "Dr. Spock," and Dr. Bronfenbrenner says in his introduction to the American edition of this book:

> It took the shock of Sputnik to cause Americans to reject the permissiveness of the 'thirties and 'forties in favor of pressure for academic excellence. It may, therefore, come as something of a surprise to learn that the primary education emphasis in Soviet society during the past ten years has been, not on academic excellence, but on character education—the development of such qualities as altruism, industry, and service to one's community and nation. Moreover, following Makarenko, Soviet leaders have emphasized that effective character training requires imposing on the child challenging responsibilities for service and self discipline not only within the family but, equally importantly, in his collective or peer group both within and outside the school.[1]

What a shock to find that while we have been going all out for hard-nosed scholarship the Russians have been stressing character and personality!

Although psychology began as a scientific discipline in 1879, it has still not found its way into the curriculum of most American schools. The same could be said of sociology, anthropology, and political science. These are the sciences of the new era expressly developed to help human beings to understand themselves and their relationships with other people, the most pressing problems of our time. Where they exist in the curriculum at all, it is usually somewhere on the periphery. They are "elective" subjects to be studied only by those students who have successfully acquired the traditional subject matter. But if humanism is truly important, these matters must not be merely peripheral; they must lie at the very center of the curriculum. After all, the most important problems deserve the most important place.

---

[1] Anton S. Makarenko. *The Collective Family: A Handbook for Russian Parents.* New York: Doubleday & Company, Inc., 1967.

TRAINING HUMANE TEACHERS

Humanness is learned from the quality of an individual's interaction with significant others. Humanistic goals, therefore, demand careful attention to the kinds of teachers being produced by our teachers colleges and our in-service programs. We have long been concerned with improving the competence of teachers, defined as what they know and how they perform. The teacher as a person, however, has been given comparatively little attention and most teacher education programs, even when they may be concerned with these matters, are woefully inadequate to deal with them.

Recently, educators have begun to understand the importance of the teacher as a human being, not merely for the effect he has upon the mental health of the students he works with, but because his humanness vitally affects the success of even the teacher's traditional role as conveyor of learning. For the teacher in training, humanness is as important to *his* success as a learner as the humanness of his future students will be in *their* growth and development.

In our studies of the helping professions at the University of Florida we have come to believe the effectiveness of teachers and counselors is not so much a question of the knowledge of the methods they use as how the helper has learned to use himself as an instrument to carry out his own and society's purposes.

The person's self is at the very heart of the problem of effective teaching. Producing an effective teacher, we have concluded, is not so much a task of teaching him *how* to teach as helping him *become* a teacher, a very human question indeed.[2]

There is good evidence to suggest that effective teachers are personally adequate people.

1. They tend to see themselves in essentially positive ways. That is to say, they see themselves as generally liked, wanted, successful, able persons of dignity, worth, and integrity.

2. They perceive themselves and their world accurately and realistically. They do not kid themselves. They are able to confront the world with openness and acceptance, seeing both themselves and external events with a minimum of distortion or defensiveness.

3. They have deep feelings of identification with other people. They feel "at one" with large numbers of persons of all kinds and varieties. This is not merely a surface manifestation of "liking people" or a question of possessing polished social graces, but a feeling of oneness in the human condition.

4. They are well informed.

---

[2]Arthur W. Combs et al., "Florida Studies in the Helping Professions." *Social Science Monograph No. 37*. Gainesville: University of Florida Press, 1969.

Selected Readings

In our research on good teaching we found that effective teachers can be distinguished from poor ones on the following bases:

- Good teachers feel identified with, rather than apart from others.
- Good teachers feel basically adequate rather than inadequate.
- Good teachers feel trustworthy rather than untrustworthy.
- Good teachers see themselves as wanted rather than unwanted.
- Good teachers see themselves as worthy rather than unworthy.
- Good teachers perceive their purpose in teaching as one of freeing, rather than controlling students.
- Good teachers tend to be more concerned with larger, rather than smaller issues.
- Good teachers are more likely to be self revealing, rather than self concealing.
- Good teachers tend to be personally involved, rather than alienated.
- Good teachers are concerned with furthering processes, rather than achieving goals.

If these human characteristics are truly qualities of the effective teacher, then it follows that our teachers colleges must give far more attention to producing these kinds of people than has been traditionally true. In another book I have tried to point out some of the changes called for in teacher education as a consequence of modern humanistic psychological thought.[3] A few of the implications of these concepts for teacher education might be summarized as follows:

> If it is true that good teachers see themselves as liked, wanted, acceptable, and able, then these are the kinds of personal perceptions that teacher-education programs must produce. And the way it is done is to treat students so. People learn that they are liked, wanted, acceptable, and able from experiences of being treated that way by the people around them and from successful experiences which teach them that they are able.
>
> Teacher-education students take their self concepts with them wherever they go and every experience they have makes its contribution pro or con in building or tearing down self perceptions. Helping to build up students' self concepts is a responsibility of every member of the teacher preparation faculty. It cannot be set aside as the exclusive task of any special group. Each staff member has his effect upon the self concepts of students whether he wants to or not. The only thing he can control is whether his impact on the student will be positive, negative, or of no account.

---

[3]Arthur W. Combs, *The Professional Education of Teachers: A Perceptual View of Teacher Preparation.* Boston: Allyn and Bacon, Inc., © 1965. By permission.

In similar fashion, the attitudes of self acceptance and openness to experience, characteristic of adequate persons and effective teachers, are the consequences of successful experiences in this realm. One learns to accept one's self from having been accepted by significant people. Openness to experience is learned in part from positive feelings about self which make risk taking possible and partly from association with open, courageous persons. A teacher preparation faculty is no place for timid souls. So, too, feelings of commitment, encounter, and oneness in the human condition are learned in the process of growing up from those around us.

It follows that teacher educators must contribute to student feelings of belonging and must provide an atmosphere of compassion and concern for people from which feelings of identification can be acquired. The characteristics of adequate personalities and the perceptual characteristics of effective professional workers are not inherent qualities. They are learned, and what is learned can be taught. Research on the nature of adequacy has pointed the way. It remains for teacher educators to set about the business of achieving such ways of seeing self in our students with greater efficiency if we are to meet our responsibilities to the next generations.[4]

DEVELOPING RESPONSIBILITY AND SELF DIRECTION

If increasing humanness is to be a major function of the schools, it will be necessary for us to find much better ways than we have to get students involved in the educational process. The complaints of students that school has little to do with life as they know it is no idle criticism. Our preoccupation with information has made of school a world apart, a place "where you learn about things that don't matter." We manage to seduce a few students into playing the game with vigor, but most have learned simply to endure the process and go through the motions of satisfying their elders. Others simply give it up as a bad job and drop out.

If schools are going to be more human it is clear that they must become more relevant to the needs and experience of students and must find more effective ways to induce students to take a major responsibility for their own learning. But of course that cannot be done without changes being made. If we really give humanism a try, it would undoubtedly revolutionize our practices and procedures and modify greatly the subjects taught. We are so far out of touch with needs of our students at present that tinkering with the machine is not enough, a major overhaul is called for.

To meet the needs of students it will be necessary to involve them deeply. This will not be easy, for traditional practices have done their work well—our students are thoroughly brainwashed into the belief that learning is a passive

---
[4]*Ibid.*, pp. 78-79.

process in which you are not learning anything unless someone is telling you something and that independent action gets you nowhere. As students in one of my classes chillingly expressed it, "The things worth getting committed to don't get you ahead!" People who do not feel that they belong do not feel under any necessity to pay their dues or look out for the members. Membership in a society is not felt by those who are cast out from it. Feelings of belonging and responsibility come about only as a consequence of feeling a part of and being given responsibility for other people.

Responsibility and self direction, we need to remind ourselves, are not learned from having these things withheld. It is hard, however, to give young people responsibility and independence because we are so afraid they might not be able to handle it. We are literally frightened to death that students might make mistakes. This fear, in turn, prevents us from giving students opportunities for the very kinds of experiences through which they could learn to be responsible and independent. Responsibility is learned from being given responsibility; it is never learned from having it withheld.

Our whole school structure is built upon a fabric of right answers, and preoccupation with being right can get in the way of creativity, independence, self direction, responsibility, and autonomy. A person afraid to make mistakes will be afraid to try. People afraid to try must live forever with the status quo. The production of self directing, responsible people calls for teachers and administrators with courage enough to let young people make mistakes. Indeed, we have leaned so far in the other direction, it would appear we could even do for a while with a campaign for *encouraging* young people to make mistakes!

Let us not be diverted from the goal of independence, either, by the cries of the young people themselves as we give them greater responsibility. In the beginning they will no doubt reject it because they do not feel able to handle it. This, however, should not discourage us from giving them more. It is only another indication that they are fearful of it, a symptom of their lack of successful experience with it. A youngster who has not had much responsibility is quite likely to be frightened by having a large dose given to him before he is ready to assimilate it. The principle of pacing that applies to everything else we know in education applies to learning about responsibility as well. Opportunities have to be congruent with capacities. Capacity, however, is achieved from experience. You cannot expect a child to read if you never let him try and you cannot expect him to be responsible without success experience.

It is a basic principle of democracy that "When men are free, they can find their own best ways." Although most of us piously subscribe to this fundamental doctrine, it is amazing how few of us are really willing to put it to the test. We do not *really* believe people can find their own best ways. They certainly cannot if they are never given an opportunity.

THE NEED FOR NEW CONCEPTS OF ADMINISTRATION

Not all of the ills of dehumanization and alienation in our public schools can be cured by reforming our teachers and the curriculum. Indeed, the likelihood of change in either of these is largely dependent upon humanizing supervisors and administrators as well. One of the great contributors to our current malaise is the feeling of frustration on the part of both students and teachers at the immovability of the structures we have created. People develop the feeling that they do not count and that their attempts to produce change in the structure are futile and useless. They feel caught in the grip of the establishment and incapable of causing it to change.

This feeling, of course, is not simply confined to the educational structure. It is much more widespread and applies to most of our human institutions including government, the churches, industry, and all of the myriad groups within which people live and move. We are in trouble because our institutions do not sufficiently fulfill the needs of their members and are not flexible enough to adjust to our rapidly changing demands. To achieve humanitarian goals, it is necessary to make these structures more readily adaptable to change and more effective in fulfilling human needs.

Many supervisory and administrative procedures only serve to increase the current feelings of people that they do not count and that education has little to offer to the human aspects of existence. Many students and teachers, after trying for a long time to produce changes, have come to the conclusion that the establishment is vicious and completely intransigent. As a matter of fact, administrators and supervisors are rarely vicious and the dehumanizing conditions which they have created are often incomprehensible to them. They see themselves as hard working and well intentioned in a comparatively thankless job.

The alienation which they produce is not a project of their intentions; it is the outcome of their beliefs about what is important. The superintendent, at great distance from the student body, deals with what is important to him: problems of the school's image, budgetary considerations, dealing with the school board, attending dozens of committee meetings and community affairs, looking out for his buildings, or dealing with problems presented to him by his second level of administrative staff. His days are full and he is likely to be a very busy man.

Meanwhile, from the point of view of students and teachers, there seems no way of getting the people with the power to pay attention to the problems of deepest concern to them. Human problems are individual problems occurring in individual people. They do not lend themselves well to mass operation and may even seem to the administration to be trivial and unimportant. When, therefore, the people rise up one day and scream in anguish, "Listen to me, damn you, or I'll tear the place down!" they are surprised, hurt, indignant, and perhaps even certain that the Communists are behind the whole thing.

If the educational structure is truly to be humanized, administrators and supervisors must come to see this communication gap clearly and turn their attention to effective solutions. The alternative is revolution. It is high time administrators gave up their preoccupation with studies of the power structure, organization charts, and the like and gave their attention fully and wholeheartedly to the problems of how to help the little man be heard, how to give everyone a voice in decision making, and how to make the administrative structure more fulfilling of human needs and more sensitively adaptable to changing conditions.

I have tried in this paper to point the way to some of the things that need to be done in the schools and the curriculum to counteract the terrible depersonalization and alienation which have become the diseases of our times. At the present time many of our inventions, and many of our customary procedures, have led us into a morass of depersonalization. We have become the victims of our preoccupation with the wrong problems. But we got into this fix because of our intelligence and it is our intelligence which can get us out again if we truly believe that humanization is important. We can find ways to humanize our schools. As a matter of fact we had better do so. Anything less means that we have failed everyone, ourselves, our students, and society itself.

The Gill Plan 1.

John H. Wright, Jr., and John C. Littleford

The plan we developed is based on a simple change in scheduling, but a change that amounts to a total departure from the traditionally fragmented school day. At Gill, every student in grades nine through twelve takes only one course at a time, five weeks at a time. We have divided the year into five-week blocks: two in the fall, two in the winter, two in the spring. We already have one in the summer. We propose two. Any six blocks (we call them Units) constitute a full year's work. At present, we follow the traditional school vacations of our Lower and Middle Schools and our neighbors; but as we develop the Plan into a twelve-month program, with regular course work scheduled over the entire year, a student may take a vacation during any Unit, completing the required six by using one of the summer blocks.

In five weeks, five hours a day, a study group more than completes the required classroom time for a high school credit. That's just the minimum. More significant educationally is the fact that by studying together one subject at a time the group becomes immersed in that subject and involved in learning to a degree not possible through traditional scheduling. Students and teachers develop a new relationship from their intellectual and personal involvement, a relationship that demands new thinking, new methods, and new goals. Teachers need no longer rely so heavily on formal testing situations to measure students' grasp of a subject. Through extended contact they have greater opportunities to get to know each student's strengths, weaknesses, potential, and achievements. Students, from their vantage point, begin to see teachers as group members and adult models, as well as scholars.

The Plan gives each learning group complete flexibility in planning its own schedule. Field trips, films, laboratory and library time, guest lecturers— whatever makes learning most interesting and valuable—become available

---

Reprinted from *The Independent School Bulletin* (February 1972). Used with permission.

naturally and conveniently. And we can finally take advantage of our location. No longer will a history trip to Washington interfere with any other subject obligations. New York's ballet, concerts, museums, libraries, colleges—even its streets—have become Gill classrooms. Students taking advanced foreign languages can make arrangements to study abroad during a five-week Unit. Others can work with schools and universities that offer unique educational opportunities in other parts of the country—and in other parts of the world: with Bucknell for Soviet Literature in Moscow; with Salem for the Arts in London; with Fairleigh Dickinson for Marine Biology in St. Croix. A girl interested in early childhood education can work in our own kindergarten or in other schools nearby. A boy interested in mechanics can try his hand in a local garage.

"The Plan clearly allows for considerably more flexibility *in* and control *over* the schedule. The new schedule can help to teach the traditional subjects more efficiently and to make many more imaginative activities possible." Dr. David E. Purpel, Associate Professor in Harvard's Graduate School of Education, summed up the Plan's advantages in this way after he visited Gill to evaluate our proposal.

Other demonstrations of this flexibility and control are the possibilities of advancement in courses and early graduation. A student who wants to move ahead rapidly in one area may do so by taking several Units in that subject in one year. It is possible, for example, for one student to take three Units of French in one year and still to take English, math, and history. Another may take Units in Algebra II, then chemistry, then biology in sequence. In this way he can move ahead in sciences in one year while still meeting his requirements in English, history, and a foreign language.

With the permission of the faculty, qualified students may use the optional summer Units to cover more than the required six courses a year. Early graduation may be possible with carefully developed faculty counseling.

The advantages are not all with those students who want to race ahead. From the beginning we recognized absences as dangerous in this concentrated program. One day's absence is equivalent to the loss of one week's work and class time. We now see, however, that after one or two days' absence a student will have the extra help of one of the team teachers who has the spare time to help the student individually. We originally stated categorically that a week's absence would mean failure of a course. Now we know that final decisions can be on an individual basis. Even so, a student who fails Introductory Physical Science in Unit II may take it again in Unit III. He does not have to wait a whole year. Also, students may contract with faculty to take an additional subject or to make up a course. While taking a Unit in ceramics, for example, a student could contract for Algebra II as make-up or as a step forward.

The burden of proof for all this has fallen on the teaching faculty. In particular, it has fallen on Gill's nucleus of well-trained, adaptable, full-time teachers, who are augmented by specialists teaching one, two, or three Units each, depending on their field. Many of these part-time teachers are professionals following other careers—in music, graphics, drama, writing—professionals who would not have been available to us one hour a day all year, but who can arrange their schedules for us for five weeks. Both full-time and part-time faculty are sometimes further supported in the teaching teams by graduate assistants from neighboring institutions and from abroad for whom this supervised teaching fulfills MAT or other requirements. This team teaching and differentiated staffing are not only necessary to vary the learning activities within the blocks of time—for the sake of teachers as well as students, but also come naturally into use with Unit teaching. This is not to say they come without their own difficulties or demand no adjustments.

But the great adjustment for all the faculty has been to planning for five hours a day, five days a week, five weeks at a time. Although most of this planning has grown out of Gill's faculty's own intelligence, background, experience, and sense of humor, they did ask for professional help. A group in New York, Human Research Laboratories, came to us with some previous success in the *systems* or *performance objectives* approach to organizing. Call it what you will, it gave the Gill faculty a concept to use as a point of departure: the simple idea that first, you determine where you want to go before you decide how to get there; second, you predetermine check points along the way to be sure you stay on the right track; and third, you develop criteria for recognizing your destination when you get there.

The teachers also realize that in all their planning they must bring variety into each day, each week, each unit. Although the day's work is automatically broken by coffee at 10:30 and luncheon at 1:00, big blocks of time still remain. Within these, each academic group establishes its own pattern of activities and movement on campus and off. We have a variety of rooms on campus—large, small, and smaller. Some have tables, some have desks, some have tablet-arm chairs. We have a few study carrels. Off campus there are the great outdoors and town and city and prisons and beaches and courthouses and studios and chemical plants and battlefields and kitchens and sewage disposal plants.

An Algebra II class of twenty boys and girls might divide its day into a combined presentation by the team of teachers, followed by smaller group question-and-answer sessions of ten students and one teacher, followed by work sessions in paired groups of students, with floating faculty giving individual help where necessary. Or half the group might go to an engineering company while the other half is graphing slopes on the athletic field or criticizing project reports in front of the fireplace in the Library.

The academic day, which starts on campus at 8:45, is over at 2:30. From then until dismissal at 3:40 there are physical education classes; a wide variety of extracurricular activities; and regularly scheduled meetings of school government organizations, of student-faculty committees, of classes, and of the faculty. An interesting note: by changing physical education class offerings and club activities in each five-week unit, we can offer a wider variety in both. And because no commitment in either area is beyond five weeks, we find that they in turn receive higher student participation. We retain only those activities that sustain interest.

From faculty-student committee meetings and from faculty workshops have come three other developments: more efficient use of space, wider offerings of courses, and a reshuffling of course requirements.

With no more than nine academic groups working on campus during any one unit, classrooms or learning areas of any kind can be established and furnished for maximum efficiency. Our science area is a good example. Limited in space (we have one lab, one adjoining classroom, and one preparation area), we had heretofore found it difficult, if not impossible, to schedule two or more sciences on the same day. Under the Unit Schedule, within this same space we offer six Units of science; two in IPS, two in chemistry, and two in biology. The only physical changes necessary occur between Units, not between classes. And the instructors make their own daily lab/lecture time allotments without conflict with anybody anywhere.

By dividing the September-June calendar into six units instead of fragmenting each day, we have also eliminated vacant periods. Each student has a six-subject schedule. More productive students demand greater depth and breadth. One result is new electives. Only the math, the foreign languages, and the sciences have familiar labels. This year the English Department is offering Introduction to Communications, Creative Communications, European Literature, American Literature, Psychology and Literature, Religion and Literature, Twentieth Century Biographies (in cooperation with the History Department), and Soviet Literature in Translation. The History Department is offering Modern European History, Origins of America, Urban America, and the United Nations Seminar (at the U.N.). There is also the possibility of an American Government Seminar in Washington, a Spanish-American Studies group in the Mexico, and an American Indian Studies group in the West.

The Fine Arts Department this year will offer Art Enrichment, Basic Studio, Ceramics, Film Making, Introduction to Music, Music Theory and Composition, and Drama—all full credit courses.

And we have an entirely new Department: Practical Arts. Never before have we found time for Child Development, for Business Skills, or for Food and Fashions. Because no department will necessarily offer the same subjects each year, we expect continuing experimentation. To aid this, we have made ourselves available to graduate schools in the area. We are willing to insert new courses into any unit on very short notice—an ideal opportunity for graduate research. With us it is possible to reduce a year's study of a classroom into a five-week span.

By requiring six units of activity, we have been able to broaden requirements considerably. Not only does participation in the arts become part of each student's program, but so does independent work under faculty guidance—as directed study or as work-study. The English Department requires each student to have four Units with them before graduation; but what these Units are (after Introduction to Communications) and when they come are individual, counseled decisions, not arbitrary departmental ones. The same is true in history: Origins of America is required. The department asks only that the other two required history courses fit the individual pattern.

Not all Gill's family approached these changes with enthusiasm. Some faculty fell by the wayside. Some parents were openly opposed. We expected the loss of some of the more conservative students. Even among the trustees there was a loyal opposition.

The academic year opened with high expectations, however—with the largest enrollment in the school's history and with the first boys in the Upper School. Anonymous questionnaires indicated after the first full day that 13 per cent had come *despite* the new Plan, 22 per cent had come *because* of the Plan, and the remaining 65 per cent were warmly disposed but would probably have come with or without it.

Among us all there is the excitement of participating in the early stages of bringing a new concept into fruition. Despite the fact that we are working within our own small school and are absorbed with our adjustment to a new situation, a great deal of this excitement grows out of the sure knowledge that our success could well have implications on a much larger scale. We think we have started something.

Academic Freedom and the Student Press

H. C. Hudgins

The preparation and publication of newspapers and magazines is an exercise in freedom of the press. Generally speaking, students should be permitted and encouraged to join together to produce such publications as they wish. Faculty advisors should serve as consultants on style, grammar, format and suitability of the materials. Neither the faculty advisors nor the principal should prohibit the publication or distribution of material except when such publication or distribution would clearly endanger the health or safety of the students, or clearly and imminently threaten to disrupt the educational process, or might be of a libelous nature. Such judgment, however, should never be exercised because of disapproval or disagreement with the article in question.

The school administration and faculty should ensure that students and faculty may have their views represented in the columns of the school newspaper. Where feasible, they should permit the publication of multiple and competing periodicals. These might be produced by the student government, by various clubs, by a class or group of classes, or by individuals banded together for this specific purpose. The material and equipment for publication such as duplicating machines, paper and ink should be available to students in such quantity as budget may permit.

The freedom to express one's opinion goes hand in hand with the responsibility for the published statement. The onus of the decision as to the content of a publication should be placed clearly on the student editorial board of the particular publication. The editors should be encouraged through practice to learn to judge literary value, newsworthiness, and propriety.

Reprinted from the *Wake Forest Intramural Law Review* (December 1969), pp. 46-47. Used with permission.

The right to offer copies of their work to fellow students should be accorded equally to those who have received school aid, and to those whose publications have relied on their own resources.

The student press should be considered a learning device. Its pages should not be looked upon as an official image of the school, always required to present a polished appearance to the extramural world. Learning effectively proceeds through trial and error, and as much or more may sometimes be gained from reactions to a poor article or a tasteless publication as from the traditional pieces, groomed carefully for external inspection.

Guidelines for the Collection, Maintenance, and Dissemination of Pupil Records

Oscar M. Ruebhausen and others

As the modern world becomes more finely organized, the search for a satisfactory human dimension to life grows in intensity. This quest is not confined to the poor, to the young, or to minority groups: it is characteristic of all men—for all of us seek personal dignity and fulfillment.

We have come to accept our society as increasingly technological and bureaucratic. What is harder to accept is that such a society, while essential to the life to which we are accustomed, in many ways threatens the quality of the lives we hope to live.

Privacy is one of the rubrics under which the persistent tensions between the natural drives for individual fulfillment and the intruding needs of society are categorized. The claim to privacy is a claim for personal freedom, the freedom of each to choose for himself the extent of his sharing with, or withholding from others. This human claim involves bodily privacy—or the right to life and physical integrity; property privacy—or, as it is usually put, the right to private property; and spiritual privacy—or the right to integrity of personality.

In no one of these aspects is the claim to personal privacy an absolute one. Privacy always yields to those needs of a community which are believed by that community to be paramount. Thus, bodily privacy yields to the draft, property privacy to eminent domain, and spiritual privacy to a free press or to a public trial by jury.

Every one of us will assess differently the tolerable limits of intrusion upon our privacy. And even a single individual will assess those limits differently at different times and in varying settings. Nor are community

---

This statement by Oscar Ruebhausen, Chairman of the Board of Trustees of the Russel Sage Foundation, is the preface to the Foundation's report of a conference on the ethical and legal aspects of student record keeping. The report was published in 1970. It is used with permission.

needs static. They, too, differ in importance, or in urgency, at differing times and under differing circumstances.

Thus, the conflict between the need for personal privacy and the claims of the community is always a contest among many powerful and constantly varying forces. The modern version of this enduring struggle between the individual and his environment is not simply a matter of urban and suburban crowding, of exploitation and prejudice, of a polluted environment, and a defiled landscape. More subtle, but by no means less important, is the increasingly intrusive capacity of modern technology, the reality of instant communication and the availability of computerized memories.

Modern science has introduced a new dimension into the issues of privacy. There was a time when among the strongest allies of privacy were the inefficiency of man, the fallibility of his memory, and the healing compassion that accompanied both the passing of time and the warmth of human recollection. These allies are now being put to rout. Modern science has given us the capacity to record faithfully, to maintain permanently, to retrieve promptly, and to communicate both widely and instantly, in authentic sound or pictures or in simple written records, any act or event or data of our choice. Technology can now transform what participants believed were private experiences into public events.

In considering the challenge of these developments, it is well to remind ourselves that not every laying on of hands is assault; nor is every technical trespass actionable; nor every taking of private property forbidden. So too not every affront to individual dignity is objectionable.

The range of tolerable invasions of privacy is ample. They include those that are purely technical, or insubstantial, or wholly inadvertent. They also encompass those invasions deemed desirable in order to further a paramount public purpose. The criteria for separating the permissible from the impermissible invasions of privacy are numerous and complex. They must be chosen with special attention to the particular setting in which the issue arises.

One of those settings is the nation's schools. And the schools have a special command upon our concerns. The promise of the human resource represented by the pupils in our schools is compelling in its importance; the plastic nature of the growing young personality underlines the delicacy of the issue; and the commitment of our society to the development of every child's full potential establishes the paramount social objective within which the human dimension must be preserved.

Part Four

The School Staff

10

Staff Selection and Organization

STAFF SELECTION

Selecting the staff of teachers, counselors, department chairmen or division heads, deans, and assistant principals who will implement the school's program is a critical administrative function, for which the principal bears a major responsibility.

Nearly every school effectiveness study lends support to the conclusion that the teacher is the most important school-related determinant of student achievement, at least in the area of cognitive skill achievement. Although there is considerable disagreement over the contribution of schooling to student achievement versus the contribution of various environmental factors, particularly family background, there seems to be little disagreement that the teacher is the most important of the school-related inputs. In *Do Teachers Make A Difference?*, a recent research report on student achievement, published in 1970 by the U. S. Department of Health, Education and Welfare, James S. Coleman summarizes the findings of many researchers by stating that

> even with the crude instruments of survey data, it is clear that variations in teachers' characteristics account for more variation in childrens' standardized performance in cognitive skills than do variations in any other characteristics of the school.

While achievement in cognitive skills should be only one of the school's goals, and a school should not be evaluated solely on the basis of students' scores on standardized measures of cognitive skill achievement, these research findings coupled with experiential and intuitive knowledge of the importance of the teacher in relation to student motivation, interest, and attitudes toward learning emphasize the importance of developing an effective staff selection process. If teachers are more important to student learning than the number of volumes in the library, or the supply of audio-visual aids and equipment, then the effort spent on recruiting and selecting the best available teachers should reflect that fact. Often schools devote more energy to obtaining bids on furniture and equipment than to employing outstanding staff members.

The employment of outstanding staff begins with recruitment. Recruitment should be an active process, characterized by initiative, energy, and skill. Unfortunately, many schools sit back and wait for candidates to find them, particularly if the district has a good starting salary and is in a desirable geographic location. However, even in times when there is an ample supply of certified teachers, the number of first rate teachers who can fill a particular role will be limited. Relying on candidates to seek out the school system may result in a staff that is composed primarily of "locals" rather than a cosmopolitan staff with a potentially greater diversity of experiences and education.

Salary, working conditions, fringe benefits, and the nature of the community will be important factors in recruiting and hiring outstanding staff members, and information pertaining to these factors should be made available to potential candidates. Many schools do an adequate job of disseminating this kind of information but neglect the opportunity to provide information regarding interesting, innovative, and challenging educational programs that the school has developed, is in the process of developing, or would like to develop. A creative teacher may be at least as interested in participating in an exciting educational program or in having the opportunity to develop new programs or to try new approaches to education as he is in economic considerations. In areas where salary schedules and fringe benefits vary little from district to district it is likely that outstanding teachers committed to the profession of education will base their decision as to where to seek and accept employment on the opportunity to become involved in challenging educational programs.

Whether recruiting potential staff members is a district office function, as is usually the case in medium to large school systems, or the responsibility of a building level administrator, the principle that those who are affected by a decision should participate in it certainly applies to the *selection* of staff members. It is to be hoped that the day is past when teachers or other staff members are employed and assigned to a school by the superintendent or personnel director without involving the principal and relevant members of his staff in the decision. It is the principal and staff who are responsible for developing the educational program in the school and who will work directly with the new employee. It is essential that they have opportunity to examine the credentials of and interview all prospective staff members, and to have their opinions considered. It is fair to the candidate that he have the opportunity to meet and talk with the principal, department or division chairman, and other staff members with whom he will be working.

If the school system has a personnel director, his most appropriate function is to recruit candidates and to perform the initial screening of credentials based on the personnel needs as described by the principal. The credentials of candidates who meet the minimum criteria should then be forwarded to the principal and his staff so that they may decide which candidates they would like to pursue. The principal and staff should assume primary responsibility for the decision regarding which candidate to recommend for employment.

Which members of the principal's staff should participate in the selection process is dependent on the way the school is organized as well as on the size of the school. In schools that are organized in subject area departments or in broader divisions, the chairman of the department or the division head should have a voice in the selection of staff members. If the principal has one or more assistants, it is advisable for those who are involved in working directly with teachers to be involved in the selection process. Involving other staff members in the selection process does not mean that the principal abdicates his responsibility to recommend to the superintendent the specific candidates to be employed. While it is his responsibility to do so, input from other staff members can help him make a more effective decision. What should be elicited from other staff members is not a vote on who should be selected; instead, information, opinions, evaluations, feelings, and beliefs regarding the candidates under consideration should be gathered.

The selection process involves the evaluation of credentials and interviews at the employing school. Unfortunately, the recommendations in a candidate's credential file are often brief, general, and vague. The principal should contact references provided by the candidate and/or other professional people in a position to provide relevant information regarding a candidate's qualifications. In many instances it is possible to visit a candidate in his present position or, in the case of an inexperienced teacher, at his college or university. It is more likely that accurate information regarding a candidate's potential can be obtained from direct contacts with his present principal, colleagues, and students or instructors than from his credential file. When one considers the importance of teachers to the learning process, the fact that it is extremely difficult to dismiss a teacher once he obtains tenure, and recent developments which have made it difficult to dismiss even a nontenured teacher, it is surprising that schools do not devote more of their resources to the recruitment and selection processes.

In selecting department chairmen or division heads and other administrative staff members, the principal can seek help from several sources. Other members of the administrative team may have insights regarding the qualifications of candidates from within the school or district. A small committee of teachers from within a department or division can help to evaluate the academic preparation, experience, and educational philosophy of candidates for department or division chairmen. When the head of a pupil personnel service department such as the guidance or dean's department is to be selected it is appropriate to involve students and parents in the process. If a candidate for such a position cannot discuss his ideas with students and parents in an interview, it is unlikely he can communicate with them effectively in the tense situations that arise on the job.

One of the aspects of staff selection which the principal will consider is diversity: to what extent should the selection of new staff members be based on a desire to maintain a reasonable balance of teacher characteristics such as age, sex, experience, and marital status. Aside from the doubtful legality of the use of such criteria, these considerations should be at most secondary, and are best ignored altogether. Unless the school is quite small, when teachers are selected solely on the basis of their potential ability to help students learn, normal probability will result in a reasonably balanced distribution of such characteristics.

A school operating as a model of a democratic community is by definition one which values diversity among the staff. Given a general commitment to the democratic philosophy, wide latitude in beliefs about how school goals should be implemented, and differences in teaching style and life style, should not only be tolerated, but encouraged. Spirited discussions about proposed changes in the school will ensure that all sides of a question are examined before a decision is reached. The essence of a democracy is the full opportunity to debate an issue. Even proposals for educational change and innovations need to be challenged, questioned, and examined from a variety of perspectives. We have earlier referred to innovative practices that fell on fallow ground because the school staff had not had opportunity to examine and accept or reject them. When change fails because of insufficient debate, the position of the "obstructionists" is strengthened. They sit back and adopt the "I told you so" attitude. What is needed are open-minded, intelligent, committed staff members who are willing to invest time and effort in exploring and deciding upon ways the school may be better and more productive for all students. Changes which are made following full discussion are more likely to be changes that last.

Another general question which the principal will have to consider arises when assistant principals, deans, and department heads are to be selected. Should the principal adopt a policy of hiring from within the school or school system, or of giving preference to candidates from within, or of hiring from outside the school system? The only policy the principal need adopt in this respect is that of attempting to fill such positions with the best available candidates, regardless of where they are currently employed. Sometimes the best is in the system, at other times from outside.

STAFF ORGANIZATION

The establishment and pursuit of common goals of secondary education are discussed elsewhere in this book but are referred to here because of their close relationship to organizational structure. In fact, staff organization should be a function of educational goals and personnel should be available for the achievement of those goals. The goals or objectives of the democratic secondary school should be determined by a wide variety of individuals and agencies. For our purposes here it is sufficient to say that satisfactory goals of the democratic school should be formulated only after lay citizens, students, teachers, and administrators have had an opportunity to contribute to their development. Furthermore, systematic means for revision will need to be established so that these elements of the school community can at any time raise questions and suggest changes.

The organization of the staff should be designed to achieve the goals or objectives commonly agreed upon by the school community. An important consideration should be the nature and types of expertise available in the staff personnel team. Therefore, the problem is "How can we best organize the staff so that its many competencies may be most effectively utilized in the achievement of the desired educational goals?"

The importance of a harmonious relationship among staff members can hardly be overestimated. People work better and achieve more when they are happy in their work and have a clear understanding of their duties and responsibilities. The ideal organization is one in which all staff members feel that their abilities are being adequately utilized in a cooperative effort. They also understand how the organization facilitates achievement of goals and how they can help in accomplishing revisions which will improve its effectiveness.

Given staff recruitment and selection procedures which result in a highly capable staff, the principal is faced with the problem of leadership in developing an organizational arrangement that will ensure the accomplishment of the various administrative, maintenance, and leadership functions that are essential if the abilities of all members of the school staff are to be fully utilized. Secondary schools vary widely in size, student body composition, and resources available, and the specific organizational plan best suited for a particular school will be dependent on these and other local factors. Therefore, our discussion of school organization will focus on common functions, and principles on which the administration of these functions can be based, rather than on the presentation of specific organizational schemes or charts.

Two key variables in any organizational design are the degree of stratification (exemplified by status levels), and the degree of centralization built into the design. A number of organizational theorists have hypothesized relationships between these two variables and various organizational goals. There seems to be considerable consistency in their estimates of the effects of more or less stratification and centralization on various types of organizations. Chester Barnard, author of *The Functions of the Executive*, believed that status systems were *a method* of providing employees with the incentive to work hard; however, he also noted that they primarily satisfy the man at the top and not the man at the bottom. Victor Thompson, author of *Modern Organizations*, suggests that status systems tend to encourage the *status quo*. The restricted, informal relationships characteristic of organizations with extensive status systems tend to inhibit free and open communication. As a result, the organization leaders remain unaware of the need for change, and with their narrowly held decision-making power, characteristic also of highly centralized organizations, they are able to discourage suggestions for change. Also, stratification may reduce the organization's ability to adapt as a result of the fact that changes frequently have consequences which upset the status system, thus causing those who have a vested interest to oppose change. An article which deals with hierarchical impediments to innovation in educational organizations is by Max G. Abbott, author of *Change Perspectives in Educational Administration*, and is included in the selected readings for Part Four.

Regarding centralization, Thompson states that organizations which require a proliferation of occupational specialties, particularly when the specialties require extensive training, will find it difficult to maintain strict centralized authority. In a complex organization requiring professionally trained personnel it is difficult for any one person, or small group of persons, to have expertise in all the areas of specialization. In order for effective decisions to be made, various specialists must be consulted. Alvin Gouldner, a sociologist, suggests that there is a motivational force, which he calls the functional strain toward autonomy, which tends to encourage the process of decentralization. It is his thesis that professionally trained specialists naturally strive for the right to make their own decisions and thus force organizational decentralization.

Utilizing the concepts of the organizational theorists already mentioned, and those of such sociologists as Max Weber and Talcott Parsons, Jerald Hage in his book *Social Change in Organizations*, has developed what might be called an eclectic theory which hypothesizes definite relationships between stratification and centralization and certain organizational ends. Interested readers may wish to examine Hage's theory in its entirety as it was presented in an article entitled "An Axiomatic Theory of Organizations," published in the fall 1965 issue of *Administrative Science Quarterly*. In this discussion, however, we are primarily interested in three particular propositions contained in his theory. These are:

1. The higher the stratification, the lower the job satisfaction.
2. The higher the stratification, the lower the adaptiveness.
3. The higher the complexity, the lower the centralization.

Schools are service enterprises, and the "labor" force is composed of persons who are striving to attain "professional" status. They are required to make many decisions about the various ways in which they accomplish their tasks. The development of programmed instruction, teaching machines, computer-assisted instruction, and teacher-aide programs appears to have done little to reduce the central position of the professional teacher in the educational process. It also seems clear that meeting the educational needs of individuals in a rapidly changing society requires organizational arrangements that enhance adaptiveness. Further, the optimum performance of personnel engaged in the performance of a complex task under conditions requiring a high degree of adaptiveness seems to be largely dependent upon their achieving a considerable measure of job satisfaction.

Admittedly, researchers have not been able to convincingly verify empirically the hypothesized relationships between organizational characteristics and organizational ends. Measuring the variables has proved a most difficult task. However, the research that is available, plus the unanimity of opinion among scholars devoted to the study of organizations, does lend weight to the contention that decentralized authority and the minimization of stratification are appropriate guidelines for the organization of a school staff.

Assistant principals, department or division heads, deans, and other members of the administrative team must be given the authority to make decisions in their particular areas of responsibility. The responsibility for the administration of a function must be accompanied by the authority necessary for its accomplishment. Such decentralization presupposes, of course, that the principal recognizes and is prepared to accept the fact that when the decision-making authority is shared, the decisions that result will not all be the ones he would prefer. Unless he can acknowledge that in certain areas other staff members have expertise that may well exceed his own, and accept their decisions as valid, he may be unable to function effectively in a leadership position in a school characterized by low stratification and decentralization.

In the secondary school, which operates along the lines of the democratic model described earlier, staff organization—in whatever form it may take—must be responsive to the needs of those it serves. It should be subject to revision and even revocation if it fails to adequately meet those needs.

In the final analysis, organization is a means to an end rather than an end in itself. Any given type of organization should be subject to continual evaluation and should be susceptible to experiment and change.

The school administrator should recognize that organization is simply a design for relating people, ideas, and materials in a harmonious and effective way for the accomplishment of desired goals. He will also need to recognize that individuals are more important than organizational designs and therefore will not insist on a particular organizational structure if it does not produce and maintain an effective and harmonious relationship among workers.

Administrative Assistance

A number of specific administrative functions must be accomplished in every secondary school. Someone must assume the responsibility for scheduling students, supervising and evaluating teachers, supervising building maintenance operations, developing and coordinating curriculum, supervising and coordinating pupil personnel services, supervising clerical personnel, supervising student activities, coordinating building usage, handling staff absence requests and other personnel matters, securing substitute teachers, and building level budgeting and requisitioning. Seeing to it that these functions are performed effectively is the responsibility of the principal, but if the principal's time is to be used effectively, he will not perform them all himself. How much help he has will depend on the size of the school and the financial resources of the school district, but ideally, it is desirable for the principal to have sufficient assistance to enable him to delegate many or all of the "maintenance" functions so that he has time available to devote to those functions that require educational leadership.

If the principal has administrative assistance available (assistant principals, coordinators, directors, etc.), some division of the administrative responsibilities must be effected. The traditional bureaucratic manner of accomplishing this is to develop an organizational chart showing each administrative position in a pyramidal hierarchy and providing some indication of its function. A written job description which defines the specific responsibilities and parameters of the job is then developed for each box on the chart. A disadvantage of this is that it assumes the individual must fit the job. However, individuals do not come neatly packaged with just the right skills, knowledge, personality, and interests to fit a particular job description—a description that was probably based on the abilities and interests of the unique individual who was holding the job at the time the job description was written. Further, rigid adherence to job descriptions would seem likely to result in the underutilization of the talents of some staff members and the inhibition of the creativity and innovativeness of highly trained professional personnel. Effective change is dependent on staff members who are able to break out of the conventional boundaries of their roles. In *Up The Organization,* Robert Townsend describes job descriptions as straightjackets. He maintains that they are:

1. Great for key punch operators and other jobs where the turnover is high and the work is largely repetitive.
2. Insane for jobs that pay $150 a week or more. Judgment jobs are constantly changing in nature and the good people should be allowed to use their jobs to see how good they are.
3. At best, a job description freezes the job as the writer understood it at a particular instant in the past. At worst, they are prepared by personnel people who cannot write and do not understand the jobs. Then they are not only expensive to prepare and regularly revise, but they are important morale sappers.[1]

---

[1] Robert Townsend, *Up the Organization* (New York: Alfred A. Knopf, 1970), p. 91.

Staff Selection and Organization

A more creative approach to the division of administrative responsibilities among the members of the administrative staff is for the principal to discuss their individual abilities and interests with them and assign the various responsibilities in a manner that maximizes their talents while providing each the opportunity to work in at least some areas which are professionally interesting and challenging. The administrative staff should periodically review the division of responsibilities in view of changes in individual interests and organizational goals and conditions. This is dependent on a minimum of stratification, the willingness to decentralize authority, and flexibility.

In delegating responsibility, the principal who would be an educational leader reserves as much time as possible for working with staff, students, parents, and others in the community in furthering the educational goals of the school. Even though certain responsibilities are placed on department or division chairman, assistant principals, and deans for curriculum matters, the principal cannot abdicate his own leadership role in the areas in which these persons function. To do so will likely result in lack of movement toward achieving the overall goals of the school or to a discrepancy between philosophy and practice. This does not mean that the principal performs all tasks, supervises all work in minute detail, or needs to be consulted about or give prior approval for all decisions made by the staff. Once the directions the school is moving have been set, day-to-day decisions which move toward the school objectives may well be left to others.

Peter Drucker, in *The Effective Executive,* emphasizes the need for executives to be able to dispense time in reasonably large segments when performing leadership tasks. He states that "Innovation and change require inordinate amounts of time.... All one can think and do in a short amount of time is to think what one already knows and to do as one has always done."[2]

The school organization must also provide for the development of instructional units within broad subject fields, assign teachers to specific classes, supervise instruction, evaluate teachers, and manage materials and supply budgets—aspects of administration that are close to the teaching-learning process. In most secondary schools the basic organization of the teaching staff is to divide it into departments along traditional subject area lines (mathematics, science, English, music, for example). A chairman or head is designated for each department and is assigned the responsibility for at least some of these administrative functions. An alternative plan is to combine several traditional subject area departments into a single unit called a division. A school may have four, five, or six such major divisions, each with an administrative assistant, chairman, head, or director in charge. In large schools these division heads are sometimes full-time administrators. When this form of

---

[2]Peter F. Drucker, *The Effective Executive* (New York: Harper and Row, 1967), p. 34.

organization is employed, the divisions are usually composed of subject areas that appear to have some relationship to one another. For example, some common divisions are: fine arts (art, music, and dance); humanities (English, social studies and foreign language); vocational education (business education, home economics, and industrial-technical education); and math-science.

Divisions may also be organized in other ways. The Committee on Reorganization of Secondary Education recommended as long ago as 1918 that a school organize its divisions around the stated purposes of the schools and pointed out that objectives must determine the organization, or else the organization will determine the objectives, a bit of wisdom which would profit any school as it plans its own organization.

When a school is divided into subject area departments with a chairman responsible for each department, the chairman is nearly always a part-time administrator. He usually spends several periods a day teaching classes, with the number of periods of "released time" available for administrative duties dependent on the size of the department. In many instances the chairman views himself as a teacher rather than an administrator. He is usually a member of the teachers' organization, and was probably selected for the job because of his teaching skill rather than his general leadership ability. He has probably had little, if any, training in administration. Frequently, the result is that the school's department chairmen exist in a "no man's land." The teachers view them as teaching colleagues, the principal views them as members of the administrative team, and the department chairman himself is uncertain as to what his role is. The result is ineffective leadership at the level closest to the teaching-learning process.

Further, when hard decisions—particularly those pertaining to personnel and the allocation of money—have to be made, the chairman's close ties to the teachers of a particular subject area may hinder his ability to base decisions on a broad perspective which encompasses the total needs of the school community. The lack of contact and interaction with staff members in other subject areas may reinforce the tendency of subject matter specialists to think in terms of narrow subject matter objectives rather than long-range educational goals. Unless the department chairman is a mature, intelligent individual, capable of placing the department role in perspective, he may be prone to view "his" department as a personal freedom to be guarded against incursions by other departments, the principal, or the central office. Such a mentality results in efforts to maintain student enrollments in order to maintain staff size rather than to meet student needs or to preserve exclusive rights to a particular area of knowledge. These attitudes are certain to thwart efforts to develop interdisciplinary approaches to meeting student needs. Only a few chairmen with these attitudes can make curriculum development difficult.

The departmental approach to school organization emphasizes the subject matter specialist orientation of teachers, which may contribute to an emphasis on specialized instruction that is inappropriate at the secondary level. The tendency is strong for subject matter specialists to teach their subject as if the goal is development of specialists rather than generalists. Science courses may be taught in a manner more appropriate for students who will major in some branch of science in college than for providing students with knowledge which will help them understand and interpret their physical environment; mathematics courses may be taught as if all students are to become mathematicians, while the real need of the majority of students to learn the mathematics necessary for the day-to-day needs of family finance, civic understanding, and job performance is neglected. The tendency of teachers to achieve personal satisfaction through the pursuit of their subject area specialties at advanced levels (calculus, physics, chemistry, English literature, etc.) rather than from helping pupils learn may be reinforced.

If this mode of organization is adopted, the principal must develop a clear definition of the role and responsibilities of the department chairman, and he must encourage a common perception of this role among members of the school staff. He must help each department chairman to view the total school rather than just his department, to think in terms of student needs rather than departmental needs, and to communicate with members of other departments in order to coordinate curriculum planning and development, and to explore interdisciplinary possibilities.

The closeness of the department chairman to the teaching staff must be turned into an advantage. One of the rationales for this type of organization is the alleged need for administrative leadership with expertise in particular subject areas. But, too often, the chairman spends most of his allotted administrative time signing requisitions, issuing chalk and erasers, and performing other clerical tasks. The principal must ensure that these tasks are kept to a minimum so that chairmen have the time to work on overall curriculum development, to provide assistance and direction to the members of his staff, and to develop course objectives, content, sequence, and evaluation in a collegial relationship with staff members. However, providing the time will make little difference unless the principal has made it clear that he expects department chairmen to devote the time to educational leadership, consistent with the broad goals of the school.

In many schools, department chairmanships are viewed in the same manner as Supreme Court appointments—for life. When this kind of tradition prevails it may be difficult to remove an ineffective chairman, but it may also be necessary. If so, the principal will need to be certain that he has the support of the superintendent and board of education. Some schools have attempted to forestall this development by establishing a policy of rotating the chairmanship of each department periodically. The rotation is usually staggered so that only a few chairmanships rotate each year. This policy has much to commend it. A review of the performance of all department chairmen should be made periodically to ensure the provision of capable leadership at the department or division level.

The organization of subject area departments into major divisions has been adopted by some schools as a means of overcoming some of the problems described above. Combining two or more subject areas into a division usually enables the school to make the division chairmanship or headship a full-time position. Since the proponents of this mode of organization believe it is more important that such chairmen have administrative ability than subject matter expertise, they view this as a distinct advantage. It is their contention that the possibility of hiring trained and experienced administrators for such positions is enhanced if the positions are full-time.

What is important is whether this organization results in better curriculum planning, coordination, and development, more effective supervision and evaluation, and more assistance and support for the teaching staff. It may facilitate the breaking down of traditional subject area lines and the development of interdisciplinary approaches. It could make the implementation of a coordinated, integrated curriculum designed to achieve broad educational goals rather than narrow subject matter objectives easier. It may also force the chairmen or division heads to become education generalists, particularly in respect to curriculum, rather than subject matter specialists.

There are also some pitfalls. Division heads or directors of instructional groups could turn into "managers" rather than educational leaders. If they became primarily an arm of the principal for accomplishing administrative maintenance and organizational tasks, even a greater leadership void in the areas of instructional planning, supervision, and evaluation might result.

There is no conclusive evidence which indicates that either of these organizational plans is inherently better than the other. It is probable that schools need to develop new school organizational forms. However, what seems more important than the particular organizational structure is the kind of relationships that are developed between the administration and the teaching staff. Relationships characterized by openness and mutual respect and trust are essential if supervision and evaluation are to be helpful and supportive rather than inspectorial. While no particular organizational plan will ensure the development of such relationships, minimizing the degree of organizational stratification and centralization in whatever plan is adopted should help. Of overriding importance, as pointed out above, is whether the objectives of the school determine the form of organization. Seldom is this taken into consideration when school organizations are established.

Teacher Assignment

When we view the secondary school as a democratic educational community, teacher assignments and teaching loads become a common concern rather than a solely administrative decision made on the basis of a fixed program. As members of the school community, teachers should share in making decisions regarding the nature and extent of their contribution to the total educational effort. Students also may provide some input with regard to optimum size of classes in various subjects, the value of setting aside periods of the school day for teacher-pupil conferences, the merits of unsupervised study periods, and similar topics.

It is the responsibility of the principal to clearly present the task of the school with regard to proposed curricular offerings to the staff. The relationship of these offerings to the total school program of which they are a major part should be made clear so that all recognize that the assignments of teachers are an integral part of a total program—the success of which largely depends on their efforts.

In this format teacher assignment becomes a common problem which all need to aid in satisfactorily solving. In small schools this approach may best be made to the total faculty; in large schools it may be made on a departmental or divisional basis. In the latter case, each department or division should give adequate consideration to its responsibilities to the total program, not merely to the academic portion of that program. In either case the central concern should be the achievement of the purposes of the program by the most effective utilization of personnel. In doing this, a primary consideration should be not only the special competency of the individual teacher but also his or her preferences and desires. Assignments should be made with due respect to the wishes of the individual teacher, and, to the extent possible, should provide for a happy teacher situation. Throughout the whole process of assignment of duties, the importance of each teacher's contribution to the success of the total educational enterprise should be stressed. Obviously, all assignments are not likely to honor the preferences of the teachers involved. However, when a teacher is convinced that the assignment is essential or at least important to the success of the total enterprise, she is more likely to accept it in good grace than if it were simply handed down by the principal.

In brief, teaching assignments should be made only after consultation with the faculty and should be assumed as responsibilities contributing to the achievement of an overall purpose to which all are committed. This format may well be put into practice during a planning session preceding the actual opening of the school term. The success of this method of teacher assignment will largely depend on the principal, and in the larger schools, on the department or division heads. While the administrator should come fully prepared with facts and figures regarding enrollments, curricular objectives, availability of personnel, teacher preferences, student interests, and similar information he should also come to the planning session with an open mind. He must encourage the expression of opinion and the offering of suggestions. He should present the *problem,* not the solution.

Only after securing the wide input described earlier should the principal complete the task of assignment. It will be his responsibility to make the final decision on assignments, but in doing so he is obligated to make use of all the information he has secured. It would be a serious mistake and a waste of teacher time if he proceeded otherwise. Teacher assignments will, of course, seldom if ever be confined to simply teaching a designated number of classes. The operation of a successful educational program involves much more. Remedial work, conferences, committee work, curriculum planning, leadership responsibilities, cocurricular duties in school clubs, musical productions, dramatics, athletics, and many similar activities are important parts of the program. Most teacher assignments will include duties related to one or more of these elements of the total program. It is in these areas that teacher and student preferences will play a most important part in assignments. While specialized preparation of the teacher in academic areas will necessarily restrict choices in assignment, such restriction is largely absent in student activity assignments.

Special problems in teacher assignment are often generated when operational or curricular practices which vary from the norm are introduced. For example, ability grouping practices pose problems in teacher assignment. A nationwide poll conducted by the National Education Association in 1968 points up this problem. In this poll, teachers were asked which types of pupils they preferred to teach. The results are shown in Table 10-1. It is obvious from this table that when students are grouped into multiple ability levels of anywhere near equal size, a considerable number of teachers are going to have to teach classes they would prefer not to teach. Since less than 2 percent of the secondary teachers prefer to teach low ability classes, teacher preference cannot be the sole criteria even if that was desired in the interest of job satisfaction. In some instances, special training and experience working with a particular type of student may be viable criteria. However, it would seem that the principal criterion should be the teacher's ability to work effectively with particular groups of students—a criterion that applies whether considering the ability level of the students or other grouping factors such as grade level or student interest.

Unfortunately, administrators frequently avoid developing criteria for assigning teachers to classes by adopting some system of rotation. This is particularly likely to happen when ability grouping is employed—teachers are simply rotated between ability levels from year to year in order to avoid

Table 10-1

Types of Pupils	Elementary Teachers	Secondary Teachers
High ability	18.4%	34.6%
Average ability	44.7%	38.9%
Low ability	4.3%	1.9%
Mixed abilities	21.3%	15.2%
No preference	11.3%	9.4%

Source: *NEA Journal* Vol. 57 (February 1968), p. 53. Used with permission.

conflict over who gets to teach the high ability classes and who has to teach the low ability classes. The rationale seems to be that each teacher should have to take his turn teaching the "problem students." The systematic rotation of teachers between ability levels, or for that matter grade levels, seems an obvious abrogation of the administrative responsibility to assign teachers to classes on the basis of their ability to help students learn in a specific knowledge area. The principal must particularly recognize that the use of ability grouping may result not only in conflict over teacher class assignments, but also that it is likely to have a direct effect on teacher assignments. When a large percentage of teachers prefer to teach the upper ability level or grade level classes, there is a strong possibility that the most experienced, best trained, and most respected teachers in the school will be able to use their prestige to avoid assignment to low ability classes. It would seem only natural for an administrator to reward an outstanding teacher with his choice of class assignments. In an article on ability grouping which appeared in the Fall 1970 issue of *Sociology of Education,* Aage Sorensen hypothesized that when ability grouping is employed, bright or high ability children get more experienced and more competent teachers, except when specific counteracting measures are employed. (Unfortunately, Sorenson does not suggest specific counteracting measures that might be effective.) He further maintains that the more selective the ability grouping, the greater the between-classroom variation in teacher competence.

Teacher effectiveness is difficult to measure. Our knowledge of which characteristics contribute the most to teacher effectiveness is extremely limited. However, a 1973 study by Richard Kamm does provide some support for Sorensen's argument. Kamm studied the allocation of teachers among 1,262 ability grouped classes in English, mathematics, science, and social studies in seven suburban Chicago high schools with student enrollments ranging from approximately 1,400 to 3,800. The distribution of three teacher characteristics (the number of hours earned in the teacher's current teaching field, the number of years of experience in his current teaching field, and the number of hours earned in his teaching field in the last five years[3]) among high, middle, and low ability classes were analyzed. In addition, variations in class size and teacher cost per pupil credit hour (the result of variations in class size *and* teacher training and experience) between ability levels were analyzed. The results shown in Table 10-2 indicate a pattern consistent with Sorensen's hypothesis, although the link between these characteristics and teacher effectiveness is admittedly tenuous in spite of the fact that they are the principal determinants of teachers' salaries. When the sample was analyzed by school and subject area, the pattern of assigning the most experienced and highly trained teachers to the higher ability classes reoccurred in nearly every department; the practice of reducing the class size of low ability

---

[3]This was considered to be a measure of continuing education which may well serve as a proxy for motivation, interest, and commitment.

Table 10-2

Distribution of Five Teacher-Related Input Variables

Table of Means

Ability Level	Semester Hours in Teaching Field	Years Experience Teaching in Current Teaching Field	Semester Hours Earned in Teaching Field in Last five Years	Class Size	Teacher Cost per Pupil Credit Hour
High(n=173)	69.0	11.6	13.1	24.9	$118.31
Middle(n=808)	65.2	8.3	10.2	27.1	$ 98.30
Low(n=149)	55.4	6.6	7.3	18.9	$136.29

classes was unanimous; and that of keeping high ability classes smaller than average classes, nearly unanimous. It would seem that ability grouping might result in the neglect of students classified as average.

In all of the schools in this study, teacher assignment was the responsibility of the chairmen of the subject area departments. There were no general school policies or guidelines pertaining to teacher assignment except for provisions in the contractual agreements with the teachers' organization, limiting the number of different courses (preparations) to which a teacher could be assigned. These chairmen were interviewed in an attempt to determine the criteria which they were using for assigning teachers to specific ability-level classes. Several chairmen indicated that they had adopted a system of rotating teachers among ability levels since the question of who had to teach the low ability classes was one of the principal sources of conflict in their department. Others indicated that their sole criterion was the teacher's ability to effectively facilitate the learning of students on a particular ability level. However, the data revealed that in nearly every department where the teacher's ability to work with a particular ability level was the alleged criterion, the department chairman had determined that the most experienced and highly trained teachers were most effective with high ability classes, and the least experienced and least trained teachers were best suited for teaching low ability classes. While it may be that younger teachers sometimes have more energy, and are possibly more tolerant and flexible than more experienced teachers and are thus better able to "handle" the "difficult" students who tend to be assigned to low ability classes, the consistency of this result would seem more likely to be due to the factors Sorensen suggests—seniority and prestige.

It is most important that the principal be aware of the potential functions of ability grouping. If he is, he can attempt to minimize this aspect of the teacher assignment problem by convincing other staff members of the wisdom of reducing or eliminating overt ability grouping or tracking in as many subject areas as possible, since the advantages seem to be illusory. However, in skill areas such as typing, music, and mathematics it may be impossible or undesirable to eliminate ability grouping entirely. In this case, the principal will need to convince the staff that it is probably unfair and unwise for one classification or another of students to be consistently exposed to either the youngest or the oldest teachers. He might also urge them to consider letting each student choose the ability level of his classes in subject areas grouped by ability rather than assigning him to an ability level on the basis of test scores.

Teacher Load

The size of the teacher's load is usually determined by the breadth of the educational program, student enrollment, staff availability, and budgetary considerations. In many schools, past practice will be a significant factor in determining teacher load. If in the past teachers accepted heavy loads, even at the risk of slighting some of their duties, the practice may well continue. If, on the other hand, teacher responsibilities have been light, increased responsibilities may be met with resentment. In either case, the approach suggested in this section will help to pave the way for change through teacher participation when necessary or desirable.

In general, teacher loads among secondary schools of the United States have been too heavy for the most effective discharge of instructional duties. Class size is now often the subject of negotiation when teachers are engaged in collective bargaining. While certain criteria may be adapted with regard to class size, they should not be applied indiscriminately. While restrictions such as limiting classes have been promulgated in the past by study commissions and teacher organizations, they are useful now only as general guidelines. The modern secondary program by its very nature does not lend itself to such formulas. Even in the traditional high school program, wide variations exist in optimum sizes of classes (in chemistry, for example, as opposed to physical education). The breadth of experiences in a modern secondary program preclude for the most part the use of class size as a criterion except as a maximum indicator.

Teachers may reasonably be expected to spend forty hours per week in performing their school duties. This is the equivalent of five eight-hour days. This time will be divided among various extracurricular activities as well as classes and instruction-related activities such as holding individual conferences, meeting with planning committees, and so forth.

Every effort should be made to equalize teacher loads so that morale will not be adversely affected. While it is common practice to provide extra payments to teachers who perform major extracurricular duties such as coaching and directing dramatic presentations, such practice should be kept at a minimum. Most teacher duties performed in connection with student activities should be recognized as integral parts of the teacher load.

Teachers should not be expected to perform clerical work in connection with their duties. It is an inefficient use of the teacher's time to require him or her to perform work which could be done by a school clerk or typist. The teacher is a professional, and his or her assignment and load should be professional in nature.

Bibliography

Abbot, Max G. "Hierarchical Impediments to Innovation in Educational Organizations." *Change Perspectives in Educational Administration.* Auburn, Alabama: Auburn University Press, 1965, pp. 40-53.

Barnard, Chester I. *The Functions of an Executive.* Cambridge, Mass.: Harvard University Press, 1966.

Bennis, Warren G. *Changing Organizations.* New York: McGraw-Hill, 1966.

Durant, Will and Durant, Ariel. *The Lessons of History.* New York: Simon and Schuster, 1968.

Hage, Jerald. "An Axiomatic Theory of Organizations." *Administrative Science Quarterly* 10, (1965), pp. 289-320.

Likert, Rensis. *New Patterns of Management.* New York: McGraw-Hill, 1961.

Smith, Ralph A. "Human Values, Modern Organizations, and Education." *Organizations and Human Beahvior.* ed. F. D. Carver and T. J. Sergiovanni. New York: McGraw-Hill, 1969.

Thompson, Victor A. "Hierarchy, Specialization, and Organizational Conflict." *Administrative Science Quarterly* 5, (1961), pp. 485-521.

U. S. Department of Health, Education and Welfare. *Do Teachers Make a Difference?* Washington, D. C.: U. S. Government Printing Office, 1970.

11

The Principal Works with the Staff

In the democratic model of the secondary school the principal works *with* the staff; he has power *with* his staff, not *over* the staff. The difference is quite significant and the "power *with*" concept reveals itself in the relaxed attitude of staff members and the general atmosphere of cooperative effort as opposed to the tensions, frustrations, and suspicions which often characterize the authoritarian type of administration. The principal is regarded as a colleague, a member of the team who exercises leadership as a means of facilitating the achievement of mutually accepted goals. A staff member feels free to raise questions, confess weaknesses, explore problems, and suggest innovations without fear of administrative disapproval or rejection. The principal and his staff work together, each fulfilling his or her unique role and all sharing the feeling of accomplishment which comes with cooperative achievement of common goals.

STAFF COMMUNICATION

Burton Fowler, onetime headmaster of the Germantown Friends School, made a speech which he titled "The Human Side of Education." Some of what he said had to do with communication or the lack of it. He described a junior high school he visited where the principal was virtually inaccessible. Seated at an intercom panel, he spent a good deal of time broadcasting administrative bulletins to harassed teachers who presumably were trying to teach. In modern practice, he was doing one-way communication. He talked and others listened. In another school, Mr. Fowler called on a principal to inquire about the progress of a beginning teacher. The principal had available all kinds of information elaborately itemized on a data card, but he knew very little about the teacher, either as a teacher or a person.

So accustomed have we become to radio, television, and advertising that we use the word *communication* only in the sense that someone gives us the message while we listen, unable to respond, or, in fact, to communicate at all. Whereas there are occasions in an organization when simple transmission of information is sufficient, particularly in schools, there are many more occasions when communication requires exchange of information, thoughts, and ideas. A principal needs to distinguish between the two.

Consider the meetings of the full faculty. Such meetings are too often formal affairs, held at the end of the school day when people are tired and want to go home. The principal uses the meeting to talk to the faculty, or reads material from mimeographed hand outs—one way communication. When such is the substance of faculty meetings, it is not surprising that they have a poor reputation among the staff. Much of this kind of communication could be better handled by informational bulletins. The faculty meetings would then be free for other purposes, and they could be centered on a problem or problems which required full faculty discussion. They could be asked to take action on issues which had originated in councils or subcommittees and which were ready for full faculty debate and advice. Items for the agenda for faculty meetings may originate with the principal or they may be proposed by individuals or committees. In many instances the question is raised and the discussion chaired by heads of committees which are reporting to and asking for advice or approval from the entire faculty.

A school characterized by low stratification will facilitate this kind of communication. If the principal gets out of his office and into the school, much person-to-person communication can be accomplished on an informal basis. Casual conversation is not the vehicle of communication that should lead to on-the-spot decisions, but it can provide the principal with a reading of a situation or problem which is not always available in group meetings.

Finally, some simple tips about communication which, if followed, may be helpful. A principal is sometimes confronted with an angry letter from a member of the staff containing what the principal interprets as unfair allegations or questioning of motives. He will be unwise to respond in a written communication. Face-to-face talk is better.

A staff member writes disparagingly of another staff member. Reply in a face to face meeting. This advice is given not for the usual reason of protecting the principal from misuse of what he has put in writing. It is because a person writing under stress needs time to talk it out. Written interchanges seldom, if ever, serve that purpose. The written memo "Please see me in my office at 3:45" conveys to the reader a threatening overtone. A personal visit or telephone call to arrange the conference is better.

Good communication is enhanced by the good listener. Few of us take the time to hear the other person out, to draw him out, to seek by a question here and there clarification of what he is trying to say. Most people are too eager to break in and present their views or their answers or solutions before the person with a problem on his mind has a chance to explain it. Good communication, the school as a good community, and the school as a humane institution are all related.

STAFF-STUDENT RELATIONSHIPS

Organization theorists, management experts, and social psychologists have devoted considerable effort to convincing administrators in all types of enterprises of the importance of harmonious and satisfying human relationships among the members of work groups. The contributions of these theorists and behavioral scientists to the body of knowledge pertaining to administration and management has had considerable effect on the training of school administrators. Professors of educational administration and practicing school administrators have attempted to adapt the developing theory to educational institutions—particularly to the problems of developing satisfactory relationships among the members of the teaching staff and between the teaching and administrative staffs. This effort is, of course, entirely appropriate. Indeed, in the discussion of staff organization included in this book we have pointed out the importance of harmonious relationships among staff members in the educational enterprise, and the attainment of job satisfaction by staff members. However, it would appear that in the course of adapting theories and practices developed in profit-making enterprises that deal in a product or service, there has been a tendency to overlook the need in schools for developing satisfying relationships between the professional staff and students.

One of the problems with attempts to apply business and industrial management practices, techniques, and organizational structures to schools is the fact that schools do not deal in a product nor simply in a service—they attempt to help individual human beings learn and grow. Consequently, attempts to view students as *products* of the organization are totally inconsistent with the democratic model. Thus, the administrative leadership of a school based on the democratic model must recognize that students are participants in the organization—in a sense, members of the working group— not products. Nor can they be viewed simply as the *recipients* of a service; rather, they must be active, willing participants in the school community. Learning is not *applied* to students; it is the result of mutual participation by teachers and students in the teaching-learning process. This means that the success of students' schooling will be dependent to a large extent on the development of human relationships that facilitate cooperation between staff members and students in the task of learning and living in the school community. We believe that to some extent the problem of developing satisfactory staff-student relationships has been overlooked in the literature pertaining to school administration.

It is to be hoped that the basic principles that should guide the development of staff-student relationships in a school based on the democratic model have become obvious from our explication of the model and from the discussions of the implications of the model for specific administrative functions. However, at this point it may be profitable to consider *specifically* some of the implications for staff-student relationships of acceptance of the democratic model and how the administrative leadership of a school may contribute to the development of such relationships.

Two basic democratic tenets—the worth and dignity of the individual and the right of citizens to participate in their governance—have particular implications for staff-student relationships. Acceptance of the first of these tenets dictates that students should be treated with basic human consideration by all members of the school staff. Further, an objective for the school should be to develop students who demonstrate consideration for the other members of the human groups in which they participate, including classroom groups, social groups, clubs, teams, their families, or the school community. In a school which acknowledges the worth and dignity of the individual, students should be treated as individuals with feelings, sensitivities, and integrity rather than as inmates in a penal institution to be catalogued, sorted, pigeon-holed, and ordered around, or as products to be managed, processed, and shipped out. The staff will operate on the assumption that students are individuals of integrity who are in the process of learning to accept responsibility rather than on the assumption that they cannot be trusted and must be under constant supervision and control.

It is true that students are not always considerate—a few are sometimes discourteous, rude, and unfeeling. However, inconsiderate and discourteous treatment on the part of the staff is unlikely to remedy this problem. If the research of Bandura and Walters regarding the effect of adult "models" on the behavior of young people has any validity, a considerate, courteous staff is much more likely to develop considerate students than one that attempts to impose one type of behavior while demonstrating another.

Not only should staff members demonstrate consideration with regard to feelings and sensitivities in their interaction with students, but they should also be considerate of students' time. The student's time is as valuable to him as the teacher's time is to the teacher; however, students are frequently kept waiting unnecessarily, required to make trips to two or three offices to obtain a simple form or an answer to a question, or are otherwise treated as if their time is of little value.

The acceptance of this tenet also implies that all members of the school community will be valued—not just those of the majority race, those from a particular ethnic background or of a certain socioeconomic status or those who conform to a particular concept of "student" or, for that matter, "teacher." In a democratic school, not only should diversity be tolerated, but it should be viewed as an asset. Staff-student relationships conducive to maximum educational growth for all students will be highly dependent on the extent to which the staff appreciates and values diverse students.

The application of the democratic principle that the members of a democratic system have the right to participate in their governance is dependent upon recognition on the part of staff members that students are intelligent human beings who are capable of contributing to the decision making process. Thus in a democratic school students should have the opportunity to voice their opinions on matters of school policy, rules and regulations, and curriculum. Further, their opinions and views should be considered, and when responses or explanations from administrators or staff members are requested they should be forthcoming.

Often staff members slough off the ideas, opinions, and evaluations of students as those of immature, unknowing neophytes who are incapable of comprehending the "true nature" of the teaching-learning process or of having any insights regarding their educational needs. Certainly students lack experience, nor do they have professional expertise; however, they do know better than anyone else how rules and regulations affect them, what their problems and interests are, and how effectively various instructional techniques and materials function in respect to generating student motivation and interest. They may also have insights into their educational needs that are unavailable to the professional staff or, at least, are unrecognized by the staff. Students are also capable of considering the overall direction of their education and the goals of their secondary schooling experience. In fact, some of them may frequently give more thought to long-range educational goals than many teachers. This is particularly true in the case of teachers who are narrowly subject-matter oriented and who never attempt to assess overall student needs, nor put the instruction they offer in perspective regarding the satisfaction of these needs. If staff-student relationships are to be characterized as a dialogue in which both students and teachers feel they can participate openly and freely, rather than as a monologue, the staff must listen to students, value their opinions and viewpoints, and acknowledge their *ability* to contribute to the decision-making process.

The following excerpt from a commencement address delivered by a high school senior in 1973 demonstrates the ability of contemporary secondary school students to consider varying educational aims and the appropriateness of the schooling they are receiving given a particular set of aims.

> ... yet I believe that the point is not whether one can read or write but *what* one reads, not whether one is technically proficient in mastering facts, but whether one is proficient in wondering about the whys of his existence, and not whether one is educated or uneducated, but what one is educated for. And what have we been educated for? Yes, a fundamental question—one that generations debate.
>
> Many declare that the function of American high school education is to train young people to absorb facts and adapt to our society as it is now. Indeed, Vice-President Agnew recently stated that this

nation has too many students in college and that 70 percent of this nation's jobs do not require a college education. He inferred that the sole purpose of education is advanced job training. Not only do national leaders hint at this, but a recent survey conducted among high school students by the White House Convention of Youth indicated that 70 percent of the students feel the main function of education is to prepare one for a good job as defined by our presently existing culture. One is indoctrinated in this way from the toddler stage through adolescence. "What are you going to be when you grow up?" "Where are you going to work next year?" "You don't know yet!" It is assumed that by one's latter high school days he already knows what his niche in the system should be. As one mother put it, "education should teach kids to understand our existing values and discipline them to conform. It's as simple as that!"

Yet this definition is being increasingly challenged by a wide spectrum of people—people who believe that education should provide a more human guide to help men evaluate and change—not merely accept—the world as it is. They seriously question the seemingly prevailing philosophy that an educated man is not one who acts morally as much as one who adjusts normally. Think about it! Schools do not seem to deal much with encouraging individuality, but more with judging the better person as the one who makes good grades, is obedient to school policy, and conforms to someone else's ideas of what is important. Between our exam pressures, our classroom experiences, do we ever take the time to wonder about the unique human being suffocated under the label of "goof-off," "smarty," or "quiet one?"

And what of the student who can parrot facts but is unable to wonder at the mysteries which engulf our world? Will he or she merely become another cog in the system? A humanized society simply cannot be run by mass produced people! So I ask, have we been helped to wonder, question, explore, challenge? Has our schooling been wonder-filled?

This excerpt certainly belies any claims that high school students are not *capable* of having a voice in the kind of schooling they are to receive. Although this student may be more articulate than most high school students, it is quite probable that the thoughts expressed represent areas of concern to many of today's secondary school students—students who are more than ever aware of the ways in which the educational system has failed them, who are more mature and better informed than ever before, and who are becoming more and more unwilling to accept what they are handed in the way of schooling because "that's the way it is." Rather than ignore the ideas, viewpoints, and feelings of students about their schooling, the staff, led by the principal, must develop ways to utilize student input to develop a more relevant, interesting, and individualized educational program and a school atmosphere conducive to the development of satisfying human relationships. Such an approach would appear to be the best antidote to student apathy and alienation that prevails in many contemporary secondary schools.

The ability of the school to elicit student input will be dependent on

The Principal Works With the Staff

staff-student relationships that are characterized by mutual trust and respect. In schools that have failed to develop satisfactory staff-student relationships, the response by students to invitations from the principal to provide input and to participate in school-related decisions may well be apathy—apathy born out of the conviction that a staff which does not listen to students or value their opinions is unlikely to give them any real voice in school affairs.

There are a number of things that the principal can do to facilitate the development of staff-student relationships which are characterized by consideration, openness, a relaxed atmosphere, and mutual respect and trust. First, we can see to it that the school's administrative staff establishes the model for developing such relationships. Administrators should be available to students and should be able and willing to discuss problems, ideas, and suggestions with them openly and frankly. Students should be able to talk with the principal or other administrators without waiting two weeks for an appointment. They should feel free to voice complaints and grievances without fear of the consequences, just as students and their parents should be able to discuss student problems with teachers without worrying that the teacher will retaliate in some way. (The use of the word retaliation, a word usually used in a military sense, is by conscious design. It is the word we have found that parents frequently use when explaining why they hesitate to contact the school regarding their children's learning or disciplinary difficulties.)

The suggestion that the principal demonstrate a willingness to listen to student complaints, suggestions, and requests and discuss them openly is not meant to imply that he should grant every request or adopt every suggestion. However, he must be prepared to change rules and regulations that are shown to be unnecessary or unreasonable, and to give student suggestions a try when possible. Experienced staff members frequently attempt to veto student suggestions on the grounds that "we tried that years ago and it didn't work." However, a new group of students and teachers may be able to refine the suggestion and make it work—and even if they can't, the experience of implementing a change, seeing it fail, and attempting to determine why it failed, may be a valuable learning experience for students. A school that attempts only those changes that it knows will succeed is doomed to the status quo. The open and frank discussion of problems and of the need for certain rules, regulations, and practices may result in better understanding on both sides, and in new means of accomplishing desirable ends that are, in the long run, more acceptable to all parties. Most students are reasonable people who are willing to accept rules, regulations, and practices which will facilitate the educational process—if someone will only take the time to explain the need for the rule, regulation, or practice to them.

By structuring the organization of the school so that students work with staff members on curriculum committees, pupil personnel policy committees, the evaluation process, and student government (as has been suggested in many sections of this book), the principal will not only broaden the base of decision-making, but will also provide an opportunity for staff-student relationships to develop in a more informal, collegial atmosphere than is often characteristic of the classroom. Teachers who participate in a collegial relationship with students in groups of this kind may discover that some of their rigid classroom procedures are unnecessary and that reducing the "press" on students results in better attitudes toward school and learning. They will certainly come to know their students better and will become more aware of their concerns, interests, attitudes, problems, and feelings.

The principal can also help to develop a genuine concern and appreciation on the part of the staff for the individual abilities, aspirations, and achievements of students. Certainly, encouraging teachers to individualize instruction to as great an extent as possible is a step in this direction; however, concern for the student as an individual learner involves more than just developing individualized approaches to traditional courses of study. The attitude of the entire school staff should reflect an appreciation of genuine student achievement in a wide range of areas. Too often schools seem to value only achievement, as demonstrated by good grades in the traditional academic disciplines; and even in the traditional subject areas it is often only achievement in college prep courses that staff members appear to value. Does it make sense for schools to value achievement in English, mathematics, and science more than achievement in art, business education, music, or vocational programs? Certainly every student needs basic communication and computational skills and a core of knowledge in the physical and social sciences in order to function economically in our society and to fulfill his role as a participating citizen in a democratic society; but our society has need for people capable of genuine achievement in a diversity of endeavors. Furthermore, individuals need to attain a sense of personal achievement by developing and utilizing their unique interests and abilities. By recognizing, encouraging, honoring, and valuing genuine achievement in all aspects of the school's program and by attempting to convince staff members of the appropriateness of this attitude, the principal can help develop a school community in which teachers and students respect and value each other. The net result should be that both teachers and students obtain increased satisfaction from their participation in the school community.

On occasion the principal may need to act as an advocate on behalf of the students. He may be the staff member best able to explain student feelings, perceptions, and attitudes to the teaching faculty, particularly to those who view any change as "lowering standards" or "giving away the school to the students." If he can act as a buffer between teachers who are threatened by the idea of a democratic school and students who are pressing for the right to participate, explaining the viewpoint of each group to the other, he may be able to contribute to better staff-student relationships. He may also be able to avoid damaging confrontations, over-reactions, and polarization. At times he will have to protect the rights and interests of an individual student in a dispute with a staff member, particularly when the staff member has used poor judgment or treated a student unfairly.

Unsatisfactory student-staff relations will increase the number of times that the principal is the "man in the middle." When students and/or parents are unable to talk with teachers about problems that arise, or are unable to resolve their problems through a conference with the teacher, they are likely to bring them to the principal. In such situations, the principal's role traditionally has been defined as that of the "defender of the profession"—in other words he has been expected to uphold the judgment of staff members, regardless of the facts. Such an attitude is, of course, antithetical to the democratic tradition. Further, the claim that such a position is necessary for the long-term good of the school does not hold water. The opposite is probably true, since the consistent application of such a principle would tend to protect incompetent, negligent, unreasonable, or unstable staff members. The principal will frequently have to acknowledge the fact that a staff member has been unreasonable or has used poor judgment. Parents and students are capable of understanding that teachers are human, that they have moments of frustration and anger and emotional ups and downs, and that the teaching profession includes a variety of personality types. However, the principal must remember that when the immediate difficulties involved in such situations are resolved, it is his responsibility to attempt to change unreasonable and unprofessional teacher behavior and to take steps to rectify obvious injustices. Nothing would seem more detrimental to staff-student relationships than blind adherence to the principle that the actions of a staff member are *always* right and proper simply because he is a staff member.

In order to increase the extent of a student's control over his schooling, a number of high schools have adopted some type of plan for implementing what is frequently referred to as "college-type" scheduling. The basic feature of these plans is that students are allowed to choose their teacher when multiple sections of a particular course are offered. Although *all* students may not, in fact, have a choice, even when this type of scheduling is employed (in most schools all teachers have to be fully utilized), the psychological effect on staff-student relationships of students having a voice in selecting at least some of their teachers should be positive. By rotating the order in which students register, the principal can ensure that all students will have some degree of choice most of the time. The principal considering a college-type plan must realize that many teachers may object to it, particularly those teachers who are insecure and those who depend on the fact that their course is "required" for student enrollment. The principal will have to use his leadership to reduce and eliminate their fears and to develop a commitment to the plan, if it is to succeed.

The principal may also foster better student-staff relationships by encouraging teachers to explain to students the objectives of their course or of shorter units of instruction. He may have to help some teachers with this task, since many teachers have little experience stating educational objectives and others have not clearly formulated the objectives of their instruction in their own minds. But if teachers help students understand the objectives of instruction and the relevance of these objectives to them as individuals and to the society of which they are a part, the groundwork for cooperative teacher-student effort should be more firm, particularly if it is clear to students that none of the objectives are writ in stone, that they are the result of a cooperative deliberation and are modifiable.

The principal can also contribute to the development of staff-student relationships by encouraging and supporting the activities program. By providing administrative support, by encouraging teachers to sponsor clubs and organizations, and by demonstrating interest in student activities, he can enhance the activities program. A thriving activities program can be one of the strongest antidotes to the tendency of schools to slip into the factory model with its attendant loss of personal involvement. Participation by teachers and students which develops from mutual interest in an activity and which occurs in a relaxed, informal, and nonevaluative atmosphere cannot help but contribute to a feeling of community. The principal cannot force or coerce staff members to attend student activities. He may be able to "assign" them to the sponsorship of a club or organization, but it is doubtful that the result will be satisfying unless the teacher has a genuine interest in the activity. However, by his own attendance at student activities and by demonstrating that he values the activities program he may be able to raise the staff's level of commitment to the program and thereby increase the number of teachers who participate in the activities program voluntarily.

One other aspect of staff-student relationships that the principal should consider is a question of time—specifically, the amount of class time that each student spends with one teacher during the course of a school year and during the duration of the student's enrollment in the school. A number of recent innovations in secondary education, such as team teaching and mini-courses, have tended to result in students being exposed to more teachers for shorter durations of time. This is particularly true of multi-unit approaches to English, social studies, and physical education. Such plans usually provide students with several six-, eight-, or nine-week units of instruction from which to choose, with each unit taught by a different teacher. These plans have advantages—students can select options on the basis of their own interest—but they may also make it less likely that teachers and students will get to know each other well. The development of personal relationships characterized by trust, respect, and confidence takes time. It would be wise for the principal and the curriculum council or committee to monitor the organization of the program of studies in order to ensure that all staff-student relationships are not short-term ones. Every student should spend enough time with at least some of his teachers to develop a personal relationship. A school where teachers do not even know the students in their own classes by name can hardly be described as a community. Particularly in large schools, the combination of size and constantly rotating classroom teachers or team-taught large groups could contribute to impersonal staff-student relationships.

In order to remedy this problem, an experimental high school in Ohio which employs team teaching and the mini-course format developed a plan for holding teacher-student rap sessions on a weekly basis. Each student was asked to select three or four members of the school staff (teachers, counselors, and administrators all participated) with whom he would like to meet. Groups of sixteen to twenty students and one staff member were formed and were scheduled to meet for forty-five minutes, once a week. The staff member and the students participated in the rap group on an equal basis—no structure was defined, no leader appointed. Any group member could bring up a topic for discussion, and the free and open interchange of ideas, opinions, and feelings was encouraged. These groups were not sensitivity or T groups, however. Counseling and psychological advice were left to the professional counselors and psychologists.

While we do not necessarily advance this plan as a means of solving the problem of developing satisfactory staff-student relationships, the very fact that a need for such a plan became evident reinforces our contention that students and teachers need to be together over time if they are to get to know each other. A recent piece of educational research also reenforces this contention. Odetola, Erickson, Bryan, and Walker conducted a study of organizational structure and student alienation in a large midwestern city which revealed, contrary to their expectations, that team-taught eighth-grade students in middle schools consistently had a lower sense of identification with school than middle school students who were assigned to a single teacher or than students in a departmentalized junior high school. They also found that middle school students who were assigned to teacher teams had a greater sense of powerlessness to use their own initiative than the students in the other two types of organizational structures. Their conclusion was that middle school students in single teacher systems were less alienated than students in junior high schools who in turn were less alienated than middle school students assigned to teacher-teams. In attempting to explain these unexpected findings they speculated that

> when teachers are organized in teams each might abandon his own responsibility to a collective whole. Relationships with students might then become specific; i.e., there may be a tendency to become less familiar with and to adopt a non-personal relationship with specific students. On the other hand, relationships with a single teacher might be primary. It is possible that students are able to develop a more intimate association with a single teacher and, thus, have a greater sense of identification with the school.[1]

---

[1]T. E. Odetola, E. L. Erickson, C. E. Bryan, and L. Walker, "Organizational Structure and Student Alienation," *Educational Administration Quarterly* 8 (Winter 1972), pp. 15-26.

While the generalizability of these findings is limited, and the findings far from conclusive, they do lend support to the argument that student association with an individual teacher over time is desirable, and possibly essential, in a school based on the democratic model in which the development of a feeling of community is considered important. In addition to this, it may well be that experiencing only brief relationships with students reduces the amount of satisfaction that teachers obtain from their work. Teachers who remain with the same groups of students only for brief periods of time, or whose only contact with students is in large groups, may be denied the satisfaction that comes from seeing one's students grow and mature intellectually and socially.

THE CURRICULUM COUNCIL

One way in which the principal may stimulate a continuing review of the educational program is to create a curriculum council. The membership of such a council would cut across department lines and would include teachers, some department chairman, and students. These could be either appointed or elected, but election is preferred. The size of such a council should be small enough that it is a working group, totalling no more than ten persons. Six members might be elected by the faculty, with the provision that at least two be department or division heads. Four would be elected by the student body. Effort should be made to see that student members are broadly representative, and if election does not result in such representation the principal should reserve the right to appoint additional student members, perhaps on nomination by the student government organization.

The Council would meet regularly to review proposals related to the educational program and to assure that these were consistent with the long range objectives of the school. The Council would also hear from teachers and students who had suggestions or complaints about the educational program as it exists. The Council would not be administrative in nature but would carry out its work in the area of policy review. Its visibility and prestige would be determined by the attention given to its deliberations by the principal. To establish the importance of the council, arrangement should be made for regular meetings, probably monthly. Agendas should be prepared, and pertinent material made available. The principal should be in regular attendance. He could chair the meetings or a chairman could be elected by the Council. If members of the faculty or students wished to appear at meetings of the Council this could be arranged with the purpose made known in advance to the Council. Reports of Council deliberations should be made available to the faculty and student body.

With a proper delineation of its purposes and functions as a deliberative advisory body primarily concerned with relating proposals and changes in practice to school goals, the principal's relationship with the Council would not be in conflict with his other associations with teachers and department or division chairmen. Nor is there any reason why the principal could not, if the occasion required, create ad hoc committees to deal with specific short range problems.

One caution needs to be observed in creating a Council as described or other kinds of committees. The deliberations of the Council or of committees must result from time to time in decisions or in resolutions of problems. Both teachers and students soon learn whether their participation is window dressing or whether what they say and recommend makes a difference and results in some change or movement. Talk alone is not enough.

IN-SERVICE EDUCATION

The democratic model suggested for the secondary school assumes the continuing development and improvement of the school staff. Such development is consistent with the principle of full participation of each individual in the educational enterprise. The contribution of each teacher can be enhanced by a systematic in-service education program. An in-service program which will be most meaningful and helpful to teachers is one which they help to plan as well as implement. With all the resources available today, every secondary school should have a well-planned in-service program which teachers will find both interesting and helpful.

The administration of a school can have a positive influence on staff development and on the induction of meaningful change by providing leadership in the development of in-service education programs tailored to meet specific staff needs. For a good many years elementary and secondary schools have depended on colleges and universities to provide the means by which their staff members could update their knowledge of their subject matter field, learn of new instructional techniques and modes, increase their knowledge of pupil growth and development, and become familiar with new developments in curriculum theory. Courses have been made available to teachers after school hours in the afternoons and evenings, on Saturdays, and during the summer months. These courses, for the most part, are part of the college or university program which leads to a degree rather than courses specifically designed to meet the needs of the teachers in attendance. Many boards of education give salary increments for courses taken as well as for degrees received.

To some extent this approach has been successful, particularly for teachers in subject areas which make them eligible to receive federal grants to attend summer institutes, seminars, or workshops. In many states, universities have done an outstanding job of providing in-service training for teachers, even in remote areas of the state, through their extension departments. However, many local elementary and secondary schools have found that the available college and university programs alone do not fully meet the in-service education needs of their staff. They have also found that teachers frequently qualify for salary increments by taking courses which are selected on the basis of convenience of time and place rather than on the basis of professional suitability.

Some schools have sought to solve this problem by developing a program specifically designed to meet the needs of their staff in cooperation with a college or university. The cooperative development of programs by the local school and a nearby college or university is a promising approach to in-service education. In some instances the universities have taken the lead in making their services available to public schools for the purpose of developing programs tailored to local needs.

The value of these programs is enhanced when the institution of higher education and the secondary school administration make arrangements for groups of teachers from a single school to form a class which can then design course content to meet the particular needs of the local group of teachers. Such an arrangement is usually both satisfying and rewarding to teachers when the instructor is flexible in his approach and when the college or university is conveniently located so that resource materials are readily available to teachers.

A cooperative arrangement with an accessible college or university is highly desirable and has proven effective in the development of the staff. However, such an arrangement is not always possible, and in some cases a more informal school-centered program may be preferable. Certainly an in-service program developed by the staff and administration can be more effectively directed toward meeting the unique needs of the local school. Such a program may be planned by the staff with the leadership of the administration and the cooperation of local agencies and individual citizens of the community. For example, one secondary school staff spent an entire year developing a carefully delineated set of educational goals for the high school. This process involved not only high school personnel but also representatives from the elementary school staff, representatives of community agencies, and citizens of the community. Problems of articulation between elementary and high school, cooperation with other service agencies, unique educational needs of the community, teamwork in pursuit of common goals, and the nature and availability of local resources for education were all considered during the project.

Resource people involved in the program were drawn not only from the local community, but from college faculties and admission offices, university extension services, and regional and state educational agencies as well.

In this type of program the local school is the center of the activity. The program is locally oriented. From its inception it is readily available to all and usually involves every staff member in one way or another. The total school community becomes the locale of the project. The staff becomes better acquainted with the community and learns more about the educational needs of the people it serves and the human and material resources available to aid in the educational enterprise.

There are numerous advantages to the development of local in-service programs, even in areas where an array of university extension courses is available. One advantage is the opportunity for the school's staff to be directly involved in planning the program. Teachers who have gone through a searching self-assessment process which leads to the identification of professional growth needs, and who have had a voice in planning the program to meet those needs are likely to have a strong interest in the program. The strong relationship that exists between interest and learning applies to teachers as well as students.

Locally developed programs can also take advantage of expertise which has proven effective under local conditions. One of the distressing facts about most schools, regardless of size, is the lack of interchange among teachers of ideas regarding instructional techniques, and materials. Nearly every school has some teachers who have developed creative, innovative solutions to teaching problems, presentations that are particularly effective or materials that are particularly designed for local conditions, or who have extensive or intimate knowledge of new educational developments. A locally designed and controlled program can provide the vehicle through which such teachers can share their expertise with other staff members. The provision of a formal program for such sharing of ideas may also contribute to the development of an attitude of cooperation in the exchange of teaching techniques, knowledge, and materials that will extend beyond the in-service classroom.

Another advantage of locally developed and controlled programs is their availability to all members of the staff. Sessions can usually be scheduled at convenient times and in easily accessible locations, usually the high school building. Even when programs are developed in cooperation with a college or university, it is usually possible to schedule sessions at a convenient time.

Both the college- or university-centered in-service educational program and the local school-oriented one have a place in staff development. Each may supplement the other. Each can contribute significantly to the development of the staff and the improvement of the educational enterprise. The former tends to broaden the experience of teachers, stimulate them to further their formal education, and improve their professional status in general. The latter program is more likely to develop teamwork, cooperative attitudes, and a sense of common purpose among teachers. Because of its community orientation it is more likely to be responsive to local educational needs.

The allocation of time to in-service programs, particularly the informal type, is always a problem. The importance of in-service education justifies the allocation of school time to that purpose as well as the provision of additional compensation for extra time spent in the program. Various ways have been devised to free teachers during the school day for in-service education. A recently developed one is the enlistment of paraprofessionals in the instructional program. Another is the utilization of parent volunteers in supervisory duties. One school allocates one afternoon each month to meetings of student activity groups such as clubs, student government, dramatic and musical organizations, and similar student organizations. Students are encouraged to carry on the business of their organizations with only an occasional appearance of a teacher at these meetings. In this way a substantial block of time is made available to the staff for in-service education while students are learning to independently conduct the affairs of their organizations. In the democratic secondary school such an arrangement is a natural outgrowth of a philosophy of self-direction and self-accountability.

STAFF SUPERVISION

The purpose of staff supervision in a school based on the democratic model is to improve instruction. Since the preceding section emphasized that one of the principal purposes for developing effective procedures and processes for staff evaluation is to provide feedback that will aid in the process of improving instruction, it is obvious that evaluation and supervision are interrelated functions. We have chosen to discuss them separately, in spite of the many ways in which they overlap, in order to make clear that while supervision involves the use of the results of evaluation it also involves considerably more.

In order to serve the purpose of improving instruction, supervision will involve the provision of support and assistance to teachers in a number of ways. Certainly the supervisor, whether the principal or some other staff member, will be involved in the process of evaluation and will help teachers obtain, interpret, and utilize evaluative feedback. However, he will also work with teachers in the development of instructional objectives—many teachers have little experience stating objectives or have not thought in terms of outcomes and will need help with this task. He will help teachers with the process of selecting and sequencing course content, planning learning activities, and developing instructional materials. Assisting teachers with the development of instruments to measure various aspects of student achievement may also be a part of the supervisory process. In addition, a perceptive supervisor will be able to help teachers develop satisfying staff-student relationships and thereby increase their ability to understand and relate to their students. In summary, supervision will consist of experienced, qualified instructional leaders providing teachers with the kind of support and assistance that will enable them to improve their teaching effectiveness.

The principal implication of the democratic model for the supervisory process is that it should be a cooperative one. The teacher must be willing to

The Principal Works With the Staff

cooperate if the supervisor is to be effective. Assistance cannot be forced on teachers, they must be willing to accept it. Just as they must be receptive to evaluative feedback if they are to profit from it, so must they be receptive to input from the supervisor if his assistance and support is to have a positive effect. Therefore, the processes of supervision must be designed and executed in a manner that will elicit receptivity and cooperation.

We doubt that the *inspectorial* approach to supervision, characteristic of schools administered in rigid, authoritarian fashion, will accomplish this goal. Improved instruction is unlikely to result from administrative threats to teachers or by snooping on them or harassing them. When supervisors are feared or disliked by teachers or when teachers feel unable to communicate with them in an open and candid manner, their contribution to the process of improving instruction is likely to be nil.

When supervision is viewed as a means of checking up on teachers or forcing them to do their jobs and obey school rules and regulations, whether the principal realizes it or not, he is operating on the basis of "Theory X" as referred to in an earlier chapter—a theory that, if implemented, would seem unlikely to lead to the development of the mutual trust and respect which are fundamental requisites for cooperation among staff members.

If supervision is to serve the purpose we have indicated it should, staff members must feel that supervisors are genuinely interested in helping them improve their teaching strategies, techniques, and materials and their ability to relate to students. Those responsible for supervision must recognize that their function is not to impose one teaching style, classroom format, or instructional approach, but rather to help the teacher refine the style, technique, and materials that fit his individual personality and that work for him. Staff members must acknowledge that there are many valid routes to the achievement of educational objectives.

If the school is large enough that supervision is the function of staff members other than the principal, the principal should make every effort to ensure that individuals who are temperamentally suited to provide support, assistance, expertise, and information to teachers in a considerate, nonthreatening, and nondogmatic manner are appointed to supervisory positions. Obviously they must possess experience, knowledge, and expertise, but their commitment to a cooperative, facilitative role rather than an authoritarian, inspectorial one is equally important. Further, pedagogical expertise and a thorough knowledge of adolescent psychology are probably more important than subject matter knowledge in a particular discipline. The role of the supervisor is not to improve the teacher's knowledge of his subject matter field, but rather to help him put that knowledge to use in order to facilitate student learning.

We have noted in the previous section that staff evaluation is frequently based solely on direct classroom observation. Similarly, the sole means for accomplishing staff supervision is too often the observation of the teacher in the act of teaching. Certainly, observation should be a part of the supervisory process, but the type of assistance we have described earlier cannot be provided if direct classroom observation, followed by a brief conference, is the only mode of interaction between the teacher and the supervisor.

Unfortunately, the same limitations regarding the reliability of direct classroom observation that were explicated in the section on evaluation apply when the purpose is supervision, and we will not repeat them here. However, if the supervisor is alert to the fact that both the teacher and the students may not behave in their normal manner when they are being observed, and if he is perceptive regarding the subtle nuances of classroom activity, he may be able to gain insights and general indications that are worth following up.

The supervisor and the teacher should meet as soon as possible after a class session has been observed to discuss the session while it is fresh in their minds. Conferences a week or two later are probably of little value. The conferences should be characterized by an open and frank discussion between the teacher and the supervisor, which concentrates less on arriving at some sort of evaluative closure than on strategies for improving instruction suggested by the clues or leads obtained through observation.

A supervisor, or even some other observer such as a colleague, may provide a valuable service to the teacher by performing some type of interaction analysis during one or more class sessions. Such an analysis can provide the teacher with an objective view of the extent to which classroom activities are teacher-dominated. Most teachers are familiar with studies that show that class sessions consist primarily of teacher talk, but few believe that this is true of their classroom unless such an analysis is performed. This type of analysis can also reveal the extent to which *all* members of a class participate in discussions and other classroom activities. Teachers sometimes fail to realize that some students fail to learn because they are, in effect, ignored.

The audio and video tape recorder can be useful tools in the process of supervision. The kind of analysis described in the preceding paragraph could be accomplished through the use of one of these pieces of equipment. The joint study of tapes of class sessions by the teacher and supervisor would seem a particularly effective means of improving a teacher's subject matter presentations and classroom manner.

A major function of the supervisory process in a democratic school will be the development of specific instructional objectives. The teacher and supervisor should cooperatively develop course objectives as well as the objectives of units of instruction. The objectives should be designed to achieve the goals of the school as determined by the board of education, staff, students, and lay members of the community. The supervisory process should include periodic reviews of the relevance and feasibility of these objectives regarding the particular students to be educated.

The supervisory process should also include periodic joint assessments of the progress that the teacher's students are making toward achieving the instructional objectives. It is, of course, at this point that the relationship between evaluation and supervision is most evident. The clear definition of instructional objectives is essential as a basis for evaluation, while the results of evaluation provide direction for supervisory activities designed to improve instruction. The success of this aspect of supervision will obviously be dependent on the development of effective procedures and processes for obtaining reliable evaluative feedback and an attitude of receptivity toward it.

In the section on evaluation we mentioned the wise use of student time as a basis for evaluating teaching effectiveness. The supervisor should help teachers plan instruction so as to make efficient use of students' time. We refer not only to class time, but also to learning activities to be assigned which require the expenditure of student time outside the class period. A supervisor with experience and pedagogical expertise can provide help with the sequencing of content and the pacing of learning activities—assistance that may help the teacher take a rather direct path toward the attainment of instructional objectives. Student interest is a powerful determinant of learning, and the relationship between well-organized instruction and interest is likely to be high. Again we emphasize that the role of the supervisor is not to dictate sequence, pace, organization, or learning modes, but to make his expertise available to the teacher. This process is probably best described as joint planning—planning in a collegial rather than a superior-subordinate relationship.

Finally, the principal must face the reality that effective supervision will require the expenditure of large amounts of time. If supervisors are to provide real assistance to teachers in the process of developing instructional objectives, selecting and sequencing content, planning learning activities, developing materials, refining teaching style, developing satisfactory relationships with students, and utilizing evaluative feedback, they will have to have ample time available to meet with teachers on a regular basis. Furthermore, they must be available when teachers are available.

In some schools the principal may be able to adequately supervise the instructional staff, but even in a small school it is possible that other administrative duties require so much of his time that he simply does not have enough time available to provide effective supervision. If a department chairman or division head is assigned the responsibility for staff supervision and at the same time is required to teach a full load of classes and perform various clerical/administrative functions, then the principal can anticipate that supervision will be ineffective. The type of organization that will best accomplish the supervisory functions described will vary from school to school, but a fundamental principle is that the assignment of responsibility must be accompanied by the necessary authority, time, and resources to accomplish the task.

STAFF EVALUATION

One of the most difficult administrative problems with which the principal will have to wrestle is developing rational and effective procedures for evaluating the members of the school's staff. Indeed, evaluating the effectiveness of teachers, department chairmen, and other administrators is such a perplexing task that it seems to be almost ignored in many schools. However, staff evaluation is a valid administrative responsibility.

There are at least two distinct purposes of evaluation that make it essential for a school that is committed to making the best possible use of the available human and material resources to meet the educational needs of its students. One of these purposes is to obtain evidence on which to base personnel decisions—decisions regarding the retention or release of probationary or nontenured teachers, the dismissal of tenured teachers, and the assignment of staff members. (This latter classification of decisions includes not only the assignment of teachers to classes, resource centers, etc., but also the assignment of staff members to department chairmanships and other supervisory and administrative positions.) These are decisions that must be made, and the principal's responsibility to the school community requires that he make every effort to initiate structures that will result in decisions based on the most valid and reliable objective data obtainable as well as on subjective data from a variety of qualified sources. The alternatives are to make little or no effort to evaluate staff members and to routinely retain them all except in flagrant cases, or to make decisions on the basis of intuition, personal whims or biases, or superficial criteria. These alternatives are, of course, an abdication of the principal's responsibility.

The principal's obligation to the community to make the best possible use of available resources is matched by his obligation to the staff to develop evaluative procedures that are as fair and objective as possible and to base decisions on relevant educational criteria. Teachers, individually and through their organizations, frequently complain that the only input into decisions regarding whether to retain or dismiss staff members is the impressions the principal obtains from his occasional classroom visits and/or from his strolls past the classroom door. They also complain that too often teacher personnel decisions are based on the extent to which the teacher maintains an "orderly" classroom and is prompt in turning in reports and forms.

Unfortunately, the limited amount of time and effort expended on staff evaluation in many schools lends credence to these claims. When the time comes that personnel decisions must be made, the only information that *can* contribute to the decisions is that which is available. If effective evaluative procedures and processes have not been developed, only limited information will be available, and, unfortunately, the information regarding teachers most readily available to the principal is usually whether their classrooms are quiet or noisy, how many students they have sent to the office for disciplinary reasons, the punctuality with which they turn in records and forms, and the neatness and accuracy of their record-keeping. While these factors may have some bearing on teacher effectiveness, they are certainly not reliable indicators of how well the teacher's students are learning. At best, they should be considered minor or tangential criteria. To retain or dismiss teachers on the basis of such evidence is unfair to teachers and to students.

It is the principal's responsibility to provide leadership in the development of evaluative criteria logically related to teaching effectiveness and processes and procedures for obtaining evaluative feedback pertaining to these criteria. He must develop an understanding of the need for evaluation among all members of the school community and he must do his best to obtain the resources necessary to implement the most effective procedures and processes known and available. In a school based on the democratic model the development of evaluative criteria will be a cooperative process, one which involves administrators, teachers, students, and parents. Procedures and processes will be developed for obtaining evaluative feedback from a variety of courses, including the staff member who is being evaluated. This does not mean that the principal should delegate his responsibility for personnel decisions—he should not and cannot do so; he will have to bear the final responsibility for them. However, the purpose of broadening the base of participation in the development of criteria and procedures is not to avoid responsibility, but to make more effective decisions. The principal must remember, however, that the participative development of criteria and procedures and evaluation of feedback will not just happen—rational means for accomplishing this must be established.

It is also the principal's responsibility to ensure that all staff members are made aware of the criteria, procedures, and processes that will be used to evaluate their performance. Teachers often complain that the criteria and procedures for evaluating them have not been made known to them or are stated or written in vague and ambiguous terms. Staff members have a right to know how they will be evaluated and the criteria that will be employed. If they are to be evaluated on the basis of their ability to maintain an orderly classroom they should be so informed; if, on the other hand, they are to be evaluated on their teaching effectiveness, as we believe they should be, they should be made aware of the criteria for determining teaching effectiveness—a set of criteria that in a democratic school will be mutually determined by administrators, teachers, students, and parents.

Probably the major purpose for developing an effective system for staff evaluation is to obtain feedback which will enable staff members to do their particular job (teaching, counseling, administering) better. That is, information should be provided that will help staff members responsible for implementing instruction (the teachers) and those responsible for supervising instruction (the administrators) to improve instruction.

It is obvious that evaluation for both of the purposes mentioned is essential if the school is to be an adaptable organization, but many schools devote even a smaller share of their resources to evaluation for the purpose of improving instruction than for the purpose of making effective personnel decisions. Schools too often simply place teachers in a classroom with a group of students and, as long as severe discipline problems do not develop, leave them to shift for themselves, providing neither helpful supervision nor evaluative feedback. However, the principal has a responsibility to students, parents, and teachers to attempt to find out whether students are learning and what they are learning and to help staff members to become better teachers, counselors, or administrators.

One of the principal's leadership tasks is to develop an attitude of receptivity to evaluative data among staff members, and we doubt that authoritarian approaches to evaluation will permit this. They are too likely to convey an implication of threat or harassment. In fact, in order to develop and maintain staff receptivity to evaluative feedback, the principal will have to be particularly careful to avoid uses of evaluative data which permit comparisons between staff members or which publicly embarrass individual staff members, and he will have to consciously strive to avoid statements and uses of feedback that staff members may perceive as threats. Effective procedures for obtaining reliable evaluative feedback are of little value if staff members are unwilling to accept it and utilize it to improve their performance. Improving instruction, in particular, requires the cooperative effort of teachers and supervisors, and when teachers perceive threat and become fearful or alienated they are not only likely to be unreceptive to and disdainful of evaluative feedback, but also reluctant to cooperate with supervisors in the process of using evaluative feedback to improve instruction. They are more likely to attempt to find ways to subvert the evaluative processes and procedures, such as teaching the answers to tests or rehearsing their students in preparation for visits by evaluators.

The commitment of the school administration and staff to the principles embodied in the democratic model should facilitate the use of evaluative feedback to improve staff performance. The willingness and ability of staff members to use evaluative feedback to improve their performance is dependent on a nonthreatening atmosphere which is characterized by mutual respect, consideration, and trust—all factors essential to cooperative staff effort. These characteristics, of course, describe a school based on the democratic model.

If evaluation is to serve the purposes defined, what means should be employed for obtaining the necessary evaluative feedback? The most common and often the sole formal means of evaluating teachers employed by contemporary secondary schools is direct classroom observation—in other words, an occasional (rare?) classroom visit by the principal, assistant principal, or department chairman is required. However, it seems unlikely that one or two or even several classroom visits can provide sufficient evidence to enable the principal to make an accurate appraisal of an individual teacher's effectiveness or adequate information to enable him to help the teacher improve his teaching style, techniques, or materials.

In addition to the obvious fact that such a process samples only a tiny fraction of the teacher's total yearly effort, and that it is often difficult to comprehend classroom activities, let alone evaluate them, without knowing what has taken place in preceding class sessions, there is considerable evidence from educational research to indicate that neither the teacher nor the students in a classroom behave in their normal manner when an observer is present. This has been found to be consistently true whether the observer is an administrator, another teacher, or an unknown researcher. In fact, researchers have found direct observation provides such unreliable data regarding various aspects of teacher and student classroom behavior that many have abandoned it as a means of obtaining data.

We are not suggesting, however, that direct classroom observation be completely abandoned, for it is probably of some value. What we are suggesting is that classroom observation alone is not adequate, either for providing evidence on which to base personnel decisions or for providing feedback for the purpose of improving instruction.

Classroom visits may enable the principal to identify teachers who have obvious difficulties relating to students or who are inconsiderate of students or unreasonable in the demands they place upon them. He may also be able to get some indication of the extent to which the teacher makes wise use of the students' time. This last factor is particularly important since one of the things it seems reasonable and feasible to hold teachers accountable for is the use they make of students' time. We suspect that one of the principal causes of student boredom and disinterest may be the waste of student time that results from poorly planned instruction. A note of caution is in order, however. Although the extent to which the teacher has planned and prepared instructional activities is an indication of his commitment to use student time wisely, the ability to implement instructional plans and the wisdom to know when to abandon them and improvise a new approach, technique, or activity or to pursue a different or tangential topic are better indicators of his ability to do so.

Classroom visits serve an additional purpose in that they demonstrate to teachers that the principal is interested in what goes on in the classroom. Veteran teachers as well as probationary teachers have a need for individual recognition, a need to feel that the principal is interested in what they are doing. Classroom visits motivated by a sincere desire on the part of the principal to fulfill the role of instructional leader can, therefore, be a source of satisfaction to teachers committed to the task of helping students learn. Such visits are also directly beneficial to the principal—they require him to get out of his office and mix with students and teachers. They give him an opportunity to gain insights regarding the general atmosphere of the school, changing adolescent norms and mores, and the extent to which actual instruction is consistent with the school's stated objectives.

The effectiveness of classroom observation will to some extent be dependent on the manner in which it is conducted. The authoritarian administrator who drops into a class unannounced with his clipboard and checklist at the ready will probably accomplish little more than the creation of teacher anxiety. The reaction of teachers to such an approach is likely to be defensive—a reaction that is dysfunctional, since a cooperative effort to utilize evaluative feedback to improve instruction requires openness and candor. The teacher should be notified several days in advance that someone will observe his class (or classes), and the observer should do everything possible to put the teacher and class at ease—being unobtrusive might help the most. If notes must be taken or lists checked, this should be done after the class session. Obviously, the observer should never make critical comments in the presence of students, nor should he interrupt or take over during the class session. Such practices are extremely inconsiderate of the teacher and will result in teacher alienation rather than staff cooperation.

In summary, what we are saying is that the principal may get some general indications of teacher effectiveness, teacher weaknesses, or the nature of teacher-student relationships by visiting class sessions, but other means of evaluation must be utilized to provide more reliable and comprehensive evaluative feedback. In addition, the process of obtaining evaluative feedback by direct classroom observation will be more effective if multiple observers are employed. If an assistant principal, department chairman, or supervisor also observes classroom instruction, information can be pooled and impressions checked—a process that is essential in view of the unreliable nature of data obtained from direct classroom observation.

An evaluative process which can serve both of the purposes defined is the mutual teacher-administrator analysis of the progress that the teacher's students have made toward attaining specified instructional objectives. If the teacher has had a voice in determining the objectives of the courses he teaches, and has specified the objectives for the units on instruction that constitute the course, he should be willing to sit down with the principal, department chairman, or supervisor and examine both objective and subjective data regarding the extent to which his students have achieved these objectives and consider ways of improving his teaching effectiveness.

Students' scores on tests may provide some of the evidence to be considered in such a mutual evaluation of the extent to which a teacher's students have attained certain objectives. However, the tests should be teacher-made tests or teacher-selected criterion-referenced tests designed to measure student attainment of the objectives of the specific instruction rather than standardized, norm-referenced achievement tests. Standardized achievement tests are primarily designed to rank students in general areas of cognitive achievement and are not adaptable for measuring the achievement of specific local instructional objectives. Objective and subjective measures of student attitudes, interests, and motivations and teacher-student relationships may also be utilized in the mutual evaluation process.

The administrator involved in a mutual evaluation process must recognize that one of the outcomes of the process might be the redefinition of objectives. Instructional objectives sometimes turn out to be inappropriate or unrealistic, at least for particular students. On occasion, teachers will discover important omissions in their specifications of objectives. Instructional objectives that are to serve as a basis for evaluation must be modifiable, although mutual agreement on new objectives may be required. To evaluate any staff member on the basis of objectives that are demonstrated to be unrealistic or inappropriate is obviously unfair.

One of the best sources of evaluative feedback regarding the effectiveness of instruction is ignored by many schools. That source is the students. Valuable evaluative feedback can be obtained from students in several ways. In a school that has developed the type of staff-student relationships that we believe should characterize a school based on the democratic model (see the section on staff-student relationships included in this chapter) it will be possible for teachers to obtain useful feedback by simply talking informally with students—individually, in small groups, or as a class. If students do not feel threatened they will offer frank opinions regarding the efficacy of various instructional techniques, learning activities, and materials, and their perceptions of the relevancy and inherent interest of content. A more systematic approach to obtaining student evaluations is to administer some type of formal evaluative instrument to entire classes of students. Instruments for this purpose can be developed locally by teachers and/or administrators, or packaged programs can be obtained from several sources.

A number of universities have developed programs designed to obtain reliable evaluations of courses and teachers from students and have made them available to public schools. The cost of these programs is usually quite reasonable. Specifically, the Educator Feedback Center at Western Michigan University has spent several years and a great deal of effort developing and refining a teacher evaluation program. The evaluative instrument used in the program is the *Teacher-Image Questionnaire* shown in Figure 11-1. The Western Michigan program specifies that the teacher select two or more of his classes to participate in the program and a colleague to administer the questionnaire. The colleague then administers the questionnaire with the teacher out of the room, places the completed questionnaires in an envelope which is provided, and seals the envelope and mails it directly to the Educator Feedback Center. The Center sends an analysis of the student responses, including an image profile and a summary of the open-ended comments, directly to the teacher—and only to the teacher. The report is completely confidential and unavailable to anyone other than the teacher. The fact that

TEACHER-IMAGE QUESTIONNAIRE

Do not begin until you are told to do so by the person in charge.

WHAT IS YOUR OPINION CONCERNING THIS TEACHER'S:

1. KNOWLEDGE OF SUBJECT: (Does he have a thorough knowledge and understanding of his teaching field?)   Poor   Fair   Avg.   Good   Exc.
2. CLARITY OF PRESENTATION: (Are ideas presented at a level which you can understand?)   Poor   Fair   Avg.   Good   Exc.
3. FAIRNESS: (Is he fair and impartial in his treatment of all students in the class?)   Poor   Fair   Avg.   Good   Exc.
4. CONTROL: (Is the classroom orderly but also relaxed and friendly?)   Poor   Fair   Avg.   Good   Exc.
5. ATTITUDE TOWARD STUDENTS: (Do you feel that this teacher likes you?)   Poor   Fair   Avg.   Good   Exc.
6. SUCCESS IN STIMULATING INTEREST: (Is this class interesting and challenging?)   Poor   Fair   Avg.   Good   Exc.
7. ENTHUSIASM: (Does he show interest in and enthusiasm for the subject? Does he appear to enjoy teaching this subject?)   Poor   Fair   Avg.   Good   Exc.
8. ATTITUDE TOWARD STUDENT IDEAS: (Does this teacher have respect for the things you have to say in class?)   Poor   Fair   Avg.   Good   Exc.
9. ENCOURAGEMENT OF STUDENT PARTICIPATION: (Does this teacher encourage you to raise questions and express ideas in class?)   Poor   Fair   Avg.   Good   Exc.
10. SENSE OF HUMOR: (Does he share amusing experiences and laugh at his own mistakes?)   Poor   Fair   Avg.   Good   Exc.
11. ASSIGNMENTS: (Are assignments sufficiently challenging without being unreasonably long?)   Poor   Fair   Avg.   Good   Exc.
12. APPEARANCE: (Are his grooming and dress in good taste?)   Poor   Fair   Avg.   Good   Exc.
13. OPENNESS: (Is this teacher able to see things from your point of view?)   Poor   Fair   Avg.   Good   Exc.
14. SELF-CONTROL: (Does this teacher become angry when little problems arise in the classroom?)   Poor   Fair   Avg.   Good   Exc.
15. CONSIDERATION OF OTHERS: (Is he patient, understanding, considerate, and courteous?)   Poor   Fair   Avg.   Good   Exc.
16. EFFECTIVENESS: (What is your overall evaluation of your teacher's effectiveness?)   Poor   Fair   Avg.   Good   Exc.

Figure 11-1

Source: Prepared by the Educator Feedback Center, Western Michigan University, Kalamazoo, Mich., 49001. Used with permission.

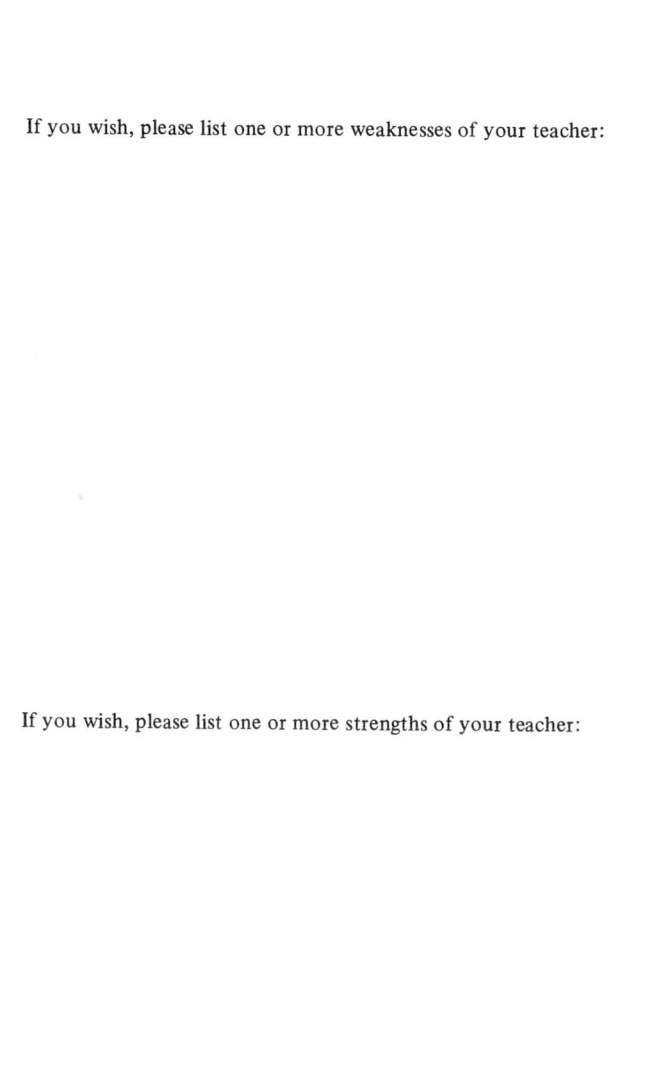

If you wish, please list one or more weaknesses of your teacher:

If you wish, please list one or more strengths of your teacher:

Figure 11-1, *Continued*

ILLINOIS TEACHER EVALUATION QUESTIONNAIRE — FORM 68

Measurement and Research Division, Office of Instructional Resources, UNIVERSITY OF ILLINOIS © By Richard E. Spencer, 1968

DIRECTIONS:
1. PRINT INSTRUCTOR'S LAST NAME HERE _____
2. COMPLETE IDENTIFICATION INFORMATION BELOW AS THE TEACHER INDICATES.
3. RESPOND TO THE ITEMS PRESENTED FRANKLY AND COMPLETELY-ONE RESPONSE PER ITEM. (SEE SAMPLE MARK AND RESPONSE CODE)
4. USE PENCIL ONLY - DO NOT USE PEN, BALL POINT OR INK OF ANY KIND.

MAKE ERASURES AS COMPLETE AS POSSIBLE

SAMPLE MARKS:
a) SA ■ A D SD
b) SA ■ A D SD
c) SA A ■ D SD
d) SA A D ■ SD

USE PENCIL ONLY

RESPONSE CODE:
- MARK SA — IF YOU STRONGLY AGREE WITH THE ITEM
- MARK A — IF YOU AGREE MODERATELY WITH THE ITEM
- MARK D — IF YOU DISAGREE MODERATELY

AGRICULTURE
ART
BUS. ED.
ENGLISH
FOR. LANG.
HEALTH
HOME EC.
IND. ED.
MATH
MUSIC
PE MEN
PE WOMEN
SCIENCE
SOC. STU.
SPEECH
OTHER

7

TODAY'S DATE
MONTH / DAY / YEAR
8 / 9

DO YOU EXPECTED GRADE IN THIS COURSE — 4
DO YOU PLAN TO GO TO COLLEGE? YES / NO — 3
GRADE — 5
TEACHER CODE — 2
SCHOOL CODE — 1

1. The teacher seems confident and knowledgeable.   SA A D SD
2. The class can easily deceive the teacher.   SA A D SD
3. The teacher knows what she (he) is talking about.   SA A D SD
4. I like this teacher.   SA A D SD
5. This teacher has 'favorites' in class.   SA A D SD
6. This subject is quite interesting.   SA A D SD
7. Quite a boring teacher.   SA A D SD
8. Discipline is a problem in this class.   SA A D SD
9. This subject is easy to follow.   SA A D SD
10. The teacher considers teaching a chore.   SA A D SD
11. The teacher seems to talk down to students

16	SA	A	D	SD	I think this teacher teaches quite well.
17	SA	A	D	SD	Out of all the teachers I have had, this teacher ranks quite high.
18	SA	A	D	SD	The pace of teaching is too slow.
19	SA	A	D	SD	The teacher seems confused.
20	SA	A	D	SD	The tests are too difficult.
21	SA	A	D	SD	Generally, the teacher seems well organized.
22	SA	A	D	SD	The teacher changes the method of teaching to suit the occasion.
23	SA	A	D	SD	An exciting teacher.
24	SA	A	D	SD	I would like to have another teacher like this one.
25	SA	A	D	SD	This class is a waste of time.
26	SA	A	D	SD	Overall, this subject is one of my favorites.
27	SA	A	D	SD	The text material is very good.
28	SA	A	D	SD	More teachers should be like this.
29	SA	A	D	SD	This class is quite rewarding.
30	SA	A	D	SD	Not much is gained by studying this subject.
31	SA	A	D	SD	The teacher encourages new ideas and viewpoints.
32	SA	A	D	SD	Homework assignments are helpful in understanding the subject.
33	SA	A	D	SD	Not enough student discussion.
34	SA	A	D	SD	The teacher has a thorough knowledge of the subject.
35	SA	A	D	SD	The types of test questions used in this class are good.
36	SA	A	D	SD	The teacher does not explain things very well.
37	SA	A	D	SD	An uninteresting teacher.
38	SA	A	D	SD	This class is one of the poorest of all my classes.
39	SA	A	D	SD	The teacher gets off the point too often.
40	SA	A	D	SD	Many other teachers I have had can teach better.

Figure 11-2.

the results of the evaluation are available only to the teacher eliminates their use as a basis for personnel decisions except in instances where the teacher may want to voluntarily make them available to the principal, however it may increase their value as a means of improving instruction. When there is no possibility of public embarrassment or administrative threat, the possibility that the teacher will react defensively is surely reduced.

The Measurement and Research Division of the Office of Instructional Resources at the University of Illinois has also developed a teacher evaluation program which is available to public schools (Figure 11-2, p. 312-3). This instrument provides students with the opportunity to evaluate course materials, pacing, organization, and other factors not included in the Western Michigan instrument; however, it does not give students the opportunity to make open-ended comments. The process for administering the questionnaire and for providing results is similar to that employed in the Western Michigan program. If a formal program for obtaining student evaluations is instituted, it might be wise to make several instruments or programs available to teachers. Some teachers might be encouraged to try more than one instrument in order to determine which provides the most helpful feedback.

The feasibility or wisdom of attempting to use student evaluations of teachers as evidence bearing on personnel decisions is doubtful. The threatening atmosphere that might well result would probably destroy the usefulness of such feedback for improving instruction. In fact, the principal may have some difficulty convincing staff members that obtaining student evaluations is a wise idea even if the results are to be used only for improving instruction and are confidential. To many teachers, particularly those overly conscious of their status and hierarchical authority, the very idea seems an affront. Some are of the opinion that students will not approach the matter seriously. They fear that students will use the process as a means of retaliation or that they will base their evaluations on personal popularity rather than teaching effectiveness. The experience of teachers who have participated in such programs indicates that none of these fears is justified, but it may take some time and effort to demonstrate to teachers that this is true.

The careful provisions for the confidentiality of evaluation results might make them a good vehicle for introducing the idea of obtaining student evaluations of staff members. The principal may want to begin by simply making one or two of these programs available to teachers on an optional basis. If teachers who participate find that the programs provide feedback useful for improving their teaching and that their egos are not demolished, it should be possible to expand the use of student evaluations.

Another approach to evaluation is through the use of audio or video tape recorders to record classroom sessions for later study and analysis. The tape recorder or video camera is likely to be less threatening to the teacher and less disruptive to the students than the presence of an observer, particularly if the process becomes frequent and common. One of the advantages of the process is that many more classroom sessions can be taped than can be visited by the principal or supervisor; thus, the amount of available evidence is increased and the likelihood of evaluation based on atypical teacher or student behavior is reduced. In addition, classroom interaction and activities can be reexamined in detail in teacher-administrator conferences which provide the opportunity for the teacher to explain his rationale for certain techniques, approaches, and activities and which give a chance for the administrator to make suggestions for improving the teacher's effectiveness. These aids would seem particularly useful for evaluating student-teacher interaction, the effectiveness of teacher presentations, and the ability of the teacher to present lucid explanations in response to student questions.

Another approach to evaluation which schools have seldom utilized is the use of some form of "peer evaluation." Such a plan might involve the teacher, principal, and department chairman or supervisor in the joint selection of a team of two, three, or four teachers whose knowledge and judgment they mutually respect, to observe a teacher's classes, obtain feedback from his students, evaluate the extent to which his students are attaining instructional objectives, and examine the learning activities and materials he is using. Their responsibility would be to provide the administration and the teacher with an overall evaluation of the teacher's effectiveness and with evaluative feedback which might aid the cooperative effort of the teacher and the supervisor to improve the teacher's effectiveness. The success of such a process is again highly dependent on a nonthreatening organizational climate which is characterized by a spirit of cooperation and a strong commitment to facilitating student learning. If teachers perceive the process as an administrative device for imposing a standardized teaching style or course of study, or for increasing their ability to spy on teachers, they will react defensively and will surely find some way of subverting it and rendering it ineffective for any of the purposes of evaluation.

What about evaluating teachers by measuring the performance of their students through the use of achievement tests? This approach to teacher evaluation seems to have considerable appeal to those who tend to think of education in terms of efficiency concepts (cost-benefit analysis, productivity, and so on) borrowed from business and industry. First, such a procedure could at best evaluate only one form of student achievement—achievement in cognitive skills. But, aside from this problem, even such a devotee of achievement testing as Ralph Tyler stressed at the 1973 convention of the American Educational Research Association that evaluating teachers on the basis of their students' performance on achievement tests is simply not feasible, given the present state of the art of measurement. Most available achievement tests are norm-referenced tests of cognitive knowledge in a general subject area. They are designed for the purpose of ranking students rather than determining whether they have mastered a particular body of content. They were not designed to be used for the purpose of teacher evaluation nor are they adaptable to it. The development of criterion-referenced tests for each course in the curriculum, which measure students' knowledge of the content of a specific unit of instruction at the beginning and end of the unit of instruction, would seem an enormous task and one that is likely to be impossible in areas of instruction based on objectives above the level of cognitive skills in the taxonomy of educational objectives. Add to this the influence on student learning of factors beyond the control of the teacher and the school such as family background, innate intelligence, community environment, and school and classroom socioeconomic class composition, and it is obviously impossible to fairly evaluate a teacher simply by pre- and post-testing his students. Testing programs can provide some *overall* evaluation of student achievement in cognitive skills at the time students enter the secondary school and when they complete their high school education, but to attempt to hold specific teachers accountable for the test scores of specific students is unrealistic.

Beyond this, we submit that the concept of evaluation through "standardized" testing is out of tune with a model which emphasizes the participative determination of objectives and the constant modification and revision of objectives to meet individual needs and changing social conditions. The use of any form of standardized achievement testing as the basic means of evaluation seems likely to result in a standardized curriculum with standardized courses of study and lockstep instruction—all of which are inconsistent with the theme of this book.

In summary, by employing a number of means for obtaining evaluations of the various aspects of teacher effectiveness, the principal can obtain more complete and reliable information on which to base personnel decisions than will be possible if direct classroom observation is the sole means of evaluation, and will, at the same time, be able to provide more help to teachers attempting to improve their teaching effectiveness. By developing a number of evaluative procedures in cooperation with teachers and supervisors, the principal may be able to hold nontenured or probationary teachers accountable for providing him with evidence obtained from these procedures which indicates that their teaching effectiveness is such that they deserve to remain on the school staff. Teachers might be given the option of using evidence obtained from student evaluations or other sources in addition to the school's formal evaluative procedures to support their position.

One particular aspect of staff evaluation of which the principal must be aware is the necessity to maintain an accurate written record of the reports of evaluations. He must also notify staff members of the results of their evaluation. It is obvious that if the evaluative process reveals the need for a teacher to improve his teaching effectiveness or change his behavior, he must be informed of the fact. Such notification will normally occur in teacher-administrator conferences, but it is essential that such conferences be followed up with written notification. Written notification eliminates future controversy over what was said and whether the staff member was, in fact, notified of certain specific problems. Because of the efforts of teacher organizations to guard the rights of teachers, often through court action, it is difficult in many states to dismiss even a nontenured teacher unless reasonably complete documentation of the teacher's deficiencies has been developed, and evidence exists that the teacher has been notified of them. Providing teachers with written summaries of evaluations and detailing suggestions for improvement in writing will require considerable administrative time; but in the interest of fairness to all members of the school community, the principal must ensure that this is done as effectively and thoroughly as possible.

Up to this point the procedures and processes for evaluation we have discussed are primarily applicable to teachers. However, in a democratic school, teachers will not be the only staff members evaluated. Providing the principal, members of his administrative staff, department chairmen, supervisors, and counselors with evaluative feedback should also be a function of the system for staff evaluation. Evaluation is necessary as a basis for future personnel decisions and to enable these staff members to improve their performance.

The Western Michigan Educator Feedback Center also has available an administrator evaluation program. It is designed to provide an administrator with feedback from teachers and other administrators regarding their perceptions of his openness, administrative skill, decision-making ability, innovativeness, technical competence, ability to communicate, and performance under stress. Since perceptions and attitudes determine behavior, feedback based on the perceptions of groups with whom he works can also be quite useful to the administrator who is sincerely interested in improving his effectiveness.

The evaluation of counselors and other pupil personnel staff members by students and parents would seem particularly appropriate. Questionnaires designed to measure the degree of satisfaction with the extent and quality of the pupil personnel services available can be administered to random samples of students and parents. A sample of an instrument developed by the members of a high school guidance department in order to obtain evaluative feedback is shown in Figure 11-3.

A survey of student attitudes regarding the general school atmosphere and student perceptions of the effectiveness with which administrative functions are accomplished can provide valuable feedback to the school's administration.

In summary, the principal should provide leadership in the development of systematic means for obtaining evaluative feedback that will enable him to retain only qualified staff members and that will help staff members provide a better educational experience for the school's students. We make no claims that the foregoing discussion of processes and procedures for accomplishing

STUDENT-OPINION QUESTIONNAIRE ON COUNSELING SERVICES

Please answer the following questions honestly and frankly. Do not give your name.

Please sit quietly or study until all students have completed their reports.

Encircle your answers to questions 1—10. Write your answers to questions 11—14.

WHAT IS YOUR OPINION ON THE FOLLOWING:

1. Has your counselor a thorough knowledge and understanding of his field?
   Below average   Average   Good   Very Good   The Very Best

2. Are suggestions and explanations made by your counselor clear and definite?
   Below Average   Average   Good   Very Good   The Very Best

3. Is your counselor fair and impartial in treatment of all students?
   Below Average   Average   Good   Very Good   The Very Best

4. Does your counselor follow through?
   Below Average   Average   Good   Very Good   The Very Best

5. Is your counselor patient, friendly, considerate, and helpful?
   Below Average   Average   Good   Very Good   The Very Best

6. Do you feel comfortable in seriously talking with your counselor?
   Below Average   Average   Good   Very Good   The Very Best

7. Are your counselor's plans well made? Is little time wasted by him?
   Below Average   Average   Good   Very Good   The Very Best

8. Are students' ideas and opinions worth something to your counselor? Do students decide how to solve problems? Do they get the real reason why certain things happen from their counselor?
   Below Average   Average   Good   Very Good   The Very Best

9. All things considered, how close does this counselor come to your ideal?
   Below Average   Average   Good   Very Good   The Very Best

10. Is your counselor tactful and courteous in dealing with students and parents?
    Below Average   Average   Good   Very Good   The Very Best

Figure 11-3

11. Please name one or two things that you especially like about this counselor.

12. Please give one or two suggestions for the improvement of this counselor.

13. Please name one or two things that you especially like about this counseling department.

Figure 11-3, *Continued*

14. Please give one or two suggestions for the improvement of this department.

Figure 11-3, *Continued*

effective staff evaluation is exhaustive. By demonstrating his own receptivity to evaluative feedback the principal will lead the way to the development of a general attitude of receptivity to evaluation which will result in the development of processes and procedures particularly suited to serve the needs of his school.

TEACHER-BOARD NEGOTIATIONS

A final aspect of the principal's relationship to the school staff is his role in the process by which a contractual agreement is negotiated between the teachers and the board of education, and in the implementation of the agreement that results from this process. Since the principal will be directly involved in implementing any agreement pertaining to teachers that is negotiated, it is fundamental that the negotiating process be structured in a way that ensures the principal the opportunity to have his point of view, problems, and perspectives considered. His knowledge of operational problems, teacher attitudes, student and parent attitudes, and the probable effect of proposed contract provisions on the teaching-learning process and school atmosphere should facilitate the negotiation of an agreement that is mutually beneficial and workable. Specifically, his participation should help prevent the ratification of provisions that are unenforceable or that cannot be implemented. For example, frequent items for negotiation are the number of preparations resulting from differing course assignments that can be required of a teacher, the number of times a teacher can be required to change classrooms during the school day, the amount of office space to be made available to each teacher, and class size.

All of these items may be affected by the physical limitations of the building, student course choices, the scope and type of curriculum offered, and the modes of instruction utilized. The principal may well be the most knowledgeable person in the school regarding the parameters imposed by these and other factors. However, the principal should not be the board's main negotiator. The strong adversary relationships that may develop in the heat of the negotiating process are too likely to affect his ability to work with teachers. To expect the principal to be an adversary in one situation and an educational leader in another is unrealistic. It is probably best for the principal to provide his input to the negotiating process in periodic meetings with the board's negotiating team held prior to their sessions with the teacher negotiators. However, if it is deemed necessary for at least one of the district's principals to be present at negotiating sessions, his role should be primarily that of an observer or consultant rather than that of spokesman.

Once an agreement is negotiated, it is the principal's responsibility to become thoroughly familiar with its provisions. He should do his utmost to administer it fairly and objectively. He will need to be particularly careful to adhere to the procedural requirements of provisions dealing with teacher grievances, teacher evaluation, and teacher dismissal. Attempts to circumvent the agreement or the failure to observe its procedural requirements will surely backfire. If the agreement contains provisions that prove ambiguous, impossible to implement, or detrimental to the educational process, the principal should ask for immediate clarification from the superintendent and board of education and should strongly suggest that the provisions be changed as soon as possible.

Bibliography

Bandura, A. and Walters, R. H. *Adolescent Aggression.* New York: Ronald Press, 1959.

Bandura, A. and Walters, R. H. *Adolescent Aggression.* New York: Ronald Holt, Rinehart, and Winston, 1963.

Cunningham, L. L. *Governing Schools: New Approaches to Old Issues.* Columbus, Ohio: Charles E. Merrill, 1971.

Findley, William and Bryan, Miriam. *Ability Grouping 1970: Status, Impact, and Alternatives.* Athens, Ga.: Center for the Study of Educational Improvement, 1971.

Griffiths, Daniel E., ed. *Behavioral Science and Educational Administration.* Chicago: University of Chicago Press, 1964.

Sherif, Muzafer and Sherif, Carolyn. *Social Psychology.* New York: Harper and Row, 1969.

Sorensen, Aage. "Organizational Differentiation of Students and Educational Opportunity." *Sociology of Education* 43 (Fall 1970), pp. 356-76.

Weldy, Gilbert R. *Administering a Negotiated Contract.* Reston, Va.: National Association of Secondary School Principals, 1973.

Selected Readings

Hierarchical Impediments to Innovation in Educational Organizations

Max G. Abbott

A discussion of the topic of change would not be complete without a serious examination of the nature of the organization in which change was expected to occur. That is, it seems obvious that the structure of the organization has important implications for the way in which that organization will function.

As I proceeded with the preparation of this paper, however, it became equally obvious that it would be necessary to limit my attention to only a few of the many structural elements which might be considered. Since, in my view, the appropriation of hierarchical prerogatives to enhance the personal status of administrative officials represents a most serious obstacle to the introduction of meaningful innovations in the educational organization, I decided to concentrate my attention on this aspect of organizational structure. Thus, the choice of the term "hierarchical impediments" rather than the term "structural impediments" as a focus for this paper has been deliberate.

During recent years, it has become respectable, or, perhaps to be more accurate, it has become popular to talk about change and innovation in education. At times one is led to the conclusion that change has become the new "royal road" to respectability for educators. During the past ten years, particularly, we have witnessed the introduction of numerous "new" practices in the schools: new math and science curricula, team teaching, large- and small-group instruction, and programmed learning, to mention only a few. Yet, not all of these practices represent genuine innovations, and of those which do, not all have been adopted and applied in such a way as to assure progress. As Professor Thelen has commented:

> In the face of all these changes... the schools' society and culture seems largely undisturbed. Comparing classrooms now with

From Max G. Abbot & John T. Lovell, eds., *Change Perspectives in Educational Administration,* School of Education, Auburn University, Auburn, Ala., 1965, pp. 40-53. Reprinted by permission.

the classrooms of 40 years ago, one notes that at both times there were numbers of students not much interested in what was being done; the typical teacher still presents material and quizzes the kids to see if they understand it; the amount of creativity and excitement is probably no greater now than then. The development of new materials and techniques has enabled us to spin our wheels in one place, to conduct business as usual in the face of dramatic changes in the society and in the clientele of the school. The operation of the educational enterprise has encountered what can only be thought of by the traditional teacher as a very large number of increasingly serious obstacles and the new devices sustain the forlorn hope of protecting and maintaining, rather than changing, the old orthodoxy in the face of the most important revolutions in the history of mankind.[1]

Thelen suggests that the changes which have occurred have gone through three distinct phases: (1) *enthusiasm,* (2) *vulgarization* and *spread,* and (3) *institutionalization.* That is, each new idea has been introduced with a flurry of activity, accompanied by widespread excitement, and followed by a period of rationalization, during which traditional practices have been redefined to make them fit the rubrics of the innovations. Thus, to cite an example, an administrator who is confronted with a lack of classroom space will combine two groups of students under the direction of two teachers, house the newly formed group in an auditorium or a cafeteria, and refer to the new arrangement as an experiment in team teaching.

How are we to account for this widespread unwillingness to deal realistically with new ideas, new practices, and new demands? How can we explain such resistance to meaningful innovation? It is neither accurate nor helpful to attribute such behavior to mere perversity on the part of teachers and other school personnel. Any formal organization is constantly subject to competing sets of forces: those that represent inertia, or the maintenance of the status quo, on the one hand, and those that represent change, or innovation, on the other.

Much of the inertia in formal organizations occurs as a result of the "sunk costs" of those organizations; in the educational enterprise, these "sunk costs" consist of a substantial investment in training and experience, and of a psychological commitment to particular ways of programming activities. Conversely, the forces for change represent some sort of dissatisfaction with the status quo.

As long as the forces for maintaining the status quo are equal to or greater than the forces to change, the organization is said to be in a state of equilibrium. As March and Simon have stated the case:

> Individuals and organizations give preferred treatment to alternatives that represent continuation of programs over those that repre-

---
[1] Herbert A. Thelen, "New Practices on the Firing Line," *Administrator's Notebook,* Vol. XII, No. 5 (January, 1964).

sent change.... Presistence comes about primarily because the individual or organization does not search for or consider alternatives to the present course of action unless that present course is in some sense "unsatisfactory."[2]

Disequilibrium occurs when the forces to change become greater than the forces to maintain the status quo. Such disequilibrium represents an occasion for innovation. Thus, we would define innovation as the adaptive response which an organization makes to a situation in which a program of action, which has been regarded as satisfying certain criteria, no longer does so.

When we employ this type of a definition, we do not attribute persistence of behavior to perversity or to a particular "resistance to change"; rather, such persistence is explained more adequately in terms of a lack of dissatisfaction with the present state of affairs and, thus, with a lack of search for new alternatives. Since change for its own sake has apparently become a valued goal in education, as it frequently does in an immature profession, school people have shown a strong inclination to board bandwagon movements, not because of dissatisfaction with present programs, but because it is fashionable to be "progressive." It is hardly surprising, therefore, that new curricula and new procedures have frequently been viewed as gimmicks, adopted and applied with little enthusiasm and even less understanding.

Assuming that meaningful innovations are necessary if the schools are to meet the challenges of the social and technological revolution that is taking place in the world today, the problem confronting us is to identify those elements in the school organization which inhibit and impede such innovations. Thus, I am led to ask two fundamental questions: (1) Are there forces in the school organization that make it difficult to determine the point at which previously satisfactory programs are no longer satisfactory? (2) Do present organizational arrangements and relationships inhibit the implementation of new programs of action when old ones have been demonstrated to be unsatisfactory?

As a prelude to a more thorough discussion of these two questions, I propose to examine briefly the school organization as it now exists. This can probably best be done by referring to the bureaucratic paradigm which Weber developed with such keen insight a number of years ago.

Weber viewed bureaucracy as the ideal type of structural arrangement for accomplishing large-scale administrative tasks. "The decisive reason for the advance of bureaucratic organization," he wrote, "has always been its purely technical superiority over any other form of organization. The fully developed bureaucratic mechanism compares with other forms exactly as does the machine with nonmechanical modes of production."[3]

---

[2]James G. March and Herbert A. Simon, *Organizations* (New York: John Wiley & Sons, Inc., 1959), p. 173.

[3]Max Weber, "Bureaucracy," in Joseph A. Litterer (ed.), *Organizations: Structure and Behavior* (New York: John Wiley & Sons, Inc., 1963), p. 45.

For Weber, the essential and distinctive characteristics of a bureaucracy were somewhat as follows:

1. The regular activities required for the purposes of the organization are distributed in fixed ways as official duties. Since the tasks of an organization are too complex to be performed by a single individual, or by a group of individuals possessing a single set of skills, efficiency will be promoted by dividing those tasks into activities which can be assigned to specific offices or positions. This division of labor makes possible a high degree of specialization which, in turn, promotes improved performance in two ways. First, it enables the organization to employ personnel on the basis of technical qualifications; second, it enables employees to improve their skills by limiting their attention to a relatively narrow range of activities.

2. The positions in an organization are arranged on the principle of office hierarchy and of levels of graded authority. This means that there is a firmly ordered system of superordination and subordination in which the lower offices are supervised by the higher ones. Although specialization makes possible the efficient performance of specific tasks, specialization also creates problems of coordination. To achieve the required coordination, it is necessary to grant to each official the requisite authority to control the activities of his subordinates.

3. The management of activities is controlled by general rules which are more or less stable, more or less exhaustive, and which can be learned. These rules are general and abstract, and they constitute standards which assure resonable uniformity in the performance of tasks. They preclude the issuance of directives based on whim or caprice, but require the application of general principles to particular cases. Together with the hierarchical authority structure, rules provide for the coordination of organizational activities and for continuity of operations, regardless of changes in personnel.

4. Bureaucracy develops the more perfectly the more completely it succeeds in eliminating from official business love, hatred, and all purely personal, irrational, and emotional elements which escape calculation. The essence of bureaucratic arrangements is rationality. A spirit of formalistic impersonality is necessary to separate organizational rights and duties from the private lives of employees. Only by performing impersonally can officials assure rationality in decision making, and only thus can they assure equitable treatment for all subordinates.

5. Employment in a bureaucracy is based upon technical competence and constitutes a career. Promotions are to be determined by seniority, or achievement, or both; tenure is to be assured; and fixed compensation and retirement provisions are to be made. Since individuals with specialized skills are employed to perform specialized activities, they must be protected from arbitrary dismissal or denial of promotion on purely personal grounds.

The American schools have been particularly receptive to the bureaucratic ideology, albeit perhaps unwittingly. Bureaucratic principles have been incorporated into the organizational practices of the educational enterprise in at least the following respects:

First, the school organization has clearly been influenced by the need for specialization and the factoring of tasks. The division of the school into elementary and secondary units; the establishment of science, mathematics, music, and other departments within a school; the introduction of guidance programs and psychological services; indeed, the separation of the administrative function from the teaching function, all represent responses to this need.

Second, the school organization has developed a clearly defined and rigid hierarchy of authority. Although the term "hierarchy" is seldom used in the lexicon of the educational administrator, the practices to which it refers are commonly prevalent. The typical organization chart is intended specifically to clarify lines of authority and channels of communication. Even in the absence of such a chart, school employees have a clear conception of the nature of the hierarchy in their school systems. In fact, rigid adherence to hierarchical principles has been stressed to the point that failure to adhere to recognized lines of authority is viewed as the epitome of immoral organizational behavior.

Third, the school organization has leaned heavily upon the use of general rules to control the behavior of members of the organization and to develop standards which would assure reasonable uniformity in the performance of tasks. Whether they have taken the form of policy manuals, rules and regulations, staff handbooks, or some other type of document, general rules have been used extensively to provide for the orderly induction of new employees into the organization and to eliminate capricious behavior on the part of all school personnel, including administrators and members of boards of education.

Fourth, despite frequent proclamations regarding togetherness and democracy, the school organization has made extensive application of Weber's principle of impersonality in organizational relationships. Authority has been established on the basis of rational considerations rather than charismatic qualities or traditional imperatives; interpersonal interactions have tended to be functionally specific rather than functionally diffuse; and official relationships have been governed largely by universalistic as contrasted with particularistic considerations. Thus, by operating in a spirit of "formalistic impersonality," the typical school system has succeeded, in part, in separating organizational rights and obligations from the private lives of individual employees.

Fifth, employment in the educational organization has been based upon technical competence and has constituted for most members a professional career. Promotions have been determined by seniority and by achievement;

tenure has been provided; and fixed compensation and retirement benefits have been assured.

The school organization as we know it today, then, can accurately be described as a highly developed bureaucracy. As such, it exhibits many of the characteristics and employs many of the strategies of the military, industrial, and governmental agencies with which it might be compared.

In many respects, this organizational pattern has served us well. It has provided the means by which reasonable control might be exercised over the behavior of members of the organization, and by which the activities of individuals and groups of individuals with diverse interests and responsibilities might be coordinated. At the same time, as Moeller has demonstrated through empirical research,[4] rational bureaucratic structure has in many respects increased, rather than diminished, the teachers' sense of personal power in the organization.

Having made this point, however, I will proceed to argue that our present organizational arrangements and practices produce some seriously dysfunctional consequences in respect to the need for innovative activities in the educational establishment. The remainder of this paper, then, will be devoted to an analysis of some of these dysfunctional consequences.

Earlier, I pointed out that Weber emphasized the importance of arranging positions on the principle of office hierarchy and of levels of graded authority; that is, he viewed a firmly ordered system of superordination and subordination as a necessary condition in large organizations. The acceptance and implementation of this principle has resulted in a monistic formulation, which is based upon a number of charismatic assumptions. Thompson has pointed out, for example, that under the monistic formulation:

> It is assumed that the superior, at any point in the hierarchy is *able* to tell his subordinates what to do, and to guide them in doing it. That is, it is assumed that he is more capable in all of his unit's activities than any of his subordinate specialists who perform them.[5]

This statement seems to capture neatly the ideology which exists in the educational establishment; yet, despite the ideology, candid observation belies the myth underlying the assumption. The concept of unity of command, which denies the relevance of nonhierarchical expertise within the organization, is applicable only in an organization where specialization refers to tasks, where activities are divided into simple, repetitive routines. In this kind of a situation, people are interchangeable in much the same way that parts of a machine are interchangeable. The foreman or supervisor, who has generally

---

[4]Gerald H. Moeller, "Bureaucracy and Teachers' Sense of Power," *The School Review*, Vol. 72, No. 2 (Summer, 1964), pp. 137-57.

[5]Victor A. Thompson, *Modern Organizations* (New York: Alfred A. Knopf and Company, 1961), p. 75.

advanced through the ranks, is frequently more capable in performing his unit's activities than are his subordinates.

In the school organization, however, specialization refers not to tasks, but to people. Through education and specialized training, teachers have been adapted or changed. They have developed the competence to perform socially valued functions which other people cannot perform. When the assumption of superordinate ability is considered in apposition to this type of specialization, the assumption takes on an aura of charisma.

Yet, charisma is an insufficient and unacceptable basis for the exercise of authority in a supposedly rationally ordered system. Therefore, educational administrators and students of educational administration have been faced with the necessity of rationalizing the charismatic assumptions which undergird the monistic formulation of authority. This rationalization has led to a general acceptance of the largely nonsensical notion that authority can be delegated to subordinates in the organization, but that responsibility rests with those in superordinate roles.

When the concept of responsibility is used in this way, it readily becomes translated into blamability; that is, the administrator who feels that he must be responsible for the decisions of his subordinates must also accept the blame for their errors. For self-preservation, therefore, he must retain the ultimate power to make decisions or to veto the decisions of subordinates. In doing so, he fails to provide for any effective delegation of authority, and he perpetuates the monistic conception of hierarchical role definitions.

Since the right to innovate represents a potent source of power in the organization, and since the monistic formulation demands that power be concentrated in superordinate roles, innovation from below is difficult to achieve in an organization which adopts the monistic formulation. This is true for at least two reasons. First, ideas that originate at the lower levels in the hierarchy encounter difficulty in receiving an adequate hearing. Second, any individual in a subordinate position, who takes the lead in introducing new programs of action, runs the risk of having sanctions imposed by his superordinate to allow that superordinate to escape the blamability which is inherent in the monistic system. It is not uncommon, for example, for a subordinate to be fired in order to protect the position of his superior.

A second major dysfunctional consequence of structuring the schools bureaucratically, and in my view a major deterrent to meaningful innovation, grows out of the hierarchical definition of roles. Although roles in general are defined in terms of both rights and obligations, there is a tendency in bureaucraticies, including the educational bureaucracy, to emphasize rights when referring to superordinate roles and to emphasize obligations when referring to subordinate roles. In analyzing this distinction, let us first consider the superordinate role. The office of "superior" in the typical bureaucracy is characterized primarily by the rights which are associated with that role. Whatever obligations exist are usually correlatives of the few rights which are guaranteed to subordinates.

Right to Veto or Affirm. One of the "rights" of the superordinate role is the right to veto or to affirm the organizationally relevant proposals of subordinates. This right applies not only to decisions which govern the organization in general, but also to decisions which govern the personal goals of individuals. Consider, for example, the difficulty a teacher encounters in obtaining a new position without a supporting recommendation from former administrative superiors.

Moreover, hierarchical relationships tend to over-emphasize the right to veto and to underemphasize the right to affirm. Frequently, there is no organizationally legitimate means for appealing a superior's decision to veto a proposal, whereas a decision to approve will often be subject to confirmation by higher officials. In one large university, for example, a proposal to introduce a new course, or to revise an existing one, must run the gauntlet of bureaucratic machinery which contains five decision points. At any one of these points, the proposal may be vetoed; however, final approval can be given only at the top of the hierarchy. Under these conditions it is remarkable that any revision of the curriculum occurs.

Such a system obviously favors the status quo and inhibits innovation from below. Yet, in an organization which consists largely of professionals, as is the case in an educational institution, meaningful and workable innovations almost necessarily originate at the lower levels of the hierarchy.

Right to Control Communications. The superordinate in the hierarchy has the "right" to control communications, both those internal to the organization and those external to the organization. There is a strong emphasis on following "channels" in attempts to communicate, particularly when the communication is upward.

The strict exercise of this right may have at least two deleterious effects on innovation. First, subordinates may be prevented from obtaining sufficient information to enable them to determine accurately the relevance of their immediate activities for achieving the terminal goals of the organization. Second, superordinates may be prevented from obtaining sufficiently accurate feedback from their activities to enable them to assess realistically the effects of their decisions.

Right to Deference. By tradition, the hierarchical superior has the right to deference from subordinates. The ranking of roles in terms of the amount of deference due them is what is generally meant by the "status system" in an organization. In this regard, the superintendent or the principal of a school need not apologize for interrupting a teacher in her classroom, either to observe her work or to transmit routine business. Such an interruption is considered to be part of the administrator's job, a right associated with his position. Yet, the same teacher may interrupt the administrator only for "good cause," and the administrator's office frequently is guarded by a secretary who considers it her mission to see that he is not disturbed.

Other Rights. A number of other rights grows out of the rights which I have just discussed. Thus, the superordinate has the right to decide the form of the organization, to determine the personnel to be employed, to *initiate activities,* to set the goals for subunits, to assign activities, to confer jurisdictions, to determine the agenda for meetings, and to settle conflicts.

Rights of Subordinates. The subordinate role is generally defined in terms of obligations, not rights. Since each of the rights defined for the superordinate role is accompanied by an obligation for the subordinate role, subordinates have an obligation to follow channels of communication, to be deferent in the presence of superordinates, and to await official approval before engaging in innovative activity. There is, at the present time, a general trend toward clarifying some of the rights of subordinates, including such things as the right to a hearing in the case of a recommendation for dismissal, the right to access to grievance machinery, and the right to academic freedom. But, such rights as do exist have been secured through collective efforts and hard bargaining, and they are granted only subject to the approval of the administrator. We have barely begun to accept the notion of rights as basic to the definition of the subordinate role.

It is true, of course, that not all occupants of superordinate positions insist on exercising fully the rights which are associated with their roles. Actual behavior may be modified by the personality of the administrator or by the social relationships which exist among the members of the organization. This fact does not alter the way in which roles are culturally defined, however, as evidenced by the observation that subordinates are pleased and grateful when a superordinate exercises his rights with humanitarian restraint.

The power of the hierarchy, and of the rights associated with superordinate roles, can be illustrated by describing what Victor Thompson has called hierarchical dramaturgy. For purely arbitrary reasons, I tend to prefer the term "status charades." To quote Thompson:

> What are the impressions fostered by hierarchical dramaturgy? As would be expected, they are the heroic and charismatic qualities—the same ones that leadership-trait studies have been seeking. The impression is fostered that occupants of hierarchical positions are, of all people in the organization, the ablest, the most industrious, the most indispensable, the most loyal, the most reliable, the most self-controlled, the most ethical, which is to say, the most honest, fair, and impartial.[6]

---

[6]*Ibid.,* p. 143.

Successful performance of status charades requires the solidarity of the performing team. Since impressions are all important, and since the control of impressions requires the discreet withholding and editing of the available information, all members of the administrative team must be trustworthy and discreet. Thus, hierarchical positions tend to be filled, not on the basis of technical competence alone, but also on the basis of the ability to create the right impressions, those of busyness, loyalty, sound judgment, and so on.

To assure adequate control, therefore, such positions tend to be filled by the sponsorship system. Promising young people with administrative timbre, that is, those who appear to be "our kind," are carefully groomed to fill positions in the hierarchy. During the grooming period, recruits for the hierarchy are made aware of the fact that they are being observed, and that if they make the team it will be because someone above trusted them. Such trust tends to be earned by those who demonstrate their ability, and willingness, to conform to established procedures.

Subordinates follow the rules of this game of charades by creating the impression that they are awed by their superiors, that the performance of the superiors has gone off well, and by creating the impression that they *need* to be told what to do and how to do it. Since the official impression is that the administrator is the busiest man in the organization, subordinates reinforce this impression by seeking conferences with him infrequently and apologetically, and by making such conferences brief.

In most school organizations, the game is played with dispatch and sincerity. The performers frequently believe that the rules represent reality. The status system aids impression management by isolating the behavior which might discredit the official impressions.

In an institution, such as the school, where superior performance occurs when superior technical competence is found at the base of the hierarchy, among the teachers, and where changes must be implemented by those who possess this superior competence, status charades are more of a tragedy than a comedy. The tendency to attach status to hierarchical positions, and the tendency to impute superior abilities to persons who occupy status positions, encourages the perpetuation of the status quo. Under these conditions, we will continue to encounter the situation which was described by Thelen in the quotation at the beginning of this paper.

A final dysfunctional consequence of adhering to rigid bureaucratic structure in the school organization, one that has important implications for innovation, relates to the extent to which such structure impedes the professional development of the teaching role.

Although the professional form of occupational life shares many of the characteristics of bureaucratic employment, there are some important respects in which professionalism is unique. In particular, the professions are characterized by a distinctive control structure which is fundamentally different from the hierarchical control of a bureaucracy. As Blau and Scott have pointed out, the control of professionals is accomplished through two sources:

> First, as a result of the long period of training undergone by the practitioner, he is expected to have acquired a body of expert knowledge and to have internalized a code of ethics which governs his professional conduct. Second, this self control is supported by the external surveillance of his conduct by his peers, who are in a position to see his work, and who have the skills to judge his performance, and who, since they have a personal stake in the reputation of their profession, are motivated to exercise the necessary sanctions.[7]

This control structure differs greatly from that employed in the typical school organization. The source of discipline in the bureaucratically organized school system is not the colleague group, but the authority vested in the hierarchy. Administrators establish regulations governing such factors as working hours, acceptable teaching procedures, criteria to be employed in determining promotions, and others. Even when such regulations are developed cooperatively, they are subject to the ratification of administrators and boards of education.

It might be argued that teachers are neither able nor willing to accept and discharge the responsibility for exercising professional control over their colleagues. Whether or not this is the case, and I seriously doubt that it is, it is highly unlikely that innovation will become common among members of the teaching force as long as teachers are subject to rigid hierarchical controls and as long as promotions consist of moving into the hierarchy and are determined by an individual's demonstrated capacity to conform.

I am not suggesting that the granting of self control would necessarily be accompanied by a flurry of innovative activity. The pressures for uniformity which groups exert upon their members are too well known for any such naive assumption. I am suggesting, however, that the freedom which could accompany professional control is a necessary condition to meaningful innovation at the point where it must occur, in the classroom.

In essence, I have argued that it is unreasonable to expect any radical departure from traditional educational practices so long as we insist on placing undue emphasis upon hierarchical status. If we are to break out of the strait jacket in which we now find ourselves, we must examine our ideology with rigor and with candor. We must be willing to admit that we do not necessarily live in the best of all possible organizational worlds. And we must display creativity in devising some type of organizational arrangement which will serve more adequately the type of institution in which we work.

I must admit that I do not now visualize very clearly what type of an organization that will be. I do suspect, however, that the educational

---

[7]Peter M. Blau and W. Richard Scott, *Formal Organizations* (San Francisco: Chandler Publishing Co., 1962), p. 63.

administrator of the future will be more like the hospital administrator and less like the industrial tycoon, who appears to be our model today.

I also suspect that in the educational organization of the future, teachers will be viewed as true professionals, and they will be able to gain reasonable status while continuing to teach. Performance in this organization will be controlled by self-imposed standards of knowledge and ethics and by peer-group surveillance, rather than by directives from administrative officials. It is my contention that the greatest obstacle to achieving this type of control structure in the public schools rests not with the inability or unwillingness of teachers to behave responsibly, but with the bureaucratic ideology which permeates the educational enterprise, particularly that part of the ideology which supports and encourages the appropriation of hierarchical prerogatives to enhance the personal status of those in administrative positions.

Part Five

School-Community Relations

12

The School Community

The term "school community" as used in this book is defined as the population the school serves. Thus an urban population center of 20,000 people served by a single secondary school may be said to be a secondary school community. In a large city school system which includes a dozen or more secondary schools, each school will have its own school community made up of the people it serves. Everyone in a school community has one thing in common: the school which serves them. In the vast majority of cases the people of the community will pay taxes directly or indirectly to support their school.

The public school system forms an integral part of practically every sociological community in the United States. Its relationship to the community varies widely, however. This relationship is likely to be quite different in the ghettos of the larger cities as compared to a close-knit rural community. In the former, the school is often viewed as a place the children are compelled to go whether they like it or not, and in the latter it is seen as a center of community interest and activity.

While in the early part of the century communities characteristically grew rather slowly, thus maintaining a stability which comes with a high population-retention rate and common concerns and values, today, by virtue of modern technology, communities spring up almost overnight. Residential developments make possible the creation of a community where three or four years earlier only farm crops were raised. The mobility of the population today makes possible a complete change in the nature of a given community in the course of five years. On the one hand, some communities have faced dissolution when their economic bases have been adversely affected. On the other, small towns on the perimeters of cities often become populous suburban communities, increasing their size ten-fold in the course of a few years. The decentralization of industry may bring an industrial development to a sleepy village of five-hundred people which will transform it into a bustling working man's community with a population of several thousand. Growth and change, and development and decay have been dramatic in the American community of the second half of the twentieth century.

The modern sociological community is quite different from the rural model of a hundred years ago. In early American history the community was characterized by close interaction of its members, a sense of common membership, and a sharing of the concerns and the accomplishments of each other and the community as a whole. Years ago it was common practice in a rural community for community members to come to the aid of one of their numbers stricken by illness, and plant or harvest his crops. While this custom persists in some rural communities, we find nothing analogous in the modern industrial urban community.

The problems and concerns of the early American community, while quite real and important, were fewer in number and much more simple than those of our time. Although once membership in a community was an end in itself, today it merely represents a means to an end. The early concept of commitment to a common purpose is largely absent in the modern community. Today members of the community characteristically assume little—if any—responsibility for the actions of other members of the community. Contacts with each other are infrequent and largely incidental. Often apartment-house dwellers regard their neighbors as strangers who are greeted with a nod as they are met in the hall.

The reasons for the change in the nature of the community and community life are not difficult to discover. The complexity of modern society growing out of scientific, economic, political, and technological changes inevitably affects the life style of the individual. The present social structure emphasizes the process of specialization of effort, division of labor, and a personal isolation from all except those who share his vocational or recreational interests. He feels a loyalty to his office staff or his bowling team, but not to the general community. He may belong to a variety of organizations, associations, unions, and special groups. His life may be said to be fragmented. This fragmentation tends to destroy or at least erode his identification with the general community in which he lives.

Another factor which has affected and is affecting community life is the extreme mobility of the population. People now move much more frequently than they did years ago. Giant corporations shift personnel from place to place. People move to a more agreeable climate for the winter, or move permanently. Summer and winter homes are becoming increasingly popular. People are no longer tied to their community by land or other real property handed down from generation to generation. Today's people are on the move. They welcome a change, whether it is for new adventures or to escape some of the pressures of their jobs or social life.

Technological advances have had a tendency to depersonalize life. The undoubted benefits conferred on us by technology have been to some extent offset by the disadvantages. A major disadvantage is the reduction of the necessity for human interrelationships and the consequent loss of a certain amount of what may be called humaneness. The elevator operator and the telephone girl have largely departed from our life scene. Automation and cybernetics are a continually increasing threat to human relationships, even as they increase our efficiency. The mechanistic nature of our life atmosphere cannot help but affect our human relationships. As we delegate activities to machines, we tend to pay less attention to people and thus we fail to develop meaningful personal relationships with others in the community.

Finally, the complexity of life, corruption and graft and broken promises in politics, inefficient and wasteful governmental operations, behind-the-scenes influences on government by large corporations and the special interest lobbies all contribute to a feeling of hopelessness and powerlessness on the part of the average citizen. The impersonal bureaucracies, the endless governmental red tape, and the lack of credibility in governmental officials at all levels leave the citizen with the feeling that he, as an individual, is powerless to affect the course of events. His natural reaction is therefore to shut himself off from the whole mess and concentrate on improving and enriching his personal life, without regard for his fellows or his community. The feeling of powerlessness forces him to adapt to, and tolerate social and political conditions which he may regard as unjust, unfair, or corrupt, simply because he feels he can do nothing to change them.

This attitude of indifference, hopelessness, and powerlessness of the individual is to some extent reflected in his attitude toward the school. It is only when his own children are involved that he is likely to become vocal and active in protest against what he believes to be wrong with the school. Thus, it is parent groups who are most vociferous in demanding quality education, accountability, excellency in teaching, and better use of educational funds. The non-parent usually expresses his dissatisfaction at the polls in the form of negative votes on educational levies and bond issues. In his case the ballot provides a dual purpose; he can protest and save money at the same time.

This attitude of disenchantment of his elders is not lost on the typical high school student. He not only feels it in his home; his own experience tends to enhance it. He has found the secondary school, in many cases, unresponsive to his needs. To him it often appears to be an impersonal bureaucracy, a part of the "establishment." His protests against the rules and regimentation, like his protests against the Vietnam war and various social injustices, have been largely ineffective.

The state of malaise generated by forces beyond the control of the individual and in some cases beyond the control of the community have had a most serious impact on school-community relations. This is true to the greatest extent in urban areas, particularly in the inner city. However even the rural areas have not escaped its influence.

The appraisal of the attitudes of the modern community in the foregoing pages does not present an encouraging picture to the secondary school and particularly to its administration. It may even cause some principals, if they share the view, to seek further isolation from an unresponsive clientele. However, the true educational leader will accept it as a challenge and attack the problem at its roots: in the community itself. He does have certain advantages as the leader of what is in most communities the top educational agency. Perhaps the major advantage is that parents, grandparents, and other relatives of students have a vested interest in the high school. While this category does not by any means include all of the people of the community it does include a very substantial portion. In the second place, the secondary school is in a strategic position to serve all the people of the school-community both directly and indirectly if its leadership is worthy of the name. How this can be done is detailed in later pages. A third advantage is the natural close relationship existing in the governmental structure which in most cases provides for elected board members and popular voting on school tax levies and bonded indebtedness. While some might look on this latter feature as a disadvantage, it is advantageous in providing an opportunity as well as an obligation for the school to justify its request for financial resources and thus strengthen its ties with the community. These and other advantageous relationships provide a fertile soil for the development of satisfactory school-community relationships despite any community apathy which may exist.

KNOWING THE COMMUNITY

The local community in which the secondary school is located forms the base of operations for that school. The nature of the community will and should influence the nature of the school. While the school serves a larger community in a very significant way, its day-to-day operations are carried on within the confines of the community it serves. This community is much more than an aggregation of people. It is composed of institutions, organizations, agencies, associations, and social structures of various types. It has an economic base which affects the operation of the school and which may well be affected by the school. It has a decision-making structure which inevitably affects the operation of the school and may even seek to dictate the direction, nature, and scope of the school program. The conflict situations which may and do arise in this context are discussed at some length elsewhere in this section.

Thus it is quite evident to even the most casual observer that a thorough knowledge of the local community, which is the real base of operations of the school, is essential. The task of making this acquaintance is one for which the principal must assume leadership. It is not an easy task or one to be undertaken lightly. Much of the success of his leadership will depend on his ability to secure the cooperation of his staff and the enlistment of lay citizens in the task of community analysis. However, the results will be eminently worthwhile for two major reasons. First, the knowledge gained in such a study will make it possible for the high school to better meet the unique educational needs of the community it serves. Second, such a study reveals the educational resources of the community and the opportunities to utilize these resources in the development of the high school program. In short then, we need to know about the high school community so we will know its educational needs and resources.

What the School Should Know About the Community

The question arises, "What do we need to know about our community?" Since the community, whether it is in a rural region or in the heart of a metropolitan area, is a complex social organism, there is much to be learned about it. Some facts will be rather easily obtained; others will require the most persistent efforts. Some information will be apparent; some will be hidden well below the surface of community life. The depth and scope of the study will in a large measure determine its usefulness.

An outline of the basic information about the community which might be included in a comprehensive study and analysis is presented here.

I. Historical background
   A. History of the community
   B. Major factors in its development
   C. History of its educational system
   D. Traditions, customs, and values
II. Physical characteristics
   A. Climatic conditions
   B. Natural resources
   C. Land usage
III. Characteristics of the population
   A. Racial composition
   B. Educational levels
   C. Occupational characteristics
   D. Numbers in each age group
   E. Health and mortality statistics
   F. Population mobility
   G. Minority grouping
   H. Recreational interests
   I. Civic responsibility
IV. Institutional characteristics
   A. Number and types of institutions
   B. Relationships among institutions
V. Economic resources
   A. Raw materials for industry

B. Business and manufacturing
  C. Financial resources
  D. Employment opportunities
  E. Transportation facilities
VI. Communication media
  A. Local
  B. Regional
VII. Organizational structure
  A. Political and economic structure
  B. Social stratification
  C. Power structure (official and unofficial)

In addition to the basic information about the nature of the community, answers to such questions as are suggested below should prove valuable in community analysis.

1. What are the emerging educational needs of the community?
2. What is the general attitude of the people of the community toward the high school?
3. What opinions do people hold in regard to local and national educational issues?
4. What is the general attitude of the community toward students, teachers, administrators, and the board of education?
5. What do people think of the high school plant and equipment?
6. What features of the high school are most popular? Why?
7. What features of the high school are most unpopular? Why?
8. What opportunities does the community offer as a learning laboratory for the high school?
9. What human resources in the community are available as aids to the school program?

The Larger Community

The local community which the high school serves is an integral part of a larger community, which in turn is part of a still larger community, and so on, until the world community is reached. The significance of this concept for the secondary school and particularly for its leadership should not be overlooked. While the school's primary interest is in the community it serves, its commitment is not to be restricted by the boundaries of the district. Education must be directed toward world citizenship as well as toward national, state, and local citizenship.

No community exists in isolation. All are part of a vast network which is characterized by an interdependence which may differ in nature and extent, but is essential to their very existence. Each community has obligations to the larger community and receives services and benefits from it. Therefore, every high school has not only a responsibility, but an obligation as an educational agency serving a particular community, to make its clientele aware of these larger responsibilities and help them prepare to meet them. In short, the high school should not be a provincial institution. While it is located in a community and serves that community, it is an educational institution whose search for truth must never be circumscribed by local prejudices or regional intolerance.

The exercise of this responsibility may sometimes generate unavoidable conflict between school and community. If this happens, it must be faced squarely and the laws and the traditions and the ideals of the larger community must be upheld, even at the expense of some local dissatisfaction. In the long run, the school which takes this position will earn the respect, if not the admiration, of opposing forces in the community. Furthermore, thinking, fair-minded members of the community will come to its support if the school has clearly and forthrightly dealt with the issue as an educational, not a political one.

The danger of serious conflict is substantially reduced when the school has built a reputation for fairness and honesty. In addition, when the school has communicated to the people it serves the nature, extent and rationale of its obligations to the larger community, it has the effect of minimizing the dangers of serious conflicts. For example, the school which has made clear, to its students and its community, the responsibility each person has to uphold the democratic principles of the larger community as they are imbedded in tradition and law, will find a smoother path through the thorns of local prejudice with regard to race, religion, or color. The consistent reminder of the democratic ideal of the worth of each individual, irrespective of his race, creed, or socioeconomic position, and that the right of each individual to equal opportunity are tenets of our democratic society, will prove most worthwhile in potential conflict situations.

In conclusion it may be said that the school which serves its community best in this respect is the one which succeeds in developing an awareness of, and a commitment to, the democratic ideals of the larger community.

The Role of the Secondary School in the Community

As early as 1936, Professor Harold Rugg proposed that the school, as the major educational agency of the community, utilize the total community as a laboratory or educational workshop. He conceived the school as a "School of Living" around which all the educational activities of the community would be built. The school would coordinate learning experiences of the community and would utilize its resources in the educational program.

A more recent proposal put forth by Herbert Thelen in his book, *Education and the Human Quest* (1960), would make education a function of the total community. Citizen education councils would be responsible for the planning, policy-making, and development of education in the community. The school would be only one of a number of agencies responsible for education. It would operate, as would the others, under the aegis of the citizen council. This council would be responsible for presenting a budget each year for all the organized educational efforts of the community. The school would be a major one of these. Others might be the hospital, the court room, the chamber of commerce, the union headquarters, and so on. Thelen sees education as composed of four basic parts: personal inquiry, group or organization inquiry, reflective action, and skill development. These areas would be developed in a number of different contexts of which the school, of course, would be an important one. Each agency would contribute in the area in which it would be most effective. An interesting and unique facet of Thelen's proposal is the assurance of a dialogue between youth and adults of the community, thus helping to bridge the generation gap.

Both Rugg's and Thelen's proposals as well as others of the same general nature are radical departures from the present form and context of education and have not met with acceptance. Despite their many obvious advantages and intriguing possibilities they have not, at least as yet, been attractive enough to force the changes in concept, structure, and program necessary to put them in effect. Nor is it likely that they will be in the near future. Involving, as they do, a number of basic changes in both school and community life, and given the nature and atmosphere of both as described earlier, there is little reason to expect their adoption in the near future.

As has been indicated elsewhere in this book, it is assumed that for the next decade, at least, the basic formal structure of secondary education will remain largely the same. This does not mean that there will not be changes. Hopefully, there will be changes for the better; however, Thelen's model is not likely to gain acceptance in the coming decade, just as it did not in the past decade. Rugg's proposal is much older, but has not achieved any greater acceptance.

Why has there been little or no acceptance in public education? Is it because the proposals are unsound? Are they based on untried theory? Are they administratively unworkable? Financially not feasible? We believe the answers to all these questions must be in the negative. Why, therefore, have such models been rejected? We believe the answer lies in the fact that they are largely inconsistent with the traditional structural pattern of education and the present life-style of the American community. Their adoption *in toto* would likely have a jarring effect on community life. This is not to say that the community might not benefit from the jolting. Rather, it is to say that the advantages offered are not likely to be achieved in an overnight transformation of educational structure.

The general concept of education beyond the walls of the school or in its more radical form "education without schools" has much to commend it. The wealth of educational opportunities available in the American community is obvious. Their meaningfulness and relevancy are beyond argument. The problem lies, as it always has, in putting these innovations into a context acceptable to the public and feasible for the school. This does not preclude change; it *requires* change both in the community and in the school. As an educational agency, the school has the responsibility to initiate change and to assume leadership in carrying out programs involving change. Change is a universal and continuous characteristic of modern society. Educational change should be initiated by educational agencies, among which, and foremost in the majority of communities, is the secondary school.

The concept of the high school as a democratic community of students and teachers, within and as an integral part of the community as a whole, has been described earlier in this book. This concept makes the establishment and maintenance of a close relationship between school and community much easier; in fact, it promotes it. In such a relationship the high school assumes a broad educational responsibility which goes beyond the walls of the school and out into the community. The community in turn provides both human and material resources which make education more meaningful, more vital, and more relevant.

Utilizing Community Learning Resources

Over the past few years a great deal has been written about secondary school programs designed to utilize various resources in the school's community in attempts to facilitate student learning. Most of the articles that have appeared in popular magazines or professional journals have described programs which involve taking or sending the schools' students out into the community. Such programs range from those which consist of a series of field trips designed to enrich classroom activity to those in which the primary learning activities take place in various areas of the community away from the school. The latter are usually described as schools-without-walls. We would like to suggest that schools have largely overlooked the possibilities for enriching and expanding the curriculum by bringing various community resources capable of contributing to student learning *into* the school—resources such as knowledgeable individuals, performing groups in the areas of drama, dance, and music, and exhibits of visual art.

Field trips and other means designed to utilize community resources in their natural setting should be a part of the school's program. However, there are many community learning resources that cannot be brought into the school. For example, the only way students can experience the court system in operation, perceive the atmosphere which pervades penal or mental institutions, or comprehend certain business and industrial operations is to make an on-site visit. Unfortunately, many public schools will be limited in the extent to which they can enrich the curriculum in this manner. Frequently there are logistical problems involved. The cost of transportation, the amount of time consumed in travel, the high cost of tickets to plays, concerts, and the like, and the limited number of students which can be accommodated in many instances are all factors which limit the extent to which the school can enrich or expand its curriculum by sending or taking students to community learning resources. Therefore, in addition to encouraging the use of field trips when they are possible and appropriate, the principal should provide leadership in the development of programs designed to bring community learning resources *into* the school.

For example, it should not be too difficult to expand and enrich the school's program in the performing and visual arts by bringing live performers and original art works to the school. Large and small musical ensembles, solo performers, ballet and modern dance groups, theater groups, poets, writers, films, and exhibits of visual art (paintings, prints, sculpture, ceramics, photography, etc.) are available to most schools from a variety of sources. In addition, it is usually possible to locate people possessed of specialized knowledge or expertise in various areas of the school's curriculum who are willing to come to the school and share their knowledge with students. This sharing may be accomplished through lectures, demonstrations, or just informal discussions. It is certainly more practical to bring a congressman, judge, or alderman to the school to share his knowledge, experience, and viewpoints with students than it is to take the students to his place of business. Similarly, it is often possible for many more students to experience musical, dramatic, or dance performances when the performer or performing group can be brought to the school than when the students must be transported to a concert hall.

Another of the advantages to this means of utilizing some of the learning resources of the community is that the resources of a broader "community" become available. It is possible to bring people, programs, and exhibits from a wide geographic area to the school, while the distance it is practical to take students to learning resources is rather limited, particularly if a number of such experiences are desired in one school year. Unfortunately, in a society which is becoming increasingly urbanized, schools some distance from a large metropolitan area are likely to have only limited educational and cultural resources available to them in their immediate community, and transporting students to an area where greater resources are available may be impossible. For such schools, enriching and expanding the curriculum by bringing learning resources from the broader community *to* the school would seem particularly appropriate and advantageous.

The resources that can be tapped for this purpose are many—it simply takes a little effort on the part of the principal and his staff to ferret them out and to develop the necessary contacts. The colleges and universities within the state in which the school is located, as well as those in nearby states, are excellent sources of programs, exhibits, and speakers. They are a particularly good source of programs in the arts—they frequently have programs of high quality that are available to public schools at minimal cost—

often entailing only transportation expenses. Many universities maintain extension departments in art, music, and so on that coordinate the scheduling of exhibits and programs in public schools throughout the state. But even those that do not will usually respond favorably to a telephone call to the particular department from which a specific program is desired. Some colleges and universities have established student and faculty speakers bureaus and provide public schools with a listing of professors or students who are willing to make their knowledge, expertise, and experience available to public school students. In many states and communities there are agencies such as a state Arts Council, Urban Gateways, the YMCA, and the YWCA, from which speakers and programs are available. Business and industry frequently make programs available to public schools; telephone companies and utility companies offer some particularly excellent science-related programs. Professional speaker's bureaus or booking agencies, film rental companies, and school assembly services can also serve as a source of programs. Although the programs obtained through commercial sources are usually more expensive than those obtained from other sources, the cost is not always prohibitive. Many performers are free during the day and will perform at a school for a reduced fee, and many lecturers, particularly those involved in politics or social causes, are willing to talk to and with students for a very small fee. Finally, there are residents in every community with talent, knowledge, and expertise in areas relevant to the school's curriculum who will be willing to come into the school to share their knowledge with students, usually at no cost to the school.

The use of community learning resources to expand and enrich the school's program need not be limited to any particular curricular areas. There are possibilities in many areas and disciplines and the principal should encourage all of his staff members to explore the possibilities in their subject area. He should also encourage suggestions from students. In fact, this would seem an excellent place to put to work the concept of a democratic school referred to throughout this book. A committee of students, teachers, and parents might well undertake the task of locating, selecting, scheduling, and coordinating the systematic use of community resources. A few creative teachers, students, and parents may take the lead and develop programs which will benefit a large number of the school's students. There are, however, two circular areas in which the use of the resources of the "outside" community seems like such a logical addition to the educational program that some of the possibilities merit specific discussion—namely, social studies and the arts.

If the social studies program in a secondary school is to deal with the operation of the political system in a democratic society and with the application of knowledge in the context of democratic principles to the solution of contemporary social and political problems, it seems evident that those people in the community who are engaged in the political process, are attempting to bring about social change, or are actively involved in attempting to solve social problems, can provide information, knowledge, insights, and perspectives that will broaden and enrich the social studies curriculum. Explanations and discussions of the political process, of the art of practical politics, and of political issues from those actively involved in the political process can add immediacy and relevance to the social studies program. The advocacy of particular solutions to social problems such as poverty, health care, the preservation of the environment, the decay of the cities, and the preservation of individual liberty in a mass society can best be presented by those committed to a particular solution. By providing students with the opportunity to hear advocates of various positions regarding contemporary social issues the school program can enhance students' ability to evaluate contradictory viewpoints and claims in the light of examined democratic principles and personal values—in other words, to practice the kind of critical thinking essential to the maintenance and renewal of a democratic society. In order to make the most of resource people who deal with politics, government and social issues programs should be structured so that students have the opportunity to ask questions. When a question and answer period is incorporated as part of the structure, students can consider the topic beforehand and prepare questions in advance. The ability to ask intelligent questions is a valuable skill for participating citizens in a democratic society.

The principal and his staff will have to gain the support of the superintendent, board of education, and the community for the free and open discussion of controversial issues if such programs are to be truly relevant. It may take a high order of educational leadership to convince them that the secondary school is an appropriate place for students to learn and practice the meaning of freedom of expression in a democratic society, and that the best route to objectivity is through a thorough examination of conflicting viewpoints. Not only must the leadership of the school help persuade and convince the community that the free and open exchange of ideas is an essential part of the democratic process, but it must also be perceptive enough to know the extent to which their persuasion has been successful—in other words, the extent to which the community is willing to sustain the school's academic freedom. An article by Lawrence Metcalf and Maurice Hunt which outlines an active role for the professional staff in developing and increasing academic freedom in secondary schools is included in the bibliography at the end of this chapter.

The use of community resources to expand the role of the arts in the curriculum of a secondary school offers at least some help toward solving a problem that has long plagued secondary school curriculum designers—how to make the arts an integral part of the common general education of secondary school students. Many secondary schools do an excellent job of providing applied training in the arts, but few have developed successful educational programs in the arts for students who do not wish to learn to perform on a musical instrument, to study ballet, or to paint, draw, or sculpt. The arts curriculum in most American high schools is heavily performance-oriented—they pride themselves on their excellent bands, orchestras, or choirs, or on their gifted visual artists, but they often devote little in the way of providing resources for developing artistic awareness, receptivity, and response in non-performing students. However, the condition of our society would seem to indicate a need on the part of all students for educational experiences which humanize, which increase aesthetic sensitivity, awareness, and values. The arts, of course, are a vital part of a liberal, humanizing education.

A number of years ago colleges, universities, and public schools devoted considerable energy to the development of music and art appreciation or survey courses, which were designed to make the arts a part of the general education of secondary school students. However, these courses were for the most part unsuccessful. They tended to be "tell 'em" courses which emphasized names, dates, and places in the lives of composers and artists, the names and histories of their works, or the recognition of their works. Students' experiencing of art was limited primarily to color slides, reproductions of visual art, and phonograph recordings of music. Evaluation was based on the *retention* of cognitive knowledge and *recognition* of art works. However, the purpose of including the arts in common general education is to develop students who are aware of art, willing to receive experiences in the arts, and willing to respond to artistic experiences. These are objectives that are more likely to contribute to the development of individuals sensitive to aesthetic values, for whom the arts become a source of delight.

Awareness is the first objective in the taxonomy of educational objectives in the affective domain. What better way is there to develop student awareness than by making the arts a basic part of the school environment? Students are much more likely to develop a willingness to receive experiences in the arts if they are regularly exposed to live performances in music, drama, and dance and to works of visual art as a natural part of their school experience than if they are required to take appreciation courses which stress the regurgitation of factual knowledge *about* the arts. Similarly, while occasional field trips to a play, concert, ballet, or museum, provide a valuable supplement to the art experiences available in the school, they alone will be insufficient to achieve the objectives outlined above. Too often, isolated trips to museums convey to students the idea that art is a collection of relics of the past rather than a part of life.

In their book on the secondary school curriculum, Harry Broudy, B. Othanel Smith, and Joe Burnett suggest four levels of response to works of art. Depending on the extent to which their awareness and perceptual skills have been developed, individuals may respond to:

1. The vividness and intensity of the sensuous elements in the work of art: the affective quality of the sounds, colors, gestures, etc.

2. The formal qualities of the object, its design or composition.
3. The technical merits of the object, the skill with which the work is carried out.
4. The expressive significance of the object, its import or message or meaning as aesthetically expressed.[1]

The distinguished American composer Aaron Copland has used a similar schema to describe levels of listening to music in his book *What to Listen for in Music*—an inexpensive paperback that can easily be understood by high school students. Attaining the fourth level of response described by Broudy et al., and Copland is probably an unrealistic goal for the secondary school program of general education. However, a series of live programs in the performing arts and exhibitions and demonstrations in the visual arts, coupled with brief, coordinated units of instruction designed to facilitate the first three levels of response, might prove considerably more effective in attaining the objectives we have suggested than the traditional appreciation course approach.

One high school has, over the last three years, attempted to make extensive use of community learning resources as a means of enriching and expanding its educational program, particularly in the arts. The school has attempted to make the discussion of contemporary social problems and issues and the performing and visual arts a natural part of the school environment. Fortunately the school has an excellent auditorium capable of seating 1,400 students, and a multipurpose room that will accommodate 200. Both are located near the student cafeteria. The multipurpose room has a small stage at one end, but does not have fixed seating, therefore it provides space that can be adapted for many types of presentations and demonstrations. In addition, in order to adapt the room for use as an art gallery, two of its walls have been lined with a six-foot wide strip of three fourth-inch plywood covered with outdoor carpeting. This provides a face on which paintings, prints, drawings, photographs, etc., of varying sizes can be mounted. The carpeting is inexpensive and provides a suitable surface for mounting exhibits of visual art.

Many of the programs, speakers, or exhibits that are brought into the school involve some cost. Financial support for the programs is provided by the student council and by the principal. The principal has made certain contingency and activity funds available for this purpose and the Council raises money by various means. Programs are suggested by teachers, students, and administrators, and final program decisions are made by a student programs committee which is a standing committee of the student council. The student council advisor is a member of the administrative staff. He works with the committee to obtain programs and is responsible for scheduling them and for making the necessary physical arrangements.

---

[1]Harry S. Broudy, B. Othanel Smith, and Joe R. Burnett, *Democracy and Excellence in American Education* (Chicago: Rand McNally & Co., 1964), pp. 226-227.

The School Community

Since the students in the school are free except when they have classes—there are no study halls or home rooms—they are able to attend presentations or view exhibits on their unscheduled time. In order to make performances available to more students they are frequently repeated two or three times during the school day. Teachers may elect to bring their classes to presentations or to view exhibits if the nature of the presentation is relevant to their course; however, they are never required to do so—there are no mandatory mass assembly programs. Teachers frequently let student interest determine the presentations or exhibits their classes attend. By scheduling multiple presentations and by scheduling programs at varied times throughout the school day, each student has access to a considerable variety of programs.

Control of the audience size is maintained by issuing reserved seat tickets (no fee is charged) for all of the programs which are made available to the entire student body. Any student or teacher may pick up a ticket for any program scheduled during one of his free periods and any teacher may obtain a block of tickets for a class he wishes to bring. Presentations designed to supplement a specific subject area or course are designated as in-school field trips and all students enrolled in the subject area or course attend regardless of the class for which they are scheduled at the time the program is presented. The proximity of the multipurpose room to the student cafeteria also enables students to visit art exhibits and view short films during their lunch hour.

In order to provide more complete understanding of the nature of the program, the complete schedule of presentations for the 1972-73 school year and a few typical programs from the two previous years are shown in Table 12-1. The presentations for 1972-73 are listed in the order they occurred during the school year. A brief description of the program, the number of presentations, the students to whom it was available, the location, the source of the program, and the cost are included.

The principal who wishes to help his staff utilize the resources of the community in order to enrich and expand the school's educational program, as this school has at least begun to do, must be willing to secure some direct financial support for the program and to develop other supplemental sources of funding. When one compares the small per pupil cost of such programs with the potential educational benefits, it would seem that the principal should have little trouble getting his superintendent and board of education to provide at least some of the necessary funds. The total cost of the program described above is about one-seventh of the average annual teacher's salary in the school district.

The principal will also need to provide administrative support to teachers, students, and parents attempting to develop such programs. Secretarial help with the correspondence involved in setting up the programs, access to a telephone, and the help of the custodial staff in making the necessary physical arrangements are essential. Ideally, someone on the administrative

Table 12-1

Programs Utilizing Community Resources

	Program Title	Description	Number of Presentations	Availability	Location	Source	Cost
1.	Mrs. Roberta Whitney Art Professor	demonstration of the process of working with clay	3	all art students	multi-purpose room	Northern Illinois University	None
2.	Under New Management	vocal and instrumental music group	1	all students	auditorium	Wheaton College	$85
3.	Charles King	folk singer	1	all students	auditorium	Wisconsin Lecture Bureau	$110
4.	Collagraphs	art exhibit	open all day for 2 weeks	all students	multi-purpose room	U. of Ill. Extension in Art	$7.65[a]
5.	Kashmir	film-lecture	1	all students	auditorium	Wisconsin Lecture Bureau	$75
6.	American Poetry	American poems dramatized by actors	1	all students	auditorium	School Assembly Service	$70
7.	T. Daniel	mime	2	all students	auditorium	Urban Gateways	$105
8.	The Great Chase and The Champion	classic films	shown continuously all lunch periods	all students	multi-purpose room	Commercial film rental agency	$15

Source: This program includes the materials presented in an Illinois high school during the 1972-73 school year.
[a] The University of Illinois Dept. of Extension in Art charges a membership fee of $50 per year (plus shipping cost).
[b] Programs 33 through 42 were part of an Asian Culture Week organized by three teachers (one each from the English, social studies, and art departments) and their students.

9.	Dirty Pictures	exhibit of original art works pertaining to ecological themes	open all day for 2 weeks	all students	multi-purpose room	U. of Ill. Extension in Art	$8.60
10.	Northern Ill. Univ. Faculty Woodwind Quintet	program of classical romantic & modern works	2	English, humanities & music classes	multi-purpose room	Northern Ill. U. School of Music	$100
11.	Eight Picassos	exhibit of reproductions of 8 of Picasso's most famous paintings	open all day for 2 weeks	all students	student cafeteria	U. of Ill. Extension in Art	$7.65
12.	James Ruddle, NBC News; Joel Weisman Political Editor of *Chicago Today*	panel discussion of freedom of the press followed by question-answer session	2	American hist. & senior social science classes	multi-purpose room	The Chicago Council on Foreign Relations	$200
13.	Valucha	Brazilian folk singer	2	all students	auditorium	Urban Gateways	$105
14.	"Musical Pig" and "The Fly"	short art films	shown continuously all lunch periods	all students	multi-purpose room	Contemporary Films	$27.50
15.	U. of Ill. Chamber Choir	program of vocal compositions by Mozart	1	music and humanities students	auditorium	U. of Ill. Extension in Music	$100
16.	Prehistoric and Early Art	exhibit of reproductions of famous works	open all day for 2 weeks	all students	multi-purpose room	U. of Ill. Extension in Art	$7.65
17.	The 1930s	multi-media presentation on the history and mood of the 1930s	1	all students	auditorium	School Assembly Service	$70
18.	Kabuki Theater: Shozo Sato	lecture-demonstration	2	English, art & social studies classes	auditorium	U. of Ill. Krannert Center for	$125

Table 12-1, *Continued*

Program Title	Description	Number of Presentations	Availability	Location	Source	Cost
19. Theodore Berland author-lecturer	lecture on noise pollution followed by question-answer session	2	jr. & sr. social studies classes	multi-purpose room	The Adult Education Council of Greater Chicago	$200
20. Early Christian Art	exhibit of reproductions	open all day for 2 weeks	all students	multi-purpose room	U. of Ill. Extension in Art	$8.65
21. Christopher Mojekwu Professor of Political Science	lecture-slide presentation on Africa and African politics	1	African History classes	multi-purpose room	Lake Forest College	none
22. Broadway in Sight	music from Broadway productions tracing the development of American musical comedy	1	all students	auditorium	School Assembly Service	$70
23. Early Frescoes and Mosaics	exhibit of photographs	open all day for 2 weeks	all students	multi-purpose room	U. of Ill. Extension in Art	$7.65
24. Jonathan Galloway Professor of Political Science	discussion of Nixon's foreign policy	1	sr. social science classes	multi-purpose room	Lake Forest College	none
25. 20th Century	exhibit of	open all day	all students	multi-	U. of Ill.	$7.65

the Performing Arts

Painting Abstract/Realism	reproductions of famous works	for 2 weeks		purpose room & student cafeteria	Extension in Art	
26. U. of Ill. Varsity Men's Glee Club	formal concert	1	all students	auditorium	U. of Ill. Extension in Music	$150
27. Paul B. Fischer Professor of Pol. Sci.	discussion of the politics of elections	2	sr. social science classes	multi-purpose room	Lake Forest College	none
28. "Dr. Nurke's Collected Silences" and "To Speak or Not to Speak"	short art films	shown continuously all lunch periods	all students	multi-purpose room	International Film Bureau	$30
29. Northern Ill. University Faculty Travelling Art Exhibit	exhibit of original prints and drawings	open all day for 1 month	all students	multi-purpose room	N. Ill. U. Dept. of Art	$16
30. U. of Ill. Contemporary Chamber Players	concert of avant-garde music	1	music and humanities classes	auditorium	U. of Ill. Extension in Music	$100
31. French School 19th-20th Century	exhibit of reproductions of famous paintings	open all day for 2 weeks	all students	multi-purpose room	U. of Ill. Extension in Art	$7.65
32. Miami University A Capella Choir	concert of music for mixed chorus	1	all students	auditorium	Miami (Ohio) University	$75
33. Japanese Life and Customs[b]	slide show	3	all students	multi-purpose room	local residents	none

357

Table 12-1, *Continued*

Program Title	Description	Number of Presentations	Availability	Location	Source	Cost
34. Yoga	demonstration (including student participation)	2	all students	multi-purpose room	local residents	$25
35. Philippine Dancers	performance of traditional dances	2	all students	multi-purpose room	Philippine Consulate	$50
36. Judo	demonstration and discussion of Japanese Martial arts	1	all students	indoor track	local resident	none
37. Introduction to Zen: Mr. Kubose	discussion of Zen by priest from Buddhist Temple of Chicago	2	all students	multi-purpose room	Chicago Buddhist Temple	$20
38. Japanese Tea Ceremony	lecture-demonstration	1	all students	auditorium	Chicago Buddhist Temple	$20
39. Asian Food	smorgasbord of samples of Asian food	available all lunch periods	all students	multi-purpose room	local residents	$30
40. Skebana: Shozo Sato	demonstration of Japanese floral art	1	all students	multi-purpose room	U. of Ill. Dept. of Art	$62.50
41. Sumi-e: Shozo Sato	demonstration of	1	all students	multi-	U. of Ill.	$62.50

42. "The Seven Samurai"	original Japanese film by Kurosawa	1 (evening showing)	all students (free)	auditorium	Commercial film distributor	$75
43. The Figure in 20th Century Painting	exhibit of reproductions	open all day for 2 weeks	all students	multi-purpose room	U. of Ill. Extension in Art	$8.60
44. The History of Rock	multi-media presentation tracing the development of rock music	1	all students	auditorium	WLS Radio and Rick-Trow Productions	none
45. Stephen Syverud Professor of Composition	electronic music and Moog synthesizer demonstration	3	all students (one for music students only)	multi-purpose room	Northwestern University	$150

(Row above 42: Japanese brush painting ... purpose room ... Dept. of Art) staff should serve as the coordinator of events in order to avoid conflicts over dates and access to building space. This task should not add too much to his work load if an effective student-teacher committee is organized. The potential for increasing the relevance of the school's program and for creating a stimulating intellectual and artistic environment would seem to justify the commitment of the necessary staff time as well as the small amount of money required.

THE COMMUNITY FORUM

As has been indicated earlier, the public high school is, in most cases, the top educational agency of the community. This position carries with it a responsibility for educational leadership in the community. Such responsibility can be met not only by formal adult education programs, but also by informal programs. One very effective means of providing stimulating and meaningful informal community-wide education is the community forum.

The high school is in a very strategic position to sponsor a variety of public educational forums based on community, state, or even national problems and issues. In accepting such responsibility the high school does not assume advocacy of any point of view, but rather seeks to make all points of view known to the public. Its purpose is to bring information before those who are concerned with the problem or issue to the end that public opinion and public decision-making may have a broad base of facts and knowledgeable opinion. In brief, the public forum is a means of raising problem-solving and decision-making in the community to a higher cognitive level. In sponsoring community forums the high school can render a vital educational service which enhances its stature and usefulness in the community.

Every community faces numerous problems and issues of broad public concern. Some are concerned with education per se, others with recreation, ecology, industrial development, public health, sanitation, and similar topics. All require study, collection of data, and presentation of relevant facts if rational and acceptable decisions are to be made. Some decisions will come as a result of popular vote, others by action of public officials. In either case an informed public is essential.

The community forum provides an effective means for the secondary school to carry out its responsibility for adult or community education. The educational leadership of the school should capitalize on it, not only as a responsibility but also as an opportunity to demonstrate its value as a community educational agency which contributes to a better understanding of the issues and which deserves the support of all citizens, regardless of whether or not they have children in the schools.

Modern techniques of communication as well as the expanded media coverage makes it possible for the school to reach practically the entire community with the forum format. Where television facilities are available, station managers are usually quite receptive to presentations of this nature. Radio is an even more readily accessible medium. The press is almost certain to cover and publicize a school-sponsored forum if it has an issue of importance and current interest as the subject.

The typical high school auditorium provides an excellent facility for a forum presentation from whence it can be transmitted by television and radio. In some cases it may be necessary to present the forum in the television studios, in which case audience questions and reactions may be relayed by telephone. Audio and video tapes may be made for later use at meetings of public and private organizations.

Essential elements of the forum are:

1. A sponsor (the school whose purpose is to convey information on the issue, not to advocate or promote or to denigrate).
2. A suitable facility which provides opportunity for audience participation.
3. A moderator who can and will conduct the forum with impartiality and objectivity.
4. Able exponents of both sides of the issue who not only present their cases but who question and are questioned by opposing presenters, who rebut and are rebutted.
5. An audience with the opportunity to raise questions and make comments.

It is not necessary, nor is it ordinarily wise, to ascertain a winner. Obviously the issue will not be decided in the forum. It is not the purpose of a forum to reach a decision, but rather to provide some basis for the average citizen to make an intelligent decision. He then may exercise his right of citizenship to influence others, to inform his government representatives of his opinion, or to express himself at the ballot box.

CITIZEN ADVISORY COMMITTEES

School systems in general, and troubled ones in particular, are increasingly turning to lay citizens for advice on educational policies and problems. The trend toward holding schools accountable to the people has added impetus to citizen participation in the educational process. If schools are to be held accountable, the professional educator must know for what they are to be held accountable. This must lead ultimately to an agreement, or at least to a common understanding of what the schools are expected to accomplish if any type of evaluation can be truly meaningful.

Citizen groups, and particularly those which are school-sponsored, can and should make major contributions to a common understanding of what the school is expected to accomplish. In fact, such a task is basic to the other legitimate tasks of lay advisory organizations.

Citizen participation in organized form can and has made very significant contributions to education, not only in the community, but also in the state and nation. Such organizations usually are most constructive when the school takes the initiative in their formation and provides them with a meeting place, typing, duplicating services, and reading materials. The provision of an experienced educational consultant and local resource people, as citizens come to grips with school problems, is usually very worthwhile even though it requires some expenditure of school funds. The importance of adequate guidance in the operation of such committees can hardly be overestimated.

Where the school system maintains a system-wide citizen's advisory committee, the secondary school receives the benefit of its counsel as an integral part of the school system. However, this does not preclude the possibility of a secondary school advisory committee working in cooperation with the overall committee. Such a committee or counsel could, within the system-wide format, provide constructive suggestions on a wide-range of secondary policies, problems, and programs. In school systems which have no formally organized citizen participation of an advisory nature, the need for an advisory council for the high school is even more compelling. In either case, every secondary school could profit significantly from the existence and operation of such a group.

In the former case the selection of the secondary school advisory council will be largely the responsibility of the principal. After securing the necessary endorsement by the superintendent, and, in some cases, the board of education, it is his job to see that a representative group of citizens is selected for the advisory council. This can only be done after a careful study of the community which the high school serves has been made. Even in a small high school community, the principal needs the help of teachers and students as well as lay citizens. He will do well to enlist their aid in selecting nominees for service on the council. He may profitably appoint a nominating committee of five to seven people chosen among students, teachers, and lay citizens. This committee should arrive at a list of fifteen to twenty-five people who are truly representative of the community—representative with regard to the social, racial, economic, political, religious, and vocational composition of the community. Further requirements would include a willingness to devote some time to the job and a genuine interest in education. Men and women of both proven and promising ability should be chosen.

In cases where the school system has an overall advisory group, the secondary school council might be a subcommittee sponsored by the overall committee which functions in cooperation with that group. In any case, the composition of the council should consist of interested men and women with time available, who are representative of the total community.

Once the membership has been established, the council should organize itself, choosing its own officers and planning its procedures. The principal and other school personnel, including students, should serve as resource people when called upon. While the council should be free at all times to study problems and policies of their own choosing, it is the duty of the principal to suggest problems, policy issues, and educational priorities for study and recommendation by the council. Furthermore, he should provide the group with a meeting place in the high school, duplicating services in connection with study materials, and reports and other such items that will facilitate the work of the council.

The council should be fully aware of the nature of the help expected of them, especially with respect to the advisory nature of their function. A set of guidelines worked out cooperatively, with the principal providing the leadership, is essential. Appropriate topics for the consideration of the advisory group might include the following:

The nature and type of reports to parents on student achievement.

The use of high school facilities by the community after school hours (consistent with school system policies).

The educational needs of adults in the community.

The nature and extent of public performances by high school athletic teams and musical and dramatic groups.

The use of paraprofessionals from the community in the high school.

The problems of juvenile delinquency.

The high school dropout problem.

The problem of drug addiction.

These and many other topics of similar nature can be thoroughly studied and discussed. Indeed, such discussion by the council may well provide new insights into old problems both on the part of laymen and professionals. Such cooperative efforts in working on solutions for the innumerable problems which face high schools will not only be helpful in solving problems, but will also inevitably improve school-community relations.

A word of caution with regard to the choice of problems, policies and activities to be taken up by the council is in order. First of all, the advisory nature of the group should be stressed. It is a study group with no administrative authority or power. Its purpose is to provide an input from the community to aid the school in satisfactorily meeting issues, solving problems, and developing and revising policies.

Problems of individual teachers, students, and nonacademic personnel are not proper topics for council discussion. The qualifications of individual teachers, the discipline problems of individual students, and the evaluation of members of the school staff as council topics must be avoided at all costs. A clear understanding of the necessity of the council limiting itself to general policy rather than individual cases should be established at the inauguration of the group.

Special Advisory Groups

The existence or nonexistence of an overall advisory group such as is described in the preceding pages does not preclude the possibility of establishing special advisory groups to various segments of the school program. For many years, high schools in agricultural areas have enlisted groups of farmers to provide advice to students and instructors in vocational agriculture programs. These special advisory groups have been quite helpful in bringing educational needs of the farm and the agriculture community to the attention of instructors who were responsible for course choices and course content. They also helped develop policies as well as programs which reflected local needs and desires. Many of these groups provided agriculture students with a variety of work experiences, not only on the farm, but in seed stores, farm implement shops, and Farm Bureau offices as well.

High school vocational-technical departments can very profitably make use of citizen advisory committees. The knowledge and insights which workers in industry can supply to these departments can be most helpful. The outmoded and outdated machines which exist in many high school shops might have been useful, had advice from industry been available. In the rapidly changing world of technology, the high school should avail itself of the knowledge and skills which industry can provide, not only in programming and purchasing equipment, but also in evaluating its work. Visits to the school by the advisory group as a group or as individuals to observe the program in action will provide an opportunity for the visitors to make some evaluation of the program with regard to its adequacy, suitability, timeliness, and effectiveness in preparing students for places in industry. Of course, such an evaluation is at best only a partial one and should not be regarded as a valid appraisal of the total program.

Other areas of instruction or departments which can profit by having special lay committees, include business education, health education, homemaking, adult education and continuing education, and education for citizenship.

Special committees, like other school advisory committees, need first to familiarize themselves with the total school program in order to give balance to their discussions and recommendations with regard to their special areas. The work of these committees will be most effective if the committees develop close relationships with the teachers and students in the area.

Unlike the general council, special committee members need not be representative of the community, but rather representative of the people in the community who have knowledge and a special interest in such areas as health, commerce, citizenship, and agriculture. Membership in such committees would include hospital administrators, nurses, public health officials, physicians, businessmen, chamber of commerce and union officials, public officials, magistrates, farmers, and agri-business operators. At first glance, one might think that people of this type would be unobtainable. Quite the contrary is true. If properly approached, most will respond affirmatively, particularly when they realize that they can render a genuine service to boys and girls of the community. The responsibility of membership on these committees is not onerous, as meetings are not frequent and the demand on a member's time is minimal.

Benefits to be Derived

In adopting a lay advisory system, the secondary school is likely to derive very substantial benefits for its program and in turn for the community itself. These committees will learn first-hand about the school, its program, its personnel, and its operation. This information will be effectively disseminated throughout the community by committee members. Many apprehensions, misapprehensions, and other types of concerns will be dissipated simply by a knowledge of what goes on at the high school and why. In addition, the needs of the school become apparent to lay people as they participate in advisory work. Thus a solid basis for support of requests for new programs, new facilities, and new equipment can be established. Bond issues and tax levies for education receive a warmer reception when the citizenry understands the needs of the school.

Citizen committees are in an excellent position to make the school aware of community attitudes toward the school and toward its programs and policies. In large communities, public opinion polls may be sponsored by such committees in their advisory function. In small communities, such polls may be unnecessary if committee members can acquire the same information in informal conversations and discussions. This sensitivity to the attitudes, opinions, and concerns of the community is a valuable committee asset and is, of course, reflected in the discussions and recommendations of these groups.

Another major benefit to be derived from lay committee work is the initiation and enhancement of relationships between the school and the many community organizations and agencies which have common or closely-related interests and functions, or can provide learning experiences, information, or materials for high school students.

One of the most significant contributions of such groups may be to inform the school of community educational needs. In many high schools today, the program of learning experiences is largely predicated on the traditional idea of what a high school program should be, with little awareness of the unique educational needs of the community. In such cases, advisory committees bring local educational needs to the attention of the school, sometimes in very strong positive terms. Where high schools are sensitive to local needs the lay advisory groups tend to keep that sensitivity alive and up-to-date. Furthermore, relating the school program to community experiences makes that program more meaningful and interesting for students. Future trends in the community and region which may affect educational needs are often recognized by intelligent lay citizens before school people are aware of them. This fact makes it possible for citizens to make very real contributions to school planning and development.

RELATIONSHIP BETWEEN PUBLIC AND PRIVATE SECONDARY SCHOOLS

Many American communities have both public and nonpublic high schools. This situation in some cases may cause friction in the school-community relationship. This is especially true in times of increasing costs of education which generate requests for public support of nonpublic schools. In some communities where the nonpublic school population is quite substantial, there is a demand that public support be provided through some means such as vouchers to parents which will avoid the constitutional inhibition so far preventing such support.

Resentment on the part of parents of nonpublic school pupils and their friends and relatives may lead to strained relationships in the community. Such a situation creates a difficult problem for the administrator. Under such conditions the passage of a public school tax levy or bond issue for school construction may be almost impossible. Friction may develop between public and nonpublic school personnel as well as among parents in these categories.

Although there are those who contend that all children should attend public schools, the courts have upheld the right of nonpublic schools to exist as long as they meet required standards set up by the state. At the same time, the courts have denied direct support to nonpublic schools. Various types of plans involving indirect subsidies have been proposed and are being proposed in order to give financial aid to nonpublic schools. Regardless of the outcome, the public school administrator will have to deal with the problem in one form or another. If indirect aid plans are invalidated, the source of irritation will remain; if they are validated, then a different form of the problem will emerge, namely, a competitive situation with regard to public funds for education. In either case, the administrator is faced with a difficult problem in school-community relations.

Nonpublic high schools fall into two major categories, namely, schools sponsored by the church, and those which are operated primarily for profit.

It is the former which have the stronger claim on public funds. High schools operated for profit are largely preparatory and vocational-technical schools which have little claim on public funds, although they would no doubt benefit significantly by an unrestricted voucher plan.

There is general agreement that public money should be spent for a public purpose only. The division comes between those who are strict constructionists in the matter and those who maintain that the providing for education is a public purpose no matter where the education is obtained. It is not our purpose to argue the merits of the case here but rather to point out ways in which this very real problem facing many administrators in the maintenance of good school-community relations may be solved, or at least reduced in its impact.

The basic philosophy expressed in preceding pages applies with particular validity in this case. The public high school is supported by all the community and serves all the community. As a democratic institution, it has a responsibility to all the people. This means that those who choose to send their children to nonpublic schools still have a very important stake in the public school. The public school is not relieved of all its responsibilities with regard to these people. Its distinct responsibilities in the areas of community and adult education remain undiminished with regard to parents of nonpublic school students. The fact that their children are not enrolled in the public high school makes it even more imperative that adequate educational services be provided for these parents.

Once this responsibility is acknowledged, the basis for satisfactory relationships can be established. It can be implemented in a number of ways, some of which are mentioned and briefly described here.

The concept of "shared time" (or "shared facilities," as it may more appropriately be called), involves opening the facilities of the public schools for the use of nonpublic students. Facilities housing physical education, home economics, science, mechanics, technologies, and other areas of study requiring special design, large spaces, laboratories, expensive equipment, and other special features are most attractive to nonpublic schools which, in many cases, emphasize academic areas of study and do not provide extensive facilities of the kind described. While the use of these facilities by nonpublic school pupils involves some administrative problems and may often require transportation services, the benefits both to education in general and school-community relations in particular far outweigh the disadvantages. Such a cooperative arrangement will tend to establish a supportive relationship in which both nonpublic students and their parents recognize a kinship with the public high school.

A formal adult education program which includes vocational and technical subjects, courses and seminars on current and relevant topics, and traditional courses as well can offer educational benefits to parents of nonpublic school students. The special facilities mentioned earlier are valuable assets in providing adult programs which will appeal to the general membership of the community.

Community forums are also an excellent vehicle for informal adult education. Issues and topics of these forums should be broad enough to encompass the interests of the total community. Parents of nonpublic school students have just as great an interest in current issues as has any other segment of the community. They will recognize the public high school as *their* school if it serves them in ways which are relevant and useful. In summary, the public high school is the main educational center of the typical community, and it should offer its services to all on an equal basis. For those who choose to send their children to private schools, the public school should still make all its educational services available. It should share its facilities and programs with all those who desire to take advantage of them.

The Secondary School and Other Community Agencies

The high school is but one of many social agencies in the nation, the state and the local community. In many communities it is the most important educational agency. However, regardless of its importance it can be most effective in its role if it has the cooperation of other agencies of the community. This is true for at least two reasons. First, the high school has much to contribute to the operation of other social agencies, and second, other social agencies have much to contribute to the school.

In the most desirable type of cooperation, each agency maintains its identity of purpose so that one agency does not duplicate the efforts of others or assume roles for which it is not intended. The purpose of the school is to educate, and its responsibility is education. It should cooperate with other social agencies so that its responsibility for education may be carried out more effectively, and so that other social agencies may perform their functions more effectively also. Such a reciprocal relationship enhances the effectiveness of all agencies and improves their contribution to community welfare.

Some critics within and without the educational profession are saying that the school is trying to do too much. They say it is spreading itself too thin and thus losing its effectiveness as an educational institution. They insist that the school program be devoted exclusively to the development of intellectual, social, and vocational competence. Restricting its practices to such programs, it is claimed, enables the school to concentrate on what it is best able to do.

Yet on the other hand, the critics insist that the school should be concerned with promoting physical and mental health, human relationships, and social, moral, and ethical values. They want a curriculum which is meaningful, relevant and suited to individual differences. Laboratory experiences, they admit, are valuable, if not essential, and the community is a learning laboratory.

The point that the school should do what it is best able to do—namely educate—is well made. There are, of course, schools which lose sight of this fact and devote time and effort to entertainment and socialization. However, to restrict or formalize the program of the secondary school to the extent that the school would tend to become isolated from the community (and particularly community social agencies) would be counter-productive. The school is part of the community and can function most effectively as a cooperating institution rather than as an isolated one. Education is not a narrow, specialized function; it is as broad as life itself. Education, like life, is enhanced by cooperation and minimized by isolation.

If we accept the proposition that the basic task of the school, and the task it can best perform, is education, we should not regard it as the sole agency which educates. Since there are other community agencies which perform educational functions even though education may be incidental to their primary tasks, the school shares a common interest with them. Furthermore, these agencies offer valuable laboratory experiences for learning which the high school cannot afford to ignore. In addition, community agency personnel form a group of resource people upon which the school may call to bring current, first-hand information to the classroom.

For these reasons and for others which could be enumerated the case for close cooperation between the school and other social agencies seems obvious. It is equally clear that the purpose of such cooperation should be the enhancement of the educational process for which the school is responsible.

For a specific example of the type of relationship between the high school and another social agency let us consider the public health service of a community. This agency is concerned with the improvement of the health of the community. It typically employs doctors, nurses, dentists, and other health specialists. It is interested in promoting high standards of health among individuals and institutions. It interacts with other agencies and institutions in the course of its work. Poor health often leads to unemployment, unemployment to poverty, poverty to neglect of children, and broken homes. This sequence of events is a matter of concern to not only the public health agency but also to the employment office, the social welfare agency, the divorce court, and last but not least, to school itself.

Even the critics of broad school involvement recognize the responsibility of the school to teach people how to achieve and maintain good health. Nor is this commitment limited to students in the high school. It can and should be a cooperative effort with the public health service to educate the total community. In the sequence described, the effect of poverty-stricken broken homes on youth is well-known. Therefore the school has a direct interest in the health of the family since it significantly affects the attitude, self-concept, and learning motivation of the student from that home.

Bibliography

Anatine, Donald. "The Concepts of Art and Teaching Art." *Journal of Aesthetic Education* 1 (Autumn 1966), pp. 95-108.

Broudy, Harry S. "The Role of the Humanities in the Curriculum." *Journal of Aesthetic Education* 1 (Autumn 1966), pp. 17-28.

??????. *Enlightened Cherishing: An Essay on Aesthetic Education.* Urbana, Illinois: Univ. of Ill. Press, 1972.

Copland, Aaron. *What to Listen for in Music.* New York: McGraw-Hill, 1957.

Graham, Grace. *The Public School in the New Society.* London: Harper and Row, 1969.

Hamlin, Herbert M. *Citizen Participation in Local Policy-Making for Public Education.* Urbana, Ill.: University of Illinois College of Education, 1960.

Lindvall, C. M., ed. *Defining Educational Objectives.* Pittsburgh, Pa.: University of Pittsburgh Press, 1964.

McClosky, Gordon E. *Education and Public Understanding.* New York: Harper Brothers, 1966.

Metcalf, Lawrence and Maurice Hunt. *Teaching High School Social Studies.* New York: Harper Brothers, 1966.

Muniz, A. J. "But Citizens' Committees Can Work." *The American School Board Journal* 157 (November 1969), pp. 41-3.

Rokeach, Milton. *The Open and Closed Mind.* New York: Basic Books, 1960.

Sumption, Merle R. and Yvonne Engstrom. *School-Community Relations: A New Approach.* New York: McGraw-Hill, 1966.

# 13

The Principal Works with the Community

The preceding chapter set forth a view of the secondary school as an integral part of the community which could attempt to serve the educational needs of the total community. This concept encourages a cooperative effort. It does not in any way preclude the recognition of the contributions which other community agencies will and should make to the total educational effort. In fact, it is a part of the role of the secondary school to promote the broadest range of educational opportunities possible for the community.

The democratic model of the secondary school requires that there be established and maintained a structured system of communication between school and community. Such a system must be two-way in nature so that information flows freely from the community to the school, as well as from school to community. Traditional practice has emphasized the latter kind of flow, often to the neglect of the return channels. The good communication system must be as effective in gathering information as it is in disseminating it.

Equally important to the democratic school is involvement of the community in the educative process. Intelligent participation requires knowledge, and the acquisition of knowledge requires study and discussion. Therefore it is incumbent on the school to provide the structure and organization for the study of school problems and issues by the community, so that the community may make constructive contributions to the decision-making process.

In his or her role as an educational leader, the principal is duty-bound to assume responsibility for establishing and maintaining an effective system for communication between the school and the community, and for establishing an equally effective structure for the participation of the community in the educational process of the high school.

The present trend toward greater autonomy of the high school will tend to increase both the need and the opportunity for the principal to achieve these goals. As a member of the community and as a professional educator his responsibility is two-fold. First of all, he is a member of the community and has the privileges and obligations of any other citizen with regard to education. Secondly, he is a professional who is in a crucial position to provide the knowledge and skills necessary to organize, develop, and maintain effective communication with, and constructive involvement of, the school community. He should be the one to initiate action and to act as a facilitator in the development of the essential instrumentation to get the job done. The remainder of this chapter will be devoted to delineating these two vital functions and describing the principal's role as a facilitator.

COMMUNICATION

The importance of good communication within the school community can hardly be overestimated. The communication system is the nervous system of the school community. When it is limited to a school-to-community flow of information or is otherwise defective both the school and community suffer. Lack of information, misinformation, and misinterpretation of information can all lead to serious misconceptions, misunderstandings, and, in some cases, grave conflicts. Good communication is essential to good education.

Each year the publicly owned corporations of the United States spend over a billion dollars in communication with their shareholders. They recognize the value of keeping their owners aware of the facts about their companies. How much more important is it that we keep the owners of the public schools aware of the facts about their schools? Furthermore, the blanket invitation of the corporate executives for comments and criticism should be greatly expanded in the case of the public school to include a wide variety of reactions (which will be discussed in subsequent pages of this book).

Objectives of Communication

It is well for the secondary school to adopt and adhere to a set of objectives for communication between itself and the people it serves. A suggested list is presented here for consideration.
1. To provide the public with adequate information about their school
2. To provide the school with information about the community and its reactions to the school program
3. To establish and maintain public confidence in the school
4. To develop an awareness of the vital importance of education in the political, economic, and social life of a democratic nation
5. To keep people informed of current developments and trends in education

6. To achieve, through a continuous exchange of information, a cooperative relationship with the people and agencies of the community
7. To help secure wholehearted support for the school and its programs

It is obvious, of course, that in the case of objectives 3, 6, and 7 it is assumed that the school is worthy of confidence, is committed to cooperation, and that it deserves the support of the community.

Characteristics of Effective Communication

There are a number of characteristics which distinguish an effective communications system. In the first place, an effective communication system is based upon a careful study of the community. Such a study as is described in the preceding chapter will furnish the necessary information. Of particular importance are the following:

1. Historical background of the community
2. The general nature of the population (educational level, occupational status, numbers in each age group)
3. Structure of the community (social, power, political, and economic)
4. Description and analysis of social agencies and institutional life of the community
5. Communication media of the community and their availability
6. Nature, scope, and coverage of available media

Basic to all effective school-community communications systems is a two-way format which provides for a flow of information from the community to the school as well as from the school to the community. Too many schools have been content with one-way communication, from school to community. In such cases there is no opportunity to profit from the community reaction, and there is little chance that the school will receive much information which would facilitate the presentation of the program of the school.

In the third place, the communication system should be comprehensive. The school should attempt to reach all members of the community. While such an attempt is not likely to be completely successful, it should nevertheless be made. The school serves all the people and has the responsibility to try to reach all of them. Such an effort involves, among other factors, carefully designed messages, proper selection of media, and effective channels for public reaction. The establishment and maintenance of a comprehensive system requires time and effort. Several years are often required to achieve reasonable comprehensiveness. It is not a task for the principal or even the administration alone; the efforts of many people are required both in the school system and outside.

Another requisite characteristic of the effective system is accuracy. Transmission of information must be reasonably accurate if essential credibility is to be maintained. Since people are inclined to place their own interpretation on news it is important that information is disseminated in a clear, concise, and understandable form. Ambiguity must be avoided.

An organized structure for communication, in which individuals have recognized responsibilities and a carefully designed framework in which to discharge those responsibilities, is requisite. A well-organized system provides communicants with exact knowledge of their duties as well as the authority and means to perform them. The basic purpose of an organized structure of communication is to provide a vehicle for the forwarding and receiving of information through proper channels to the proper persons at the proper time.

Finally, the best communication system will be one which is developed and operated on a long-range basis. School-community communication is a long-range process and requires long-range planning. Current information provides the foundation for the future program. A consistently favorable image is not built in a day or a month or even a year; rather, it is the result of years of accurate, credible, and comprehensive reporting over two-way communication channels. The public secondary school is a long-range institution and its communication system must be geared to long-range objectives.

Agents of Communication

In the technical sense, the agents of communication may be defined as those who send and those who receive messages. In the practical sense, as applied to the school community, everyone of communicating age and ability is an agent of communication. In planning for school-community communication the principal should recognize the fact that almost all members of the population are communication agents. In the school such agents include the administrators and teachers, and—perhaps even more importantly—the pupils, the secretarial staff, and the maintenance workers. In any structure of communication that may be developed, each one of these school-associated persons should have a place. Too often the students and the nonacademic staff are overlooked. Whether we like it or not, every person involved with the school, whether employee or student, contributes somewhat to the image which the school presents to the community. In fact, the greatest number of contacts with the community in school-related situations is surely made by students. Their large number virtually assures that this is true. The student who enjoys his school work, profits from his study, participates in school decision-making, admires his teachers, respects his principal, and finds the school program a satisfying experience is perhaps the best communication agent a school can have. Likewise, teachers who enjoy their work, feel free to teach, are involved in the decision-making of the school, and have confidence in the administration are important contributors to communication and will reflect favorably on the school. On the other hand, students who dislike school, have no influence in decision-making, are subject to unreasonable rules and regulations, regard their course material as irrelevant, and are generally dissatisfied will communicate and reflect unfavorably on the school. The dissatisfied, disgruntled, and nonparticipating teacher can be a very destructive agent of communication. The careless secretary, hostile receptionist, and slovenly custodian all convey impressions of the school which may seriously affect its image in the community.

Outside the walls of the school there is an infinite number of communication agents to be found in the community. They may be divided into two classes: individuals, and organizations. The latter term includes agencies, business enterprises, industrial corporations, community power structures, and a variety of social groups, such as the family, the bridge club, and the Masons and other fraternal orders.

While the school may be of secondary concern to most individuals not directly associated with the school, it nevertheless has important meaning to most parents, taxpayers, and to all those who are interested in community development and improvement. As individuals they communicate their concerns, criticisms, and praise to other individuals and to those groups and organizations to which they belong.

Organizations, in many cases, concern themselves with the school program and often take formal positions on issues which directly or indirectly affect the school. Business enterprises and industrial companies may praise or blame the high school on the basis of the quality and competency of its graduates. They may compliment or complain about the high school program on the basis of its effectiveness in meeting educational needs which are important to them. A "re-teaching" program for employees forced out of their jobs by technological advances is a case in point. As taxpayers, organizations often take strong positions on proposed tax levies and bond issues. They communicate their opinions in no uncertain terms. They are effective communication agents and the wise principal will not overlook them. He will realize that organizations, although composed of individuals, are separate and abstract entities, pose different problems, and operate differently. Not infrequently organizations with strong leadership take positions on community issues with which a substantial minority or, in some cases, even an apathetic majority do not agree. Therefore it is necessary that the structure for communication take into consideration the nature of the organization and its potential as a favorable communication agent with respect to the secondary school.

Communication Media

Most high school communities have a varied array of communication media, and the mass media are, in most cases, available to the school if the school leadership takes the initiative in securing the necessary cooperation. The administrator who is willing to go more than half way to secure the cooperation of the media in establishing and maintaining a communication system will usually be well rewarded for his efforts. Most media executives will be found to be sympathetic with an honest effort to enlist their help in improving communication between school and community. They will welcome a well-planned program, if such is presented, and will freely explain the conditions, limitations, and adaptations which they may find necessary to impose on any plan presented. Usually a meeting of minds will result and a general set of guidelines will emerge which will be mutually acceptable and workable.

Sumption and Engstrom suggest the following general guidelines for selecting and utilizing the mass media to build an effective program of communication between school and community.

1. Identify and catalog all available media.
2. Develop long-range plans for the utilization of the most promising media.
3. Choose the medium or media best adapted to the time, the message, and the coverage desired.
4. As far as possible, develop a balanced usage of available media.
5. Establish and maintain a fair and equitable policy for news releases through the various media available.
6. If possible, make use of all available media over a period of time.
7. Utilize media in such a way as to involve a maximum number of people in the transmission of messages as long as it does not detract from the effectiveness of the message.
8. Other factors being equal, select the media which require the least time and effort to encode the message, since facility of preparation is important.
9. Encode the message to suit the medium to be used in order to achieve maximum effectiveness.
10. Maintain a close professional relationship with those in charge of community-based media, and respect requirements as to form, space, accuracy, and deadlines.
11. Accord public recognition to media and individuals who have made special contributions or rendered outstanding service to school-community communication.
12. Conduct periodic evaluations of the adequacy, appropriateness, and effectiveness of the media used.[1]

While mass media make it possible to reach the largest number of people in the shortest time, the use of direct contact media such as the telephone, personal correspondence, the grade report to parents, opinion surveys, and

---

[1] Merle R. Sumption and Yvonne Engstrom, *School Community Relations: A New Approach* (New York: McGraw-Hill Book Co., 1966), p. 146.

personal interviews should not be neglected. The advantages of direct contact include the opportunity to get specific and usually immediate reactions and the opportunity to build personal rapport between the school staff and the community it serves.

WHAT SHOULD THE SCHOOL COMMUNICATE?

The public secondary school as a public enterprise should seek to inform the community about its operation, its staff, its students, and its program. Likewise the community should know about its policies, plans, and problems, and, as indicated in the latter part of this chapter, it should participate in their formulation and solutions. Full disclosure is not only good policy, it is good public relations.

A few examples of the type of information which should reach the community via a systematic and coordinated communication structure follow.

1. The broad goals and objectives of the school as agreed upon.
2. The nature and breadth of the secondary program.
3. The extramural services of the school.
4. The number, classification, and activities of the student body.
5. The role of student organizations and student government in high school life.
6. The measurement of student program and attainment.
7. The nature, scope, and limitation of the student counseling and guidance programs.
8. The general policies with regard to use of school facilities after school hours by community organizations.
9. Cooperative programs with other educational agencies of the community.
10. The cost of the local educational operation and the means of financing it.

The community also needs to know about education in general, about education in the broader context of a national concern. The people of the community should know about the profession of education and its contribution to human welfare, its importance to the national economy, and its place in a democracy. The late President Lyndon B. Johnson, speaking of his quest for the Great Society, said "Poverty has many roots, but the tap root is ignorance." The people of the community need to know about the importance of education not only to the community but to the nation and to the world as well. In most communities the secondary school is the public agency best suited to convey this information to its clientele.

What kinds of general education information should be communicated? A descriptive list taken from Sumption and Engstrom's *School-Community Relation, A New Approach* is presented here.

1. *The essential nature of education in the preservation and progress of a democracy.* In a democracy people have a freedom of choice, but that freedom can be preserved only if people make enough right choices. Ignorance is a handicap in making right choices of governmental officials and on public issues. Democracy depends to a great extent on the common man, and his educational level is a crucial factor in his ability to make wise choices.

2. *The relationship between education and freedom.* The Bible states, "Ye shall know the truth and the truth shall make you free." That statement is as true today as it was two thousand years ago. It is the ignorant masses who live beneath the heel of the oppressor. In no country in the world is freedom so cherished and so enjoyed as in our own. It is hardly a coincidence that although our country has only about 6 percent of the world's population, it includes more than half of the high school graduates in the world.

3. *The concept of equal educational opportunity for all.* This is an ideal which is fundamental to the democratic way of life. It is not easy to achieve, yet it is important that people be reminded of it and the necessity of constantly striving for it. As educational demands grow and educational tax rates rise, it is essential that the school keep the ideal of equal educational opportunity before the people at all times.

4. *The social and economic values of education.* The social and economic values of education are, of course, immense. Educational expenditures are in a real sense an investment. In the technological age in which we live education is an investment we must make to ensure reasonable productivity and a minimum of unemployment. Adlai E. Stevenson, onetime United States Ambassador to the United Nations, said, "From the start of the Republic we in America have recognized that our strength as a nation, our wealth, our welfare, yes, our love of country all depend on what happens in our schools. Now in the middle of the twentieth century, in an increasingly crowded and complex world, we understand more urgently than ever how necessary it is to give our children the education they need to play an effective role in modern life."

5. *The concept of individual needs.* It is important that people understand the significance of individual differences and consequent individual educational needs. The school must make clear that the diversity of human abilities and interests requires a broad curriculum. The parents of a student bound for college must be made to realize that his neighbor's son who will not go beyond high school needs and deserves a different type of education.

6. *The trend in education.* If the educational process is to keep pace with changing times and conditions, it must innovate. Some innovations are not welcomed by the community, largely because of lack of information. It is the duty of the school to keep the community informed of educational trends and to explain why they developed and how they affect learning and teaching.[2]

THE PRINCIPAL AS THE FACILITATOR OF COMMUNICATION

The principal in his role of democratic leadership has much of the responsibility of seeing that effective communication between his school and the community is established and maintained. The nature and scope of his role will be determined to some extent by the policies of the system of which the high school is a part. However, systemwide policies, if they are well-founded, will serve as a base upon which an appropriate and effective communication structure may be developed and maintained. It follows, of course, that the greater the autonomy given to the high school, the greater is the freedom to develop a structure of communication which will be most responsive to the unique needs of the high school.

It is not the purpose of this book to suggest a specific type of communication structure, as different types of secondary schools, different personnel, and different communication indicate different structures. The structure adopted should be the one which seems to best fit the existing conditions. However, there are a number of general elements of which the principal should be aware and a number of principles of communication which should guide him in his efforts. While it is incumbent on the principal to assume leadership in achieving effective communication, and to be responsible (in cooperation with the head of the school system) to maintain such communication, he should keep in mind that the task will require the efforts of many people. As was pointed out earlier, communication agents are legion. The primary task is to provide the organizational structure in which those agents may function most constructively. The principal should assume the responsibility of initiating action leading to the development of such an organization—if none exists, as is the case in many schools. If one does exist he may find it necessary to revise it in the light of changing conditions or to adapt it more closely to emerging needs.

An effective communication structure will have a staff member, usually on a part-time basis, who is responsible for communication. He or she will serve as a coordinator of the communication system. This person may be called a public relations director, a school-community relations agent or simply a communications coordinator. It will be his job to administer the communications organization.

---

[2] From *School Community Relations: A New Approach,* by Merle R. Sumption and Yvonne Engstrom. Copyright 1966 by McGraw-Hill. Used with permission.

The organization will have its center of operations in the school but it will reach out into the community. The principal as a facilitator will work with the person designated for communication responsibility in developing the communications structure and securing the cooperation of staff, students and community.

The principal should provide assistance in securing the cooperation of the available media and in contacting community organizations saluting their cooperation. In short it is his responsibility to do whatever he can to insure that an efficient system is developed, provided with responsible leadership, and the full cooperation, as nearly as he can obtain it, of school personnel and community organizations and individuals.

Such a system will reduce conflicting publicity, duplication, and misunderstandings to a minimum. The two-way flow of information as described in earlier pages will be invaluable to the principal in his day to day administrative duties. It will provide the essential contacts, associations, and communication which are essential to effective and constructive participation by the lay community in the operation of the secondary school. It may, in some cases, open new vistas of community educational needs for the principal and extend his horizons with respect to the role of the school in meeting those needs.

COMMUNITY INVOLVEMENT

The concept of the school community as a democratic model, with the school as the central agency for education, is accompanied by the necessity for broad community involvement in the educational process. The high school is in a favored position with regard to the involvement of members of the community. It can offer a great deal to adult members of the community, not only through adult education programs, but also through the broader informal education activities which have been described in earlier chapters. It is in an excellent position to capitalize on the educational resources, both human and material, which the community has to offer. The preceding chapter delineated ways and means of utilizing these resources in the development of a broad and relevant secondary program.

The secondary school can be a vital force even in the lives of those senior citizens who have retired and no longer are interested in vocational education or other utilitarian programs. Adult classes in current events, modern literature, great books, and recreational skills will be attractive to them. One enterprising high school initiated what is known as the Golden Pass Plan. In this program, each citizen of the school community who reaches the age of sixty-five receives a pass to all high school functions. Thus the senior citizen is in effect the guest of the school for athletic contests, musical presentations, dramatic productions, and similar functions. The cost to the school is negligible since in most cases the senior guest occupies a seat which would not have been occupied by a paying guest. The good will generated by such a program will be reflected in the support of the school by these people who, in most cases, would otherwise have no direct connection with the school. The Golden Pass Plan is being adopted by a growing number of high schools where administrators recognize the desirability of serving the total community membership.

The school has much to gain from the involvement of the community, but to achieve these gains there must be skillful and dedicated leadership. That leadership must be knowledgeable about the appropriate ways, procedures, and techniques of involving the community in a constructive and productive fashion. Nothing will more quickly negate an attempt to secure involvement than a lack of skill in organizing and providing instrumentation for effective involvement. The typical interested citizen is willing to give time and effort if he or she feels that such time and effort is productive. Citizens do not, as a general rule, enjoy the passive role of listening to school personnel extolling the virtues of the school buildings, the equipment, the staff, and the program, and expressing the need for more tax money. Successful involvement is characterized by inquiry, study, discussion, and action on the part of the citizens. The professional educator makes his contribution by providing the mechanism through which the citizens can work effectively and by serving as a resource person for lay citizens.

DEVELOPMENT OF EDUCATIONAL GOALS

The principal, above all others, should recognize the need for the establishment of accepted goals for the high school. The practice of having a teachers committee draw up a philosophy of the school and file it for future reference will not suffice. The school must join with the community in developing mutually acceptable goals for the secondary school. This task serves quite well as an introductory phase of community involvement or as a reorientation process where involvement has become more or less mechanical or ineffective.

Perhaps at no other time in our history has public education been so closely examined as to its purposes and effectiveness. Historically, "home rule" has largely determined policy and direction for the local educational system; however, home rule, which was designed to reflect the general consensus of the citizenry, has too often abrogated its responsibility to local boards of education and school administrators. If schools belong to the people, then citizens have the inherent responsibility to join with the school in determining the purposes and goals of the educational institution which they support.

No social institution can expect intelligent support from a constituency that does not understand the function and purpose of that institution. Too many citizens' purposes and goals for public schools are vague, intangible, or even undetermined, and subsequent support is reduced to the degree that such support is legally mandatory or socially required.

Predetermined goals give direction to the educational program. When those who learn and those who teach and all those who support the school have a common understanding of the goals of the school, then leadership has a real sense of purpose. A feeling of security from unjust criticism emanating from misunderstanding, coupled with a sense of purpose and direction, creates a climate for capable leadership.

In most instances, causes of misunderstanding and conflict between the lay public and the professional staff can be substantially reduced when areas of responsibility are defined. As previously stated, the total citizenry should determine educational goals and should elect a representative board of education to enact policy to attain such goals. Professional educators should organize and execute an educational program commensurate with such policy.

The desire for accountability is becoming more pronounced as time passes. It is logical that the schools be held accountable; but it is imperative that it be known for what they are being held accountable. If the school community can arrive at a set of commonly accepted goals, it has a valid basis on which to seek accountability. Without such a basis there can be no realistic accountability.

An example of a tentative list which was developed through cooperative effort of lay and professional citizens is presented here.

GOALS FOR THE ELGIN, ILLINOIS, SCHOOL SYSTEM

Self-Realization

The purpose of the school is:

To encourage and assist in the development of a desire for knowledge and self-improvement;

To develop appreciation and respect for thought and knowledge;

To inspire respect for intellectual freedom and creative thought;

To develop the basic skills of reading, writing, mathematics, and speech as aids to the acquiring of knowledge for the purpose of self-expression and communication;

To develop individual initiative, good study habits, the ability to think clearly and reason objectively; to recognize honest differences of opinion; and to develop a sense of judgment and confidence in one's own abilities;

To develop the basic elements of character, such as integrity, truthfulness, kindliness, courage, tolerance, and gratitude;

To teach students to recognize and appreciate the physical self, its requirements, its protection against disease and accident, its limitations, and its constant dependence upon the good health of others; to recognize and learn to live with one's own mental and

physical limitations so that a failure of effort will not result in mental or physical distress sufficient to harm or retard good mental or physical well-being;
To help students to understand basic scientific facts concerning the nature of the universe and of men, the methods of science, and the gathering of scientific information; to recognize the importance of these facts and their influence upon human progress; to develop an interest in the promotion of science for the betterment of all;
To encourage and aid the development of purely personal interests which afford mental and physical satisfaction such as an appreciation of the arts, the intelligent use of one's own leisure time, and the enjoyment of, and participation in, sports and hobbies.
To teach a recognition of, and an ability to adapt to, ever-changing economic, social, political, and scientific conditions and patterns.

Economic Evaluation and Realization

The purpose of the school is:

To furnish guidance and information so as to assist individuals in the selection of a suitable and desirable occupation;
To develop natural aptitudes and abilities along particular lines of economic endeavor;
To provide all educational prerequisites necessary for educational experience;
To furnish certain basic courses in trades and commercial subjects;
To help students learn basic economic theories and principles and to recognize the interrelation of all economic endeavor;
To help students appreciate the economic importance of, and recognize the need for, conservation of our natural resources, including wildlife;
To develop consideration of one's personal economic demands, requirements, and limitations, the need for economic planning, and the acquisition of good saving, buying, and spending habits.

Political Integration

The purpose of the school is:

To teach respect for the laws and a general knowledge of how they are made and enforced;
To impart an understanding of the basic principles underlying the developments of the American system of government and the basic rights and privileges guaranteed by our Constitution;
To impart a general knowledge of the Constitution of the United States, the Constitution of the State of Illinois, the doctrine of separation of powers, the Australian ballot system, and the important documents in our history;
To develop a clear understanding of the history of the United States, the reasons for its growth, and its position in the community of the world;
To impart a knowledge of various types of government and an ability to compare and evaluate their principal characteristics;
To develop a loyalty to, and appreciation for, democratic ideals and a

determination to protect them, preserve them, and assume personal responsibility for them.

Social Attitudes

The purpose of the school is:

To develop a thoughtful consideration for the welfare of all members of a society; to recognize the equality of all people, the equality of rights and duties of all members of the community, and the right to benefit commensurate with one's contribution, whether individual initiative, capital, skill, or labor;

To develop a charitable attitude and a sense of obligation to aid in the correction of social inequalities and relieve human misery and want;

To develop personality for a full social life, the friendship of others, and the ability to cooperate with others at work and at play;

To help students learn and respect the rules of social behavior and common courtesy;

To develop a recognition of the family as a vitally necessary social institution, and to prepare the student to be a contributor to its welfare and to accept its responsibilities.

In summary, the establishment of the goals of the school is the responsibility of all the people. The professional staff can and should give effective leadership in their development, and the board of education, as legal representatives of the people, should facilitate their implementation. The goals of education, if they are to be realistic, meaningful, and effective, must arise out of a consensus and be recognized by the public.

PLANNING AND POLICY-MAKING

Every responsible enterprise, whether public or private, must plan for the future. The secondary school is no exception. Among those things which should be planned for are future enrollments, whether increasing or decreasing, plant development, equipment for laboratories and shops, extracurricular activities, informal community education, future instructional programs, and financing of all these activities. Members of the community at large as well as school staff and students should participate in such planning. Each group has much to contribute to the planning process. Furthermore, plans developed by the total community are more likely to be brought to fruition than those made independent of broad community involvement.

The secondary school will, of course, operate in accordance with the general policies established by the board of education. In addition, each secondary school will have policies for its own operation which are not inconsistent with general school system policies. Again, community involvement, both at the system and school level, will yield more satisfactory policies if the community is brought into the development process. Recognizing that the board of education has the responsibility to enact school policies, it is equally true that the board can profit by the enlistment of community opinion. Likewise, the secondary school will profit by seeking advice and counsel from the community in the formulation of its own policies and regulations. Some examples of policies in which the input of the community will be found most helpful include policies for community use of school facilities after school hours, policies with regard to transportation of students and others to away-from-home athletic contests and similar activities, and policies with respect to reporting student achievement to parents.

In both the area of planning and that of policy-making, the administration must exert professional leadership in organizing for effective community participation. Obviously some form of representation must be established, and such representation must make it possible for every citizen of the community to consider the issues and have the opportunity to express an opinion. Furthermore, the relevant facts should be made available so that citizen opinion will be based on fact rather than custom or prejudice.

The preceding chapter presents a brief description of one effective method of citizen involvement. There are many variations, but the general principle of responsible participation through a representative committee is common to almost all of them and is consistent with the concept of a representative democracy. The principal must be familiar with the total process of community involvement and should exert leadership in initiating, organizing, and maintaining such involvement so that citizens may make their contribution to the successful operation of the school.

EVALUATION

How well is the school performing its job? This is a question of paramount importance not only to the students and the staff, but also to the school community. The taxpayers are stressing the necessity of an accounting by the school. They want to know whether or not their money is being spent effectively in achieving the purposes for which it is appropriated. They believe that a public enterprise should be held accountable by taxpayers in much the same way that a corporation is held accountable by its shareholders.

The principal and his staff are, of course, cognizant of the importance of evaluating the program of the school and of making some assessment of the vocational and college success of the school's graduates. Since the community shares this interest, why not ask citizens to join with the school in making a periodic evaluation? There seems to be no good reason for not doing so. The argument that evaluation of the educational process is a task for professional educators only is hardly persuasive when we realize the people of a community have a very direct knowledge of educational needs, of the success or failure of graduates, and of the impact of the school on community life. Furthermore, the involvement of lay citizens lends greater credence to the evaluation, and thus encourages broader acceptance in the community.

Of course, shared evaluation requires knowledgeable leadership on the part of the administration. Not only must an organization of educators, students, and lay citizens be set up, but an assignment of tasks which will ensure the most effective contribution by each category of participants must be made. Obviously, each category has a vantage point from which it views the educational process. Each has certain unique knowledge about the work of the school. It is the task of the administrator to provide the ways and means through which the contributions of each category may be translated, transmitted and assimilated in the total evaluation. While this is no easy task, it will prove to be a rewarding one if performed with skill and enthusiasm.

Joint or shared evaluation may take the form of an overall survey which encompasses the entire responsibility of the school or it may be directed toward one or more aspects of the school program. In the former case a rather large and varied group of evaluators will necessarily be involved. On the other hand, if only one segment of the program is to be evaluated, the required personnel will be considerably fewer in number. For example, the evaluation of the business education program might be undertaken by two students in the program, two business education teachers, an administrative staff member, and three or four businessmen or women of the community (at least one of whom is a graduate of the high school). In some cases, an outside expert from a university or educational organization may be brought in as a member of the evaluation team.

Regardless of the type or scope of the evaluation, the responsibility for it rests squarely on the shoulders of the principal. He must have the cooperation of his superintendent and the board of education, as well as that of students, teachers, and community, and it is up to him to secure that cooperation and use it effectively to achieve an evaluation that is satisfactory not only to school personnel, but to the school community as a whole.

THE PRINCIPAL AND THE POWER STRUCTURE

Every type of community, including the school community, possesses a structure of power. Such a structure is essential to decision-making and is not at all inconsistent with the democratic form of government. Unlike the oligarchy, the democratic model presupposes a power structure representative of the people, responsive to the people, and exercising power for the benefit of all the people. However, history presents a patchwork story of power subverted and corrupted by selfish interests which assume no social responsibility for their acts. Democratic government at all levels is subject to almost continuous attack. Public officials are corrupted and the very processes of democracy are subverted by those whose sole concern is the accomplishment of personal ends without regard to the effects of their acts upon society.

For purposes of identification we will use the term "informal power structure" to designate a structure which is an interrelationship of vested interests exercising power without social responsibility. This is in contrast to the formal power structure which has a legitimacy growing out of the fact that it exercises only power given it by the people and is responsible to the people. In some cases—fortunately not in any substantial number of cases—the informal power structure permeates the legitimate structure to the extent that it is difficult to make a clear-cut distinction between the two. It is characteristic of the informal structure, which secretly operates to either infiltrate the legitimate power structure or to control those who are members of that structure or both.

The typical administrator has a general idea of how to work with the formal power structure of the community and can easily obtain information about it. On the other hand, he knows little about the informal power structure and its potential influence on his leadership in the community. Fortunately, sociologists, political scientists, and educators have been doing research and publishing some materials on the nature of the informal power structure and how it affects community decision-making. The secondary school principal would do well to study the literature in this field and to seek to understand and appreciate the power which this behind-the-scenes structure can exert. He should be able to identify in broad outlines at least the identify power figures. Kimborough, Dahl, Lynd, Hunter, and others have must recognize that in attempting to involve the community in the various activities described in this and the preceding chapter he is very likely to encounter the influence of the informal power structure of the community. His ability to deal with this group without sacrificing his personal integrity or that of the school will frequently determine his success not only with respect to community involvement, but as an educational leader in the community.

The identification of an informal power structure is not an easy task and will be doubly difficult for an administrator who is new to the community. However, it can and must be done if the administrator is to exercise effective leadership over a period of time. The scope and influence of informal structures vary greatly from one community to another. In some communities, their power and influence may be negligible, yielding to the formal power structure. Unfortunately, some communities are ruled almost despotically by informal power structures which completely overshadow the legitimate structure and may even use it as a front for their own activities. In such cases, the duly elected representatives of the people resemble puppets who mechanically respond to those who control them. The vast majority of American communities fall some place between these two extremes.

In seeking to identify the informal power structure, the administrator may find it helpful to first examine the legitimate structure. Do those elected act independently? Do their decisions appear to be in the best interests of the community? Is decision-making solely a function of institutional government? Are decisions made openly in meetings of formal agencies, boards, and legislative bodies which are open to the public? If at any point the concept of formal institutionalized exercise of power breaks down, that is the place to begin a careful scrutiny behind the scenes. Why does it break down? How is it broken? Who benefits? The answers to these questions may lead to the identification of some power figures and eventually to an understanding of the outlines of a structure. The testing over a period of proponents of successful issues and opponents of unsuccessful ones may yield some insights as to who wields power. Sociologists have used the reputational technique to identify power figures. Kimborough, Dahl, Lynd, Hunter, and others have suggested means of identification which have been used with varying degrees of success. However it must be kept in mind that the identification of the key figures in an informal structure is only part of the task. It is essential also to discover the source of their power and the nature of the relationship existing among them—in other words, what holds the structure together and keeps it operative. The sources of power are usually wealth, the ability to confer favors (political or otherwise), the capability of providing opportunities to make money, the ability to confer social, political, or vocational advancement, and the capacity to inflict punishment on those who refuse to cooperate. The types of such punishment are many and varied, ranging from the denial of financial credit to mental and physical harrassment, and, when the criminal element is involved, even persecution.

Although the school administrator will seldom if ever find himself in a situation which might cause him to fear for his life, mental and physical harassment are certainly not unknown to administrators who incur the displeasure of the structure. In any event, for his own protection and for the protection of the school he represents, he should be aware of the possible forces which may be brought to bear upon him, not only in his direct relationship with the community, but also in the performance of his regular administrative duties in connection with the internal operation of the school.

Once the informal power structure is identified, at least in broad outline, and when its mode of operation is recognized, the administrator has a knowledgeable basis on which to deal with it. He will find that it is not consistently perverse, as many of its goals are consistent with the development and progress of the community and the school system which serves it. On the other hand, it may promote projects which will adversely affect both school and community or which may oppose and attempt to sabotage constructive programs which conflict with its interests. It may seek to "use" individuals who by virtue of their position have some legitimate influence in decision-making.

In order to deal effectively with these situations, the administrator must maintain his independence and must never become obligated to the informal power structure. Once he obligates himself he loses the freedom of action which is so necessary if he is to fulfill his commitment to his school and his profession. As an educational leader he is responsible to all the people of the community. He cannot favor any group, no matter how powerful, at the expense of the people he serves and still maintain his moral and professional integrity.

He must insist on a policy of full disclosure in his school. Secrecy, concealment, intrigue, shady deals, half-truths, and deceptions of any kind have no place in the administration of the school. In dealing with the informal power structure, there is no better strategic position than that which comes with free, complete, and uncompromising publicity. Those who would use the school or its program to advance selfish ends do not want people to know about it. When the school has a policy of full disclosure it does not provide fertile ground for those who would secretly use the school for selfish ends. The administrator is fully justified in insisting on full disclosure, as the school is a public enterprise, supported by the public and responsible to the people. The people are entitled to know all the facts all the time. The only exceptions are in the area of staff and student personnel and the purchase of school sites.

While the school administrator, like the politician, must effect compromises, he himself must never be compromised. In the give-and-take nature of his relations with the community the principal will of necessity make compromises. However he will never compromise truth, the rights of individuals, justice, fair play, the rule of law and the equality of all under the law. These elements of the democratic society are not subject to compromise. If he keeps this in mind the administrator will avoid many situations which might involve him in serious difficulties with the community.

He must judge each issue which faces him on its merits. He must never promote an issue or acquiesce to a plea simply because some power figure wants him to do so. He must think for himself and weigh the issue in terms of its effect on the school and the community. He should never allow himself to become aligned with any group or organization which is self-serving at the expense of those he is committed to serve. Ideally he should conduct himself in such a way that he will gain a reputation for fairness, impartiality, and truthfulness in all his dealings with community groups.

Bibliography

Cunningham, Luvern. *Governing Schools: New Approaches to Old Issues.* Columbus, Ohio: Charles E. Merrill, 1971.

Dahl, Robert. *Who Governs?* New Haven, Connecticut: Yale University Press, 1961.

Hunter, Floyd. *Community Power Structure*. Chapel Hill, North Carolina: University of North Carolina Press, 1953.

Jackson, R. B. "Schools and Communities: A Necessary Relevance." *Clearing House* 44 (April 1970), pp. 488-90.

Kimbrough, Ralph B. *Political Power and Educational Decision Making*. Chicago: Rand McNally, 1964.

Lurie, Ellen. *How to Change the Schools*. New York: Random House, 1970.

Meranto, Phillip. *School Politics in the Metropolis*. Columbus, Ohio: Charles E. Merrill, 1970.

Norton, M. Scott. "School-Community Relations: New Issues, New Needs." *Clearing House* 44 (May 1970), p. 538.

Selakovich, Dan. *The Schools and American Society*. Waltham, Massachusetts: Ginn and Company, 1967.

Summerfield, H. L. *The Neighborhood-based Politices of Education*. Columbus, Ohio: Charles E. Merrill, 1971.

Sumption, Merle R. *How to Conduct a Citizens School Survey*. New York: Prentice-Hall, 1952.

Selected Readings

Community Relations

J. Lloyd Trump

The position of the secondary school of the future in its community will be on a sounder basis than it is today. The school today creates community understanding through the P.T.A., citizens' advisory councils, newspaper-radio-television publicity, and personal contacts of its students and teachers. These means of communication will be augmented by the fact that the future school's program will take place in the community rather than being limited to a somewhat isolated school building.

Large numbers of adults will be used as part-time instructors and teaching assistants. Community resources will be utilized more frequently by students. Moreover, education will be a continuous process as graduation becomes less important because of adult education programs and closer integration of secondary school and college or employment. Some students in the upper years of the secondary school will gradually spend less time in formal classes and more time at jobs, until the major part of their time will be spent as workers. After they begin full-time employment, many will continue as students in adult education classes. This does not imply any lowering of standards on the part of organized secondary education, but actually quite the opposite. Professional teachers and counselors will help students decide whether they will benefit most from full-time study in secondary school or college, from full-time employment, or from some division of their time between study and work.

This integration of school and community will bring about a new type of school-community relations. It will be difficult to tell where the school ends and the community begins because the two will be so completely interwoven. When the community thus plays an integral part in the education program, there will be better understanding of what teachers do, what is expected of students, and what it costs to provide an education program that will produce superior results.

From *Images of the Future,* by J. Lloyd Trump, p. 35. Copyright NASSP. Reprinted by permission.

America's Social Imperative

Ernest O. Melby

Rather slowly, but surely, even we educators have been forced to reach the conclusion that our present educational system is a stark failure with the poor, with the inner city, and with the black people and other minority groups. An even darker cloud is on the horizon, and that is the growing realization that in large measure the whole system is obsolete. We have been so enthralled by our problems with the disadvantaged that we have failed to see our larger failure with all children and all people. It is of course urgent that we be concerned with our inner cities and about race prejudice. But we are beginning to ask other questions. Why is it, that in the most schooled nation in history, our white affluent people tolerate slums? Why is it that we white people generally fail to see what it means to be black in America? Why do many of us steadfastly refuse to give equality and full citizenship to our minority groups? Why have we so little perception of injustice? Why have we so little compassion?

Had our education given our white people (that is the middle-class white) compassion, had this education given our affluent people a sense of oneness with their fellow men and a feeling of responsibility for their welfare, we would long ago have done something about the problems that now give us a crisis for which we have no sure solution. The fact is our failure with the white middle class is more basic than our failure with the poor, though the reality is that, faced with the society we now have, our total educational system from first grade to graduate school is obsolete.

There can be no doubt of the seriousness of the present social crisis. We are in the beginnings of a revolution. Our black citizens will no longer tolerate second-class citizenship, slum living, inferior education, unemployment, unemployability, and general alienation. They have sought integration, only to

---

Reprinted from *The Role of the School in Community Education,* edited by Howard Hickey et al. Copyright 1969 by Pendell Publishers. Used with permission.

be rebuffed so badly that many of them now have given up on us and seek instead to develop a separate black society. To discuss the implications of separatism would take all the time at our disposal. Suffice it to say here that we want one America and not two. The human horrors of apartheid would ruin the American Dream forever. Widespread violence with hard-line "law and order" police work without more justice can only lead finally to a police state, in which case the American Dream goes down the drain.

We just cannot and must not give up the American Dream. For me and, I am sure, for you, human brotherhood has been and must continue to be our basic national aspiration. This leaves us with no alternative but to develop an educational system which will truly prepare all our citizens to build and live in an integrated society, in what Senator Edward Brooke calls "a magnificent pluralism."

We are, by history and usual national mood, an optimistic profession. No group in our society has been more dedicated to the American Dream than the teachers. We have not only believed in the ultimate triumph of freedom and democracy, we have tried to convince the American people that regardless of the problems we face, education holds the solutions. This has been true from Jefferson through Horace Mann to John Dewey to John Gardner. Especially we have held that education is the escalator that moves people from lower-class poverty and misery to middle-class affluence and comfort. Now within the short space of a decade we discover that the escalator has stopped running for great masses of the poor. It has been extremely difficult for us as educators to face this reality. We just cannot, or perhaps will not, face our stark failure with the poor in our large cities and in the remote rural areas, for here we not only fail to provide cognitive learning, but we damage the children to the point where their rehabilitation is difficult, if not impossible. We have known about this failure now for years, but generally speaking we have done very little about it. In fact sociologists, politicians, and lay civic leaders are way ahead of us in social perception as well as action. It is this slowness to perceive and to act which disappoints me the most when I look at my profession.

To be sure, it is not only our schools that fail in the city. Government, police, sanitation, and health do not fare much better. The problems confronting education are exacerbated by all these failures, yet the school's failure is central. It is central because without education people can no longer get jobs, or at least jobs that provide a decent standard of living. No longer can schools assume that their failures will get lost in unskilled jobs. These jobs are getting fewer and fewer. Somehow we must now comprehend the fact that in our kind of society every individual must be educated. We can no longer tolerate educational failure. It has become too costly in money, social injustice, and unrest.

I want to come back, however, to an earlier statement to the effect that it is our total educational establishment that is at fault. It proceeds on assumptions that sooner or later defeat both children and their teachers. The first assumption is that the child's cognitive learning is more important than the child; second, that this learning must take place on schedule; third, that all first graders must read no matter what the effort to teach them does to their personalities, to their self-concepts; and fourth, that acquiring cognitive learning on schedule is so all-important that we make a desperate attempt to achieve it even if, in the words of Jonathan Kozol, it means "death at an early age." What we need is an educational program in which the child as a person is more important than his day-to-day cognitive learning—a school, a home, and a community which in close coordination help the child to respect himself more each passing day.

Another assumption is that we can do it all in the school. It is appalling, even frightening, to witness the efforts of the teaching profession—administrators and teachers alike—to avoid the parents and the community. Even community schools provide rich programs for the adults at our school buildings but often do little to improve the homes or the community and especially to help the people of the community to help themselves. Were we to do the latter we would have to take our chances on what the people would do and we fear we might not like their ideas. The struggles in New York City over decentralization bear out the point being made here.

Even though we have found remedial work with inner-city children very difficult, we have learned a great deal in trying; in fact I believe our work in the inner-city has been a veritable mirror in which we can see not only our failures, but in some measure our greatest needs. No one can work with disadvantaged children without getting a dramatic proof of the influence of the child's total environment on his growth and development. Here we learn that middle-class children succeed academically in all kinds of schools, good and poor: that the children of the poor need not only especially good schools, but an improvement of their total lives. Here the community school is a must if children are to have any real chance to become employable and full members of our society.

I am often asked, "Is the community school necessary in a prosperous community?" My answer is that in such communities our present schools are giving most children academic success, college entrance, and middle-class status. But we are not giving these people a sense of social responsibility and compassion, nor will we ever—unless we get out of the schoolhouse, unless we bring people together around great ideas, unless we give children and their parents a chance to meet and work with people of other races and economic position, unless the people and their children have a chance to act and give of themselves in the improvement of life for others.

I have spent most of my effort in recent years trying to improve the education of the disadvantaged. It has begun to dawn on me lately that even our grandchildren will have to do the same thing unless we change the education of the advantaged, the affluent, the white middle class in such a way that they will not tolerate poverty, slums, and racial injustice. I have decided to place my efforts on bringing about changes in the white community. This does not mean we don't do everything we can to improve ghetto education—it does mean we work to get rid of the ghetto.

A great part of our work with the disadvantaged in the last decade has been remedial and/or compensatory. Having been close to people who work at such education, I know how hard and discouraging it is. Even more discouraging is the fact that the number and proportion of children who need such remedial education is not being reduced from year to year, but often increases. Our present school system is a machine for producing potential dropouts who must somehow be salvaged. While the salvage operation for this year's remedial group goes on, the teachers in the system are preparing another batch for each of the years to come. This situation is intolerable. It is expensive in money and destructive of human beings.

I come more and more to the conclusion that we do not really have an educational system. We have a scholastic establishment. It is the establishment that has first priority: our graded school with standards for each grade, not for each child; our marking system; our notion that school is a kind of cafeteria where we set out the same educational food for all children and that this gives them all the same chance—it is this establishment mindedness that defeats the children of the poor and leaves the children of the rich with no great sense of responsibility for others.

We had better get a true educational system and get it in a hurry, before it is too late. Make no mistake about it, people will not tolerate much longer the human waste and destruction our present establishment produces. If we in public education do not come up with an education for the poor soon, the federal government will be forced to set up a special system for the poor. Can you think of a better way to produce a class society than to have two separate systems—one for the poor and one for the middle class?

No, I do not believe we are going to permit America to become a rigid class society. We are not going to have two Americas, one white and the other black, nor are we going to have a police state in which violent revolution by the poor is held in check by armed force. We are going to be one society with freedom and equal opportunity for black and white. We are going to replace the obsolete scholastic establishment of the past with a true educational system, a system which maintains only schools that are for all, young and old—true community schools. We can call this system the education-centered community—a community which makes education for all the focus of its life.

We can visualize this new system beginning with the four-year-olds as a part of an ungraded school. We will have no grades and no destructive marking system. Each child will be studied. So will his community and his home life. We will work with his parents. With us they will constitute a team which thinks first of the child's welfare, not of the school or of a subject. Cognitive learning will be seen as important, but the child's self-concept will be considered more important. Constant effort will be made to send each child home every day liking himself better than when he came in the morning. Parents, students preparing to teach, and especially employed paraprofessionals will provide much individual attention and relieve teachers of many duties so the teacher can spend more time in studying and counseling each child.

Teacher-pupil ratios will vary with the kind of community and the previous experience of the children. The ablest teachers will work with the children presenting the greatest learning difficulties. Such a teacher assignment, for example to an inner-city school, will be viewed as a special recognition of one's skill and professional competence.

Cities and urban areas will be redistricted on something like the park plan permitting the poor to go to school with the rich, as was the case in the little towns and still is true there to some extent.

The administration of our city school districts will be decentralized. The really important educational decisions will be made by teachers and principals. Budgets for schools and districts will take account of the problems to be met in each school and with each group of children, the largest allocations going to inner-city and perhaps remote rural areas. When this is done, no heavy-handed bureaucracy will hang over the teacher and the child. When decisions are made as to what can be done, the teacher will answer most questions herself and any she can't decide can be decided by the principal of the building without waiting for a slow-moving bureaucracy.

In these schools the evening program will be part and parcel of the daytime program. There will be no cold war between the two. The same attitudes toward children—toward human beings generally—will be exhibited regardless of time of day. The community school director will be an assistant principal. There will be one or more home counselors who will maintain constant communication between the parents and the principal and the teachers.

Finally what we have visualized for the community school thus far will have only partial meaning unless we have the right teacher attitudes and behaviors. Here we need changes in teacher education. Our present teacher education is even more obsolete than our educational system itself. Present teacher education assumes that the teacher's knowledge is the prime factor in his success. We know this is not true. Teachers succeed more in terms of what they are than in terms of what they know. The teacher's attitude toward himself and toward other people conditions his behavior. Knowledge can be acquired on a college campus but the process of becoming is another challenge. We would do better to have prospective teachers spend half of their four or five years of preparation actually at work with children in a community.

If the new community education is to become a reality, teacher education must deal more fully with the problems of the urban community, with racial backgrounds, with poverty, its causes and cultural impacts. We have too many teachers who are brittle, middle-class oriented, unable to understand the poor or the children of the poor. It is a paradox, yet it is a fact that the school which should be the door to opportunity for the child from the poor home, is too often the agency that delivers the final blow to the child's self-image. It is in the school that this child learns he cannot learn and thus gets what he believes is final proof that he does not belong in our affluent society, that he isn't wanted.

When we work with disadvantaged children we need a creative teacher with a high estimate of human potential of the worth of each child. Such a teacher respects each child regardless of the circumstances from which he comes. The great teacher has faith in every child. He is humble enough to learn with the child. He knows he cannot teach those whom he does not love. Consequently he truly cares about each child as a person. He sees every child not only as he is today but in terms of what he has the potentiality of becoming.

The teacher we have just described is a symbol of the spirit of the true community school. Its cornerstone is faith in people, all of the people—rich and poor, black and white. The true community school has no colonial attitude; it sees itself as an agency whereby the people themselves in large part through their own efforts create the favorable environment for human growth. It does not consider itself the repository of all teaching talent or as the only real educational agency in the community. It seeks to mobilize all the people for education, and mobilizing the people for education means building a good community because it is the community as a whole that educates. Before we can have effective education we must first build a good community.

The community school is a social imperative because only this kind of school can help the white middle class to the compassion and social responsibility which will bring an end to the poverty and the alienation of the ghetto. It is a social imperative because only this kind of school gives the poor child a door to education and opportunity. It is a social imperative because without the education it provides, America cannot heal the divisions which now threaten her life as a free society. For us in education it is an imperative because it is the only way we can make good on the promise we have held before the American people for a century, namely, that through education mankind can become the master of its own destiny.

Toward a Dynamic Administration

Ernest O. Melby

In American education we have the most elaborate machinery for administration in the world. No other country has such a big investment in administration or expects so much from administration. In quantitative terms administration has delivered handsomely. When it comes to extending the years of education and expanding educational facilities our administrative structure has done well. When, however, one turns to quality we have another story. The children of the poor were in trouble in school 50 years ago—they are still in trouble. Moreover, the administrators themselves are in trouble. No experienced observer of educational administration in the current scene can fail to note the trauma through which both the administrators and their organizational personnel are passing. Short tenures, precipitate firings, heart attacks, ulcers, and resignations because of discouragement, are reported from all sections of the nation. It is, of course, easy to blame the administrators themselves for this situation. Postmortems are frequently held during which the critics point out the errors committed and/or the weaknesses in personality in each case. In all this there is great injustice, over-simplification and faulty diagnosis. I believe an historical review will show that a great part of the administrator's problem comes, not so much from his own deficiencies as from a faulty theory, system and practice. As long as educators continue to blame the superintendents and the boards of education, as well as community people, there will be no significant change in the theory and practice of administration and the scrap heap of administrators who seem to have been found wanting will grow larger.

More important, however, than the educational administrator's own problems is the growing feeling that the educational enterprise itself lacks dyna-

---

"Toward a Dynamic Administration" is excerpted from an address given by Dr. Ernest O. Melby to Mott internes. Reprinted from Ernest O. Melby and Clyde Campbell *The Community School and its Administration,* Vol. 10 (November, 1971). Used with permission.

mism and that it has little internal capacity for change. The slowness with which educational change takes place has been noted by many an observer over several decades. Someone has said that it takes 50 years for a new idea to find its way into practice in our schools. This may be an exaggeration, but one cannot deny that the educational profession is supercautious, that much of what we now do in schools is obsolete and highly ineffective, so ineffective that millions of children fail to get the education they need to function in our society with benefit to society and adequate reward to themselves. This situation is now so widely known that no documentation is needed at this point.

This failure with the poor becomes all the more disturbing and baffling when we take account of the elaborate machinery for supervision and administration that has grown up in the last half century. No other country in the world has invested so heavily in administration, evidently on the assumption that this structure would exert a lifting force on our education, that expert supervision would compensate for the teachers' shortcomings. Surely the data about the effectiveness of our schools with the disadvantaged do little to support the view that the big investment in middle management has brought a satisfactory return.

When one turns to the literature on educational administration one finds plenty of diagrams and theory but little analysis of the nature of the educational enterprise. The administrative systems are described without reference to any assumptions about what is meant by education, to any learning theory, or to any goals of the educational system. There seems to be an assumption that there are several kinds of administration but we are not told what each of these kinds of administration are supposed to administer. Rarely, if ever, have we in the field of education based a theory of administration on the nature of learning, on the climate required for learning and growth, on the nature and role of the community. We study administration but we do not study education to see what kind of administration we need. What results is the present plight of administrators, the plethora of studies, models, theories, arguments, most of which assume that the way one sees the educational process has nothing to do with whatever theory of administration we follow.

As an example let us look at children, teachers and parents—people of the community all trying to learn. What support, stimulus, control, intervention do they need? They need places to work, materials and equipment, opportunities to work together. Most of all they need freedom to use their imagination, to tap the available resources, to be free from fear.

Unfortunately, current research in administration is of little help. Studying different theories does little good when no effort has been made to see what the educational enterprise needs. The books on administration are of little value except as history. They delineate administrative theories and practices, nearly all of which are failing because on the one hand they do not fit education, and on the other they are out of tune with community needs.

This is an opportune time in the history of education to build a new theory of administration. The inner city has us baffled. Racial problems continue to challenge us. The old psychology is passing out of existence.

Community education, now spreading rapidly, can hardly be provided by the old bureaucratic organization. Parents want to be involved and must be if we are to educate all. Teachers and community school directors must have more freedom of action. They cannot function effectively if they are subject to rigid controls from some district office. Educational programs must fit particular communities.

It is time we began to see that it is the structure itself and the theory on which it is based that is out of gear with the educational enterprise. We should stop wasting our time in an effort to improve the functioning of a badly adopted organization and put our efforts on studying the learning setting and building a new theory in terms on this study.

Why have we not developed a theory in this way before? Our reason is that to do so required us to leave the campus, and work largely as learners with teachers, children and the people of the community. We feel secure on campus—insecure with the masses.

We in the university have rarely faced the realities of an educational system, the complexity of a large city, the problems of learning, in building our theories. Too often we begin with administrative theory often developed in industry and see how we can modify this to meet the problems of education. The result has been a structure of great complexity with much power to control but little power to liberate, much power to manage, but little to stimulate, great inertia against change but little power to effect change. The obsolescence of existing education bears eloquent testimony to the need for a new theory and a more creative and dynamic practice.

In this presentation I am not arguing for a specific organization. My conviction is that the classical organization with its assumptions and its practices has become an obstacle to the changes we desperately need in American education. If we are ever to have the education we need, administration must create the climate for change. We are not likely to develop this kind of administration by simply trying to improve our practice of the present theory. We must, instead, study the needs of learning groups of people and set out to supply those needs. We need experimentation and out of it we'll find a way of putting dynamism into education and its administration.

Community Education and its Organization

Clyde M. Campbell

As Dr. Melby and Dr. Moore have so succinctly pointed out, what is learned in classrooms often contradicts what is learned in communities, causing young people to lose the good that could be won from joint motivation, joint guidance, and joint teaching efforts. To be sure, when men and women step in perfect unison toward the same destination a kind of unitive power inescapably follows. Ideas expressed by laymen may stir young people immeasurably, give a lift to their hearts, and move them into action immediately far more than when the same ideas are presented by teachers from a lofty academic tower. Yes, laymen and professionals conversing together, thinking together, performing together, has an aura about it of bible class worthiness. Citizens and teachers learn from each other. Conceivably their mutual strivings toward a common goal may be much more fruitful than the aggregate of their contributions made separately. Beyond doubt, the philosopher's statement that the whole can be more than the sum of its parts is applicable in this instance. Yes, all this and more too. The efforts of laymen and professionals should be commingled for many reasons, one reason perhaps more important than all others. Decisions made daily in schools and in communities influence significantly the life patterns of children. Teachers should not exercise this persuasive power alone. Healthy boys and girls have exuberantly active minds that develop attitudes, ideals and beliefs almost continuously from their daily contacts, resulting often in fixed patterns of behavior. True it is that a road first traveled may be a highway traveled frequently thereafter far into the future. Once set, convictions and habits can be as binding as chains. Indeed, what young people become is determined by many motivations, many inspirations, many suggestions from parents, from siblings, from relatives, and

---

"Community Education and its Organization" is taken from Ernest O. Melby and Clyde M. Campbell, *The Community School and its Administration* Vol. 10 (November, 1971).

from close friends, to mention a few. Let it be said over and over again that everyone in a community is a teacher in some respects. Some are harmful it is true, often exposing young people to incidents that are damaging to them; others are not hurtful, but by their example dampen the ambition of youthful associates. But still remaining are those few who can inspire youth to standards of excellence that neither the youth nor their parents had ever dreamed possible. I am sure that a number of these non-professionals are much more effective as teachers than many educators are willing to admit.

. . . .

In this period of great social change there should be a different kind of social organization.

What we have now was transported from Germany to the United States in the nineteenth century, particularly the cell-like classroom with one teacher instructing a limited number of students. The way high schools were organized in the 1900's is in essence the way they are organized today. Oh, admittedly, a few courses have been added and a few dropped but the Carnegie Unit with its sixteen or seventeen credits required for graduation still prevails in high schools nation-wide.

It has been alleged that approximately one-fourth of the youngsters in schools today do not thrive under this system; and even asserted by some that the remaining seventy-five percent would do better if they functioned in a different setting and were taught in a different manner. How true it is that our guidance, our instruction, our goals for youth have tended to fly off in all directions. Really, we haven't tried to direct a laser beam focus on young people, a beam that would bind together all the forces that impinge upon their lives. Why can't professionals and nonprofessionals blend their motivation and instruction so that young people can better become what they are capable of becoming. How beautiful a concept it is to visualize a unity of effort which might flow toward a common purpose.

Mary Follett, that classical writer on administration, told us much about organization in the 1920's but apparently we didn't listen or at least we didn't listen well. Today we find that her principles of organization still are as solid as the Rock of Gibraltar. Let me illustrate.

These passages are taken from her papers published in the book, *Dynamics of Administration:*

> "One of the characteristics which seems to set apart the successful and effective administrator from the unsuccessful and relatively ineffective administrator, is the degree to which the successful person is able to organize whatever is to be done so that it moves in a flow from step one to step two to step three. . . . The chief task of organization is how to relate the parts so that you have a working unit. Then you get effective participation. . . .

Four fundamental principles of organization are: coordination by direct contact of the responsible people concerned; coordination in the early stages;

coordination in the reciprocal relating of all the factors in a situation; coordination as a continuing process."

Our organization in schools today encourages a cacophony of experiences more than an orchestration of experiences. Really, the setting today in large part is each for himself irrespective of what it may do to anyone else. Let me repeat again how inspiring it would be if administrators, teachers, pupils, and citizens could function with the precision of a superb athletic team, with the beautiful blending of a tabernacle chorus, with the synchronization of a symphony orchestra. Organization today, as I see it, needs to help all forces flow toward those larger social confluences in the schools and in society.

What Could We Build If We Worked Together?

U Thant

What could we build if we worked together?

This simple but tantalizing question is a sharp reminder of the irony of the present state of mankind. It dramatizes the persistent struggle between our wisdom and our foolishness, our strength and our weakness, our creativeness and our self-destructiveness, our idealism and our baseness. It serves to remind us that the predominant rivalries of our era, political, military, or ideological, are also the most wasteful consumers of our time, spirit, talent, resources and even of life. It reminds us of the strange fact that even now, with an unprecedented range of knowledge at their disposal, men in all parts of the world passively continue to accept policies and programmes of all kinds which not only fritter away their substance and the bountiful legacy of nature, but at times endanger their very existence.

The simplest citizen can grasp the fact that a fraction of the money that will be spent throughout the world on armaments in 1967 could finance economic and social programmes, both national and global, on a scale hitherto undreamed of. It is obvious that a small part of the ingenuity, effort, expertise and resources deployed in building an intercontinental missile system, for example, would almost certainly, if applied to the more immediate problems of human misery or of future human development, produce a series of breakthroughs which might well illuminate and inspire man's whole concept of his own future. It is a commonplace that, if nations could only lay down the sword and live in harmony, the world might, with judicious leadership and management, well become a place which could rival all the utopias of the philosophers—and certainly be far more interesting.

Why do these totally obvious and desirable developments fail to come about—fail, moreover, in an age which prides itself on its new mastery of communications of every kind? Why do we have to live in fear rather than in hope, in antagonism and distrust rather than in harmony and cooperation?

"Human nature" is popularly held to be responsible for this deplorable state of affairs, the assumption being that "human nature" is in some way a force which cannot possibly be controlled or improved. It is high time this comfortable pretext was exploded. Men should aspire to be the masters of their fate, rather than the victims of their own "nature." If we presume, as we do, to change and improve everything else in nature, why do we leave ourselves out of the process? Improvement and progress should surely begin at home.

If, then, we discard the facile notion that "human nature" is to blame and that nothing can be done about it, what is the real reason for our inability to shape our affairs as reason and self-interest tell us that they should be shaped? How does it come about that greed, prejudice, arrogance, envy, fear, misunderstanding and all the other less desirable human characteristics play such a large part in the affairs of the world, so that the common denominator of international life is fear and lack of mutual confidence? It is perhaps because we think more of our differences than of our opportunities. We are still in a state of mind where the traditional attitudes born of our past wants and conflicts influence us more than the abundant, and so far largely unexploited, opportunities of the hopeful present. The note of hope and idealism in the world is still tremulous at best, and tends all too often to be drowned out by a jangle of qualification, compromise and cynicism. We must sustain that note of hope, which our achievements in many fields so amply justify, until it overpowers the voices of fear, cynicism and reaction. We must gain enough confidence in ourselves and in each other to turn our ideals and our potential into reality.

The opening question—What could we build if we worked together?—certainly provides us with a powerful incentive to solve this basic problem, and it may even provide us with a clue to the problem itself. It is a historic fact that when men have worked together in enthusiasm and loyalty to a commonly held ideal the results have benefited all succeeding ages, and have even on occasion—as for example in Athens or Florence in their greatest days—inspired enduring works of genius of an extraordinary quality, vitality and variety. We may not hope to find the conditions of Athens or Florence in large modern states, let alone in the world. But we can at least recognize that working together in the pursuit of practical aims provides men with an unusual solidarity and vitality, an environment in which their differences are a stimulus rather than an obstacle.

In this century political ideology has taken the place formerly occupied by religion as a main source of strife in the world. We have been, perhaps, too anxious to define and agree, by force if necessary, upon the ideal to be pursued before making a practical start in cooperation on fundamental problems. The world is, mercifully, an infinitely varied place. If we could start pragmatically by working together on the problems which urgently concern all peoples, differences of ideology and other apparently insoluble conflicts might be seen in a new light as wasteful and unnecessary, and may thus work themselves out over a period of time.

If we were to ask ourselves: What could we work on together *now?*, a vast range of fascinating possibilities for enhancing the condition and the quality of human life opens up before us.

....

We have too often in the past been forced to regret some aspects of scientific progress, and have been driven to act belatedly to mitigate them. We are now in a position, if we work together, to foresee and, to some extent, to determine the future course of human development. We can do this, however, only if we cease to fear and harass each other and if together we accept, welcome and plan the changes that must inevitably come about.

If this really means a change in "human nature," then it is high time we began to work toward such a change. What is certainly required is a change in some human political attitudes and habits. Intelligent self-interest is reason enough for making this change, already long overdue. In this process, I believe that the United Nations, as a centre for harmonizing the actions of nations, may have a vital role.

Part Six

Management in the Secondary School

14

The Principal and Management Functions

Although the greater part of this book has been concerned with general principles which should guide the leader of the secondary school, we recognize that for all in leadership positions, management responsibilities must be carried out efficiently. Such responsibilities require only a moderate amount of organizational ability and planning. Done well, the organization functions smoothly, permitting the members of the organization to carry on their respective tasks, free from distractions caused by breakdown in the organizational procedures. Most of the management responsibilities of the principal are associated with the school. Others, however, are related to the school system as a whole, of which the secondary school is a sub-system.

SYSTEM-WIDE RELATIONS

The typical district organization is that of a unit encompassing education from kindergarten through the secondary school. A board of education, most typically elected by citizens of the district, serves as the public body in which the control of education in the district is centered, pursuant only to state legislation and rules and regulations. The board of education employs, as its executive officer, a superintendent of schools who is responsible to the board of education for recommending policies, for carrying out the policies adopted by the board of education, and for the general administration of the district. Even the smallest secondary schools are in most instances a part of a larger system.

As we pointed out in an earlier section, the secondary school principal functions within a larger system. He is bound by the general policies laid down by the board of education. He works within district policies which set the length of school year, the vacation periods, the overall budget, purchasing procedures, employment and dismissal practices, and student-teacher ratios. Negotiated contracts with teacher organizations apply to a district as a whole. Boards of education have great interest in high school athletic programs and other student activities, such as bands, dramatic activities and the like, which involve public appearances.

In some districts, the superintendent of schools, as the chief educational agent of the board of education, is so insistent on central control of all aspects of the educational program that it is difficult for a principal to exercise the kind of leadership necessary to improve and change the secondary school. We recognize that such conditions exist. However, as we stated earlier, it is coming to be recognized that in order to encourage flexibility of programs, professional growth of staff, and adaptations of education to a changing world outside the school, as much decision-making as possible must be decentralized to the building level. Risk-taking cannot be discouraged in the name of efficient central administration. Many modern superintendents recognize this and will actively support intelligent leadership at the school level.

Leadership of the secondary principal within the system requires that the principal persuade the superintendent of the necessity for latitude of action and of the necessity for the superintendent to convey to the school staff support for the leadership efforts of the principal. Together, superintendent and principal should occasionally appear before the board of education to discuss educational issues and problems, to recommend policy statements, and to approve changes in internal school programs, policies, goals, and procedures. We have already referred to the need for policy declarations in such areas as academic freedom, and teaching of controversial issues, and the conduct of athletics. Other policy statements will be added as changes occur or are proposed.

Whether in a unit district or in a district confined to secondary schools, the principal will find himself involved with the schools at levels below the secondary school. A working arrangement between the secondary schools and the elementary schools which feed into it is more easily accomplished in a unit district where all schools are within the scope of a single administration. The necessary cooperation is often more difficult when the elementary schools are within another jurisdiction.

In either form of organization, the secondary principal and his staff must forego the privileges which seem to be associated with being higher in the pecking order. Elementary schools and their principals should be accorded the same latitude for experimentation as are argued here for secondary schools. The most frequent exercise of the pecking order privilege is that used by subject departments in the secondary school. Too frequently, mathematics teachers proclaim publicly that elementary pupils are ill-prepared in mathematics, or the English department states publicly that elementary pupils cannot write or spell properly, or they attempt to prescribe the books that should be read. Proper articulation can be achieved on a professional basis, featuring mutual respect. The schools embrace a wide variety of talents, abilities, interests, and aptitudes, and no amount of effort will satisfy some secondary teachers who expect all who come to the secondary school to be "prepared" (as they define preparation). The secondary school principal must exercise leadership in his work with the schools that "feed" his schools.

We pause here to comment on the management team concept currently held in considerable esteem by superintendents of schools and to put this in the context of the leadership role of the secondary school principal. The concept emerged in great part as a response to collective bargaining by organizations of teachers, although as it developed into practice it became associated with a new form of administration. As the bargaining procedure was carried on in the early period in most districts, negotiators representing teachers became pitted against the board of education or its negotiating representative (in many cases the superintendent of schools) in an adversary relationship patterned after the industrial labor-management model. In these early stages of collective bargaining, the question arose as to who constituted management. Was it the board and superintendent? Did it include not only these, but also other administrative personnel, including principals? Boards of education and superintendents concluded that management was made up of all administrative employees. Teacher organizations soon began to make it clear that their membership did not include administrators. Caught in the changing patterns of relationships that evolved, principals discovered that their roles placed them with management.

Concurrently, the concept of the administrative team evolved. Instead of administering a school system by the long established, hierarchical chain of command model, teams of administrators, made up of central office administrators and principals, shared the decision-making process. The superintendent became a leader among equals, and although he retained his central position of authority and responsibility by virtue of his unique relationship with the board of education, he deferred to the team in identifying problems and arriving at solutions. He often appeared before the board with the team or with parts of it, depending on the nature of the decision facing the board.

The management team idea can have advantages, both to the superintendent and to team members. It can provide a forum where the changes in school program and practices proposed by the principal can be presented and examined. The team can offer support to proposals which are carried over into practice. Meetings of the team give an opportunity for dissemination of information which can be helpful both to the superintendent and to team members.

Used unwisely, however, the management team concept can be used to produce uniformity of thought and conformity of action. In other words, it lends itself to increased inflexibility if the superintendent wishes to use the team for such a purpose. Like any form of organization, it can be used to further different kinds of goals. The purposes for which we hope the administrative team will be used are implicit in this book. We hope it will contribute to the full development of the leadership capacities and opportunities for the secondary school principal within the school for which he is responsible, above all else. We hope the management team concept will come to stand on its own merits, apart from the early conflicts which led to its development.

THE PRINCIPAL'S OFFICE

We have observed schools where the principal has been crowded into a space large enough only for a desk and perhaps two straight-back chairs, and a file cabinet. Such an office is not one where a visitor is likely to feel comfortable or would want to linger. While the principal's office need not be lavish, it should contain enough space to accommodate six or eight persons comfortably in a conference setting. It should contain comfortable chairs for visitors or for conferences, a conference table, and a table which could be used for serving coffee. It is surprising how the tone of the school may be set by the way the principal uses his office. There should be many opportunities for informal meetings with staff, students, parents, and other citizens. At such meetings, the principal can create a condition of participation by removing himself from behind his own desk, generally symbolic of his authority, and joining his visitors around the conference table or over a cup of coffee or tea.

No matter how pressed for time he may be, or thinks himself to be, the principal should reserve some time for the less structured meeting arising from the need of others to talk about personal or professional concerns, problems, or hopes, or simply to speculate with others about how the school may be changed and improved. Time for such unstructured conversations and meetings should include opportunities to chat with students. Too many principals isolate themselves from both faculty and student body, appearing only on ceremonial occasions, in formal faculty meetings, in the inspectorial role associated with walking through the halls, strolling through the lunch room, or visiting classrooms for evaluation purposes. To students, the principal is too often seen almost exclusively as an authoritarian figure, as one who is an arbiter of discipline.

We recognize the many demands on the time of a principal. We know he must adhere to some kind of work schedule. We know he must have some time to himself to sort out events and ideas, to plan for the future. Yet we maintain that some of his time must be set aside for the human, face-to-face, informal meetings as described above.

THE ADMINISTRATIVE AREA

The center of the communication network of the school is the administrative area, including the principal's office and other administrative space. It is usually centrally located and is the first area a visitor encounters when entering the school. It is also the area where teachers usually go on arriving in the morning and is often the last place they go before departing for the day. It is the principal who creates the climate of the office area. It can be friendly or forbidding, calm or chaotic, cheerful or depressing.

The importance of the secretaries who usually man the outer office space, monitor the telephones, and respond to faculty and student questions cannot be overestimated. The impression they should try to create by their manner and their efforts will determine whether others see the administrative offices as a command post or as a service center. It is the latter impression that should prevail.

When parents or other citizens call, every effort should be made to provide them with the assistance or information needed. In most instances the secretary can take care of the call or visit without further referral. The principal cannot always be available to respond to telephone inquiries or complaints. If it is something the secretary cannot handle satisfactorily, she can elicit the purpose of the call, summarize it for the principal, and arrange for him to return the call; or, if necessary, she can make an appointment for a personal visit. In no instance, no matter how irate the caller, should the secretary respond in kind, or pass judgment on the merits of the call. The same applies also to those who come personally to the office. The secretary's attitude should be one of wanting to help the caller or visitor. Unfortunately, few parents and citizens have direct opportunity to see the inside of the classrooms. Many perceptions about the school come from telephone or personal communications with the school offices. The cornerstone is courtesy. Gossip about office affairs is taboo.

The same objective—service—should characterize the relations of the secretary to members of the staff. Secretarial officiousness is a cause of resentment. Teachers and parents sometimes express impatience or criticism. When this occurs the secretary should not respond in kind, but should objectively seek a way to resolve the difficulty.

Students too have frequent need to visit the office. They often want to see the principal, or in larger schools, one of the assistants. How their inquiries or complaints or requests are received can create the impression of the office as either helpful and considerate or unpleasant.

In times of budgetary restrictions, which seem to be most of the time, secretarial assistance in the principal's office may seem to have a low priority. Yet failing to recognize the importance of such service may result in the unwise use of a principal's time, which could more profitably be spent in improving education. Collecting and counting money from various school activities, distributing and accounting for supplies, preparing lists of absentees, processing records, sending records to other schools for students who are transferring, preparing book orders, providing routine information for the central office, and keeping schedules of school use by community groups, are activities which can and should be carried out by the secretarial or clerical staff. Such activities can be routinized so that they are done smoothly and efficiently. For the principal, even in the small school, to busy himself with such tasks is an uneconomical use of his time.

In both small and large schools, teachers occasionally need the service of a typist and assistance in duplicating materials. In the very small school, the typing service needed is usually limited by lack of secretarial help. The same is true of duplicating services. For the latter, a space housing duplicating equipment can be provided for use of teachers as well as instruction as to the use of the machines.

In order to provide some assistance in both typing, cutting stencils, and reproducing materials, students taking classes in typing and office practice can often be of considerable help, at the same time gaining practical experience. As always, exploitation of students must be avoided. In large high schools, a secretarial pool of two or more persons may be established, one of whom will be responsible for channeling work requested by teachers, counsellors, and others, and scheduling a steady work flow.

RECORD KEEPING

Many kinds of records are kept in the administration area of the school. These should be filed for ready use and easy access. Examples of records for which a filing system should be devised include, among others:

Student cumulative records
Health records
Enrollment cards
Transfer cards
Individual daily schedules
Schedules for use of the building
Custodian schedules
Teaching and extracurricular assignments
Transportation schedules
Minutes of faculty meetings
General correspondence
General policy statements (board of education, superintendent, school)
Reports required by the system and by other agencies, such as the state education agency, accrediting agency, etc.
Budget information
Requisitions
Invoices
Purchase orders
Supply and equipment inventories
Accounting statements for student funds
Information about various student activities

Record keeping should be kept to essential information. One of the plagues of present-day organization is the paper work which engulfs all who work in the organization. Easy access to copying machines compounds the paper problem. Being alert to the need for ways to simplify record keeping, reduce paper work, and keep files from being clogged with information no longer needed is quite as important as knowing what is necessary to retain and file for ready reference.

THE CUSTODIAL STAFF

Even though the school system may employ a general supervisor for custodial and maintenance services, it is important that the principal be clearly responsible for, and have authority over, such employees during the day-to-day operations of the school. Custodians need to be selected with as much care as any other staff member and should be accorded the full respect given to all co-workers. Custodians are in frequent association with teachers, students and parents, and often have insights into school problems and understanding of students which are denied to other staff members. On occasion their presence at staff meetings is desirable, as fully participating members.

The principal, along with the custodians, will plan the work schedules. He will also make necessary arrangements for scheduling custodial service for after-school use of the building, and will see that the custodians are responsible for locking and securing the building when it is not in use.

BUILDING SECURITY AND SPECIAL EVENTS

Generally, some arrangement is made with local or county police officials for providing security. Unfortunately, in some areas, night vandalism is a problem of considerable concern. Police patrol cars making a periodic tour of the school grounds reduce the possibility of vandalism.

Police assistance is usually required for special events, held both inside the school and at athletic events on school playing fields. Such assistance is usually paid for from district budgeted funds, but arrangement for the service rests with the principal and the security police are responsible to the principal at school events.

Use of the Buildings

School buildings in most communities are used for a variety of community activities. Evening use for extensive programs in adult education are increasing. In addition, various civic groups are permitted to use school facilities for a variety of purposes. In a well-managed school system, use of buildings is regulated under policies adopted by the board of education, covering conditions of use, times available, and rental fees (if any). Usually, once a general policy is adopted, permission to use a building is given by some person in the central administration. This calls for close communication between the one who issues the permit and the building principal in order to mesh civic use with use of the building after hours by student groups. After policies are determined and a routine is established, scheduling use of buildings is a task that may well be delegated, as indeed can most of the other tasks described above.

TRANSPORTATION

Many high school districts located in more sparsely populated areas of the country draw their students from a wide geographic area, necessitating extensive use of buses to transport students to and from school. In most states, large subsidies are provided local districts for transportation costs. Two principal methods of providing bus service are (1) district owned and operated buses, and (2) contracted service. Regardless of the method used, the principal has responsibilities related to transportation. If transportation is provided by district owned buses, operators must be employed. As much care must be taken in their selection as for any other staff, as each day a driver holds in his hands the safety of from forty to seventy boys and girls. He or she must also be one who can establish rapport with students, control behavior on the bus, and present a good example in personal appearance and conduct. School-owned buses must be maintained and checked for safety. Routes must be established which reduce the time any child spends in being carried to and from school to a minimum. Provision must be made for late buses to accommodate those who, for any one of a variety of reasons, must remain at school after the regular school day has ended. Although the school district cannot exercise as much direct control over drivers and vehicles when bus service is contracted, nevertheless standards of driver competence, personal behavior, and, above all, safety must be insisted upon as part of the contract.

Where busing is extensive, the area to be covered large, and the complexity of scheduling routes great, some person should be employed to manage the transportation system other than the principal. We have all observed schools where principals, either by choice or compulsion, are directly responsible for the operation of an extensive busing system. Large portions of their time every day are spent on transportation. This, we suggest, is time not well spent.

Finally, the country has shown an increasing concern about bus safety. Fatal accidents involving school children have raised questions about school bus construction and about the adequacy of inspections of both vehicles and drivers. The school principal should have, as a major concern, all aspects of safety of transportation, even though he does not directly supervise it.

SCHOOL PLANT PLANNING

Taking the United States as a whole, secondary school enrollments will decline well into the 1980 decade. This reflects the decline in number of births which began in the last half of the 1960 decade. This decrease was reflected in smaller enrollments in primary grades in the late sixties, and in the upper elementary grades in the early seventies. The early junior high grades began to be affected in the middle of the 1970s. The numbers in the age group 14-17 will be 10 percent fewer in 1980 than in 1970. Even if the number of births should begin to increase again, it takes fourteen years for this to affect secondary enrollments.

For most communities, the need to build to accommodate an increasing enrollment will not be present in the years ahead, in contrast with the great demand for more building space which characterized the period 1958–1970. This does not mean that building planning will come to a halt. Many secondary plants are so old they have reached the stage of obsolescence. Others, while still structurally sound, are in need of extensive rehabilitation in order to accommodate a modern educational program.

If either a new school is to be constructed or an older school rehabilitated, one fundamental principle of planning applies. This is that determination of the educational program to be housed precedes the drawing of plans. School building and renovation are almost always financed by a bond issue which is presented to the public by the board of education of the district. To determine the amount the voters will be asked to approve, an estimate of the cost must be made. Even at this preliminary stage, educational program needs are primary considerations. Usually, in arriving at the sum to be requested in a bond issue, the board of education employs an architect to develop preliminary sketch plans on which a cost estimate may be based. School architects do not sit in their offices and prepare plans out of their own ideas alone. The good architect wants to know the program needs before he begins to design a structure to house them properly. If it is a new building, the educational requirements must be provided in considerable detail. The number to be housed must be estimated, presently and into the future.

Although board of education and superintendent are essential parts of the planning team, it is the building principal who must further their efforts by providing a clear and complete list of educational specifications. At this point, the principal involves as many others as possible—teachers, secretaries, counselors, and custodians. A full year of preliminary work is required to develop the educational requirements. Behind every request for space should be an educational justification. As the educational planning proceeds, close association with the architect is imperative. For one reason, requests, even though well justified, usually exceed what can be financed. Compromises usually have to be reached. Nevertheless, the educational priorities should be firmly established as planning goes forward.

If the bond issue is successful, detailed drawings begin. All through the procedure, from rough preliminary plans to final working drawings, the principal and staff will be involved. If it is a new school for which a staff has not been chosen, the principal works with those in existing schools. If a complete staff is to be transferred, he works with those who will occupy the new school. It is equally important to have as full participation as possible if the project calls for rehabilitation of an existing building. This presents an opportunity to identify needs which were not apparent when the building was constructed.

The list of needs not satisfied in older buildings is extensive. They seldom contain enough locker space. The cafeteria may be inadequate. The library may not meet modern standards, and restructuring may present an opportunity to develop a complete learning center, requiring much more space and provisions, not only for books but also for tapes, records, slides, films, along with areas for listening or viewing. It should be possible to eliminate the study hall, both as a space requirement and as an educational anachronism, replacing it with a learning center and with a student lounge or commons, and space for student council and newspaper and yearbook staffs, for example.

Vocational areas in older buildings are almost always absent or inadequate. Gymnasiums are often under-sized. Lighting is usually below acceptable standard. The principal's office and the administrative area are drab and limited in space in many old schools. Teachers' rest rooms either do not exist or are completely unsatisfactory. Rehabilitation of an older building presents a principal and staff with almost as many opportunities as planning for a new building.

Size of Schools

The work of the secondary principal is conditioned by the size and type of school he heads, even though the principles of leadership described in this book apply to all secondary schools.

A survey of 15,000 public secondary schools carried out for the National Association of Secondary School Principals in 1965 by a committee under the chairmanship of James Conant showed that 45.5 percent had enrollments of under 500. In eleven states, 75 percent had enrollments under 500. Although consolidation efforts have reduced the number of very small secondary schools in the intervening years, the small school continues to exist in large numbers. At the other end of the range, 19.3 percent of the secondary schools had enrollments from 1,000-1,999, and 6.1 percent had enrollments of 2,000 or more.[1]

When one contrasts a school of 200 students with one enrolling 2,000 it is evident that administrative organization will vary greatly between the small and large high school. In some schools the principal is part-time teacher, part-time principal. He may have one secretary in the office, full or part-time. Guidance becomes the job of the classroom teacher, or perhaps the school will have a part-time counsellor who also teaches. Because of its small size, the range of curricular offerings is likely to be narrow. At the other end of the enrollment scale the principal may have two or three assistant principals, a dean of boys, a dean of girls, and six or eight full-time counsellors, along with department chairmen who have some freedom from teaching duties. In the larger schools, delegation of responsibility and authority is necessary but such delegation does not relieve the principal from his obligations of leadership. Despite the delegation of authority, the ultimate responsibility rests with the principal.

Many opinions have been expressed about the minimum and optimum size of secondary schools. No precise enrollment figure can be stated with complete conviction. Schools with very small enrollments, perhaps those under 500, face two possibilities. Either the range of curricular offerings will be too small to accommodate the needs of all students, or the per pupil expenditure will be inordinately large. In an effort to provide services to small schools in sparsely populated areas, cooperative arrangements are made on a county or regional basis to furnish psychological services, services for the mentally and physically handicapped, and, to provide vocational opportunities, area vocational schools have been established.

Minimum size is to some extent conditioned by geographical considerations. In some sections of the country, even if all other factors were favorable, it would be difficult to assemble in one school as many as 500 students without excessive time spent on busses and extreme distances to be travelled. At the other end of the scale, many observers have concluded that schools can be too large. Unless some organizational scheme is adopted to reduce the effect of large numbers in a single school, students can get lost in the impersonality of the institution. Various schemes have been used to overcome the difficulties of super-size, including organizing schools within schools, assigning a group of teachers to a group of students for the three or four years of their student life in the school, or variations on these plans. If we had to give a rule of thumb on the question of size we would suggest a maximum of 750–800 for a junior high school, and 1,500 for a senior high school. Some research, although not conclusive, seems to support this estimate of size.

[1] James Conant, *A Study of the American Secondary School: A Preliminary Report* (Washington, D. C.: NASSP, 1966), pp. 1-6.

TYPES OF ORGANIZATION

Just as there is difference in size of schools, so are there differences in types of organization. The NASSP survey revealed that 22.9 percent of the principals were responsible for schools with grades 7–12; 5.5 percent were responsible for schools with grades 8–12; 32.3 percent for schools with grades 9–12; 16.8 percent for grades 10–12; .2 percent for grades 11–12. Responsibility for grades 1–12 was carried by 19.3 percent, and some other grade combination by 2.7 percent of the principals. It can be assumed that principals carrying responsibilities for all grades in the system were in very small districts. Perhaps the only constant is the age group of pupils, covering early and late adolescence, roughly ages 12–18.[2]

Bibliography

"A Guide to Pupil Transportation." *School Management* (November 1965), pp. 103-25.

Anderson, Lester and Van Dyke, Lauren A. *Secondary School Administration.* New York: Houghton-Mifflin Co., 1972.

Boles, Harold W. *Step by Step to Better School Facilities.* New York: Holt, Rinehart and Winston, 1965.

Featherstone, Glen and Culp, D. P. *Pupil Transportation: State and Local Programs.* New York: Harper and Row, 1965.

McClurkin, William A. *School Building Planning.* New York: The Macmillan Company, 1964.

Ovard, Glen F. *Administration of the Changing Secondary School.* New York: The Macmillan Co., 1966.

———. *Change and Secondary School Administration.* New York: The Macmillan Co., 1968.

Toffler, Alvin, ed. *The Schoolhouse in the City.* New York: Frederick A. Praeger, 1968.

Yaeger, William A. *Administration of Noninstructional Personnel and Services.* New York: Harper and Row, 1959.

---

[2]*Ibid.*, p. 2.

Selected Readings

The Dominion of Economic Accountability

Ernest R. House

While recognizing that accountability may be a passing fad, and that some manifestations are as ephemeral as this paper, I believe that the idea is going to be around for a while. If for no other reason, it is a way of lassoing the wild stallion of educational spending. Groups competing for funds at the federal, state, and local levels insure that educational spending will not continue to climb as rapidly as it has in the past. So whatever else accountability may be, it is a way of holding down spending. And although some good may come from it, I am disturbed at the form it is taking.

It has been said in support of accountability that it will result in favorable changes in professional performance "and these will be reflected in higher academic achievement, improvement in pupil attitudes, and generally better educational results."[1] I would contend that accountability will not automatically do good things, that we are already accountable for many things that we do, that being accountable, in fact, makes our lives miserable in certain ways, and often actually prohibits favorable changes in professional performance and better educational results. For example, college professors are quite accountable for publishing articles, yet one would be hard pressed to show how this arrangement helps, say, the public schools. Similarly public school teachers are accountable for keeping their classrooms quiet, and I've heard it said that this is an impediment to good teaching.

So when one hears talk about accountability as if it did not now exist and about all the good things that are going to happen when we get it, one must

---

"The Dominion of Economic Accountability" was presented to the Ninth Annual Conference of the California Association for the Gifted, (Monterey, California, February 27, 1971). It is reprinted with the permission of Kappa Delta Pi, An Honor Society in Education.

[1] Stephen M. Barro, "An Approach to Developing Accountability Measures for the Public Schools," *Phi Delta Kappan,* 52, 4 (1970).

regard this argument as too simplistic and look more squarely at what is being proposed. It is safe to assume that somebody wants something he is not now getting.

ECONOMIC ACCOUNTABILITY

Not long into any discussion on accountability, someone always raises the question, "Who is accountable to whom?" Almost invariably the response is that one is accountable to his superior. In fact, most people apparently perceive the society as being a vast hierarchy in which each person is accountable to his boss and his boss is accountable to someone else and so on. In this conception the school district, the society, the world is perceived as being organized like a vast bureaucracy, a gigantic corporation. Accountability is upward. Each person is accountable to the institution.

Nowhere is this better illustrated than in a recent issue of the *Phi Delta Kappan* (December, 1970) devoted to the theme of accountability. Explicitly or implicitly several articles in the magazine harbor this view, but the apotheosis of it is the lead article written by a Rand Corporation economist. He proposes that pupil performance measures be given to all the students in a school district; then, through a series of multiple regression equations, each teacher, each principal, and the superintendent be held accountable for that bit of pupil performance that the analysis attributes to him. Mrs. Smith, for example, is responsible for three percent of verbal reasoning while Mr. Jones only managed to get in one percent. Presumably Mrs. Smith and Mr. Jones will be differentially rewarded for those contributions. Good girl, Mrs. Smith. Bad boy, Mr. Jones.

The technical and political problems that this approach would encounter are insurmountable. Technically the conditions necessary for employing the statistical analysis cannot be met: none of the current measures are adequate indices of the relevant variables; the variables cannot be made independent of one another; and there is no way of specifying all the critical variables that should be included. The political problems are even more formidable. If the teacher organizations are anything like the rascals I know them to be, they would never allow such a thing.

But I must confess I am intrigued by the prospects of Mr. Jones sabotaging Mrs. Smith's lesson plans so he can pick up a few points on her. Or the kids in eleventh grade algebra organizing to throw the math test and send the despised Mr. Harms into bankruptcy. My mind slips back to those exciting days of comparative anatomy practical exams when the desperately competitive pre-meds would pull the numbered pins from one part of the cat's brain and stick it into another in order to fool their rivals.

Although this particular scheme is not going to be widely employed, this conception of accountability is so widely accepted that I would not be surprised to read in an education newsletter that the superintendent in Lockjaw, California, or Bone Gap, Illinois, having secured a batch of army surplus tests and a slide rule for the business manager to work the regression equations on, has decided to institute the system.

The point I'm trying to make is that discussions of accountability always lead us down this dismal road. In fact, we are so far down the road that it is impossible for many people even to imagine another type of accountability. For the dominant theme today is economic efficiency and its purpose is control—control over pupil behavior, control over staff behavior, control over schooling.

At the risk of oversimplification let me outline this mode of economic accountability. It is an economist's view of the world. Basically it assumes that the purpose of education is to supply manpower to other institutions of the society, particularly the economic ones. The skills needed to run the societal machinery can be formulated in specific terms, so educational goals are mandated by technological demands. The goals being specific and set, the job of educators is to maximize these goals, (usually forms of student achievement) with the greatest efficiency possible. Ultimately then the goals of education become economic and the attendant accountability system is economic.

Economic analysis always has to do with maximization of *known* objectives.[2] It provides a descriptive theory of how maximization will happen or a prescriptive analysis of how to get it to happen. Thus we get analytic tools like systems analysis, cost/benefit analysis, PPBS, and performance contracting. Perhaps the technique *par excellence* is regression analysis against a production function, in which the most efficient combination of inputs is related to output.

There are serious problems in applying economic analysis to education in a pluralistic society. Where objectives or outcomes are not known, economic theory offers no way of determining them. And where there are competing viewpoints of what education should be doing, the maximizing solution does not even apply. In a pluralistic society like ours, there are irreconcilable differences as to what the outputs of education should be. At best one can compile a great list of possible outputs and try to relate inputs to them, thus assembling a collage. But this solution does not have much practical appeal to administrators who want to make decisions. For example, it would not tell them what would happen if an attempt were made to increase a particular output.

The alternative is to reconcile these differences into a few set goals, which is what I believe the demands for economic accountability are attempting to do. The ultimate form of accountability then is to tighten the system to the

---

[2]John E. Brandl, "Public Service Outputs of Higher Education: An Exploratory Essay," in *The Outputs of Higher Education: Their Identification, Measurement, and Evaluation* (Boulder: Western Interstate Commission for Higher Education, 1970).

point that each person is held personally accountable for his contribution to those few goals—just as the Rand economist suggested. In this scheme students are shaped to prespecified ends, educators are efficient at producing those ends, and education is more closely wired to the economic institutions of the society. The whole social system is more efficient, but the cost is terribly high: it is our cultural pluralism and our humanity. For this mode of accountability reduces to simply this: the individual is accountable to the institutions, but the institutions are not accountable to the individual.

DOMINANCE OF MANAGERIAL EDUCATION

Inextricably bound to economic accountability is what Thomas Green[3] calls "managerial" education. The same principle of economic efficiency shapes both the accountability system and the nature of education. Managerial education dominates when the schools are assessed by the utility of their "product" to the dominant institutions of the society. In our society this means that the schools are held accountable for effectively and efficiently meeting the demands for educated manpower. To the extent that the economic institutions maintain their voracious appetite for technical skills and to the extent that school credentials become the primary means of placing people in the structure, managerial education will predominate.

Contrast this with "humanistic" education in which schools are assessed in terms of what they do for people—independently of their contribution to other institutions. The humanistic *credo,* often expressed as the impossible goal of "developing each individual to his fullest," is the official ideology of most educators. It seeks not to shape the individual to a predetermined end, to some criterion of external utility, but to cultivate independence and individualism.

Yet, according to Green, in spite of this *credo,* managerial concerns now shape the schools and will increase their dominance substantially over the next two decades. One reason is that each lower educational level must at a minimum prepare its students for the next higher level, and at the top of the pyramid are the graduate and professional schools, which feed into the economic institutions.

Down this road a few decades Green foresees a very high level of managerial education for an elite and a lower level for the majority of people. To a certain extent this has already happened. As we investigated gifted programs across Illinois we found gifted children being educated toward some kind of vocational marketability. In shaping the child toward these distant and pre-specified goals the classes tended to be dull and repressive, often requiring that both teachers and parents exert great pressures on the child in

---

[3] Thomas F. Green, "Schools and Communities: A Look Forward," *Community and the Schools* (Cambridge, Mass.: Harvard Educational Review Reprint No. 3, 1969).

order to get him to perform. The rationale underlying these classes was usually "This may be painful now but it will help the child when he wants to get ahead."

Here are some excerpts from one of our case studies. First, excerpts from an interview with the teacher Mr. Harms:

> *Q: What would you say your major goal is for this particular class?*
> Mr. Harms: I'd say the major goal is to prepare them for advanced math. Most of the students will probably go ahead and take college work in math as either a science, math, or engineering major.
>
> *Q: What do the students do that is especially appropriate for the gifted?*
> Mr. Harms: It's primarily a matter of acceleration and an enrichment of mathematics. Projects are good but I feel that in math there really is no substitute for hard work; there just isn't any royal road to mathematics. I'm afraid I probably assign more problems than some teachers do, but even the good students need practice.
>
> *Q: How would you describe a successful student in this class?*
> Mr. Harms: A successful student would be one that studies regularly every day, pays attention in class, does well in his tests, and does his homework pretty regularly. I have some students that ask questions and others that don't. I believe that I like to have them ask questions but some students have gotten to the place where they get it pretty much on their own and they don't have to ask questions. Others don't ask questions because they're ... well, they don't.
>
> *Q: What does it take to get an 'A'?*
> Mr. Harms: Well, my feeling is you have to be pretty good to get an 'A'. You have to be an outstanding student, have to almost have an A on every test. It depends somewhat on how many tests we have during the quarter but unfortunately with an A, you don't have a grade above the A to average with one below to bring it up, and so it's a little tough.

The student enthusiasm is extremely low, and, what is rare for a gifted group, there is no humor in the class. Here is a brief excerpt from an interview with Donna, the best student in the class:

> *Q: What kind of things do you do in this class?*
> Donna: Mr. Harms will ask us if we have any questions over the problems we did, and if we do, he'll discuss them and write them on the board. He'll also give us at least one proof a day. And he kind of yells at us a little because we don't like them. But he keeps saying that we should like them, and we should do them because that's all we're going to do in college.

Q: What kinds of things are you supposed to learn in this class?

Donna: I think we're supposed to learn the generalities with proofs and just learn the technique of proving. He doesn't give us too much busy work, like some teachers do. He is concerned about us knowing proofs because he keeps saying we have to know this for college.

We have to learn how to do the proofs; we are going to have to realize that we can't skip over them. Some of us work the problems and don't have enough time to get to all of them so we'll do the rest of the problems and skip the proofs. And say we didn't get them because we probably wouldn't get them anyway.

Q: Do you get graded in this class?

Donna: Yes, and I need to be graded so that I have some drive to get me going. It makes me feel real good when I can bring home an A and my Dad is real proud of me.

Mr. Harms' class is the stereotypical math class that students through the years have come to dislike intensely. Of more than 100 classes examined, this one is lowest on student enthusiasm. The unremitting aim of the teacher is to ingrain the subject matter into the heads of his students so that they can "get ahead" vocationally. The future orientation of the teacher and the degree to which he impresses it on the students is a significant feature of the class. The rationale for the future utility of the subject attempts to mitigate current unpleasantness.

To the teacher's credit he does manage to teach for the higher thought process of "analysis." This emphasis occurs in all math classes we have studied. In all probability, the students will perform well on the Advanced Placement tests he keeps reminding them about. Since this is the main goal, the class may be a success in that regard. The cost is high, however. The strict humorless classroom atmosphere and total domination of the class by the teacher results in a particularly uninspiring class. There is no joking, no questioning—only the grimmest pursuit of subject matter. When he wishes to "enrich" the class he does so by showing the students other ways of solving equations. His pathetic attempts at "making the students independent" consist of occasionally not giving them any help on their homework.

When Mr. Harms tries to start a discussion in class, he asks recall questions that leave nothing to discuss and that no one cares to answer. In addition, he is a very hard grader. The extreme emphasis on grades is strong in the entire school—quite typical of all the middle-class suburbs studied—and the teacher manifests these pressures. The severe competitive environment is very real to the students. There is one thing that the students like about his class—he doesn't collect and check their homework. However, unknown to them, he does check on them covertly.

Even the best student stresses the dullness of the class and claims that the only thing that keeps her going is pressure from her father to make good grades. At best the other students are resigned. As a helpful crutch, Mr. Harms relies on his ultimate rationale—that learning math is unenjoyable ("There is no royal road") but one must do it in order to get ahead in college and eventually gain a competitive advantage in the job market. The philosophy of the community is embodied in the classroom of the teacher—learning is not intrinsically worthwhile but is unpleasantly necessary to "success." The honors classes reveal a considerable trace of elitism. Parents and students see the classes as quite a status symbol.

In summary, strong community pressure for competition and success, a subject difficult to teach enjoyably, and a teacher who has little flexibility, humor, or ability to enliven the class combine for an unhappy learning experience and a negative feeling toward the subject. As one of Mr. Harms' students says, "Math is a lot more 'cut and dried' than most subjects. I'm sorry to say it seems mostly dried, and I don't think anything can help."[4]

Atkin[5] has called attention to the paradigm of this type of education in which educational services are perceived as "products" to be mass produced. This production-line model calls for elaborate prespecification and quality control. Emphasis is placed on that which is replicable, easily quantifiable, readily discernible, and unambiguous. Education becomes engineering and finally industrial production. Evaluation becomes greatly simplified: one need only compare the prespecification to the final product.

PPBS—AN ACCOUNTANT'S DREAM

Thus we get simple business management tools applied to education—like the PPB system California is implementing soon. The system promises no less than providing "information necessary (1) for planning educational programs that will meet the needs of the community; and (2) for choosing among the alternative ways in which a school district can allocate resources to achieve its goals and objectives."[6] According to their state's lucid and well-written manual here is how the system works:

The school arrives at a set of *goals* which are the cornerstone of the system. From the goals is derived a set of objectives which must be measurable. Based on these objectives the *program* is developed, which is a group of activities to accomplish the objectives including attendant resources and schedules. This completes the program development. Then the *program*

---

[4] Joe Milan Steele, Ernest R. House, Stephen Lapan, and Thomas Kerins, *Instructional Climate in Illinois Gifted Classes* (Urbana, Ill.: Center for Instructional Research and Curriculum Evaluation, University of Illinois, August, 1970), 55 pp.

[5] J. Myron Atkin, "Curriculum Design: The Central Development Group and the Local Teacher," prepared for *Institute für die Pädagogik der Naturwissenschaften*, Invitational Symposium (Kiel, West Germany, October 14, 1970).

[6] California State Department of Education, *Conceptual Design for a Planning, Programming, Budgeting System for California School Districts* (1969).

description package is drawn up which includes the course content, objectives, and method of evaluation. Then the *program structure* is set up which is a hierarchical arrangement of programs. (The system is very big on hierarchies; about 15 of the 18 charts in the book are some kind of hierarchy.)

Finally the *program code* is built, which means each program is assigned a number; the *program budget* is completed; and the *multiyear financial plan,* a five-year cost projection, is constructed. All neatly rational and internally consistent—if you believe in an abstract "economic man." Actually any relation between the PPB *system* and reality will be purely coincidental.

First the problem of defining goals in a pluralistic society has already been noted. The PPBS manual spends no time on how to arrive at goals, and with good reason. Defining goals is a political not an economic process. Empirical studies of business organizations have shown that their goals are changing, multiple, inconsistent—and the organizations survive quite nicely.[7] Upon close inspection even the profit goal in business organizations turns out to be quite elusive.

Assuming that the goal problem is overcome, one must then develop a set of objectives which are measurable—the old behavioral objectives problem. Here is a behavioral objective for students from *Educational Technology:*

> The student will be given a problem which is totally unfamiliar to him. He will be able to respond by stating ideas or solutions to the problem. The responses (as measured by a choice of checklists, teacher observations, teacher evaluation, and teacher-made exercises) will be rated on the basis of newness and uniqueness.[8]

How many of these would one have to write to cover fully what a child should be doing? One Office of Education project set out to compile a complete set of behavioral objectives for the high school. Before it was abandoned, they had 20,000. Teachers must teach and measure each one. No wonder they want a raise.

There are many other objections to behavioral objectives, most of which revolve around the impossibility of specifying a complete set for anyone and the difficulty of specifying any but the most trivial tasks. I might add that of all the gifted programs we investigated in Illinois, not one employed a set of behavioral objectives.

The program description package is prepared after the program has been "developed." If you compare the simplicity of this program description with even the brief excerpts from our case study example, you will see how something as complex as a classroom cannot be reduced to a ledger sheet. I

---

[7] James G. March, "Organizational Factors in Supervision," in *The Supervisor: Agent for Change in Teaching.* (Washington, D.C.: NEA, Association for Supervision and Curriculum Development, 1966).

[8] Miriam B. Kapfer, "Behavioral Objectives and the Gifted," *Educational Technology* (June 15, 1968).

submit that with this form completed you would know almost nothing worthwhile about any program. Here is also implicit the interesting idea that "program development" is completed when these activities are specified. This is not how good programs develop. Our own data indicate that program development is a complicated process that occurs when an "advocate," perhaps a parent or teacher, becomes interested in developing a program for pupils. This advocate organizes a group of people, secures resources, and proceeds to build a program. The development of the program is never complete.[9]

Finally these artifacts are coded and related to the budget—which I suspect was the purpose all along. The code numbers can then be manipulated as if they meant something—which they clearly do not. The manual is peppered with statements like "Assessment of results is essential" and other exhortations to evaluate these programs, do cost/benefit analyses, and so on. But actual procedures for doing so are glossed over at great speed, and well they might be, for there is absolutely no legitimate way to collect the measures and make the comparisons the system demands.

The end result is what I always find in dealing with systems analysis—a lot of hazy generalizations that seem reasonable on the surface but are actually impossible to implement. All the objections to this system that I have raised are based on either empirical evidence or experience. But I have found that systems people are never disturbed by data. They simply say "You aren't doing it right," which means that people are not behaving in accordance with the rationalistic-economic model that underlies the system. If they did behave properly the model would work—a brilliant piece of circular logic.

In short this system seems to be an accountant's dream of how the world should work. Its implicit message is economic efficiency, promoting economic rationality at the expense of other human characteristics such as political rationality.[10] Significantly, the California system was drawn up by an accounting and budgeting commission and almost all the examples used are in business education.

My prognosis is something like this. My worst fears are that the system will actually succeed in doing what I see as its real design. In that case, we will have a very high level of managerial education. The repression and dullness of the classroom will increase and we will have succeeded in crucifying our kids on the cross of economic efficiency. My most hopeful prediction is that people will realize the restrictiveness of this system and subvert it into an

---

[9]Ernest R. House, Joe M. Steele, and Thomas Kerins, *The Development of Educational Programs: Advocacy in a Non-Rational System* (Urbana, Ill.: Center for Instructional Research and Curriculum Evaluation, University of Illinois), 30 pp.

[10]Aaron Wildavsky, "The Political Economy of Efficiency: Cost-Benefit Analysis, Systems Analysis, and Program Budgeting," in Fremont J. Lyden and Ernest R. Miller (eds.), *Planning, Programming, Budgeting: A Systems Approach to Management* (Chicago: Markham, 1968).

PPBS ELEMENT FORM
GOAL STATEMENT
To provide all students the opportunity to develop skills in typing, shorthand, bookkeeping, and office machine operation. Developed By_____
OBJECTIVE STATEMENT AND EVALUATIVE CRITERIA
Ninety percent of graduating Business Curriculum students shall meet the following standards: Typing—70 words per minute as measured by the IBM Test with 90% accuracy Shorthand—100 words per minute as measured by the Gregg test. Bookkeeping—Demonstrate understanding of journals, income statements, and balance sheets as determined by decision tests. Office Machine Operation—Mean score equal to national average on NCR test Developed By_____
PROGRAM DESCRIPTION SUMMARY
This program is designed to allow students to develop skills in the areas of typing, shorthand, bookkeeping, and office machine operation sufficient to gain employment using these skills. This program will include practice with typical problems and situations found in actual employment situations. Contacts will be maintained with the local business community to aid students in obtaining employment. Developed By_____
PROGRAM TITLE _____ PROGRAM ID NO. _____ PROGRAM NO.___ PROGRAM LEVEL___ SUPPORTED PROGRAMS_____ SUPPORTING PROGRAMS_____

information system that attends to the needs of the pupils instead of simply shaping them to the needs of the institutions.

But neither of these projections is likely in the near future. Schools will stay pretty much as they are now. Schoolmen will get by just as they got through chemistry lab—by filling out forms regardless of what is happening in reality. In California the PPB system will take more people to fill out the forms, more destroyed trees to provide the paper, and more people in Sacramento to shuffle them around. As one economist says, most PPB systems have culminated in "sterile accounting schemes."[11] But one can see the public and certain government leaders providing more money for the schools now that "sound business procedures" have been adopted. The end result will be a slightly less efficient system that looks more efficient. But even that is preferable to the first choice.

INSTITUTIONAL ACCOUNTABILITY

Here is a newspaper clipping from *The Wall Street Journal* dated June 24, 1970, datelined San Francisco. The headlines read:

EDUCATED DROPOUTS

COLLEGE-TRAINED YOUTHS
SHUN THE PROFESSIONS
FOR A FREE-FORM LIFE

John Spitzer of Harvard Is
Cabbie; Clara Perkinson,
Smith, Carries the Mail

OPTING OUT OF "THE SYSTEM"

The article goes on to say that increasing numbers of highly talented and educated young people do not want to join the system. John Spitzer says, "When I was a senior, Dylan's 'Subterranean Homesick Blues' came out. Remember that's the one when he says 'twenty years in school and then they put you on the day shift.' That touched so many nerves for so many people; that said it all." Although we might not agree on whether those young people are refuse or martyrs, saboteurs or saviors, we would agree that PPBS is not going to solve the problem. In fact, it would make the situation worse.

I wish I had a well worked out alternative to economic accountability that would solve all our problems. I don't. But let me suggest a different mode of accountability in which institutions are accountable to persons rather than persons being accountable to the institution. Such an

---
[11] Brandl, *op. cit.*

accountability scheme would provide feedback on the clients' well-being instead of just how well they are "shaping up." Teachers must be responsible to students and administrators to teachers. The information system attendant to this mode of accountability would revolve around the question, "Is this information going to help the institution adjust to characteristics of the student or will it result in shaping the student to the demands of the institution?"

With this in mind here are some recommendations for dealing with any kind of information system.

1. *Examine the function of the system, not just its rationale.* The true nature of the system is revealed by how it works, not what it promises.
2. *Try to respect the complexity of reality.* Good programs do not result from establishing a few objectives and selecting appropriate activities. Establishing any program successfully necessitates complex political processes. Any model of development that denies this is dysfunctional.
3. *Insist on multiple outcomes.* No educational program should be judged on the basis of one or two measures. Resist attempts to reduce educational output to simple achievement scores.
4. *Look at classroom transactions.* Regardless of outcomes, the atmosphere in which a child spends a good portion of his life is important. Many instruments for doing this are available.
5. *Collect many different kinds of data.* In light of all the above, the more kinds of data the better. Testimonials, interviews, classroom interaction analysis, objective tests—almost any data are appropriate. They provide a picture of the richness of classroom life and mitigate against making decisions based on highly abstract information. One thing we did in a recent evaluation was combine 25 different kinds of information to produce a case study of the class. The resulting image of the class was much superior to combining just a few kinds of data.
6. *Collect data from different sources.* It is especially important to find out what students are thinking, even if one asks only "What are the three things in this class you would like to change most?" Students can give as good a reading of what is going on as anyone else. Information should also be collected from parents and other groups.
7. *Report to different audiences.* For example, parents have a right to know something about what's going on in class. So do many other people.
8. *Rely on intuition and professional judgments.* Many experts on PPBS

emphasize that analytic tools should only provide assistance to intuition. There is no substitute for human judgment.
9. *Promote diversity within the system.* The most difficult task for organizations is to generate alternative ways of doing things.[12] An information system should promote the development of divergent ideas, not inhibit them. There are many places where even economic efficiency should be the criterion. For example, recently we did a cost/benefit analysis comparing the efficacy of demonstration centers and summer training institutes. But the circumstances were proper—a few short-range goals were at stake. Ordinarily, life is not that simple.

Breaking the exclusive hold of economic accountability is not easy to do. I hope that economists and those who control our economic institutions will stop maximizing economic gains long enough to assess the long-range consequences of doing so. There is some hope. Even an economist has remarked "When my son Christopher got all A's in first grade but found school repressive and dull, the arguments that his grades indicated a successful and lucrative future was little consolation to him or to me."[13]

---

[12]March, *op. cit.*
[13]Brandl, *op. cit.*

Looking Ahead

We began this book by saying that it is difficult to predict what the future will hold for a fast changing, post-industrial society or what the effect of change will be on American institutions, including the secondary school. Can man, by thought, influence the direction of change? Will the benefits of technology be used to serve the human quest for freedom, self-fulfillment, and a richer, more satisfying life for all? In the future will we value pluralism and the uniqueness of the individual? Will the long cherished principles of self-government survive? Or will the demands of the corporate state and the material rewards of a producing-consuming society persuade people to accept a large measure of regimentation, uniformity, and conformity in life style and beliefs? Assuming alternatives will be open, who will make the choice? Will it be a few, or will everyone have the opportunity to think about, discuss, and participate in decisions about which options to choose before the options are narrowed or closed out?

These are questions for the larger society, but they are also related to the secondary school and to what it will become, to the philosophy which will guide it, and the practices which derive from its organization, administration, and teaching. The secondary school embraces an age group which is at its most formative stage, insofar as the emergence of beliefs and attitudes and the development of concepts about themselves and society are concerned. Secondary school students are nearing adulthood, approaching the full rights of citizenship, thinking about vocations and about the quality of the lives they wish to lead. They are always the next generation, the ones for whom decisions about the future are most important, because so much of it lies ahead of them.

This book has been based upon a set of beliefs about the school, elaborated throughout its pages. Not everyone who works in the school at present nor everyone in the community will share the same beliefs. Many

Looking Ahead

current proposals about what schools should be doing and about their administration run counter to the general point of view expressed. Having acknowledged this, we can look ahead to suggest some changes which may occur in the future. Whether they do come about will depend in great degree upon the quality of leadership in the schools and the willingness of the professional staff to examine current practice, to adapt where adaptation is called for, and to include in discussions of needed changes students, parents, and the community.

Some of the changes will take place in the school as we know it. Students will become more involved in their own education, will participate in an ever-increasing degree in evaluating it and will take a full share in the decision-making leading to policy formulation which governs their lives in school and their relationship to faculty and administration. They will be chosen as a matter of course to serve actively with boards of education in advisory and consultative capacities. Given responsibilities, they will be listened to and their opinions will be given weight. As a fuller understanding of the meaning of court rulings affecting student rights develops, a new and more healthy relationship will evolve between adults and students. Students as well as teachers and administrators will be considered a part of the system when decisions about the organization are under consideration.

New ways of evaluating student progress will be developed, greatly expanding measures currently based upon traditional grading practices. The uses of standardized tests will be reexamined, and testing will be used more for diagnostic purposes than for the establishment of norms. A student's progress will be measured against himself more than against others, taking into consideration his own capacities and goals. The success of the school will be measured less against the number who succeed and more against the number who do not.

Time allotments for learning will become much more flexible. Compulsory attendance as presently measured by minutes in class, hours per day spent in school, and the length of the school day and year will be modified. Formulas for allocating state funds based on average daily attendance and average daily membership will be modified to accommodate a more flexible learning arrangement. Reentry into the school for students who have chosen to leave for one reason or another will be greatly simplified and encouraged.

Within the school and the school system many alternatives will be available to provide for a wide range of needs, interests, and vocational aspirations, and to test different methods of teaching and patterns of learning. Definitions of what it means to learn will be greatly expanded, and more emphasis will be placed upon discovering meanings than on memorization and recall of isolated pieces of information. Creativity will be valued, and those who show evidence of it will be given support. As conditions dictate, reevaluation of programs will result in more rapid elimination of material which is no longer relevant and addition of material that is more relevant.

More justification will be demanded for retaining what is taught as well as for substituting something else. The curriculum will become less rigid and less resistant to modification.

Much more valid information about careers will be made available including the kind and extent of preparation needed for pursuing successfully any particular career. Guidance will become more a matter of providing authentic information, answering questions, and less effort will be expended on trying to influence the choice of a student in one direction or another. Since, in the future, lifelong opportunities will be provided for workers to acquire new skills, to upgrade themselves, and to change occupations, it will not be thought desirable to guide a student into highly specific career choices at an early age.

Much of the educational program will be in the nature of general education and will be designed to be helpful to the student as a person, as a citizen, as a consumer, and as a member of a family. Segregation of students in those aspects of learning that are related to general rather than specialized education will be abandoned, including tracking and homogeneous grouping arrangements as presently conceived. An emphasis will be placed upon seeing that all secondary school students have the basic reading and number skills to enable them to survive in the modern world. Reallocation of resources within the school will be needed to accomplish this objective.

Leadership in the school will include more participation by staff in setting goals and in determining whether goals have been reached or whether they should be modified as circumstances dictate. The labor-management division between teachers and administration will become less and less distinct as the entire staff moves toward mutually agreed upon objectives.

If the school is to serve all its students as the future will require, an increased willingness on the part of the school to include parents as co-partners in the education of their children and in helping to find solutions to problems of learning and behavior will become evident. No longer will the school administrators and teachers be the ones who talk to parents while parents only listen. Mutual exchange of knowledge and ideas will become essential. A partnership will be established.

We have written so far about possible changes in the school as we know it. Some of the changes in the future, however, will alter the image of the school as a building, and education as something that takes place only within its walls. Unless school leaders obstruct it, and probably even if they attempt to do so, education in some, perhaps many, of its aspects will be carried on outside the school—in the community, in cooperation with community agencies, businesses and industries, yet under the aegis of the school as more broadly defined. If there is continuing reluctance on the part of school leaders to move in this direction, out-of-school education will go forward, but not under the mantle of the school.

Looking Ahead

Planning for new and expanded educational programs within the school and outside it will include people from the community, school graduates, and parents, as well as teachers and administrators. The human resources of the community will be brought into the school building, and the resources of the school will be taken into the community. Those in trades, businesses, professions, and politics will be occasional teachers. The definition of teacher will be enlarged. Leadership in secondary education will involve working in and with the community.

The kind of changes in the education of boys and girls of secondary school age described as possibilities here will not result in sameness and mediocrity; quite the contrary. Most people do not have the opportunity to develop to their full potential either as persons or in their careers. In the future, a wide variety of talents will be discovered and encouraged, including those that lead to major contributions to civilization—in medicine and medical research, in technology, in the creative arts of literature, graphic arts, architecture, and the theatre. Students will be given the opportunity to pursue the education needed to reach their goals, whatever their goals may be, in relation to their talents and desires. It can no longer be said that "many a flower is born to blush unseen and waste its sweetness on the desert air," as Gray reflected in thinking of those buried in the English country churchyard.

More human and financial resources will be invested in education, for society will discover that the investment will be returned with interest and it will be thereby enriched.

As schools look to the future and reexamine themselves, professional associations of teachers, curriculum workers, and administrators will devote more of their financial and human resources to study of educational and social questions. This will be reflected in their written reports, and studies and in their communications with the public. This trend is already evident. We have referred to some of these studies and reports and articles in the body of the text.

For example, the Report of the Task Force on Compulsory Education of the National Education Association, referred to in the text, includes a number of statements bearing on future needs and changes.

> Different people need education of different forms as well as different content. They learn best in different ways, within different structures of the educational system.
>
> Everyone, however, needs the guarantee that the school will offer him the kind of education he needs to carry out his plans. Everyone needs to know that when he leaves the school he will be competent to survive, to look forward to a life free of the fear of hunger and cold. He must be enabled to earn or win the economic freedom to make choices about his life if he was born without that freedom.
>
> Everyone needs respect for himself, his ideas, his opinions, his feelings. One way for the school to show that respect is to accord

students more and more responsibility in making decisions about the school and about their own education as they grow older. Although the form and content of education must vary, the attitude of the staff towards the students must be unswerving human respect.

... There is no question that all Americans require education; but as society's needs have come to change so rapidly there has also come the need for a much wider variety of alternatives for securing the desired education; and many of these alternatives will need to be pursued in ways other than those by which most schools presently operate and are organized.[1]

The report from which this quotation was selected is not alone in being in general accord with the tenor of this book and with speculations about future needs. The Bulletin of the National Association of Secondary School Principals reflects in recent years a concern about issues of change, as articles and editorial comment testify.

To the young person now entering a career of leadership in secondary education, the recital of such possibilities may read like impossible idealism. But we are thinking about the future, and the future can be quite different from the present, given vision on the part of those who will have a part in shaping it. The full dimensions of democracy as a form of government which releases the full creative energies of all people have not yet been realized.

The young person about to undertake or who has recently assumed a leadership role in the secondary school can look forward to a career of thirty years or longer. Many will be active until the year 2,000 and beyond. The young principal or other administrator will be faced with two perspectives. The first and shorter one will be related to the school as he finds it. He will inherit a staff, a student body, a program, a mode of operation, and a system of organization. He will also inherit from past practices and experiences a series of role expectations, for himself, for the teachers and for students. He will live in a community where these role expectations will be reinforced by those who see the school in the image of the ones they attended. Since the young principal has been a student in a school similar to the one he now leads, and since he has probably been a teacher in such a school, the pull to act in defense of the status quo will be strong. He will be tempted to settle down to the tasks associated with maintaining the school much as he finds it, making minor improvements and concessions here and there, but avoiding fundamental or disquieting issues.

Prudence, of course, requires a period of getting acquainted with staff, students, and community and in assessing the school as it is. The new principal will find much on which to build. He will not immediately institute changes, knowing that time is required to involve all concerned in an appraisal of the school and agreement on some short-range goals. Yet the principal who lets his thinking rest at this point risks the possibility of complacency.

---

[1]*Op. cit.,* p. 2.

Looking Ahead

To avoid this, the administrator-leader will also have a second, long range perspective constantly in mind. While working toward short range improvements, he will have his sights set five or ten years ahead. He will be reading widely, not solely on topics covered in educational periodicals but perhaps more importantly, reading in other fields which are related to social problems and trends. He will try to move from the viewpoint of educational manager to educational statesman. He will be developing a personal commitment, a personal philosophy, a set of beliefs which are his own because he has given thought to them and made them a part of himself.

His longer range goals will be more tentative than the short-term objectives. They will be subject to modification as new information and insights become available. But there must be longer-range goals, nevertheless. Since education as well as society is in a state of flux, the principal will be confronted with a variety of proposals about what secondary schools should be and what their purposes should be. Some of these will be in conflict with others, and he will have to have the knowledge and discernment to discover the difference; otherwise, he will be in the embarrassing position of espousing proposals which, if both are followed, will have effects which are diametrically opposed.

The long range objectives established by the young leadership of the secondary school can affect what education will be a quarter of a century from now. That it will be different, few would doubt. It is the nature of the difference that is important.

Index

Abbott, Max G., 272, 325
Ability, 46, 54, 74, 192, 230, 275, 289, 292, 411
Abington v. Schempp, 129
Academies, 4–6, 10, 12
Accountability, 38, 52, 58, 87, 91, 93, 195–8, 221, 341, 382, 425–37
Achievement, 51, 55, 69, 141, 190, 230, 267, 292, 363
Activism, 105, 106, 110
Activities: extracurricular, 15, 27, 412; fund raising, 218–9
Advanced placement, 26, 430
Alienation, 140, 241, 242, 244, 254, 255, 280, 295, 308, 394
Altruism, 70
American Association of School Administrators, 20–1, 34, 208
American College Testing Service, 181
American Council on Education, 3, 18
Apathy, 105, 290, 291, 342
Arts, 23, 27, 350, 351
Association for Supervision and Curriculum Development, 34, 35
Athletics, 212–5, 280
Attitudes, 13, 22, 30, 31, 53, 105, 115, 138, 140, 141, 142–3, 150, 179, 242, 267, 292, 320, 384, 403, 408, 438
Autonomy, 84, 272, 379
Awareness, 91, 351

Baker v. Downey City Board of Education, 124
Bandura and Walters, 288
Barnard, Chester, 271
Behavior, 62, 68, 71, 80, 91, 115, 141, 155, 179, 316, 398, 403; problems in, 234–6
Bennis, Warren G., 62, 77
Blackwell v. Issaquena, 125
Blake, Robert R., 82
Bloomberg, Warner Jr., 67
Borton, Terry, 141
Breen v. Kahl, 127
Bronfenbrenner, Urie, 249
Broudy, Harry, et al., 349–50
Brown v. Topeka, 115
Budget, 36, 198–201, 411
Bureaucracy, 77–86, 328, 341, 398
Burnside v. Byars, 125, 162, 163, 164
Butts and Cremin, 5

Campbell, Clyde M., 403
Carnegie Unit, 7–8, 190, 404
Centralization, 271, 272, 278
Challenge, 71, 131, 398
Change, 11, 25, 28, 44, 46, 48, 52, 53, 57, 77, 111, 113, 137, 139, 272, 273, 291, 325, 340, 401, 438, 441, 442; cultural, 19; program for, 148–53; social, 42, 115; technological, 83
Charisma, 60, 331
Cheerleaders, 216–7
Choice, 37, 113
Coleman, James, 141, 150, 267
College, 8, 18, 24, 67, 181–2, 233–4; community, 22
Combs, Arthur W., 35, 241
Commission on the Relation of School and College, 15, 195
Commission on the Reorganization of Secondary Education, 8, 15, 276

445

Commitment, 217, 243–4, 293, 294, 307, 340, 443
Committee on Secondary School Studies. *See* Committee of Ten
Committee of Ten, 7, 8, 10–1, 26, 28
Communication, 14, 73, 89–90, 112, 116, 132, 154, 156, 272, 285, 287, 332, 360, 371, 372–80, 393, 407, 418; agents of, 374–5; characteristics of, 373–4; media, 375–7; objectives of, 372–3
Competence, 14, 29, 35, 38, 78, 79, 80, 279, 317, 329, 368, 398, 418
Competition, 27, 50, 83, 155, 214, 246
Complexity, 59, 79, 81, 272, 340, 402
Compulsory attendance, 34, 118, 439
Compulsory education, 10, 29–32
Conant, James, 26–7, 193, 420
Conant Study, 26–7
Conduct, 46, 51, 55, 71, 119, 132, 211, 214
Confidence, 60, 107, 139, 372, 407
Confidentiality, 231, 232, 233, 234, 237, 314
Conflict, 60, 61, 82, 84, 90, 112, 116, 119, 120, 155, 382
Conformity, 71, 140, 143, 175, 190, 226, 247, 413, 438
Confrontation, 292
Consensus, 53, 223, 381, 384
Content, 51, 171, 277, 303
Contests, 217–8
Controversy, 44, 60, 81, 179–81, 197, 316
Cooperation, 14, 50, 287, 298, 299, 301, 308, 316, 343, 362, 369, 373, 375, 376, 379, 380, 407, 412, 440
Copland, Aaron, 352
Cost, 185, 198, 205, 419
Councils, student, 210–2
Counseling, 31, 53, 220, 223, 225–8, 234, 295, 305, 377
Counselors, 111, 113, 145, 187, 317
Creativity, 45, 50, 53, 71, 85, 113, 139, 141, 150, 226, 439
Credibility, 60, 97, 210, 341
Criticism, 28–32, 40, 41, 44, 46, 52, 53, 67, 69, 97, 113, 123, 193, 208, 222, 250, 372, 375, 382, 415
Cronkite, Walter, 94
Customs, 10, 44, 116, 151, 385
Cybernetics, 341

Davis v. Firment, 127
Decentralization, 57, 91, 93, 272, 273, 339, 396
Decision making, 11, 48, 49, 51, 53, 57, 61, 87, 90–1, 104, 112, 141, 156, 194, 200, 212, 289, 374, 387, 388, 412, 413, 439
Dehumanization, 241, 242, 254
Delinquency, 27, 363
Democracy, 12, 13, 17, 22, 24, 40–6, 48, 130, 132, 133, 200, 233, 253, 378, 395
Denker, Joel, 147
Depersonalization, 242, 255
Deschooling, 28–9, 37
Destiny, 41, 42, 84, 150, 399
Dewey, John, 33, 49, 70, 395
Dignity, 33, 46, 149, 227, 288
Diploma, 16, 29, 69
Discipline, 9, 37, 38, 122, 125, 145, 148, 155, 414
Discrimination, 29, 151, 216
Discussion, 44, 45, 50, 53, 180, 210, 211, 295, 364, 371, 381
Dishonesty, 139, 140, 143
Dissent, 109, 120, 125, 223
Diversity, 80, 102, 112, 270, 288, 437
Dixon v. Alabama, 119
Dress codes, 146
Dropout, 9, 14, 15, 24, 27, 28, 69, 111–2, 143, 173, 183, 233, 244, 245, 363, 435
Drucker, Peter, 82, 275
Dynamism, 400–1, 402

Educational Policies Commission, 20–3
Educational Testing Service, 181
Educator Feedback Center, 309, 317
Effectiveness, teacher, 59, 84, 85, 281, 305, 308, 314, 315, 364, 381
Efficiency, 52, 220, 221, 233, 427, 428, 433
Eight-Year Study, 15–8
Eisner v. Stamford Board of Education, 124
Elementary and Secondary Education Act of 1965, 27
Eliot, Charles W., 7
Employment, 22, 24
Engel v. Vitale, 129
English, 5, 7, 15, 16, 27, 46
Enrollment, 19, 276, 279, 283, 293, 294, 419, 420, 421
Enthusiasm, 326, 386, 407, 429, 430
Environment, 58, 82, 83, 104, 200, 277, 316, 352, 399, 407
Equality, 109
Evaluation, 16, 44, 45, 46, 48, 112, 150, 196, 245, 247, 277, 278, 291, 300, 301, 303, 304–19, 364, 383, 385–6
Experience, 22, 24, 34, 83, 301, 433
Experimentation, 57, 273, 412
Expertise, 289, 299, 301, 303, 406
Exploitation, 188, 213
Expulsion, 199, 235

Index

Extremists, 107

Facilities, 363, 367, 377, 385, 400, 417
Failure, 246, 394
Fairness, 236, 389
Fear, 139, 293
Feedback, 89–90, 143, 148, 149, 150, 222, 226, 233, 247, 300, 301, 303, 306, 307, 308, 309, 314, 315, 317, 320, 332, 436
Field trips, 54, 191, 347
Flexibility, 7, 30, 48, 57, 112, 113, 147, 149, 151, 152, 190, 191, 236, 256, 257, 275, 412, 431
Follett, Mary, 404
Forum, community, 360–1, 368
Freedom, 33, 41, 51, 52, 57, 81, 86, 94–8, 113, 139, 144–6, 276, 335, 378, 379, 395, 397, 438; academic, 179–81, 261–2, 412; of assembly, 118, 125–6, 132; of expression, 118, 119–25, 132, 141, 145; of personal appearance, 118, 126–9; of religion, 118, 129–30; of speech, 122
Frequency, 190
Friedenberg, Edgar, 33, 183, 226
Friedman, Milton, 32
Frustration, 109

Gardner, John, 83, 93, 395
Ghetto, 10, 27, 397
Gill Plan, 191, 256–60
Glasser, William, 185
Golden Pass Plan, 380–1
Goodman, Paul, 69, 141, 183, 226
Gouldner, Alvin, 272
Grading, 150, 186–9, 211
Grievances, 61, 212
Griffin v. Tatum, 127
Grouping, 26, 34, 75, 192–5, 282–3, 440
Growth, 46, 78, 79, 133, 138, 299, 340, 399, 412
Guidance, 19, 24, 26, 28, 31, 53, 224–8, 377, 403, 404, 421, 440
Guidelines, 214, 233, 376; for records, 364-4

Hage, Jerald, 272
Harmony, 85, 407
Health, 9, 13, 22, 46, 47, 132, 236–7, 368, 369, 395
Heritage, cultural, 16, 17, 44, 47
Hierarchy, 274, 325–36
History, 7, 15, 27, 46, 401
Holmes, Oliver W., 41
Holt, John, 33, 34, 141, 183
House, Ernest R., 425
Hudgins, H. C., 261
Humaneness, 341

Humanism, 241–55
In loco parentis, 118
Incentive, 81, 271, 407
Incompetence, 141
Individualism, 81
Individuality, 46, 54, 139
Individualization, 30
Industrial Revolution, 10, 35, 78
Industrialism, 70, 81
Industrialization, 10, 69, 77
Industry, 34, 339, 364
Inequality, 36–8
Influences, 37, 81
Initiative, 45, 46, 50, 53
Innovation, 48, 51, 61, 68, 71, 91, 92, 113, 146–7, 177–9, 294, 325–6
Input, 35, 36, 149–50, 196, 223, 279, 290, 291, 301, 304, 363, 385, 427
Inquiry, 44, 46, 50, 200, 381
Insight, 59
Institutionalization, 326
Insubordination, 124
Integration, 14, 79, 81, 83, 383–4, 3933, 394
Integrity, 60, 112, 288
Intelligence, 41, 42, 192, 316
Interdependence, 83
Involvement, 111, 117, 208–10, 371, 380–1, 385
Isolation, 340, 344, 369

Jencks, Christopher, 36
Job Corps, 27
Judgment, 45
Junior high school, 7
Justice, 42

Kamm, Richard, 281
Keppel, Francis, 197
Knowledge, 9, 13, 17, 41, 52, 60, 67, 83, 116, 144, 174, 235, 244, 267, 274, 276, 301, 371, 372, 398
Kozol, Jonathan, 141, 183, 396

Languages, 7, 15, 26, 217
Latin schools, 3, 5, 6, 10
Leisure, 9, 13, 18, 22, 23, 200
Libel, 208
Likert, Rensis, 80
Literature, 23, 173, 380
Litigation, 120
Littleford, John C., 256

Makarenko, A. S., 249
Malaise, 155, 341
Manipulation, 155
Mann, Horace, 70, 395

Materialism, 103, 104
Materials, 51, 54, 173, 289, 301, 303, 307, 314, 365
Mathematics, 7, 15, 26, 46, 217
McGregor, Douglas, 62, 80, 88
Meetings, faculty, 286
Melby, Ernest O., 394, 400, 403
Methods, teaching, 9, 30, 191
Miller v. Gillis, 127
Mini-course, 195
Mobility, 84, 339
Model, 49–56; bureaucratic, 61; corporation, 49, 51–2; democratic, 52–6, 285, 287, 296, 371; factory, 49, 50–1, 67–76, 294; family, 49–50; newer, 61–3
Modules, 191
Mores, 44, 108, 308
Motivation, 14, 28, 62, 81, 85, 143, 230, 247, 267, 289, 369, 403

National Association of Secondary School Principals, 22, 34, 35, 106, 177, 209, 420, 422, 442
National Commission on the Reform of Secondary Education, 31
National Congress of Parents and Teachers, 31
National Council of Education, 6
National Council of Teachers of English, 185, 186
National Defense Education Act, 26, 27
National Education Association, 6, 8, 12, 13, 20, 29, 34, 197, 198, 280, 441
National Merit Scholarship Examination, 230
National School Public Relations Association, 108, 187
National Teachers Association, 6
National Youth Administration, 12, 27
Needs, 57, 132, 141, 143, 220, 222, 298, 365, 439; educational, 45, 47, 304, 344, 363, 365–6, 375, 386, 419; of individual, 24, 53, 54, 62, 63, 70, 81, 131, 149, 378; of youth, 15, 22
Negotiations, 320–1
Neighborhood Youth Corps, 27
New York Times v. Sullivan, 208
Newspaper, underground, 110–1

Objectives, 301, 302, 309, 316, 377, 427, 443; behavioral, 201–3, 432; course, 277; curricular, 279
Objectivity, 181, 241, 242, 245
Obligations, 42, 119, 236, 304, 372, 421
Observation, 301, 306
Occupation, 18, 29, 58

Office of Economic Opportunity, 27, 32
Opinion, 30, 48, 53, 61, 102, 131, 146, 155, 176, 181, 187, 192, 209, 279, 289, 291, 295, 385
Oppenheimer, Dr. Robert, 77
Opportunity, 34, 378, 399; equality of, 18–9, 41, 397
Ordway v. Hargraves, 157–61
Organization, 17, 84–5, 270–84
Originality, 149
Output, 35, 36, 196, 201, 427

Paraprofessionals, 300, 363, 399
Parsons, Talcott, 272
Participation, 31, 47, 52, 53, 57, 67, 84, 104, 109, 110, 111, 112, 125, 131, 149, 155, 200, 205, 215, 223, 287, 292, 294, 297, 305, 320, 362, 371, 414, 440
Patriotism, 121
Perceptions, 110, 292
Performance, 237, 306, 425
Personality, 60, 71, 81, 131, 274, 301, 400
Personalization, 30
Pluralism, 395, 428, 438
Polarization, 292
Poll, opinion, 186, 365
Poverty, 103, 369, 377, 395, 399
Power, 43, 80, 83, 363
Preference, 54, 176, 279
Prejudice, 40, 43, 45, 140, 385, 394
Press, student, 206–10, 261–2
Pressure, 144, 247
Prestige, 34, 281
Privacy, 129, 246
Privilege, 42, 372, 412
Process, 9, 24, 189
Productivity, 69, 70, 196, 241, 315
Professionalism, 91
Progressive education, 24, 25, 49
Progressive Education Association, 15, 195
Protest, 101, 105, 117, 120, 125
Psychology, 14, 248, 301, 402
Punishment, 31, 139, 140, 143, 148, 155, 235, 246
Purpose, 7, 9, 16, 24, 30, 35, 37, 59, 63

Rabbie, Jaap, 82–3
Reaction, 102, 121, 140
Receptivity, 301, 303, 306, 317, 320
Recognition, 52, 307
Records, 231–3, 247, 416–7
Reform, 244
Regents' Inquiry, 19–20
Reich, Charles, 103
Reinforcement, 202

Index

Reliability, 302
Reorganization, 19, 30
Repression, 208, 433
Requirements, 24, 31, 138, 419
Research, 84, 85
Resources, 55, 152, 200, 220, 274, 298, 303, 304, 305, 306, 347–60, 393, 433, 441
Respect, 23, 30, 40, 45, 131, 132, 200, 291, 301, 306, 413
Restrictions, 144, 151, 152, 181
Retaliation, 291, 314
Revitalization, 83, 86
Rewards, 81, 139, 140
Richards v. Thurston, 127, 165–7
Rickover, Hyman, 26
Rights, 208–10, 233
Rigidity, 150
Role, 277, 331, 401
Rotation, 280, 281
Ruebhausen, Oscar M., 263
Rugg, Harold, 345
Rules, 38, 55, 94, 106, 111, 119, 132, 211, 214, 236, 289, 291, 301, 329, 341, 375, 411

Santayana, 3, 221
SAT, 181, 227
Satisfaction, 52, 58, 277, 296, 307
Scheduling, 22, 171, 173, 190–2, 273, 293, 418
Science, 15, 23, 26, 217
Scores, 34, 143
Scoville v. Board of Education, 122, 123
Security, 232, 233, 237, 417–8
Self-concept, 58, 63, 150, 369, 397
Self-confidence, 143
Self-direction, 250
Self-examination, 105
Self-expression, 140
Self-fulfillment, 438
Self-image, 399
Self-realization, 52, 81, 382–3
Self-respect, 139, 143
Self-understanding, 88–9
Sensitivity, 141, 173, 236, 242, 245, 351, 365, 366
Separatism, 395
Sequence, 277
Silberman, Charles, 33
Sims v. Colfax, 127
Skills, 17, 22, 29, 52, 53, 55, 59, 69, 274, 372, 380
Skinner, B. F., 202
Social studies, 5, 15, 46, 349
Socialization, 369
Sorenson, Aage, 281, 282

Sorokin, Pitirim, 229
Specialization, 35, 78, 80, 340
Sputnik, 7, 25, 27, 28, 101, 192, 225, 249
Standardization, 67, 75
Status quo, 41, 52, 97, 102, 253, 272, 291, 326, 327, 332, 442
Stratification, 271, 272, 273, 275, 278, 286
Sullivan v. Houston School District, 124
Sumption and Engstrom, 376, 378–9
Support, 294, 300, 301
Suppression, 121
Suspension, 119, 235

Teachability, 194
Teacher aides, 51
Team teaching, 51, 90, 177–9, 294
Techniques, 51, 67, 147, 289, 299, 301, 307, 381
Technology, 67, 79, 81, 82, 339, 441
Tension, 85, 105, 109, 111, 112, 148, 150
Testing, 228–31, 247
Textbooks, 31, 140, 179
Thant, U, 406
Thelen, Herbert, 193, 325, 326, 343–6
Thompson, Victor, 272, 333
Tinker v. Des Moines, 120, 122, 124, 160, 161–4, 206
Toffler, Alvin, 103, 172
Toleration, 132
Totalitarianism, 163
Townsend, Robert, 274
Tracking, 192–5, 247, 282–3, 440
Traditions, 10, 155
Transportation, 418–9
Trump, J. Lloyd, 107, 393
Trust, 60, 132, 291, 301, 306
Tyler, Ralph, 315

Understanding, 17, 22, 23, 59, 141, 225, 242
Unemployment, 11, 27
Uniformity, 45, 335, 413, 438
United States Commission of Education, 7
United States Employment Service, 111
United States Office of Education, 112, 125
Unity, 16, 17
Urbanism, 69
Urbanization, 241
Utility, 91, 430

Values, 26, 40, 78, 84, 103, 104, 116, 138, 242, 244, 248, 378; democratic, 54, 81; ethical, 23, 368; individual, 45–6; job, 113; moral, 368; organizational, 80; societal, 43–5, 52, 115, 368; subject, 9

Vietnam, 117, 120, 145, 161, 163, 164, 171, 341
Vocational Act of 1963, 27
Voucher system, 32

Weber, Max, 272, 327, 328, 329, 330

Welfare, 13, 41, 42, 43
West Virginia v. Barnette, 120
Westin, Alan F., 108
Whitehead, Alfred North, 83
World War II, 18, 24, 25, 79, 101, 171
Wright, John H., Jr., 256